Devil's Game

DEVIL'S GAME

HOW THE UNITED STATES
HELPED UNLEASH
FUNDAMENTALIST ISLAM

ROBERT DREYFUSS

METROPOLITAN BOOKS

HENRY HOLT AND COMPANY · NEW YORK

Metropolitan Books
Henry Holt and Company, LLC
Publishers since 1866
175 Fifth Avenue
New York, New York 10010
www.henryholt.com

Metropolitan Books ® and Ⓜ ® are registered
trademarks of Henry Holt and Company, LLC.

Library of Congress Cataloging-in-Publication Data
Dreyfuss, Robert.
Devil's game : how the United States helped unleash fundamentalist Islam /
Robert Dreyfuss.—1st ed.
p. cm.—(American empire project)
Includes bibliographical references.
ISBN-10: 0-8050-7652-2
ISBN-13: 978-0-8050-7652-3
1. Islamic countries—Relations—United States. 2. United States—Relations—
Islamic countries. 3. Islamic fundamentalism—Political aspects. I. Title. II. Series.
DS35.74.U6D76 2005
327.73 056'09'045—dc22   2005043881

Henry Holt books are available for special promotions
and premiums. For details contact: Director, Special Markets.

First Edition 2005

Designed by Victoria Hartman

Printed in the United States of America

1   3   5   7   9   10   8   6   4   2

For Anna and Justin

CONTENTS

INTRODUCTION

I

THERE IS AN unwritten chapter in the history of the Cold War and the New World Order that followed. It is the story of how the United States—sometimes overtly, sometimes covertly—funded and encouraged right-wing Islamist activism. *Devil's Game* attempts to fill in that vital missing link.

Vital because this little-known policy, conducted over six decades, is partly to blame for the emergence of Islamist terrorism as a worldwide phenomenon. Indeed, America's would-be empire in the Middle East, North Africa, and Central and South Asia was designed to rest in part on the bedrock of political Islam. At least that is what its architects hoped. But it proved to be a devil's game. Only too late, after September 11, 2001, did Washington begin to discover its strategic miscalculation.

The United States spent decades cultivating Islamists, manipulating and double-crossing them, cynically using and misusing them as Cold War allies, only to find that it spawned a force that turned against its sponsor, and with a vengeance. Like monsters imbued with artificial life, radical imams, mullahs, and ayatollahs stalk the landscape, thundering not only against the United States but against freedom of thought, against secular science, against nationalism and the left, against women's rights. Some are terrorists, but far more are just medieval-minded religious fanatics who want to turn the calendar back to the seventh century.

During the Cold War, from 1945 to 1991, the enemy was not merely the USSR. According to the Manichean rules of that era, the United States demonized leaders who did not wholeheartedly sign on to the American agenda or who might challenge Western and in particular U.S. hegemony. Ideas and ideologies that could inspire such leaders were suspect: nationalism, humanism, secularism, socialism. But subversive ideas such as these were also the ones most feared by the nascent forces of Muslim fundamentalism. Throughout the region the Islamic right fought pitched battles against the bearers of these notions, not only in the realm of intellectual life but in the streets. During the decades-long struggle against Arab nationalism—along with Persian, Turkish, and Indian nationalism—the United States found it politic to make common cause with the Islamic right.

More broadly, the United States spent many years trying to construct a barrier against the Soviet Union along its southern flank. The fact that all of the nations between Greece and China were Muslim gave rise to the notion that Islam itself might reinforce that Maginot Line–style strategy. Gradually the idea of a green belt along the "arc of Islam" took form. The idea was not just defensive. Adventurous policy makers imagined that restive Muslims inside the Soviet Union's own Central Asian republics might be the undoing of the USSR itself, and they took steps to encourage them.

The United States played not with Islam—that is, the religion, the traditional, organized system of belief of hundreds of millions—but with Islamism. Unlike the faith, with fourteen centuries of history behind it, Islamism is of more recent vintage. It is a political creed with its origins in the late nineteenth century, a militant, all-encompassing philosophy whose tenets would appear foreign or heretical to most Muslims of earlier ages and that still appear so to many educated Muslims today. Whether it is called pan-Islam, or Islamic fundamentalism, or political Islam, it is an altogether different creature from the spiritual interpretation of Muslim life as contained in the Five Pillars of Islam. It is, in fact, a perversion of that religious faith. That is the mutant ideology that the United States encouraged, supported, organized, or funded. It is the same one variously represented by the Muslim Brotherhood, by Ayatollah Khomeini's Iran, by Saudi Arabia's ultra-orthodox Wahhabism, by Hamas and Hezbollah, by the Afghan jihadis, and by Osama bin Laden.

II

The United States found political Islam to be a convenient partner during each stage of America's empire-building project in the Middle East, from its early entry into the region to its gradual military encroachment, to its expansion into an on-the-ground military presence, and finally to the emergence of the United States as an army of occupation in Iraq and Afghanistan.

In the 1950s, the enemy was not only Moscow but the Third World's emerging nationalists, from Gamal Abdel Nasser in Egypt to Mohammed Mossadegh in Iran. The United States and Britain used the Muslim Brotherhood, a terrorist movement and the grandfather organization of the Islamic right, against Nasser, the up-and-coming leader of the Arab nationalists. In the CIA-sponsored coup d'état in Iran in 1953, the United States secretly funded an ayatollah who had founded the Devotees of Islam, a fanatical Iranian ally of the Muslim Brotherhood. Later in the same decade, the United States began to toy with the notion of an Islamic bloc led by Saudi Arabia as a counterpoint to the nationalist left.

In the 1960s, despite U.S. efforts to contain it, left-wing nationalism and Arab socialism spread from Egypt to Algeria to Syria, Iraq, and Palestine. To counter this seeming threat, the United States forged a working alliance with Saudi Arabia, intent on using its foreign-policy arm, Wahhabi fundamentalism. The United States joined with King Saud and Prince Faisal (later, King Faisal) in pursuit of an Islamic bloc from North Africa to Pakistan and Afghanistan. Saudi Arabia founded institutions to mobilize the Wahhabi religious right and the Muslim Brotherhood. Saudi-backed activists founded the Islamic Center of Geneva (1961), the Muslim World League (1962), the Organization of the Islamic Conference (1969), and other organizations that formed the core of an international Islamist movement.

In the 1970s, with the death of Nasser and the retreat of Arab nationalism, the Islamists became an important prop beneath many of the regimes tied to the United States. The United States found itself allied with the Islamic right in Egypt, where Anwar Sadat used that country's Islamists to build an anti-Nasserist political base; in Pakistan, where General Zia ul-Haq seized power by force and established an Islamist state; and in Sudan, where the Muslim Brotherhood's leader, Hassan Turabi, marched toward power. At the same time, the United States began to see Islamic fundamentalism as a tool to be used offensively against the Soviet Union, above all in Afghanistan and Central Asia, where the United States used it as sword aimed at the Soviet Union's underbelly. And as Iran's revolution unfolded, latent sympathy for Islamism—combined with widespread U.S. ignorance about Iran's Islamist currents—led many U.S. officials to see Ayatollah Khomeini as a benign figure, admiring his credentials as an anticommunist. As a result, the United States catastrophically underestimated his movement's potential in Iran.

Even after the Iranian revolution of 1979, the United States and its allies failed to learn the lesson that Islamism was a dangerous, uncontrollable force. The United States spent billions of dollars to support an Islamist jihad in Afghanistan, whose mujahideen were led by Muslim Brotherhood–allied groups. The United States also looked on uncritically as Israel and Jordan covertly aided terrorists from the Muslim Brotherhood in a civil war in Syria, and as Israel encouraged the spread of Islamism among Palestinians in the occupied territories, helping to found Hamas. And neoconservatives joined the CIA's Bill Casey in the 1980s in secret deals with Iran's Ayatollah Khomeini.

By the 1990s, the Cold War was over. The political utility of the Islamic right now seemed questionable. Some strategists argued that political Islam was a new threat, the new "ism" replacing communism as America's global opponent. That, however, wildly exaggerated the power of a movement that was restricted to poor, undeveloped states. Still, from Morocco to Indonesia, political Islam was a force that the United States had to deal with. Washington's response was muddled and confused. During the 1990s, the United States faced a series of crises with political Islam: In Algeria, the United States sympathized with the rising forces of political Islam, only to support the Algerian army's crackdown against them—and then Washington kept open a dialogue with the Algerian Islamists, who increasingly turned to terrorism. In Egypt, the Muslim Brotherhood and its offshoots, including a violent underground movement, posed a dire threat to President Mubarak's regime; yet the United States toyed with supporting the Brothers. And in Afghanistan, shattered after the decade-long U.S. jihad, the Taliban won early American support. Even as Osama bin Laden's Al Qaeda took shape, the United States found itself in league with the Islamic right in Pakistan, Saudi Arabia, and the Arab Gulf.

And then came 9/11.

After 2001, the Bush administration appeared to sign on to the neoconservative declaration that the world was defined by a "clash of civilizations," and launched its global war on terrorism, targeting Al Qaeda—the most virulent strain of the very virus that the United States had helped create. Still, before, during, and after the invasion of Iraq—a socialist, secular country that had long opposed Islamic fundamentalism—the United States actively supported Iraq's Islamic right, overtly backing Iraqi Shiite Islamists, from Ayatollah Ali al-Sistani to radical Islamist parties such as the Supreme Council for Islamic Revolution in Iraq and the Islamic Call (Al-Dawa), both of which are also supported by Teheran's mullahs.

III

The vaunted clash of civilizations, that tectonic collision between the West and the Islamic world, if that's what it was, began inauspiciously. Amid the wreckage of World War II, America stumbled willy-nilly into the Middle East, into a world it knew little about. If the United States made mistakes in dealing with Islam in the second half of the twentieth century, it was in part because Americans were so profoundly ignorant about it.

Until 1941 the Middle East, for young America, was a fearsome and wonderful place, a fantasyland of sheikhs and harems, of turbaned sultans, of obscene bath houses and seraglios, of desert oases, pyramids, and the Holy Land. In early literature—novels, poems, travelogues—it was a place of mystery and intrigue, inhabited by the unsavory and the irreligious. Its people were often portrayed as scimitar-waving "Mussulmen" and "Mohammedans," uncivilized and uncouth. It was the land of pirates and "Turks," a term that retains its pejorative connotation today.

Since its appearance in 1869, Mark Twain's *The Innocents Abroad* has come to symbolize a peculiarly American sort of naïve blundering overseas. Yet few realize that Twain, perhaps America's most acute satirist and observer, used the book to describe a months-long sojourn in the Mediterranean and the Middle East. It was hugely influential among nineteenth-century U.S. readers. But Twain unfortunately contributed to, and took advantage of, built-in prejudice against things Islamic. Meandering through Turkey, Syria, Lebanon, and Palestine, Twain seems to be fairly holding his nose, marveling at the barbarism he is surveying. Dwellings are "tastefully frescoed aloft and alow with disks of camel dung placed there to dry." Damascus ("How they hate a Christian in Damascus!") is the "most fanatical Mohammedan purgatory out of Arabia." He added: "The Damascenes are the ugliest, wickedest looking villains we have seen." Comparing the Holy Land to a classical engraving of Nazareth, Twain wrote:

> But in the engraving there was no desolation; no dirt; no rags; no fleas; no ugly features; no sore eyes; no feasting flies; no besotted ignorance in the countenances; no raw places on the donkey's backs; no disagreeable jabbering in unknown tongues; no stench of camels; no suggestion that a couple of tons of powder placed under the party and touched off would heighten the effect and give to the scene a genuine interest and charm which it would always be pleasant to recall.

By the early twentieth century—with the advent of World War I, the forced disintegration of the Ottoman Empire, and the start of the British-sponsored "Arab Awakening," led by the likes of Winston Churchill, T. E. Lawrence ("of Arabia"), and Gertrude Bell—the modern Middle East had begun to intrude on the American consciousness. Still, it was filtered through a layer of romanticism and ignorance. Lawrence's sexually charged, desert-romantic accounts, including his famous *Seven Pillars of Wisdom,* became U.S. bestsellers, as did oasis-to-oasis travelogues by various adventurers. For most Americans, the Middle East was most memorably encapsulated in film and song. Rudolf Valentino's *The Sheik* (1921) embodied what would become the standard-issue American idea of the Arab, along with its accompanying 1921 song, "The Sheik of Araby," whose lyrics included the vaguely threatening: "At night, when you're asleep / Into your tent I'll creep." Its influence lasted decades. Benny Goodman recorded the song in 1937, as did the Beatles in 1962 and Leon Redbone in 1977.

Little if any professional American Middle East expertise existed in the years leading up to World War II. From the nineteenth century until well into the twentieth, pretty much the only Americans who ventured into the region were members of a band of Protestant missionaries, educators, and doctors who took it upon themselves to bring the gospels to the heathen masses and to preach among the Christians of the Ottoman Empire, in Syria and Lebanon especially. Pioneers such as Daniel Bliss, his son Howard Bliss, and the Dodge brothers (Reverend David Stuart Dodge and William Early Dodge), who built and ran Syrian Protestant College—renamed the American University of Beirut in the 1920s—and Mary Eddy, a missionary's daughter who founded a clinic in Lebanon, alighted on the shores of the Ottoman Empire's Arab provinces. The Blisses, Dodges, and Eddys would become the parents, grandparents, and great-grandparents of America's priesthood of "Arabists" who emerged after World War II.

IV

In 1945 Franklin Delano Roosevelt went east in search of oil—and found Islam. He conducted a fateful shipboard encounter with the king of Saudi Arabia, Ibn Saud, and for the United States, it marked the real start of its political and military engagement with the region.

Flushed with victory, the United States found itself in the role of a worldwide superpower. Its activism then was naïve in the extreme—endearingly so for its partisans, and frighteningly so for others. The post–World War II generation of U.S. leaders believed wholeheartedly that the American spirit would conquer all, figuratively speaking—or, if necessary, on the ground in real life. This was, after all, Henry Luce's "American Century."

The Middle East was then emerging as the most strategically vital area outside the industrial West and Japan. Though it lacked expertise, language skills, and cultural familiarity with the region's complex civilization, the United States was called to its imperial mission by the very logic of its immense power. In Norman Mailer's *The Naked and the Dead,* General Cummings presciently described the inexorable growth of American power that would be unleashed by World War II:

> I like to call it a process of historical energy [says Cummings]. There are countries that have latent powers, latent resources, they are full of potential energy, so to speak. . . . As kinetic energy a country is organization, coordinated effort. . . . Historically, the purpose of this war is to translate America's potential energy into kinetic energy. . . . When you've created power, materials, armies, they don't wither of their own accord. Our vacuum as a nation is filled with released power, and I can tell you that we're out of the backwaters of history now.

But as America's energy flowed into the Islamic world, the United States began its long-running engagement with little or no comprehension of the forces it was dealing with.

Until after the Second World War, Middle East studies in the United States were virtually nonexistent or relegated to a subset of theology. Partly sponsored by the government, centers for Middle Eastern affairs began springing up after 1947, when Princeton University created the first Near East center in the United States. But it would be many years before the United States would have a cadre of academic experts who had a grasp of Islamic politics, culture, and religion.

From FDR on, leading U.S. politicians were prisoners of misguided stereotypes. They seemed entranced by the almost other-worldly appearance of their Arab interlocutors. FDR, after meeting Ibn Saud, returned to Washington and "could not shake the image of the hawk-like Saudi monarch, ensconced in a gold chair and surrounded by six slaves." Harry Truman, two years later, described a leading Saudi official as a "real old biblical Arab with chin whiskers, a white gown, gold braid, and everything." And Eisenhower dismissed the Arabs as "a very uncertain quantity, explosive and full of prejudices." The official record is full of such uninformed stereotyping of Arabs and Muslims by U.S. officials. For the next sixty years, the handful of American Arabists who actually knew something about the Middle East would try to combat those stereotypes. But they would fail.

V

The American attachment to a romanticized fantasy of Arab life and a racist-fed, religious disdain for the Arabs' supposed heathenism proved a deadly combination when the time came for America to engage itself politically and militarily in the Middle East. Perhaps those stereotypes led American policy makers to see Muslims as fierce warriors. Perhaps they believed that the fanaticism of their religious tenets would lead them to resist atheistic communism. Perhaps it was the notion that in southwest Asia the traditional religious establishment was a bulwark of the status quo. But it never dawned on U.S. officials that Islamist organizations such as the Muslim Brotherhood were a qualitatively different phenomenon from the comprador clerical establishment. Certainly, as the Cold War progressed, the big enemy, the USSR, and its alleged accomplice, Arab nationalism, seemed to have a common enemy: Islam.

In some ways, the Cold War itself began in the Middle East. President Harry Truman proclaimed U.S. responsibility for Greece and Turkey, replacing Great Britain in that role, in 1947, and confronted the Soviet Union in northern Iran's Azerbaijan. England's imperial presence was shrinking: London abandoned Greece and Turkey, then India and Palestine, and the retreat was on—with only the United

States to fill the vacuum, an allegedly tempting target for Soviet expansion. (Later scholarship would show that neither Stalin nor Khrushchev had either the intention or the capability to seize control of the Persian Gulf and the Middle East.)

The strategic importance of the Middle East was obvious to all: it was (and is) the indispensable source of energy for America's allies in Europe and Japan. At the time, the United States did not depend on the Persian Gulf for oil, relying instead on Venezuela and Texas, Louisiana, and Oklahoma. But Europe and Japan desperately needed the Gulf for day-to-day survival. It is no exaggeration to say that U.S. strategists realized that the defense of Western Europe was inconceivable without a parallel plan to control the Gulf. Despite important internal tensions among the Western powers, they forged a series of alliances in the region: NATO, the abortive Middle East Defense Organization, the Baghdad Pact, CENTO—all directed against the USSR. More quietly Washington and London supported the Islamic right against the left in country after country and encouraged the emergence of an "Islamic bloc."

For those who knew little about the religion and culture of the Middle East—presidents, secretaries of state, CIA directors—the Islamic right seemed like a sensible horse to ride. They could identify with people inspired by deep religious belief, even if the religion was an alien one. In their search for tactical allies, Islam seemed like a better bet than secularism, since the left-wing secularists were viewed as cats'-paws for Moscow, and the centrist ones were dangerously opposed to the region's monarchies and traditional elites. In the aftermath of World War II, the list of nations ruled by kings included not only Saudi Arabia and Jordan, but Egypt, Iraq, Iran, and Libya.

By the 1950s, the military-intellectual complex of Middle East studies was up and running in many U.S. universities, producing Arabists and Orientalists who were called on by policy makers for advice in grappling with the region's complexities. The CIA and the State Department gobbled up Ivy League graduates who spoke Arabic, Turkish, Farsi, Urdu, and other Middle East languages, and a core of U.S. government Arabists emerged with at least a working understanding of the region. Yet, by their own testimony, few of them learned much about Islam or Islamism, concentrating instead on the nuts-and-bolts economic and political questions. Most of the Arabists were secularists, and did not have much sympathy for fundamentalist Islam. Many, in fact, instead sympathized broadly with Arab nationalism. Many of them saw Islam as the bygone symbol of a past era.

As the Cold War unfolded, however, State Department and CIA officers who sided with Arab nationalism were increasingly ignored. Their views were attacked by Cold Warriors, and by the supporters of Israel, who were determined to undermine anyone who considered himself or herself "pro-Arab." By the 1970s, the very term Arabist had become indelibly tainted. Since then, pro-Zionist activists have piled on, waging an ideological blitzkrieg against those Arabists who remained in government or academia. Robert D. Kaplan's tendentious 1993 book, *The Arabists: Romance of an American Elite,* marked the high point of this effort. Ever since its publication, attacking Arabists has become a cottage industry. Virtually all of them were excluded from prewar planning on Iraq. To a man, most Arabists were strongly opposed to the preemptive war. But by excluding them, the Bush administration guaranteed that planning for the war would be carried out by know-nothings.

VI

Some may argue that the United States created neither Islam nor its fundamentalist variant, and that is true. But here we need to consider an extended analogy with America's Christian right.

Conservative and evangelistic Christians have been present in large numbers in America since the colonial era. But in another sense, the emergence of the Christian right in the United States can be dated to the late 1970s, with the formation of the Rev. Timothy LaHaye's California alliance of churches, the creation of the Moral Majority by LaHaye and Jerry Falwell, and the role of those two men and others in the rise of the Council on National Policy, the Christian Coalition, and organizations like Pat Robertson's broadcast empire and Dr. James Dobson's Focus on the Family. Until then, conservative Christians were a politically inchoate force. Relentlessly organized over the past three decades, they have become a self-conscious, politically powerful movement.

The same is true for the Islamic right. The reactionary tendency within Islam goes back thirteen centuries. From Islam's earliest years, obscurantists, anti-rationalists, and Koran literalists competed with more enlightened, progressive, and moderate tendencies. In more recent times, Muslim reactionaries have been a drag on modernization, opposing progressive education, liberalization, and human rights. But it wasn't until the creation of the pan-Islamic movement of Jamal Eddine al-Afghani in the late 1800s, the founding of the Muslim Brotherhood in Egypt by Hassan al-Banna in 1928, and the creation of Abul-Ala Mawdudi's Islamic Group in Pakistan in 1940 that the Islamic right had its LaHayes, its Falwells, and its Robertsons. Those early Islamists sharpened the culture wars in the Middle East just as their Christian right counterparts did in the United States, and for the same reasons.

Just as the Christian right found support from wealthy right-wing donors, especially oil men from Texas and the Midwest, the Islamic right won financial support from wealthy oil men, too—namely, the royal families atop Saudi Arabia and the Gulf. And just as the Christian right formed a politically convenient alliance with right-wing Republicans, the Islamic right established a similar understanding with America's right-wing foreign policy strategists. In fact, support for the Christian right and the Islamic right converged neatly during the Reagan administration, which eagerly sought alliances with both. So blinded were some Americans by the Cold War that militant Christian-right activists and fervent Zionist partisans of Israel cheerily supported Islamist fanatics in Afghanistan.

The analogy between Christian and Islamic fundamentalists holds in other areas, too. Both exhibit an absolute certainty about their beliefs and they tolerate no dissent, condemning apostates, unbelievers, and freethinkers to perdition. Both believe in a unity of religion and politics, the former insisting that America is a "Christian nation," the latter that Muslims need to be ruled either by an all-powerful, religio-political caliphate or by a system of "Islamic republics" under an ultra-orthodox version of Islamic law (sharia). And both encourage a blind fanaticism among their followers. It's no accident that among followers of both Christian and Islamic fundamentalism, the world indeed appears to be engaged in a clash of civilizations.

VII

A war on terrorism is precisely the wrong way to deal with the challenge posed by political Islam.

That challenge comes in two forms. First, there is the specific threat to the safety and security of Americans posed by Al Qaeda; and second, there is a far broader political problem created by the growth of the Islamic right in the Middle East and South Asia.

In regard to Al Qaeda, the Bush administration has willfully exaggerated the size of the threat it represents. It is not an all-powerful organization. It cannot destroy or conquer America, and it does not pose an existential threat to the United States. It can kill Americans, but it has never had access to weapons of mass destruction, and it almost certainly never will. It does not possess large numbers of cells, assets, or agents inside the United States, although after 9/11 the U.S. attorney general made the unfounded charge that Al Qaeda had as many as 5,000 operatives in America. None of the many hundreds of Muslims arrested or detained after 9/11 were found to have terrorist connections. In three and a half years after 9/11, not a single violent act by Al Qaeda—or any other Islamic terrorist group—occurred in the United States: no hijackings, no bombings, not even a shot fired. No ties were ever proved linking Al Qaeda to Iraq—or to any other state in the Muslim world: not to Syria, not to Saudi Arabia, not to Iran. In short, the threat from Al Qaeda is a manageable one.

Using the U.S. military in conventional war mode is not the way to attack Al Qaeda, which is primarily a problem for intelligence and law enforcement. The war in Afghanistan was wrongheaded: It failed to destroy Al Qaeda's leadership, it failed to destroy the Taliban, which scattered, and it failed to stabilize that war-torn nation more than temporarily, creating a weak central government at the mercy of warlords and former Taliban gangs. Worse, the war in Iraq was not only misguided and unnecessary, but it was aimed at a nation that had absolutely no links to bin Laden's gang—as if, said an observer, FDR had attacked Mexico in response to Pearl Harbor. The ham-handed use of the armed forces against a nonstate actor like Al Qaeda is useless and self-defeating. Like some grotesque ancient legend, for every head lopped off by laser-guided missiles, Marine-led raids into Islamist redoubts, Israeli gunship attacks on Hamas and Hezbollah enclaves, and cruise missile attacks on remote strongholds, three new heads grow in its place. But because the Afghan and Iraq wars fit nicely with the Bush administration's broader policy of empire building and preemptive war, and because they allowed the United States to construct a vast political-military enterprise stretching from East Africa deep into Central Asia, those two wars went forward. A problem that could have been dealt with surgically—using commandos and Special Forces, aided by tough-minded diplomacy, indictments and legal action, concerted international efforts, and judicious self-defense measures—was vastly inflated by the Bush administration.

Still, Al Qaeda can be defeated.

The larger problem, that of the growing strength of Islamic fundamentalism in the Middle East and Asia, is far more complicated.

Naturally, the first problem is related to the second. Unless the Islamic right is stopped, it is possible that Al Qaeda could resuscitate itself. Or, as in Iraq after the U.S. invasion, new Al Qaeda–style organizations might emerge by drawing on anti-American anger and resentment. Or, one of the other Islamic-right terrorist groups, such as Hamas or Hezbollah, might metastasize from a group with a mostly local focus to one with larger, international ambitions. The violence-prone and terrorism-inclined groups in the Middle East draw financial support, theological justification, and legions of recruits from among the more established Islamic fundamentalist institutions that have sprung up in the past three decades in virtually every Muslim country. Like a kettle of water boiling on a stove, out of which only a small volume of steam steadily escapes into the air, in the Middle East the forces associated with political Islam are kept simmering. Out of it, a steady stream of radicals is constantly emitted—extremists who are immediately absorbed by one of the already existing terrorist groups.

So what can the United States do to turn down the heat? To lower the political temperature underneath the Islamist movement?

First, the United States must do what it can to remove the grievances that cause angry Muslims to seek solace in organizations like the Muslim Brotherhood. Not all of these grievances, of course, are caused by the United States, and not all of them can be softened or ameliorated by U.S. actions. At the very least, however, the United States can take important steps that can weaken the ability of the Islamic right to harvest recruits. By joining with the UN, the Europeans, and Russia, the United States can help settle the Palestinian-Israeli conflict in a manner that guarantees justice for the Palestinians: an independent state that is geographically and economically viable, tied to the withdrawal of illegal Israeli settlements, an Israeli return roughly to its 1967 borders, and a stable and equitable division of Jerusalem. That, more than any other action, would remove a global *casus belli* for the Islamic right.

Second, the United States must abandon its imperial pretensions in the Middle East. That will require the withdrawal of U.S. forces from Afghanistan and Iraq, the dismantling of U.S. military bases in the Persian Gulf and facilities in Saudi Arabia, and a sharp reduction in the visibility of the U.S. Navy, military training missions, and arms sales. Many U.S. diplomats who have worked in the region know that the provocative U.S. presence in the Middle East fuels anger and resentment. The United States has no claim to either the Persian Gulf or the Middle East, whose future economic ties and political relationships can and must be determined solely by the leaders of the region's states, even if it redounds to the detriment of U.S. interests.

Third, the United States must refrain from seeking to impose its preferences on the region. Since 2001, the United States has done incalculable damage by demanding that the "greater Middle East" conform to American visions of democracy. To be sure, for the more radical idealists in the Bush administration, Bush's call for democracy in the Arab world and Iran is seen primarily as a pretext for more intrusive U.S. involvement in the region. Even taken at face value, however, the initiative ignores the fact that the nations of the Middle East must find democracy at their own pace and in their own time. An obsessive drive for democratic reform in the region is self-defeating and insulting to the states and peoples of the Middle East. Some of those states may be ready for reform, and some may not. Democratic changes that end up empowering the Islamic right and catapulting the Muslim Brotherhood to power in Cairo, Damascus, Riyadh, or Algiers will not serve their intended purpose. They will only deliver additional states into the hands of the Islamists. The United States should adopt a hands-off policy in connection with democracy in the Islamic world.

And fourth, the United States must abandon its propensity to make bellicose threats directed at nations in the Middle East, including those—such as Iran and Sudan—that are still under Islamist rule. The wave of Islamism may not yet have crested. Other nations may succumb to its tide before it recedes, since it is a force that has gathered momentum for decades. But the United States must get used to the fact that threats of force and imperial-sounding diktats strengthen Islamism. They do not diminish it.

The true emancipation of the Middle East will require action by the secular forces in the region to uplift, educate, and modernize the outlook of people who have been captured by Islamism. It is an effort that will take decades, but it must begin now. There is nothing about Islam that requires it to remain mired in the seventh-century belief that the Koran must govern the world of politics, education, science, and culture. It means changing a culture that allows millions of deluded Muslims to think that back-to-basics fundamentalism is somehow an appropriate answer to twenty-first-century problems and concerns. Fundamentalism, whether it takes the form of Islamism, or whether it appears in the form of America's Christian right or Israel's ultra-Orthodox settler movement, is always a reactionary force. In the Muslim world, a rational division of the secular and the divine is far from unheard of. Tens of millions of Muslims are able to separate their religious beliefs, held privately, from their politics, just as millions of Muslims, Christians, and Jews do in the United States. It is they—the true silent majority—who must seize the initiative from the fundamentalists. They may ask for, and should receive, support from civil society in the West: from NGOs and universities, from research centers and think tanks, and more.

The peoples of the Middle East must engage not only in nation building but in "religion building." As the hothouse temperatures in Middle East political discourse are lowered, Muslim religious scholars, philosophers, and social scientists can come together in a great debate to hammer out a twenty-first-century vision of a tolerant, modern Islam, to create a new culture no longer held hostage by self-dealing mullahs and ayatollahs. A consensus can emerge organically in the Muslim world that reinterprets ancient texts and traditions in a manner appropriate to an enlightened world outlook, and then that consensus must find its way into every nook and cranny, beginning in the major cities—Istanbul, Cairo, Baghdad, Karachi, Jakarta—and spreading to every village and mosque. It will mean reforming the educational curriculum in the Muslim world, deemphasizing religious universities and so-called madrassas in favor of modern education. It will require new mass-media outlets in places where they can flourish, and the use of radio, satellite television, and the Internet to reach places where they cannot. All this will take many years. It cannot occur unless the armed conflicts that roil the region are ended, and unless economic conditions move steadily upward. Religion building, like nation building, can take a long, long time.

1

IMPERIAL PAN-ISLAM

IN 1885, EXACTLY one hundred years before officials of the Reagan administration made a secret initiative toward Ayatollah Khomeini's Iran, a century before the United States spent billions of dollars in support of an anti-Soviet jihad in Afghanistan led by Islamic fundamentalist mujahideen, a peripatetic Persian-Afghan activist met in London with British intelligence and foreign policy officials to put forward a controversial idea. Would Britain, he wondered, be interested in organizing a pan-Islamic alliance among Egypt, Turkey, Persia, and Afghanistan against czarist Russia?[1]

It was the era of the Great Game, the long-running imperial struggle between Russia and England for control of Central Asia. The British, owners of India, had seized control of Egypt in 1881. Turkey's Ottoman Empire—which included, among other lands, what is now Iraq, Syria, Lebanon, Jordan, Israel, Saudi Arabia, and the Gulf states—was wobbly, too, and important pieces of it were up for grabs, although the final dismantling of Turkey's holdings would await World War I. The biggest imperial land rush in history was under way in Africa and southwest Asia. And the British, masters of manipulating tribal, ethnic, and religious affiliations, expert at setting minorities at one another's throats for the greater good of Her Majesty's realm, were intrigued with the idea of fostering a spirit of Islamic revivalism—if it could serve their purposes. Both Russia and France had the same idea, but it was the British, with their tens of millions of Muslim subjects in the greater Middle East and South Asia, who had the advantage.

The man who, in 1885, proposed the idea of a British-led pan-Islamic alliance was Jamal Eddine al-Afghani. From the 1870s to the 1890s, Afghani was supported by the United Kingdom, and at least once, the record shows—in 1882, in India, according to a secret file of the Indian government's intelligence service—Afghani officially offered to go to Egypt as an agent of British intelligence.[2]

Afghani, the founder of pan-Islam, is the great-great-grandfather of Osama bin Laden—not biologically, but in ideological terms. Were we to construct a biblical genealogy of right-wing Islamism, it would read like this: Afghani (1838–1897) begat Mohammed Abduh (1849–1905), an Egyptian pan-Islamic activist who was Afghani's chief disciple and who helped spread Afghani's message. Abduh begat Mohammed Rashid Rida (1865–1935), a Syrian disciple of Abduh's, who moved to Egypt and founded a magazine, *The Lighthouse,* to advocate Abduh's ideas in support of a system of Islamic republics. Rashid Rida begat Hassan al-Banna (1906–1949), who learned Islamism from Rashid Rida's *The Lighthouse,* and who founded the Muslim Brotherhood in Egypt in 1928. Banna begat many offspring. Among them were his son-in-law, Said Ramadan, the Muslim Brotherhood's international organizer, whose headquarters were in Switzerland, and Abul-Ala Mawdudi, the founder of the Islamic Group in Pakistan, the first Islamist political party, who was inspired by Banna's work. Banna's other heirs set up branches of the Brotherhood in every Muslim state, in Europe, and in the United States. Another of Banna's offspring, a Saudi who took part in America's Afghan jihad, was Al Qaeda's Osama bin Laden, the family's blackest sheep.

In the half century between 1875 and 1925, the building blocks of the Islamic right were cemented in place by the British empire. Afghani created the intellectual foundation for a pan-Islamic movement—with British patronage and the support of England's leading Orientalist, E. G. Browne. Abduh, Afghani's chief disciple, founded, with the help of London's Egyptian proconsul, Evelyn Baring Lord Cromer, the Salafiyya movement, the radical-right, back-to-basics fundamentalist current that still exists today. To understand the proper role of Afghani and Abduh, it is important to see them as experiments in a century-long British effort to organize a pro-British pan-Islamic movement. Afghani, a quixotic and slippery ally, shopped his services to other imperial powers, and ultimately his mystical, semi-modernist version of fundamentalist Islam failed to rise to the level of a mass movement. Abduh, his chief disciple, attached himself more firmly to the British rulers of Egypt and created the cornerstone of the Muslim Brotherhood, which dominated the Islamic right throughout the twentieth century. The British backed Abduh even as they launched two other pre–World War I schemes to mobilize Islamic fervor. In the Arabian Peninsula, the British helped a desert band of ultra-fundamentalist Arabs, led by the family of Ibn Saud, create the world's first Islamic fundamentalist state in Saudi Arabia. At the same time, they encouraged the Hashemites of Mecca, a second Arabian family with a spurious claim to be descended from the original prophet of Islam, whose sons London installed as kings of Iraq and Jordan.

Originally, the Hashemites, as guardians of the Arabian holy cities of Mecca and Medina, were supposed to have assumed the leadership of the entire Muslim world, with the idea of establishing a pro-British caliphate to replace the faltering one in Turkey. That plan never quite came together, but a parallel one did. From the 1920s on, the new Saudi state merged its Wahhabi orthodoxy with the Salafiyya, now organized into the Muslim Brotherhood—and the resurgence of Islam was under way.

It was Afghani, however, who started it all. Like many of his progeny, Afghani made common cause with the imperial powers as they competed for influence over the vast swath of territory between east Africa and China. Years after his death, many—but not all—of his biographers and chroniclers have painted him as a believer, consistently advocating a renaissance of Islam; as an anti-imperialist, thundering against the great powers; and as a liberal reformer, seeking to blend medieval Islam with the scientific rationalism of the Enlightenment. While elements of all this are present in Afghani's career, he was above all a political magician who invoked religion for temporal ends, and who was at once ally, errand boy, and tool of the imperial powers. Although Afghani rarely missed an opportunity to offer his services, in serial fashion, to the British, to the French, and to the Russians, and served as an agent for all three, his followers—Abduh especially— became increasingly Anglophilic.

Born in 1838, apparently in Persia, Jamal Eddine adopted the name "al-Afghani" in order to create the impression that he was born in Afghanistan. By claiming Afghan origins, Afghani could disguise his identity as both a Persian and a Shiite, the minority branch of Islam, thus giving him a broader appeal in the mostly Sunni Muslim world. Lying about his place of birth was just Afghani's first dissimulation. According to Elie Kedourie, a leading British Orientalist, Afghani's followers (including Abduh and Rashid Rida) "practiced economy of truth."[3] Throughout his life, Afghani dissembled. Although he is rightly credited with having developed the theoretical basis for a pan-Islamic political and social movement spanning the entire Muslim world, he was a heterodox thinker who was a Freemason, a mystic, a political operative, and, above all, someone who believed, as Kedourie wrote, in the "social utility of religion."[4] Afghani treated religion as a tool. He was outwardly pious, constructing a detailed scheme for a politics governed by the pared-down, seventh-century version of the simple Muslim society of Mecca during the era of the Prophet. But in his more esoteric writing, Afghani was explicit about his beliefs:

> We do not cut the head of religion except with the sword of religion. Therefore, if you were to see us now, you would see ascetics and worshippers, kneeling and genuflecting, never disobeying God's commands and doing all that they are ordered to do.[5]

Noted Kedourie: "This letter makes absolutely clear that one of Afghani's aims—of which his disciple Abduh knew and approved— was the subversion of the Islamic religion, and that the method adopted to this end was the practice of a false but showy devotion."[6]

In fact, although he preached Islamic orthodoxy to the masses, Afghani was a closet atheist who railed against not only Islam, but all religions, to more esoteric groups of listeners:

> Religions [wrote Afghani], whatever they are called, resemble one another. No understanding and no reconciliation is possible between these religions and philosophy. Religion imposes its faith and its creed on man, while philosophy liberates him from them wholly or in part.

However, Afghani concluded: "[But] reason does not please the mass and its teachings are understood only by a few choice spirits."[7] The elitism of this passage is an essential part of Afghani's mystique. Throughout his life, Afghani had one message for the "mass" and another for the "choice spirits": for the masses, pan-Islam; for the elite, an eclectic brand of philosophy. And while he posed as an anti-imperialist when it suited his purposes, Afghani and those in his inner circle engaged in conspiratorial alliance with those very imperialists.

Many historians, however, take the Afghani story at face value: that as an Islamic activist, he helped to create a movement that would restore Islam to its former glory, to recapture the pristine, golden days of the Prophet's rule in Mecca and Medina. Much conventional wisdom portrays Afghani as a crusader against imperialism, and as a reformer who sought to bring enlightenment and rationalism to a fogbound Islamic intellectual tradition controlled by a stodgy clergy. Sadly, that is the view propounded by some of the leading Anglo-American Orientalists. H. A. R. Gibb, author of the classic *Modern Trends in Islam* (1947), wrote that Afghani believed in a state governed by "sound Koranic orthodoxy"[8] mixed with a modernistic outlook, while Wilfred Cantwell Smith called Afghani "the complete Muslim of his time." In his landmark work, *Islam in Modern History*, Smith wrote breathlessly about Afghani's alleged anti-imperialism:

> He [Afghani] saw the West as something primarily to be resisted, because it threatened Islam and the community. . . . He was vigorous in inciting his Muslim hearers to develop reason and technology

as the West was doing, in order to be strong. . . . Indeed, this urging to action, from a non-responsible quietude to a self-directing determination, was carried further into an almost irrepressible or effervescent dynamism.[9]

Smith wrote admiringly of Afghani that

geographically, his career encompassed Iran, India, the Arab world, and Turkey, as well as the European West. He was both Sufi and Sunni. He preached a reconciliation with the Shiah. He united with traditional Islamic scholarship a familiarity with Europe and an acquaintance with its modern thought. . . . He inspired political revolutionaries and venerable scholars. He advocated both local nationalisms and pan-Islam. A very great deal of subsequent Islamic development is adumbrated in his personality and career. In fact, there is very little in twentieth-century Islam not foreshadowed in Afghani.[10]

Correctly, Smith added that Afghani was "the first Muslim revivalist to use the concepts 'Islam' and 'the West' as connoting antagonistic historical phenomena."[11] That makes Afghani the true originator of the concept of a clash of civilizations, as popularized a century later by Bernard Lewis and Samuel Huntington.

Whether Afghani was, as Smith maintains, irrepressibly dynamic or merely opportunistic, there is no question about his role as godfather to the Muslim Brotherhood and similar groups on the Islamic right. The devout and militant Brothers of today would no doubt be shocked to learn that their inspirational forerunner Jamal Eddine al-Afghani was an atheist and a Freemason. Nonetheless, Richard P. Mitchell, whose book *The Society of the Muslim Brothers* is the definitive work on the organization, observed that the pedigree for the militant, terrorist organization that rose to prominence in Egypt after World War II goes directly back to Afghani. "The Brothers saw themselves clearly in the line of the modern reform movement identified with the names of Jamal al-Din al-Afghani, Mohammed Abduh, and Rashid Rida," he wrote. "Towards Afghani the Brothers felt a special kinship. Many felt him to be the 'spiritual father' of the movement and to him Banna was most often compared."[12]

AFGHANI AND HIS FOLLOWERS

Afghani's public life began in 1869, when he left Afghanistan. Little is known about his life before that. He claimed to have been involved in Afghan politics in the 1860s, and according to a leading scholar he did so while acting as a Russian agent.[13] But his lasting impact began only in 1869, when he undertook a remarkable, quarter-century-long odyssey.

Even in brief outline, it is dizzying. He went first to India, whose British-led colonial authorities welcomed the Islamic scholar with honors, graciously escorting him aboard a government-owned vessel on an all-expenses-paid voyage to Suez. After visiting Cairo, he traveled to Turkey, where his unorthodox religious views caused a furor among the religious establishment, leading the Turkish government to expel him unceremoniously. Back in Cairo, Afghani was adopted by the Egyptian prime minister, Riad Pasha, a notorious reactionary and enemy of the nascent nationalist movement in Egypt. Riad Pasha persuaded Afghani to stay in Egypt, and allowed him to take up residence at Cairo's 900-year-old Al Azhar mosque, considered the center of Islamic learning worldwide, where he received lodging and a monthly government stipend. It was Afghani's first official post as an Islamic scholar, and the first (but not last) time he would be on the payroll of one of the imperial powers or their stand-ins. Afghani spent eight years in the midst of Egypt's tumultuous politics, up to the eve of England's shelling of Alexandria and the British occupation of Egypt.

Feted by the British in India, transported by London to Egypt, and sponsored by England's agents in Cairo, Afghani patiently laid the cornerstone of pan-Islam. But the vicissitudes of Egyptian colonial politics were not always kind to him: as nationalism in Egypt gained strength (until crushed by the British), Afghani's influence declined. In 1879, he was expelled from Egypt, beginning a sojourn that took him to India, London, Paris (where he stayed three years), Russia (where he spent four years), Munich, and Iran. In Iran, the shah made him war minister and then prime minister, but Afghani and the shah soon parted ways, and Afghani began agitating against the Persian monarch. Foreshadowing

Ayatollah Khomeini's 1970s revolution, Afghani took refuge in a mosque and organized the clergy to support him, until he was arrested and deported to Turkey. In 1896, his followers would assassinate the shah, ending that king's fifty-year reign. Afghani died in 1897.

Always it was Afghani's secret activities that set him apart.

In the 1870s, in Egypt—while outwardly professing to be a pious Muslim—Afghani frequented the lodges of the Anglo-Egyptian and Franco-Egyptian Freemason societies. He delved into mysticism, including Sufism. On his expulsion from Egypt, the British consul-general, in an intelligence report, said that Afghani "was recently expelled from the Freemasons' Lodge at Cairo, of which he was a member, on account of his open disbelief in a Supreme Being." According to Kedourie, Afghani was a member of the General Scotch Lodge,[14] which was organized around the alleged mysteries of the Egyptian pyramids and the so-called Grand Architect, the Freemasons' concept of a god. Many British and French officials in the nineteenth century were caught up in an obsessive fascination with the "Orient," the pyramids, Masonic lore, and assorted cults of secret brotherhoods, and used these fraternities as channels of imperial power, often competitively.

It was in the late 1870s that Afghani met the man who would become his chief disciple, Mohammed Abduh. As a fixture at Al Azhar, Cairo's historic mosque, Afghani gathered around himself a burgeoning group of acolytes, none more attached to him personally than Abduh. Born in Egypt in 1849, Abduh was raised by a family of devout Islamic scholars, and by the age of ten he had memorized the Koran and was able to recite it in the precise, singsong fashion venerated by the elders. Like Afghani, Abduh was also drawn to the mystical Sufi brotherhoods, with their transcendent view of spiritual life. Sufism, an ancient current within Islam, challenged many orthodox Muslim beliefs in favor of a meditative, introspective approach to "oneness" with God, and the movement gave rise to many *tariqa,* or brotherhoods, some organized as tightly bound secret societies and others as hierarchical mass movements spread over vast geographic areas.

Abduh was taken with Afghani almost instantly, and they developed a bond. According to Kedourie, the biographer of Afghani and Abduh,

When Abduh met Afghani he was some twenty-two years old, an ardent young man going through a crucial phase in his spiritual life, and this no doubt made him impressionable; but Afghani must have had a powerful magnetic personality to have exercised over Abduh then and for many years afterward so strange and tenacious an influence. The link between them is very much that of the master and disciple in some secret, esoteric cult.[15]

For eight years, between 1871 and 1879, the two men worked closely together. They organized not only in Egypt, but throughout the region, and built a diverse collection of followers, some of whom—including a group of mystical Christians from Syria who were attracted to Afghani's offbeat message—founded the Young Egypt secret society. Gradually, Afghani and Abduh amassed a coterie of devoted followers around Al Azhar. In 1878, Riad Pasha, the prime minister and Afghani's protector, went out of his way to appoint Abduh to a prominent post as a history teacher at Dar al-Ulum, a newly launched Islamic school, and as professor of language and literature at another institution. Eventually, when Riad Pasha's power ebbed, Afghani and Abduh left Egypt. In Cairo, nationalists in the army were gaining momentum, led by the famous Egyptian hero, Ahmad Arabi, a colonel and war minister, who led an uprising against the British role in Egypt. Arabi's movement was crushed, the British completed their occupation of Egypt, and Arabi was exiled to Ceylon. Abduh opposed the military's resistance to the British, advocating a middle ground, decrying violence, and trying to arrange a compromise between the army's fierce nationalism and London's imperial designs. Abduh's chief acolyte and biographer, Rashid Rida, summed it up: "He was the opponent of the military revolution even though he was a directing spirit to the intellectual movement. He hated the revolution and was opposed to its leaders."[16]

There was a pattern here that would endear right-wing Islamists to Western imperial strategists for generations to come. The opposition of Afghani and Abduh to Egyptian nationalism, and their support for vague notions of an Islamic state, foreshadowed the Muslim Brotherhood's opposition to President Gamal Abdel Nasser in the 1950s, the resistance of the Muslim Brotherhood–led Hamas in Palestine to the nationalism of the Palestine Liberation Organization, and countless other instances in which Islamists opposed nationalism and left-wing movements during the Cold War.

Afghani and Abduh did not confine themselves merely to intellectual theorizing and Islamic scholarship. When Afghani was finally expelled from Egypt, he and Abduh were accused of organizing "a secret society composed of 'young thugs,'" apparently a reference to unruly members of the Masonic lodge that Afghani led,[17] foreshadowing the paramilitary organization established by the Muslim Brotherhood in the 1930s. Leaving Egypt, Afghani endorsed Abduh as his fit successor: "I leave you Shaikh Mohammed Abduh, and he is sufficient for Egypt as a scholar."[18] Abduh was temporarily exiled to his village in Egypt, though he would later join Afghani in Paris and then return to Egypt in triumph, with the full support of the representatives of Her Majesty's imperial officers.

Upon leaving Egypt in 1879, Afghani went to Arabia, then to India. Soon afterward Afghani, later joined by Abduh, migrated to Paris, where the two men began their most productive collaboration. It was in Paris, in the mid-1880s, that Afghani and Abduh built the network that would continue after their deaths. In 1884, the two men began publishing a weekly newspaper called *The Indissoluble Bond*. Though it lasted only eighteen issues, the paper had great influence. Exactly how it was financed is unclear, though Kedourie suggests that it was supported secretly by the French government, to which Afghani turned after his formal offer in India to become a British agent was rejected.[19] C. C. Adams, who in 1933 wrote the most complete biography of Abduh, notes that *The Indissoluble Bond* was "the organ of a secret organization bearing the same name, founded by [Afghani], composed of Muslims of India, Egypt, North Africa and Syria, the purpose of which was to 'unite Muslims and arouse them from the sleep and acquaint them with the dangers threatening them and guide them to the way of meeting these dangers.'"[20] Afghani also organized a pan-Islamic society in Mecca that had as its goal the creation of a single caliphate to lead the entire Muslim world.

Whether Afghani and Abduh were acting on their own initiative at this time, or—more likely—in cooperation with London or Paris, is unclear. Immediately afterward, however, the French government halted publication of *The Indissoluble Bond,* and Afghani and Abduh traveled to London, ostensibly to discuss the crisis in the Sudan, where they proposed the notion of a pan-Islamic alliance with Great Britain. The proposal was advanced in the midst of a tribal-religious rebellion against the British in the Sudan, led by the charismatic Mohammed Ahmad, a Sudanese sheikh who proclaimed himself the Mahdi, or savior, and led a puritanical Islamic revolt. Two versions of Islamism came into conflict: the Mahdi's, a feral, angry revolt in which nationalist sentiments were in part disguised by religious language, and Afghani's, an Anglophilic version of Islamism that viewed the Mahdi as primitive and uncouth. In 1885, the forces of the Mahdi, calling themselves the Helpers of the Prophet, defeated and killed the celebrated British general, Charles Gordon, and captured Khartoum. Afghani sought to maintain his pan-Islamic credentials by paying lip service to the Mahdi, but—continuing to cultivate his British patrons—he opposed the Sudanese rebel behind the scenes. "I fear, as all wise men fear, that the dissemination of this doctrine [mahdism] and the increase of its votaries will harm England and anyone having rights in Egypt," wrote Afghani. In a separate piece, entitled "England on the Shores of the Red Sea," Afghani argued that the Mahdi was attracting the support of the "simple-minded." He suggested in another article that the Mahdi's revolt could be met only by an opposing challenge that used Islam as its organizing principle. "The strength of an Islamic preaching," he wrote, "cannot be met except by an Islamic resolution, and none but Muslim men can struggle with this pretender and reduce him to his proper stature."[21]

Afghani, in other words, proposed fighting fire with fire—Islam with Islam. The British, apparently, did not take him up on this proposal, a rejection that angered Afghani, though Abduh remained faithful to London. In going their separate ways, Afghani went to Russia while Abduh journeyed to Tunis, in North Africa. From there, Abduh "then traveled incognito in a number of other countries, strengthening the organization of the society they had founded."[22] Their message, to the masses at least, was one of pan-Islam in its purest form:

The religion of Islam is the one bond which unites Muslims of all countries and obliterates all traces of race or nationality. . . . The Muslim peoples were once united under one glorious empire, and their achievements in learning and philosophy and all the sciences are still the boast of all Muslims. It is a duty incumbent upon all Muslims to aid in maintaining the authority of Islam and Islamic rule over all lands that have once been Muslim. . . . The only cure for these nations is to return to the rules of their religion and the practice of its requirements according to what it was in the beginning, in the days of the early Caliphs. . . . The supreme authority over all should be the Koran.[23]

Today it seems standard Islamist boilerplate, and could be taken from the pages of a Muslim Brotherhood tract or an Al Qaeda communiqué. But in the 1880s, it was a new concept, and a revolutionary one. Not in centuries had Muslims heard a challenge to renew their societies according to the methods of the early caliphs. And the message in this call to arms, published in *The Indissoluble Bond,* about restoring Islamic rule "over all lands that have once been Muslim," read like a jihad-style summons to recapture parts of Spain, central Europe, and lands where provinces had fallen to Christianity or other religions. It was a challenge whose promise would seize T. E. Lawrence and his British intelligence cohorts at the Arab Bureau in Cairo during World War I, when London posthumously took up Afghani and Abduh's proposal to mobilize Muslims for a new caliphate, one that could at once undermine the crumbling Turkish empire and threaten Russia.

Abduh, who had returned to Egypt on occasion in disguise during his travels in the 1880s, watched as Egypt's nationalists were scattered by the British. By the late 1880s Abduh openly cast his lot with Lord Cromer and the British administration in Egypt. In 1888, with Cromer's help, Abduh returned openly to Egypt and took the first of several official positions in Cairo. Like Afghani, Abduh spoke quietly about the "social utility of religion."[24] Kedourie, analyzing his collected lectures from Beirut, published as *Risala,* concludes: "It is clear that . . . the erstwhile mystic, outwardly a divine, was secretly a free thinker, like his master." On returning to Cairo, Abduh forged a partnership with Lord Cromer, who was the symbol of British imperialism in Egypt. Born Evelyn Baring, he was a scion of the enormously powerful Baring banking clan of the City of London, and he had served in the 1870s as the first British commissioner of the Egyptian public debt office and then controller general. After London crushed Arabi's revolt, Baring returned to Egypt in 1883 as British agent and consul general, and he served as the virtual ruler of the country until 1907. Abduh and Cromer became friends and confidants, the militant Islamist and the aristocratic British empire builder who became his patron. With Cromer's backing, Abduh was named to lead a committee to reorganize Al Azhar, became the editor of Egypt's *Official Journal,* and was appointed to Egypt's Legislative Council, where he became "its leading member whose opinion on every question was heard with respect. He was chairman of its most important committees."[25]

Finally, in 1899, two years after Afghani's death, Abduh was named mufti of Egypt. As mufti, he "was the supreme interpreter of the canon law of Islam (the sharia) for the whole country, and his fatwas, or legal opinions, touching any matters that were referred to him, were authoritative and final."[26] It also gave him significant patronage power, since he helped oversee the rich religious endowments, or *waqfs.*

As Abduh's influence in Egypt grew, Afghani spent a few years in Russia, where he had gone to sulk after London rejected his offer to help build a pan-Islamic alliance. According to Kedourie, Afghani, for a time at least, was "a client and subsequently an agent of Russia."[27] He reportedly tried to sell Moscow on the idea that he could help spark a revolt in India, the very heart of the British Empire. According to a British intelligence report from 1888, Afghani "had impressed upon some Russian officials the prospect of a general uprising in India whenever the Russians chose to give the signal."[28] It seems that the Russians didn't buy what Afghani was selling, and soon afterward he was back in London.

Afghani's London contacts were diverse. He plunged into a world that included a swirling mix of freethinkers, Masons, Gnostics, mystics,

Sufis and other experimenters in religion and the divine, blended with writers, travelers, and Orientalists fascinated with the so-called Near East. It was a heady time. London in the late nineteenth century was like a gigantic melting pot of religious activism. Many British intellectuals, and not a few imperialists, were seized with a desire to find a sort of holy grail, a unified field theory of religious belief. Religious syncretism won followers among the elites, along with the idea that perhaps some new cult, some new system of belief, would emerge, one that could unite the empire's many cultures. Experimental religions, some of whose roots went back into the early nineteenth century, began to flourish—and Afghani, whose view of Islam was tempered by a deeper commitment to mysticism, the Sufi brotherhoods, Freemasonry, and philosophical skepticism, was open to it all.

One of Afghani's most important contacts in London was the renowned British Orientalist Edward Granville Browne. Browne, a Cambridge University professor, is perhaps the godfather of twentieth-century Orientalism, especially in the area of Persian and religious studies, and he exerted enormous influence not only over academics but policy makers as well, until his death in 1926. As we shall see, E. G. Browne was a teacher and friend to the powerful, including two leading British intelligence operatives, Harry St. John Bridger Philby and T. E. Lawrence, during Britain's intense engagement in the Middle East in World War I. In the 1880s and 1890s, Browne traveled widely in the Arab world, Turkey, and Persia, and he specialized in cultlike movements, Sufism, and the alternative mystery religions springing up in the Middle East.

Browne's Persian teacher was Mirza Mohammed Baqir. "Having wandered through half the world," wrote Browne, "learned (and learned well) half a dozen languages, and been successively a Shiite Muhammadan, a dervish, a Christian, an atheist, a Jew, [Baqir] had finished by elaborating a religious system of his own, which he called 'Islamo-Christianity.' "[29] The two men became close, and Browne, inspired by the works of an eccentric specialist in the religions of central Asia, Joseph de Gobineau, delved into movements like the Baha'is, developing a lifelong fascination with that odd religious cult.

Like Mirza Baqir's Islamo-Christianity, the Baha'is promoted an odd, syncretistic faith based in Persia, with outposts in Haifa and elsewhere. For years, the Baha'is were viewed with suspicion in the Middle East, with many conspiracy-minded political and religious leaders accusing them of Masonic connections and ties to British intelligence. But the Baha'is were openly Anglophiles, and after World War I, one of the Baha'is' founders, Abdul Baha, was knighted by the government of Great Britain. Browne became perhaps the chief publicist in the West for the Baha'is, and he apparently believed that the Baha'i movement was destined to play a shaping role in the future of religion in the Middle East.

Both Afghani and Abduh had multiple contacts with Browne, Mirza Baqir, and the Baha'is. According to Kedourie, Abduh and Baqir debated theology and the Koran in Paris during the time when Afghani and Abduh were publishing *The Indissoluble Bond*, and Afghani sent the newspaper to the Baha'i movement's leaders in their Middle East headquarters. Another person who played an important role in furthering Afghani's increasing involvement in Persia—where he would eventually become prime minister—was Malkam Khan. Malkam Khan was the Persian ambassador to London for many years, the son of the founder of the Persian Society of Freemasons. Like Afghani, the Baha'is, and Baqir, Khan believed that a reformed, universalist "religion of humanity" was the prerequisite for political action in the Middle East, especially in Persia. Even though Afghani never abandoned his rhetorical support for a fundamentalist version of Islam, under Khan's influence Afghani formed the "Arab Masonic society."[30] The chameleon-like Afghani seemed to believe in combining a simplistic version of Islam for the "simple-minded," or the masses, with a top-down, syncretistic one-world religion above it.

But Afghani's career ended, partially at least, in failure. With the support of Malkam Khan, he spent most of his final years in Persia, as war minister and prime minister, but his ideas didn't succeed in winning over either the shah or the Iranian elite. Tired of Afghani's appeals to Iran's mullahs, the shah acted. "The Shah finally violated the sanctuary of the mosque and had Jamal arrested, although on a sick bed at the time, and conveyed to the Turkish border."[31] He would bounce back and forth between Turkey, Afghanistan, and Persia during the 1890s, "attracting," Kedourie says, "the attention . . . of security and intelligence departments."[32] At the very end of his life, the British bailed him out once more. "In 1895 Afghani, then at Istanbul, some two years before his death finding himself in Sultan Abdul Hamid's bad books, and threatened with extradition to Persia where he was wanted for subversion, applied to the British Ambassador for protection as an Afghan subject."[33] The British consulate gave Afghani a pass, allowing him to leave the sultan's territory. He eventually returned to Turkey, where the itinerant pan-Islamist died of cancer in 1897. E. G. Browne ensured that Afghani's fame would last long beyond his death by lionizing him in his 1910 classic *The Persian Revolution*.

But Lord Cromer, ever the practical imperialist, wrote perhaps the ultimate epitaph for Afghani, Abduh, and the first generation of Islamic revivalists. "They were much too tainted with heterodoxy to carry far along with the conservative Moslems. Nor were they sufficiently Europeanized to win the mimics of European ways. They were neither good enough Moslems, nor good enough Europeans." Like a scientist closing the books on an experiment that failed, Lord Cromer concluded that the pan-Islam of Afghani and Abduh needed a major revision. Its Masonic-tinged, universalist modernism didn't blend well with a call to return to seventh-century Islamic purism, and so it had failed to win the allegiance of either the clergy or the modernizers. Eventually, Afghani's ideas, preserved by the journalist Rashid Rida, who founded *The Lighthouse,* the publication that brought Afghani and Abduh's ideas to the Egyptian Salafiyya and the Muslim Brotherhood, would find more fertile soil. In the meantime, the British would turn to a much less ambiguous version of Islamist radicalism in the next phase of their colonial policy in the Middle East: Saudi Arabian Wahhabism.

ABDULLAH PHILBY'S BROTHERHOOD

From 1899 through the aftermath of World War I, Great Britain embarked on one of the most remarkable imperial gambits ever conceived. The Ottoman Empire, the nineteenth century's "sick man of Europe," was finally in its death throes. The rise of the imperial navies, railroads, and finally the development of the internal combustion engine and the automobile created an insatiable demand for oil. Despite the growth of Texas, Romania, and Baku as centers of oil production, it had also begun to dawn on imperial strategists that Persia, Iraq, and Arabia had untold petroleum wealth. Hard-headed imperialists saw southwest Asia as a gigantic chess board, and they were playing for keeps. London's gambit was to make a play for the loyalty of the world's Muslims, not by appealing to the Islamic world's enlightened, modernizing Muslim elite but to its traditionalist-minded masses and autocrats.

While fending off the French in the Middle East, the British had simultaneously to deal with three other powers. The Russians, seeming to press inexorably down from the north, were one concern. The Germans, whose global power was expanding under the Kaiser, were fast building ties to Turkey while making plans to construct a rail line from Berlin to Baghdad. And the Turks, whose empire's life force was ebbing, still had an ace in the hole, namely, the existence of a caliphate in Istanbul that, nominally at least, could claim the allegiance of orthodox Sunni Muslims everywhere.

London was firmly in control of India (including, of course, what is now Muslim Pakistan), and thanks to Lord Cromer the British had locked up Egypt and the Suez Canal as their lifeline to India. They had significant, even dominant influence in Afghanistan and Persia. And they had important surrounding real estate, from Cyprus to East Africa to Aden that could be used to bring power to bear in the Persian Gulf. For their gambit to seize control of Iraq and Arabia, they needed a force to challenge Turkey's control of that vast expanse of sand-covered territory.

The first step in accomplishing that feat was the forging of an

alliance for the English throne with the future king of Saudi Arabia—
and with the long-established Wahhabi Islamic movement. To understand how the British-Saudi alliance developed, we must first take a
step back into the eighteenth century, when the entente between the
Al Saud, the future royal family, and the Al Shaikh, the Wahhabi family of the Islamists, was first cemented.

In the middle of the eighteenth century, an itinerant Muslim
preacher, sort of an Arabian Elmer Gantry, began crisscrossing the
northern reaches of the peninsula and the Fertile Crescent, from
Mecca and Medina to the al-Hasa Oasis in the east to Basra, Baghdad,
and Damascus. Mohammad ibn Abdul Wahhab, born in 1703, was
not a city dweller, and he didn't bother with the kind of learning that
occurred in the Arab world's intellectual centers. Spreading the
Islamic version of fire and brimstone, Abdul Wahhab thundered that
the Muslims needed to purge themselves of everything that had been
learned since the days of the Prophet a thousand years before. It was a
revivalist movement in the classic sense, with eager followers packing
tents thrown up by Abdul Wahhab's organizers.

Abdul Wahhab's most important convert was the founder of the Al
Saud dynasty, Mohammed ibn Saud. Ibn Saud apparently saw himself
as an eighteenth-century version of the Prophet Mohammed, conquering lands for Islam and imposing his faith on the conquered. To
reinforce their message, Abdul Wahhab, Ibn Saud, and their followers
had the unfortunate habit of slaughtering anyone who disagreed with
them and demolishing their cities, their mosques, and their shrines.

Abdul Wahhab was called "the Teacher," or *al-shaikh* in Arabic,
and from then on the descendants of the Abdul Wahhab clan were
called the Al Shaikh.[34] The alliance between the Al Saud and the Al
Shaikh families evolved into the Saudi state in the 1920s. It wasn't
without its ups and downs, however; from the 1700s through the
1920s, the Al Saud repeatedly founded states that would, in turn, be
swept away either by the more worldly, and less fanatical, Ottomans
and their allies in Egypt, or by rival Arabian tribes.

In standard accounts of the rise of the Wahhabis, it is usually said,
often with respect, that the Wahhabis were reformers and modernizers, or that they united the Arabian Peninsula around the idea of

tawhid, or monotheism. (The term *Wahhabism* is considered somewhat insulting by its adherents, who prefer the term *Unitarians,* from "unity of God.")[35] And Wahhab is often described as a thinker, whose philosophical work and interpretation of the Koran were groundbreaking. Not so. Hamid Algar, author of *Wahhabism: A Critical Essay,* notes that the Arabian desert and Abdul Wahhab's so-called theology had something in common. "Its topographical barrenness seems always to have been reflected in its intellectual history," he writes.[36] In discussing "what might charitably be called the scholarly output of Muhammad b. Abd al-Wahhab," Algar says that his works are simplistic and superficial, comprised mostly of reprinted collections of the Prophet's sayings and containing little or no "elucidation or commentary." Even the custodians of Wahhabism, notes Algar wryly, are "embarrassed by the slightness of [his] opus."[37] A great thinker he was not.

But Abdul Wahhab was a master at hurling polemical thunderbolts at moderate Muslims, accusing them of abandoning Islam, of apostasy, of heresies, and worse. Joining forces with the Al Saud, the Wahhabis assembled a mighty army of followers, who spent centuries wreaking havoc across Arab territory. They were, in the words of a nineteenth-century English writer, notorious for "preferring slaughter to booty" in their conquests.[38] The slaughter never ended. In the 1700s, the Saud-Wahhabi alliance began a "campaign of killing and plunder all across Arabia," first in central Arabia, then in Asir in southern Arabia and parts of Yemen, and finally in Riyadh and the Hijaz.[39] In 1802 they raided the Shiite holy city of Karbala in what is now Iraq, killing most of the city's population, destroying the dome over the grave of a founder of Shiism, and looting "property, weapons, clothing, carpets, gold, silver, [and] precious copies of the Quran."[40] In fact, Wahhabism would be weirdly marked by a "signature activity of dome demolition."[41] Domes in Mecca, too, would be destroyed in the early part of the nineteenth century. (It is a practice that continues today. In the former Yugoslavia, Saudi Arabia would demand radical changes in Islamic sites. "Saudi aid agencies," wrote John Esposito, "have been responsible for the destruction or reconstruction of many historic mosques, libraries, Quran schools, and cemeteries in Bosnia and Kosovo because their Ottoman architecture, decorations, frescoes, and tombstones did not conform to Wahhabi iconoclastic aesthetics.")[42]

As the dome-destroyers expanded their power in Arabia, they ultimately came into contact with Great Britain. England's ties to the Al Saud began in the mid-nineteenth century, when a British colonel made contact with the House of Saud in Riyadh, the sleepy desert city that would eventually be the capital of Arabia. "The first contact was made in 1865, and British subsidies started to flow into the coffers of the Saudi family, in ever growing quantity as World War One grew closer," reports Algar.[43]

In 1899, Lord Curzon, then viceroy of India, carved out the protectorate of Kuwait, and London's ties to the Al Saud and the Wahhabis began in earnest. The Al Saud, struggling to impose their will in Arabia, were invited to establish a base in Kuwait, a tiny emirate south of Basra that was increasingly an outpost of British imperial power and control.[44] Just three years later, the Al Saud would begin the final effort to secure control over the whole of the Arabian Peninsula. "The Amir of Kuwait," according to an account, "dispatched Ibn Saud, then just twenty years old, to try to retake Riyadh from the [pro-Ottoman] Rashids."[45] Riyadh fell to Ibn Saud in 1902, and it was during this period that Ibn Saud established the fearsome Brotherhood, known by their Arabic name, the Ikhwan.[46] He collected fighters from Bedouin tribes, fired them up with fanatical religious zeal, and threw them into battle. By 1912, the Brotherhood numbered 11,000, and Ibn Saud had both central Arabia's Nejd and al-Hasa in the east under his control.

Between 1899 and the outbreak of World War I, rumors of oil in the Middle East became reality. The first oil "concessions"—really one-sided, imperialist deals imposed by oil men backed by great-power gunboats on weak vassal states and captive tribal leaders—were signed. Suddenly the Persian Gulf emerged as a strategic site. Arabia and the Gulf had been viewed by Great Britain as one link in a chain that ran from Suez to India, the two anchors of the empire. Slowly, the reverse seemed truer: Suez and India would, increasingly, be seen as bases from which the British would be able to protect their burgeoning oil interests in southern Persia, Iraq, and the Gulf. William Shakespear, the felicitously named British officer who was appointed political agent in Kuwait, became the first of several legendary British liaisons to the Al Saud, and he forged the first formal treaty between England and Saudi Arabia, which was signed in 1915. Punctuating his accomplishment, Shakespear died in battle alongside the Al Saud in a desert confrontation with the rival Al Rashid tribe. But the treaty he designed bound London and Arabia, years before Saudi Arabia was a country. "It formally recognized Ibn Saud as the independent ruler of the Nejd and its Dependencies under British protection. In return, Ibn Saud undertook to follow British advice."[47]

With the outbreak of war in 1914, Great Britain saw a golden opportunity to oust Turkey from Arabia. As the Ottoman Empire wobbled, two British teams backed two distinct—and opposing—Arab players in the barren, desert stretches of the Arabian peninsula.

The first team was led by Harry St. John Bridger Philby, a British operative well schooled in the political utility of religious belief by none other than E. G. Browne. Scion of a modestly distinguished British family with ties to Ceylon and India, Philby was a product of England's most prestigious schools, including Westminster, where he was a Queen's Scholar, and Trinity College, Cambridge, where he became a disciple of E. G. Browne's.[48] At the dawn of the twentieth century, Cambridge was a training ground for empire builders, and he rubbed elbows there with England's (and the world's) best and brightest. Grounded in the ties between church and state in England, and with an intimate familiarity with the Anglican establishment, Philby, though an atheist, exhibited a strong appreciation of religion's influence on politics, and he described religious belief as "of all conventions the greatest, . . . so strong in its resistance to all opposition."[49] At Cambridge he studied philosophy, oriental languages, and Indian law, and then joined the Indian Civil Service. Philby—who would later undergo a sham conversion to Islam, adopting the name "Abdullah"—would carry Browne's lessons with him to India, where he served as a minor functionary, and then to Arabia, where he succeeded Shakespear as Great Britain's liaison to Ibn Saud.

While Philby's team, Britain's India Office, backed the Al Saud, their friendly rivals were based in Cairo at the Arab Bureau, a branch of British intelligence, which sponsored the famous T. E. Lawrence ("of Arabia"). The Arab Bureau backed the Sharif of Mecca, Hussein, head of the Hashemite dynasty, and his sons, Abdullah and Faisal. They were the rulers of the Hijaz, the province in western Arabia that included Mecca and Medina. The Al Saud, meanwhile, controlled most of central Arabia's Nejd from Riyadh, which is now the Saudi capital. In the end, of course, the Al Saud would conquer Arabia and name the country after their family. The Hashemite sons, Abdullah and Faisal, having lost to the Saudis, would be installed like replacement parts as kings of two other nations whose borders were drawn up by Winston Churchill: Abdullah as king of Transjordan, and Faisal as king of Iraq.

In both cases—the Al Saud and the Hashemites—the British sought to mobilize Islam. The Hashemites boasted that their family was directly descended from that of the Prophet Mohammed, a claim made by any number of scurrilous would-be rulers in the past century. The British, naturally, saw the Hashemites as potential claimants to a new, and pro-British, caliphate based in Mecca. The Al Saud, propelled by the warriors of Wahhabism, were a formidable Islamic strike force that, the British believed, would help London gain control of the western shores of the Persian Gulf.

Initially, around 1916, it seemed that the Hashemites had the upper hand. Because of their position atop Mecca and Medina, the British believed that Hussein and his sons could rally Muslims from North Africa to India to the British cause. At the time, the tottering Ottomans controlled a decrepit caliphate, which nominally exercised sway over religious Muslims worldwide. But the Ottomans were besieged on all sides, and the British took the lead trying to use Islamic loyalties as a force against the Turks. It was a policy cooked up by London's Middle East team: Lord Curzon, the ultraimperialist foreign secretary and former governor of India; the aristocratic Robert Cecil, and his cousin, Arthur Lord Balfour, who with Rothschild backing promised Palestine to the Jews; Mark Sykes, the duplicitous chief of the Foreign Office's Middle East section; and David George ("D. G.") Hogarth, the head of the Arab Bureau, the author of *The Penetration of Arabia,* and an archaeologist, Orientalist, and keeper of the Ashmolean Museum at Oxford. Churchill, Arnold Toynbee, and other leading lights of British imperialism joined in. Outlining the policy, Lawrence said:

> If the Sultan of Turkey were to disappear, then the Caliphate by common consent of Islam would fall to the family of the prophet, the present representative of which is Hussein, the Sharif of Mecca. Hussein's activities seem beneficial to us, because it marches with our immediate aims, the breakup of the Islamic bloc and the disruption of the Ottoman Empire, and because the states he would set up would be as harmless to ourselves as Turkey was. If properly handled the Arab States would remain in a state of political mosaic, a tissue of jealous principalities incapable of cohesion, and yet always ready to combine against an outside force.

The idea seemed simple enough. The Hashemites would stage an anti-Ottoman revolt, complete with swashbuckling, romantic images of Arabs led by Lawrence charging across the sand to liberate themselves from Turkish rule. Behind the scenes, Britain would try to forge an alliance between the Hashemites and the Zionists, with the goal of installing a pro-British Jewish state in Palestine, and with the Hashemites ruling present-day Syria, Lebanon, Iraq, Jordan, and the Hijaz along Arabia's west coast. Uniting it all would be a Mecca-based, and British-controlled, Arab caliphate. Egypt and Sudan, of course, would remain in the British camp, too.

Philby, meanwhile, was working the eastern flank. Sir Percy Cox, the political representative of the India Office in the Persian Gulf, was the man in charge of England's effort to secure the precious oil territories, whose potential was just beginning to emerge. Philby, then a junior officer, worked with Cox and with the legendary explorer and super spy, Gertrude Bell, whose intimate knowledge of Arabian tribal lore and the genealogies of its families, along with her expert linguistic abilities, made her an essential member of the team. Cox dispatched Philby to meet Ibn Saud in 1916. While London was mobilizing the Meccans against the Turks in western Arabia, Philby was assigned to marshal the Al Saud against another warlord clan, the Al Rashid, who had the misfortune to ally itself with the Turks in eastern Arabia.

Beginning in January 1917, Ibn Saud was put on a £5,000 monthly retainer, and Philby was the bagman.[50] Off and on after that, Philby would serve as Ibn Saud's British handler, and met him on dozens of occasions. In 1919, he escorted Ibn Saud's fourteen-year-old son, the future King Faisal of Saudi Arabia, on a tour of London that included visits to Philby's old Pied Piper, E. G. Browne, and to Wilfred Scawen Blunt, perhaps England's leading advocate of pro-British pan-Islam.

Britain's imperial exercise in redrawing the map of the Middle East and building a new caliphate foundered, however. Great Britain, of course, remained the dominant player in the region by virtue of its sheer imperial power. But the Arab-Zionist deal didn't quite work, and Iraq proved troublesome, and deadly, for British troops. Furthermore, the French insisted on booting the British out of Syria and Lebanon, and the Bolsheviks took over Russia and revealed details about secret Anglo-French understandings that proved exceedingly embarrassing to London. And, though London placed most of its chips on Hussein's Hashemites, Ibn Saud's legions swept through Arabia, conquering all before them—including Hussein's mini-realm in the Hijaz. Gertrude Bell, speaking of Iraq but in a manner that could have referred to Britain's entire Middle East policy, said, "We have made an immense failure here."[51]

Philby, still in British service, maintained his connection to the Al Saud. Indeed, he seemed almost to worship the uncouth Ibn Saud and his Bedouin thugs, the Ikhwan:

> The Arab is a democrat [wrote Philby], and the greatest and most powerful Arab ruler of the present day is proof of it. Ibn Saud is no more than *primus inter pares;* his strength lies in the fact that he has for twenty years accurately interpreted the aspirations and will of his people.[52]

Though Philby often postured as an advocate of democracy and Arab republicanism, he never wavered from supporting the brutal Al Saud dynasty.[53] Even some of Britain's most hard-core imperialists, including D. G. Hogarth, saw the Al Saud, and in particular their Wahhabi warriors, the Ikhwan, as rather unsavory. "To men [like Hogarth] with experience of Islam in India, Egypt, Syria, Turkey and the Hijaz, the proselytizing of Ibn Saud's *Ikhwan* was a menace, and Wahhabism a fanatical creed unsuited to most of the Islamic world," wrote Philby's biographer.[54]

In the 1920s conquest of Arabia, Philby's "democrats," the Al Saud, left 400,000 dead and wounded, carried out 40,000 public executions, and ordered, under its strict interpretation of Islamic law, 350,000 amputations.[55] The scorched-earth battles by which the Ikhwan conquered Arabia for the Al Saud gave Britain an unbroken chain of vassal states and colonies from the Mediterranean to India. Yet even as the Saudi state was being established, the bloody Ikhwan were seen by some in London, and by some Arabs, as a double-edged sword. A Lebanese friend of Ibn Saud's described the Ikhwan thus: "Today a sword in the hand of the prince, a dagger in his back tomorrow."[56] Hussein, the British-backed Sharif of Mecca, pleaded with London to force Ibn Saud to dismantle the Ikhwan. In a missive to the British Agent in Jeddah in 1918, Hussein wrote: "What concerns me above everything else . . . is that H.M.G. should compel [Ibn Saud] to abolish and disperse what he calls the Ikhwan—the political society in the cloak of religion." The British coolly refused.[57]

Ibn Saud tried to maintain that the Ikhwan were an independent force, but the British knew otherwise, of course. "He does not want it to be known that he himself is at the bottom of the whole thing, and is fostering and guiding the movement for his own ends," cabled a British official in 1920. Yet, other, far less well informed British officials warned, rather stupidly it would now seem, that the Ikhwan were Bolshevik-inspired![58]

Theoretically, at least, Ibn Saud still had the option of creating a secular state, one in which fundamentalist Islam would not have an official part. But he was propelled by the momentum of his alliance with the Wahhabis and with the Ikhwan, as the shrewd British political officer Percy Cox realized:

> In late 1915 or early 1916 Ibn Saud found that Ikhwanism was definitely gaining control of affairs in Najd. He saw that he had to make one of two decisions: either to be a temporal ruler and crush Ikhwanism, or to become the spiritual head of this new Wahhabism. . . . In the end he was compelled to accept its doctrines and become its leader, lest he should go under himself.[59]

The Islamic fundamentalist movement that Ibn Saud rode to power was essential to the origin of Saudi Arabia. He utilized Islam to break down tribal loyalties and replace those loyalties with adherence to the cult. "In a desert, tribal society, where the family was an individual's security, identity, and legitimacy, the renunciation of all this was no light matter," wrote John S. Habib. "It underscored the degree to which Ibn Saud was able to substitute the brotherhood of Islam domiciled in the *hijra*[60] for the protection, security, and identity which they surrendered when they left the tribe."[61]

When the dust had cleared after World War I, and after the various imperial conferences that established the boundaries of the Middle East's states, the Ottoman Empire had been dismantled, Britain reigned supreme in the region, and Ibn Saud controlled the bulk of Arabia. According to Philby, Ibn Saud's Ikhwan numbered more than 50,000 by the 1920s.[62] To the west, in the Hijaz, the Hashemites still ruled, but their time was running out. In 1924, the new Turkish government under the modernizing Mustafa Kemal Ataturk disdained the backwardness of official Islam and shocked conservative Muslims worldwide by peremptorily abolishing the caliphate. Hussein, the Anglophile Sharif of Mecca, tried to capitalize on Ataturk's action. Perhaps remembering T. E. Lawrence's grand design, Hussein proclaimed himself caliph, but unfortunately for him, no one was listening. The British had essentially abandoned Hussein by then, having chosen to ride with Ibn Saud and another up-and-coming Muslim fanatic, Hajj Amin al-Husseini, the mufti of Jerusalem. "Philby," wrote Monroe, "returning from Syria in this moment of Muslim uncertainty, entered in his diary that Hussein's power in Arabia was confined to the Hijaz coast, and that his gesture about the caliphate was meaningless when set against the bright light of Ibn Saud's star rising over the Arabian desert."[63] Soon afterward Ibn Saud's hordes swept into the Hijaz, ousting the Hashemites, slaughtering hundreds of men, women, and children, and unifying Arabia under the control of Riyadh. So began the modern Saudi state. And Philby, still close to Ibn Saud, was there at the creation.

Ibn Saud set out immediately to establish himself as the uncrowned king of Islam, but it was a process that developed slowly. "A formal treaty between Ibn Saud and Great Britain, recognizing the full independence of the kingdom, was signed on May 20, 1927," wrote Bernard Lewis. "Muslim recognition was slower and more reluctant." He added:

> A Muslim mission from India visited Jeddah and demanded that the king hand over control of the holy places to a committee of representatives to be appointed by all Muslim countries. Ibn Saud did not respond to this demand and sent the mission back to India by sea. In June of the same year he convened an all-Islamic Congress in Mecca, inviting the sovereigns and presidents of the independent Muslim states and representatives from Muslim organizations in countries under non-Muslim rule. Sixty-nine people attended the congress from all over the Islamic world. Addressing them, Ibn Saud made it clear that he was now the ruler of the Hijaz. . . . At the time he evoked a mixed response from his guests. Some dissented and departed; others accepted and recognized the new order.[64]

Ibn Saud also finally had to confront the Ikhwan. By the late 1920s, their job done, the Ikhwan were restless, and increasingly resented Ibn Saud's monarchy. They clashed, and by 1929 Ibn Saud had dismantled the Ikhwan and transformed remnants of the Bedouin force into the Saudi armed forces. Still, having crushed the Ikhwan, Ibn Saud did not abandon Wahhabism. Indeed, to consolidate his power in the more worldly, and less religious, Hijaz, the king created the religious police to enforce five-times-a-day prayer, dress codes, and other strictures of orthodox Wahhabism. In the early 1930s Ibn Saud also created the Society for the Propagation of Virtue and the Suppression of Evil, who were composed of "illiterate, fanatical

Bedouin who were only too eager to enforce the literal prescriptions of prayer, and the closing of shops during prayer time, in addition to the prohibition of smoking and other 'immoral' habits."[65] It still exists.

For the British, the emergence of the state of Saudi Arabia gave London a foothold at the very heart of Islam, in Mecca and Medina. For the more pragmatic among Britain's imperial strategists, it seemed that Ibn Saud's armed forces proved themselves to be of greater worth than the mystic-theological currents advanced by Afghani and Abduh and their secret societies. And clearly, London's experiment with Afghani and Abduh was not completely successful. Afghani, in particular, proved to be an elusive imperial asset, and while his vision of a pan-Islamic alliance might have appeared attractive to the British elite, it failed to capture the imagination of the masses and it met with determined opposition from rulers in Turkey and Persia.

The creation of the Saudi state by the British gave Islamism a base out of which it would operate for decades to come. For England, and then for the United States, Saudi Arabia would serve as an anchor for imperial ambitions throughout the twentieth century. Yet Wahhabism, for all its power, was still primarily a religious, not political, force. It could win the devout allegiance of Saudis, and it could be proselytized to Sunnis far and wide. But in the modern sense, true political Islam had not yet emerged. Missing was a mass-based Islamist political force that could hold its own against the new century's most attractive anti-imperialist ideologies, communism and nationalism. Yet the seeds planted by Afghani and Abduh were about to sprout. Watered and carefully tended by Saudi Arabia's Wahhabis and the British intelligence service, a new Islamist force was about to arise on soil sown by Abduh. For the first time, a true grassroots Islamic fundamentalist party would begin in a city on the Suez Canal, not far from Saudi Arabia: Ismailia, Egypt.

2

ENGLAND'S BROTHERS

IN ITS POST–WORLD War I struggle to maintain its empire, Great Britain made deals with many devils. From the late 1920s until the failed invasion of Suez in 1956, those pacts included support for two fledgling Islamist movements in Egypt and Palestine. In Egypt, in 1928, a young Islamic scholar named Hassan al-Banna founded the Muslim Brotherhood, the organization that would change the course of history in the twentieth-century Middle East. And his Palestinian confrère was Haj Amin al-Husseini, the demagogic mufti of Jerusalem. Both Banna and Haj Amin would play important roles in the growth of Islamism in the decades after World War I—and, like the Saudi royal family, both owed their start to British support.

Banna's Muslim Brotherhood was established with a grant from England's Suez Canal Company, and over the next quarter century British diplomats, the intelligence service MI6, and Cairo's Anglophilic King Farouq would use the Muslim Brotherhood as a cudgel against Egypt's communists and nationalists—and later against President Gamal Abdel Nasser. Meanwhile, in Palestine, Haj Amin, the Nazi-leaning, viciously anti-Semitic firebrand, climbed to power beginning in the 1920s with overt backing from the British overseers of the Palestine Mandate. Together, Banna and Haj Amin would be responsible for the worldwide spread of political Islam. The two men tied Wahhabi-style ultra-orthodoxy to the pan-Islamic ideals of Jamal Eddine al-Afghani and—with Saudi funding—created the global enterprise that spawned Islam's radical right, including its terrorist wing.

London's relationship with the Muslim Brotherhood was complex.

Although the British supported the organization at its founding, and although the organization may have received support from British intelligence in the subsequent years, the Brotherhood—and political Islam—was only one force in an ever-shifting political universe in Egypt and the broader Middle East. The British and the king used Banna's group—especially its underground, paramilitary arm and its assassins—when it suited them, but kept a wary eye on the organization, which sometimes turned against them. As the Muslim Brotherhood gained strength, eventually claiming several hundred thousand members in Egypt alone, with branches in Jerusalem, Damascus, and Amman, it became an important player in Egyptian politics. As such, it drew attention from a number of foreign intelligence services over the years, from the Nazis and the KGB to the U.S. Office of Strategic Services and the CIA.

The Muslim Brotherhood exploded onto the scene at a time when British power in the Near East, though nearly universal, was also unsettled.

As the smoke cleared after World War I, England reigned supreme in the region, but uneasily so. The flag of the British empire was everywhere from the Mediterranean to India. A new generation of kings and potentates ruled a string of British-dominated colonies, mandates, vassal states, and semi-independent fiefdoms in Egypt, Iraq, Transjordan, Arabia, and Persia. To varying degrees, those monarchies were beholden to London, but not without occasional, tentative attempts to claim some authority for themselves. The kings were trapped between two conflicting forces: on the one hand, in each of those states, an anti-monarchical nationalist movement began to take shape; on the other hand, the British Foreign Office and London's colonial officials were breathing down their necks. Juggling factions like balls in the air, the British spent the years between 1918 and 1945 trying to balance the king, the tribal leaders, the emerging middle classes, the army, and the clergy in each of these states, always with an eye toward preserving British power. Sometimes the king would get too strong, and form an alliance with the army; in that case the British would try to break the alliance of king and generals by favoring tribal chieftains instead. Sometimes, if the tribes or ethnic groups got too uppity, the British would deputize the army to crush them.

The Islamic right emerged amid this shifting balance. It provided a vital counterweight to England's chief nemeses: the nationalists and the secular left.

Islam's Anti-nationalists

The Muslim Brotherhood, founded in 1928 by Hassan al-Banna, was the direct outgrowth of the pan-Islamic movement of Afghani and Abduh. The transmission belt for that influence was Rashid Rida, a Syrian who had arrived in Egypt in 1897. Rashid Rida, who had received a religious education in Tripoli, in what is now Lebanon's Sunni stronghold, had been an avid follower of *The Indissoluble Bond,* Afghani and Abduh's weekly, and when he arrived in Cairo he sought out Abduh, the soon-to-be mufti of Egypt, and became his chief acolyte. In 1898, Rashid Rida founded the publication *The Lighthouse,*[1] a weekly eight-page newspaper that was explicitly aimed at carrying on the tradition of the pan-Islamic *Bond.* Unlike Afghani and Abduh, who operated through secret societies, underground groups, and the Masonic movement, Rashid Rida advocated the establishment of an aboveground "Islamic Society," with its headquarters at Mecca and with branches in every Muslim country.[2]

Though Rashid Rida never managed to found the society he wanted—that would await Hassan al-Banna—he created the Society of Propaganda and Guidance as an early forerunner of the Muslim Brotherhood. At the time, Abduh enjoyed the patronage of Lord Cromer, the absolute ruler of Egypt at the turn of the century, and the work of Rashid Rida could not have occurred without British acquiescence.

According to C. C. Adams, *The Lighthouse* consistently attacked the nascent nationalist movement in Egypt, which was secular in nature, and the nationalists hit back at Rashid Rida. *The Lighthouse* also welcomed the growth of Saudi power:

> A new star of hope has appeared with the rise of the Wahhabi dynasty of Ibn Saud in Arabia. The Government of Ibn Saud is the greatest Muslim power in the world today, since the fall of the Ottoman dynasty and the transformation of the Government of the Turks into a government without religion, and it is the only government that will give aid to the Sunnah and repudiate harmful innovations and anti-religionism.[3]

Nationalists, in both Egypt and Turkey, were deemed "atheists and infidels" by Rashid Rida.[4]

The Society of Propaganda and Guidance, and its related Institute of Propaganda and Guidance, were established in Cairo with financing from wealthy Arabs from India. Its enrollees included students from as far away as Malaysia, Indonesia, India, Central Asia, and East Africa. They formed a second wave of the international cadre for an Islamist movement, after the secret societies tied to *The Indissoluble Bond*. Prominent Egyptian sheikhs and other religious leaders formed what came to be known as the "Lighthouse Party," made up of followers of Abduh and Rashid Rida collected around Al Azhar and including various leaders of the mystical Sufi brotherhoods. In opposition to the new Nationalist Party, they helped establish a second Egyptian political formation called the Peoples Party, which included followers of Abduh and Rashid Rida. The Peoples Party, reputedly created with British support, openly supported the British occupation of Egypt, and it won plaudits from Lord Cromer, who described its members as a "small but increasing number of Egyptians of whom comparatively little is heard." In his 1906 Annual Report, Lord Cromer wrote: "The main hope of Egyptian Nationalism, in the only true and practicable sense of the word, lies, in my opinion, with those who belong to this party."[5]

Rashid Rida's chief acolyte was Hassan al-Banna.

It is impossible to overestimate the importance and legacy of Hassan al-Banna. The twenty-first-century War on Terrorism is a war against the offspring of Banna and his Brothers. They show up everywhere—in the attorney general's office in Sudan, on Afghanistan's battlefields, in Hama in Syria, atop Saudi Arabia's universities, in bomb-making factories in Gaza, as ministers in the government of Jordan, in posh banking centers in the Gulf sheikhdoms, and in the post–Saddam Hussein government of Iraq.

To get the Muslim Brotherhood off the ground, the Suez Canal Company helped Banna build the mosque in Ismailia that would serve as its headquarters and base of operations, according to Richard Mitchell's *The Society of the Muslim Brothers*.[6] The fact that Banna created the organization in Ismailia is itself significant. Ismailia, today a city of 200,000 at the northern end of the canal, was founded in 1863 by Ferdinand de Lesseps, the canal's builder. For England, the Suez Canal was the indispensable route to its prize possession, India, and in 1928 the sleepy backwater town happened to house not only the company's offices but a major British military base built during World War I. It was also, in the 1920s, a center of pro-British sentiment in Egypt.

Mitchell reports that Banna was closely associated with Rashid Rida.[7] Banna's father, an influential scholar, was a student of Abduh's, and Banna himself avidly read *The Lighthouse* as a young man, later calling Rashid Rida one of the "greatest influences in the service of Islam in Egypt."[8] The relationship between Afghani, Abduh, and Rashid Rida was seen by Banna as a kind of Blessed Trinity. According to Mitchell: "Afghani was seen [by Banna] as the 'caller' or 'announcer' and Rida as the 'archivist' or 'historian.' . . . Afghani sees the problems and warns, Abduh teaches and thinks ('a well-meaning *shaykh* who inspired reforms in the Azhar'), and Rida writes and records."[9] *The Lighthouse* halted publication soon after the death of Rashid Rida in 1935, but in 1939 Banna revived it in tribute to his mentor.[10]

The political program of the early Muslim Brotherhood was hardly complex. Banna insisted that Muslims should return to the simple days that prevailed during the era of the Prophet Muhammad and his immediate successors, rejecting modern scholarly interpretations of

Islamic law and what he saw as the Westernized impurity of thought that had started to beguile Muslims, especially youth. For Banna, the Koran was enough. "Confronted by the Egyptian nationalists of the [1920s]—who demanded independence, the departure of the British, and a democratic constitution—the Brothers responded with a slogan that is still current in the Islamist movement: 'The Koran is our constitution.' "[11] Indeed, the Koran and the *Sunna* (the tradition associated with the prophet's way of life) were enough to guide society, and Islamic law (sharia) could replace man-made, secular jurisprudence. Yet Banna had a very weakly developed concept of an Islamic state, whose elaboration would await his heirs: Sayyid Qutb, Pakistan's Abul-Ala Mawdudi, Khomeini, et al. According to Mitchell, for Banna:

> The political structure of the Islamic state was to be bound by three principles: (1) the Quran is the fundamental constitution; (2) government operates on the concept of consultation (*shura*); (3) the executive ruler is bound by the teachings of Islam and the will of the people.[12]

Islam, for Banna, was an all-encompassing, cultlike system of belief. Referring to the Salafiyya, the back-to-the-basics purists, and the Sufis, the mystical, Freemason-like movement within Islam, Banna described his movement thus: "a Salafiyya message, a Sunni way, a Sufi truth, a political organization, an athletic group, a cultural-educational union, an economic company, and a social idea."[13]

In 1932, Banna moved to Cairo and established the Muslim Brotherhood in the Egyptian capital. For the next twenty years, until the revolution of 1952, the Brotherhood would serve as an anchor of the Egyptian right, allied to the palace, to the right wing of the nationalist Wafd Party, and to conservative officers in the Egyptian army. In 1933, Banna convened the organization's first national conference, which took place in Cairo. Soon afterward, youth clubs and athletic associations tied to the Muslim Brotherhood began to form paramilitary units, first called the Rovers in 1936. Explicitly organized along the lines of European fascist movements, the Rovers (later called the Battalions),[14] were a unique presence in Egypt: disciplined, menacing, and utterly devoted to Banna. In 1937, at the coronation of King Farouq, the Brotherhood's thugs were enlisted to provide "order and security" for the king's ceremony.[15]

The Muslim Brotherhood's chief rival between the wars was the nationalist Delegation (Wafd) Party. Assembled from the ranks of the pre–World War I anti-British political movement, the Wafd Party was named for the "delegation" led by Saad Zaghlul, who attended the postwar conferences at which the victorious imperialists decided the future of the region, creating entire states and assigning them to various European capitals. The Wafd, as a coalition, had left-, center, and right-wing components, and it variously aligned itself for or against the monarchy and other Egyptian political forces over the years. The Wafd left would eventually toy with an alliance with Egypt's communists, while the smaller right wing of the Wafd often maintained secret relations with the Brotherhood.

For the next decade, Banna played a complex game of three-dimensional chess in Egyptian politics. He enjoyed intimate relations with the royal entourage around King Farouq, getting financial support and political assistance and providing the king with intelligence and shock troops against the left. "Certainly by the 1940s the Ikhwan has an on-and-off close relationship with the palace, and a lot of money was changing hands, and the British would be involved in that," says Joel Gordon, a Muslim Brotherhood expert. "Anything the palace does is linked to the British."[16] Banna also developed close ties to two key Egyptian officials, Prime Minister Ali Mahir, an ardent advocate of pan-Islamism, and General Aziz Ali Misri, the commander in chief of the Egyptian armed forces. Through various channels, mostly secret, Banna was connected to the palace, sometimes through the king's personal physician, or through various government officials or the army. He was consulted by the king on the appointment of Egyptian prime ministers, and at least once received an official invitation to a royal banquet.

"The Society of the Brothers," wrote Mitchell, "was obviously conceived of as an instrument against the Wafd and the communists."[17] Right-wing Wafdists, primarily big landowners and capitalists, viewed the Muslim Brotherhood as an ally, while the mainstream Wafdists considered the Brotherhood a reactionary force.[18]

THE BROTHERHOOD'S SECRET APPARATUS

During World War II, the Muslim Brotherhood first established its intelligence service and a secret, terrorist-inclined unit called the Secret Apparatus. "The intelligence service gathered information at military installations, foreign embassies, government offices, and so on," a 1950s analyst wrote.[19] This clandestine unit is what gave the Brotherhood its well-deserved reputation for violence. Created in 1942, over the next twelve years (until it was smashed by Nasser), it would assassinate judges, police officers, and government officials, burn and ransack Egyptian Jewish businesses, and engage in goon-squad attacks on labor unions and communists. Throughout this period, the Brotherhood operated mostly in alliance with the Egyptian king, using its paramilitary force on his behalf and against his political enemies. As the king began to lose his grip, the Muslim Brotherhood distanced itself from Farouq while maintaining shadowy ties to the army and to foreign intelligence agencies—and always opposed to the left. According to Mitchell, the Apparatus operated precisely the way an Egyptian intelligence unit would: "In 1944 the secret apparatus also began to infiltrate the communist movement, which during the war had taken on new life and which the Muslim Brothers considered to be one of their principal enemies."[20]

Without doubt, the vast majority of the membership of the Muslim Brotherhood was zealously dedicated to the creation of a right-wing Islamic government, and they were militantly opposed to imperialism. Yet the leadership of the Brotherhood played politics at the highest level, collaborating with the palace, the secular political parties, the army, and the imperial powers. Whether the Muslim Brotherhood's leaders were indeed true believers who decided to make their own temporary deals with the world's Great Satans, or whether they were cynical politicians and even outright agents of foreign powers, is not known for certain. But there seems little doubt that while some leaders of the organization were sincere, others were double-dealers and agents.

The Brotherhood existed in a kind of political netherworld. Its overt branch, and its political stars—above all, Banna himself—hobnobbed with kings and generals, while its covert branch engaged in espionage and assassinations. As long as the Brotherhood's violence was aimed at the enemies of the king and the British, it managed to operate with impunity. When it crossed the line, as it did from time to time, the government would crack down on it or ban it temporarily. At other times, when it was either useful to the palace or to the army, or when it was simply too powerful, it was tolerated and even supported by the regime. Throughout its entire existence, too, the Muslim Brotherhood had an ace-in-the-hole, namely, the political support and money it received from the Saudi royal family and the Wahhabi establishment.

The Muslim Brotherhood was organized into cells, or "families," groups of five to seven members who "underwent indoctrination and systematic, sometimes extended military training in the various branches of guerrilla warfare to qualify as 'active brothers.' When the training was completed, they were instructed to pretend that they had given up their membership in the Brotherhood and to join some other organization active in religious affairs or sports."[21]

The British, with two centuries of deep involvement in religious and tribal politics, were well aware of the power of Islamism. A British intelligence officer tied to the king recognized the power of the Islamic revival at the end of World War II. MI6's David "Archie" Boyle was liaison to Farouq's *chef de cabinet* Hassenein Pasha, a British intelligence asset. Boyle "sensed the 'murmuring resurgence of Moslem renaissance, which as in 1919 was again in 1946 commencing to affect the Middle Eastern countries as a whole. This time it was to be coupled with the race for oil.'"[22] The British embassy, and later the U.S. embassy in Cairo, had regular contact with Banna's Brotherhood.

After World War II, the faltering Farouq regime lashed out against the left, in an intense campaign of repression aimed at the communists. The Cold War was beginning. Prime Minister Ismail Sidqi of Egypt, who was installed as head of the government with the support of Banna, openly funded the Muslim Brotherhood, and provided training camps for its shock troops. Its sweeping anti-left campaign was enthusiastically backed by the Brothers:

> In this campaign the Muslim Brotherhood, bitterly antagonistic to the communists, could join wholeheartedly. Their press reported the course of the governmental campaign in a daily column entitled, 'The Fight Against Communism.' The 'intelligence' of the Society passed on information useful to the government in its continual round-ups of real and suspected communists, especially in labour and university circles.[23]

In addition, the Brothers organized right-wing trade unions, undermined strike actions, and bitterly opposed the Wafd nationalists (often secretly in conjunction with the Wafd's right). Concludes Mitchell: "For the moment, the palace, the conservative heads of government, and the Muslim Brotherhood shared common foes: communism and the Wafd."[24]

Anwar Sadat, the future Egyptian president, was a key member of the Muslim Brotherhood in the 1940s. During World War II he was associated with a loosely organized movement of junior officers that, in 1949, was formally established by Nasser as the Egyptian Free Officers in the wake of the Palestine war and who seized power from the king in 1952. The Free Officers included men from a wide variety of ideologies, from communists and left-wing nationalists to Wafdists and members of the Muslim Brotherhood, all united in their belief that Farouq was hopelessly corrupt and servile. England's imperious treatment of Farouq during the war by British ambassador Miles Lampson—who reportedly[25] called the young Farouq "boy" to his face—had enraged them, and they maintained contact with one another in the postwar years.

Sadat, a right-wing member of Nasser's Free Officers movement, was the liaison between the dissident military officers and Banna, and during the war Sadat conducted regular tête-à-têtes with the Brotherhood founder. In his autobiography, *In Search of Identity*, Sadat provided a detailed account of his relationship to Banna.[26] Sadat warmly praises Banna: "His understanding of religion [was] profound, and his delivery impressive. He was indeed qualified, from all points of view, to be a religious leader. Besides, he was a true Egyptian: good-humored, decent, and tolerant. . . . I was struck by the perfect organization of the Muslim Brotherhood, and by the respect, even extraordinary reverence, which the Supreme Guide commanded."[27] In 1945 Sadat tried to arrange a meeting between Banna and King Farouq, through Yusuf Rashad, a contact of Sadat's and the king's personal physician. That meeting didn't happen, but in a frank discussion between Sadat and Banna, they agreed to cooperate in building the Free Officers, and Banna started recruiting military officers for the group.[28]

But was Banna recruiting members for the Free Officers—or infiltrating it? It isn't clear. The Brotherhood was more than a movement. It was a cult, it was a revivalist party, it was an intelligence operation, it was a paramilitary unit, and it was an international organization that was rapidly building branches in many Middle East countries. What is clear is that during the 1940s, the British, the Nazis, and the Soviets had thoroughly penetrated the Brotherhood. In the 1930s, many right-wing Arab nationalists and many on the Islamic right, including the Brotherhood, found succor and support in ties to German Nazi intelligence. According to Miles Copeland, a legendary Central Intelligence Agency operative who spent years in Egypt, during World War II Banna's organization "had been virtually a German Intelligence unit."[29] In saying so, Copeland no doubt exaggerates, perhaps willfully, though countless Islamists had Nazi affiliations in the 1930s and 1940s. After World War II, many of the Nazi-linked Islamists migrated back to British, and then into Anglo-American circles, sometimes with generous financial inducements. In the 1950s, when Nasser arrested the leadership of the Muslim Brotherhood, his security services found out how tangled were the organization's ties. "Sound beatings of Muslim Brotherhood organizers who had been arrested revealed that the organization had been thoroughly penetrated, at the top, by British, American, French, and Soviet intelligence services, any one of which could either make active use of it or blow it up, whichever best suited its purpose," wrote Copeland.[30]

As it became ever more clear to London and Washington that Farouq could not survive, the search for an alternative regime developed. The main options were first, the combination of the Wafd and the communists; and second, the secretive alliance between the Muslim Brotherhood and the military officers. Neither the British nor the Americans wanted the Wafd-communist option; the British seemed insistent on propping up the monarchy, while the Americans opted for supporting Nasser's Free Officers. The Brotherhood, with ties to both the monarchy and the Free Officers, played a double game.

The Wafd Party itself was divided into competing factions and plagued by corruption. Yet an important section of the Wafd sought an alliance with the left and the communists, which worried the palace, the British—and the Muslim Brotherhood. The Brothers worked hard to destroy any possibility of a Wafd-communist axis, and the Wafd struck back at the Brotherhood, portraying Banna's thugs as being in the pay of the British and the pro-British prime minister, Ismail Sidqi. The communists and the Wafd accused the Muslim Brotherhood of being "tools of the imperialists." The Wafd charged that "phalanxes of the Muslim Brothers" were carrying out "acts of fascist terror." It called for dissolution of the Brotherhood's (government-funded) paramilitary units, and it documented numerous instances of strike-breaking by Muslim Brotherhood goons.[31] But the Brotherhood would gain strength from an unexpected direction in 1948: the war in Palestine.

BANNA AND THE MUFTI

The Arab-Jewish war strengthened the Muslim Brotherhood immensely. It was a chaotic moment in the Middle East, as a new Jewish nation established itself on part of the territory of British-occupied Palestine. The war, the defeat of Arab armies by paramilitary Jewish units, and the creation of Israel forever changed the dynamic of politics in the Middle East, and it spurred political Islam in several ways. First, the Brotherhood created paramilitary units during the war itself, forces that won official backing from Arab states—and, like the Afghan jihad of the 1980s, created legions of battle-hardened Islamist veterans. Second, the Arab defeat discredited the Arab regimes, including the monarchies. It created space for new political forces such as the

Muslim Brotherhood, and the fledgling Islamists took full advantage of the propaganda value that attached to the loss of Palestine. And third, the Islamists generated political capital by raising the alarm over the Jewish threat to Jerusalem and its Islamic holy places and used that threat as a rallying cry.

The war also bolstered ties between the Brotherhood and another key British-sponsored Muslim operative, the conspiratorial, Nazi-leaning mufti of Jerusalem, Haj Amin al-Husseini. Their connection went back more than a decade. Haj Amin had his first recorded encounter with the Muslim Brotherhood as far back as 1935, when he met Banna's brother, Abdel-Rahman al-Banna, who'd helped Banna found the group and who headed its Secret Apparatus.[32] Like Banna, Haj Amin played an immensely important role in founding the twentieth-century Islamic fundamentalist political movement.

The creation of Israel spurred more than Islamism, of course, providing fodder for Arab nationalists, such as Nasser, who wanted to rid the Arab world of its fraternity of dissolute kings. For nationalists, Israel was a symbol of Arab weakness and semi-colonial subjugation, overseen by proxy kings in Egypt, Jordan, Iraq, and Saudi Arabia. But Banna and the Brothers argued that the Arab nationalists were wrong, that no solution could be found in secular nationalism and nation building, and certainly not in Westernization. The only way to restore the former glory of the Islamic world was to return to fundamentalist Islam, they proclaimed.

A multidimensional struggle was developing that would decide the future of the Middle East. The Islamists were just one of many forces competing against one another: There were the nationalists, the left (including the growing Arab communist parties), the secular intellectuals, and the urban working class; there were the wealthy merchants and businessmen engaged in international trade and commerce; there were traditional elites, tribal leaders, and aristocratic landowners; and last, there were the monarchies and their armies. The burgeoning Islamists were a kind of wild card: Bitterly opposed to the nationalists and the left, they maintained ties to the traditional elites and had the support of many merchants, and they also had covert alliances with army officers and royals. For the British, and the Johnny-come-lately

Americans, it was hard to know where to place one's bets. The Palestine war had vastly complicated the Anglo-American calculations, since both the left-nationalist forces and the Islamists blamed "the West" for the Israeli debacle.

The Brotherhood grew by leaps and bounds in the late 1940s. Banna's son-in-law, Said Ramadan, helped organize chapters in Palestine and Transjordan. Under cover of arming themselves for war with the Zionists, the Brothers collected and stored stockpiles of weapons, often supplied by members of the Secret Apparatus who had ties to the Egyptian army. And the Banna–Haj Amin alliance, forged in the crucible of the Palestine war, helped the Brothers extend their reach into Syria, Jordan, Lebanon, and Palestine.

To say Haj Amin al-Husseini had a checkered career is an understatement. His paranoid worldview, centered on fierce hatred of Jews, and his open support for Hitler make him an object of scorn by historians. But from the beginning Haj Amin was a British creation. He exercised a spell over generations of British spooks, including Freya Stark, a legendary British intelligence operative who described Haj Amin in almost reverential terms: "The Mufti sat there all in white, spotless and voluminous, a man in his early forties, wearing his turban like a halo. His eyes were light blue and shining, with a sort of radiance, as of a just fallen Lucifer."[33]

Haj Amin's career began modestly, to say the least. A scion of an important Arab Palestinian family, he studied at Egypt's Al Azhar Islamic university, but didn't do well and failed to finish. After World War I, he took a job with the Reuters news agency in Jerusalem, as a translator. Gradually, he immersed himself in Palestinian politics, but he showed a flair both for violence and for fanatical, anti-Jewish conspiracy theories, among them the Protocols of the Elders of Zion. He was arrested for his role in anti-Jewish riots, but in 1920, Sir Herbert Samuel, the British High Commissioner for Palestine (and a Jew), singled him out for a dramatic special pardon, and then "engineered his spectacular rise to power."[34] Though Haj Amin's credentials as an Islamic scholar were nil, Sir Ronald Storrs, the governor of Jerusalem, rigged an election on his behalf and then appointed Haj Amin as

Jerusalem's mufti. According to the *Political Dictionary of the Middle East in the 20th Century*, a mufti is a

> Muslim religious official who issues rulings (fatwa), in general in response to questions. In most Islamic countries the mufti is government-appointed. A mufti has a highly respected status and great spiritual and social influence, but plays no executive or political role. An exception to this was the mufti of Jerusalem, Haj Amin al-Husseini (appointed 1921, dismissed 1937), who exploited his position to consolidate his political leadership.[35]

A year later, Herbert Samuel established the Supreme Muslim Council, which assumed control of Palestine's rich religious endowments, and named Haj Amin president. The two posts gave the erratic Muslim demagogue enormous political power.[36]

Parallel with the establishment of the Muslim Brotherhood, in 1931 Haj Amin convened an Islamic Congress in Jerusalem and traveled to India, Iran, Afghanistan, and other Muslim countries, raising funds and building support. He enjoyed a modicum of British support and protection even as he veered into a political alliance with Germany; when sixty Arab militants were arrested in Palestine in 1936 during an anti-British rebellion, Haj Amin—who'd taken part in the revolt—went free.[37] Eventually, his Nazi sympathies forced him to flee, first to Lebanon, then to Iraq, then to Iran, and finally—after pledging Adolf Hitler his "loyal collaboration in all spheres"[38]—to Berlin. In Germany, Haj Amin oversaw Axis propaganda broadcasts into the Middle East, directed a network of espionage agents, and organized all-Muslim units of the Nazi SS, made up mainly of Bosnians.

With the collapse of the Third Reich, however, the mufti quietly left Germany via Switzerland, settling in France, where the Allies refused to arrest or detain him. The British, in particular, declined to seek his extradition, and Great Britain's undersecretary for foreign affairs made a point of saying: "The mufti is not a war criminal."[39] In 1946, Haj Amin al-Husseini arrived in triumph in Egypt, where he was welcomed as a guest of the king. "The new shrine of political Islam is the mufti's house, Villa Aida, near Roushdy Pasha Station of the street car line that runs out from Alexandria to the suburb of Ramleh," a *New York Times* report in August 1946 proclaimed. "There is an Egyptian soldier about every eight or ten yards around the garden, and the mufti has private bodyguards inside."[40] Another report said that the mufti's political work was "lavishly financed" by Saudi Arabia's King Abdel Aziz and Egypt's King Farouq.[41]

Apparently, the British didn't hold a grudge against the mufti, because they soon hired him as a propagandist. In Cairo, British intelligence had established the Arab News Agency and the Near East Broadcasting Station (NEABS), whose "first director was Squadron-Leader Alfred Marsack, a devout Muslim who had served in the Middle East before the war and who had devoted the best part of his life to Arab affairs, and had even converted to Islam."[42] Perhaps impressed by his experience as a Nazi broadcaster, the MI6 outlet hired Haj Amin. The man who oversaw NEABS, through MI6's Near East Association, was Sir Kinahan Cornwallis, an aristocratic British banker who'd headed the Arab Bureau, the Cairo headquarters of British intelligence during World War I and T. E. Lawrence's base of operations.[43]

In 1946, the mufti and the Muslim Brotherhood jointly organized a paramilitary force in Palestine called the Rescuers, with up to 10,000 men under arms.[44] The Rescuers were either tolerated or ignored by the British authorities. In Egypt, meanwhile, Banna and the mufti established a working relationship. One of the Muslim Brotherhood's military units, stationed in Gaza, was put under the command of a Sudanese aide to the mufti.[45] And in Cairo, Hassan al-Banna backed Haj Amin as the head of a new Palestine government. Perhaps the high point of the mufti's career came with his triumphant return to Gaza in September 1947, where he proclaimed the state of Palestine and himself as "President of the Republic."[46] With the Arab defeat by Jewish forces, however, Haj Amin's fledgling state was no more. But Haj Amin would survive, prosper, and return to battle in the 1950s.

Banna, meanwhile, was nearing the end of his fiery lifetime. The regime of King Farouq was on its last legs, and the political vultures were circling. The 1948 Palestine crisis fatally undermined Farouq's regime, making it difficult for any of Egypt's political forces to ally with the king. An economic crisis, too, engulfed the country, accompanied by riots, demonstrations, strikes, and growing violence. The accord between the Muslim Brotherhood and the palace broke down, and both nationalists and Islamists sought political advantage by blaming the corrupt and feckless regime of King Farouq for the Palestine defeat. Finally, in December 1948, the Egyptian government outlawed the Muslim Brotherhood, and weeks later, a Brotherhood assassin murdered Prime Minister Mahmud Fahmi Nuqrashi.

Two months later, in January 1949, Banna's career came to a sudden end. Hassan al-Banna was assassinated, shot to death on the streets outside the Young Men's Muslim Association headquarters in Cairo, apparently by Egyptian security officers.[47]

Banna's death provided an exclamation point for the end of the first era of the Muslim Brotherhood, and the beginning of another. In the wake of Banna's death, various factions of the Muslim Brotherhood competed for control, and the party itself drifted in and out of legality, first banned and then tolerated. The new supreme guide, succeeding Banna, was Hassan Ismail al-Hudaybi, an Egyptian judge whose brother was chief of Farouq's royal household, and whose appointment was engineered by a wealthy landowner in Upper Egypt. (Fifty years later, Hudaybi's son would also serve as the Muslim Brotherhood's supreme guide.) The Brotherhood's factions would each maintain ties to parts of the Egyptian body politic, keeping lines open to the palace, infiltrating the army and the police, and establishing covert contacts with the burgeoning movement of Free Officers who, in 1952, would seize control of Egypt.

Despite the factional divisions, however, it was clear that the Muslim Brotherhood would outlast Banna. Thanks to Said Ramadan, the Brothers were extending their range and influence worldwide, and in Egypt they remained a potent force with hundreds of thousands of adherents. Money from Saudi Arabia helped sustain the movement when other Arab governments, especially Egypt's, moved against them. And thanks to the Cold War, the Muslim Brotherhood would draw energy from the global crusade against communism. Its combination of elite insider politics and underground violent militancy marked the true start of what we now call "political Islam." The Islamist regimes in Pakistan, Afghanistan, Iran, and Sudan that came to power beginning in the late 1970s were the direct result of the groundbreaking work done by Banna, Ramadan, and their allies.

Amid the wreckage of World War II, the United States would make its first, tentative steps into the Middle East. The vast area stretching from Greece and Turkey through Pakistan and India was fated to become a major battleground during the Cold War. What set the Middle East apart from other arenas for the East-West struggle was its proximity to the USSR and the fact that two-thirds of the world's oil was concentrated in a tiny area surrounding the Persian Gulf. The strategists who built the NATO, Baghdad Pact, and CENTO alliances, the Rapid Deployment Force, and the U.S. Central Command attached extraordinary importance to securing the Gulf. Unfortunately, those same strategists confused the alleged threat from the Soviet Union with the homegrown forces of Arab and Persian nationalism, who saw the region's oil as part of their national patrimony. To defeat the nationalists, and to build a tier of nations aligned in opposition to the Soviet Union, the United States would reach out to the Islamic right.

The Muslim Brotherhood was waiting.

3

ISLAM MEETS THE COLD WAR

I FIRST MET Hassan al-Banna in Saudi Arabia," recalls Hermann
Eilts, then a young American diplomat in Jeddah, who says that he
knew Banna reasonably well. "He used to come to Saudi Arabia for
money, actually," he says. "I met him at the home of the then-Saudi
deputy minister of finance, who was a man who was himself very
pious and who handled Banna. His name was Shaikh Mohammed
Sorour [Sabhan], who was a slave who had been manumitted, and it
was Sorour who handled most of the major financial matters with the
Muslim Brotherhood. He was a black, and he was from Sudan."[1]

It was 1948, just a few months before Banna was assassinated in
Cairo. Eilts would often see Banna in Sorour's home. "He was a frequent visitor, because Saudi Arabia was his principal source of financing," Eilts remembers. Since its founding twenty years earlier, the
Brotherhood had become a powerful, even frightening force in Egypt,
with a secret paramilitary arm that sponsored terrorism, infiltrated
the Egyptian army and intelligence services, and intimidated its political opponents. "I found him to be very, very friendly," says the former
U.S. diplomat, who would become one of America's leading Arabists
and ambassador to Egypt and Saudi Arabia. "There was no hesitation
in meeting Westerners."

Eilts didn't discuss Banna's movement with him, but U.S. political officers in Cairo in the 1940s did so on a routine basis. "I know that some of my colleagues at the American embassy in Cairo had regular meetings with Hassan al-Banna at the time, and found him perfectly empathetic," he says. "We kept in touch with them especially for reporting purposes, because at that time the Muslim Brotherhood was one element that was viewed as potentially politically important, so you kept contact with them. I don't think we were alarmed by them, though there was concern when the Brotherhood's Secret Apparatus assassinated the prime minister [of Egypt]. We were concerned about stability, primarily, and our judgment was that these assassinations were worrying but that they did not forecast serious political instability."

It's not surprising that U.S. diplomats in Egypt and Saudi Arabia in the 1940s would maintain regular contact with the Muslim Brotherhood, despite its violence-prone nature and fascist orientation. The regime of Egypt's King Farouq was on its last legs, and it wasn't clear what might replace it. According to Said Aburish: "The growing Muslim Brotherhood, which by then had 1.5 million members, represented the only potential challenge to the ruling establishment."[2] Yet many early U.S. representatives in the region were attracted by its militant anti-communist outlook.

The Brotherhood, the broader community of the Islamic right, and the underlying institutions of traditional Islam in the region stood at the center of a swirling debate in Washington: Was Islam a bulwark against godless communism? Or was organized Islam a backward-looking, ultra-conservative force whose inherent anti-Western outlook made it receptive to the class-warfare politics of the left? Could the United States help shape Islamic institutions that could be the backbone of a new civil society in the Middle East, or did America's interest lie in allying itself with the region's secular modernizers?

The United States was just beginning to feel its way around the Middle East. Few American officials had any experience in the region, U.S. universities were abysmally weak on Middle East studies, and despite its leading role in winning World War II the U.S. military had virtually no significant presence in either North Africa or the Persian Gulf. The fledgling Central Intelligence Agency, which was gobbling up Ivy League graduates and virtually anyone who could speak Arabic, was inexperienced at best. From its founding in 1947 until at least the 1950s, the CIA took a backseat to British intelligence.

"Our attitude," according to Miles Copeland, a CIA officer who served in the region in those years, "was one of let's-wait-until-we-know-what-we're-doing."[3]

The Middle East was British turf, and the British were exceedingly turf conscious. Egypt, Iraq, and Iran, though nominally independent, were under de facto British suzerainty. Palestine and Transjordan were officially British mandates. The states that make up Kuwait and the other Gulf sheikhdoms were British colonies, as were India and Pakistan. Yet the British hold on the region, and on its oil, was eroding, and America's post–World War II engagement in the Middle East was growing fast. It began with Saudi Arabia, the country that would be the entry point and anchor for the American presence in the region. But that country's policy of supporting and financing the Muslim Brotherhood would forever entangle the United States with fundamentalist Islam. The U.S. connection with Saudi Arabia and the Middle East was spurred by the desire for oil and the logic of Cold War containment. Yet U.S. inexperience in the region, and its near-total lack of understanding of the region's culture, including Islam, bedeviled American policy from the start.

According to standard histories, the official U.S. entry into the region is said to have begun in 1945, on a yacht anchored in the Great Bitter Lake astride the Suez Canal. There, in February, on his journey back to Washington from Yalta, Franklin Delano Roosevelt met King Abdel Aziz ibn Saud, the first meeting between an American president and a Saudi monarch, setting the stage for a half century of relations between the two countries.

But two other crucial events preceded the FDR–Ibn Saud encounter.

First came the signing, in 1933, of the U.S. oil concession in Saudi Arabia that would grow into that global petroleum superpower, the Arabian-American Oil Company (Aramco). And the man who brokered that all-important deal was the British spook, Harry St. John Bridger ("Abdullah") Philby, the operative who had helped Ibn Saud and his Wahhabi Brotherhood take power during and after World

War I. In the late 1920s, Philby, trading on his Saudi connections, left official government employ and went into business for himself. Increasingly tied to the Al Saud, Philby distanced himself—at least publicly—from British policy. To the bemusement of his friends and the consternation of his wife and family, he converted to Islam, taking the name "Abdullah." His conversion, however, was a lark—or a subterfuge. In his diary, he wrote jocularly "how nice it would be for me when I became a Muslim and could have four wives."[4] Having been an atheist since Cambridge, it was clear that Abdullah Philby "needed Islam not as a faith but as a convenience," and he told friends exactly that.[5] Yet he plunged into Islam, visiting Mecca, taking multiple wives, and marrying a slave girl who was a gift from Ibn Saud. His real interest, however, was making money, and in Jeddah it was said that Philby "should be called not Abdullah, slave of God, but Abd al-Qirsh, slave of halfpence."[6] The born-again wheeler-dealer ran businesses, becoming Ford Motor's official representative in Saudi Arabia (though he said: "I hate the sight and sound of motor cars").[7] Eventually he became an agent for Standard Oil of California (Socal) and, using his friendship with the king, Philby sealed the deal for Socal's entry into what would become its ultimate El Dorado, achieved at a bargain price: £50,000 ($250,000) down and annual rent of just £5,000 in gold. The concession was to last sixty years and cover 360,000 square miles, half again as large as all of Texas.[8] For a pittance, the king had signed away his country's richest treasure. And the United States, represented by Standard Oil of California—eventually joined by Texaco, then Exxon and Mobil, the four Aramco partners—was in.[9]

FDR's proclamation, in 1943, that Saudi Arabia would henceforth fall under the U.S. defense umbrella was the second crucial development. "I hereby find that the defense of Saudi Arabia is vital to the defense of the United States,"[10] the president announced.

Roosevelt's embrace of Saudi Arabia had multiple aims. There was the obvious one, namely, that its oil was a precious resource. There was a strategic one, in which the threat (remote though it was) of Soviet encirclement of the Persian Gulf was a concern. And there was a tactical one, aimed at America's allies, especially the British. Although London was dominant in the region, including southern Persia and Iraq, there was a sometimes bitter rivalry between the United States and the British—and to a lesser extent, France and Italy, too—over oil in the Middle East. All jealously guarded their companies' advantages.

Four years before his shipboard encounter with the king, FDR had seemed willing to let Saudi Arabia be handled by Great Britain, since London was virtually all-powerful in the region, and the United States had little experience there. "Will you tell the British I hope they can take care of the king of Saudi Arabia?" FDR asked an aide. "This is a little far afield for us."[11] But Standard Oil of California and the Texas Oil Company, partners in what would soon be renamed Aramco, would have none of it. They convinced Interior Secretary Harold Ickes, FDR's right-hand man, and then FDR himself, that the United States must stand up to the British, who, they said, were "trying to edge their way into" Saudi Arabia.[12] In the midst of World War II, the two allies eventually struck a deal, carving up the region's oil. Roosevelt told Lord Halifax, the British ambassador, "Persian oil . . . is yours. We share the oil of Kuwait and Iraq. As for Saudi Arabian oil, it's ours."[13]

To Winston Churchill, FDR cabled: "Please do accept my assurances that we are not making sheep's eyes at your oil fields in Iraq and Iran." Replied Churchill, who'd almost single-handedly built London's overseas oil empire, "Let me reciprocate by giving you the fullest assurance that we have no thought of trying to horn in on your interests or property in Saudi Arabia."[14] (Both men, of course, were lying. The British had long coveted Saudi oil, and the United States would soon elbow its way forcefully into the oil concessions in Iran and Iraq.)

FDR's meeting with Ibn Saud did mark a consummation of the U.S.-Saudi partnership. To transport the king, who'd never been outside of Arabia before, the United States bundled him onto the U.S.S. *Murphy,* complete with family, retainers, servants, and sheep for slaughter, and the desert potentate set up a tent on deck for sleeping. Elliott Roosevelt, the president's son, described FDR's encounter with Ibn Saud, as the king was known, aboard the *Quincy:*

Discreetly, my sister Anna had taken her leave of Father that day for a trip to Cairo, out of deference for the Moslem custom of secluding the women of the family. . . . Father ended up by promising Ibn Saud that he would sanction no American move hostile to the Arab people. . . . And Ibn Saud, looking enviously at Father's wheelchair, was surprised when Father promptly made him a present of it.[15]

Actually, it was a spare wheelchair, and it was too small for the bulky monarch. But it was enough for the Saudi king to declare himself FDR's "twin," and it symbolized the formal beginning of the U.S.-Saudi alliance. C. L. Sulzberger, writing in the *New York Times,* was excited at the prospect of the United States getting its hands on Saudi oil: "The immense oil deposits in Saudi Arabia alone make that country more important to American diplomacy than almost any other smaller nation," he wrote.[16] Roosevelt, too, it is clear, cared a lot about oil, and not much about Islam.

FDR's 1943 proclamation that America would defend Saudi Arabia would be reaffirmed by every American president, most prominently in the 1957 Eisenhower Doctrine and the 1980 Carter Doctrine. In 1944, the United States sent its first military mission to Saudi Arabia, and in 1945 the United States and Saudi Arabia signed a military cooperation agreement that established a major U.S. Air Force base at Dhahran in the Persian Gulf, a facility that would serve as an American base until the 1960s. That agreement was quickly followed by a 1949 accord, which provided for a U.S. survey team to cover the entire Arabian peninsula, with recommendations for creating a U.S.-equipped, 43,000-man army and air force, and a 1951 accord setting up a permanent U.S. Military Training Mission in the country.[17]

From the beginning, America's relationship with Saudi Arabia was a no-nonsense one, involving a rapidly expanding oil output, bilateral defense arrangements, and a vast influx of Texans, Oklahomans, and Louisianans into the kingdom. The United States, joined by Great Britain as a rival and junior partner, began to surround Saudi Arabia with military alliances. In 1951, the United States and Britain proposed a "Middle East Command," linking the United States, the United Kingdom, and France with Turkey, Israel, and Jordan. They began by approaching Egypt, but abandoned the idea when Egypt's king, pressed by nationalists and deeply unhappy about the new Jewish state, politely declined. Next, the British took the lead in signing treaties with Turkey, Iraq, Iran, and Pakistan, calling the new constellation the "Baghdad Pact." The United States, which was building its own ties to those states and was simultaneously intent on elbowing the British out of the oil-rich Persian Gulf, didn't join the Baghdad Pact, and an astute U.S. observer of the time, writing for the Council on Foreign Relations, rather snidely noted that the British had assembled the pact "in order to save its position in Iraq and to bolster a flagging influence throughout the Middle East."[18] The Baghdad Pact, too, soon fell part when Baghdad, its center, underwent a revolution in 1958. The British-installed king of Iraq was toppled and executed by an alliance of army nationalists and the Iraqi Communist Party, and the Baghdad Pact was no more. It was replaced by the Central Treaty Organization, linking the United States, the United Kingdom, Turkey, Iran, and Pakistan. Pakistan was also linked to the West by its membership in the Southeast Asia Treaty Organization.

The Anglo-American alliances in the Middle East rested on the traditional levers of external influence—military power, economic muscle, and diplomacy. More quietly, though, as the Cold War evolved, an additional factor emerged to bolster the U.S. and U.K. presence, namely, the religious and cultural power of political Islam. Especially important in that regard was Saudi Arabia's would-be role as Islam's Vatican. As Saudi Arabia emerged as America's counterweight to Egypt, Nasser, and nationalism, a number of Muslim Brotherhood organizers emerged as emissaries for the Islamic right across the region—none, perhaps, more important than Said Ramadan.

Ramadan, a key Brotherhood ideologue, served as Saudi Arabia's unofficial ambassador of Islamism. As the Muslim Brotherhood struggled to maintain its presence in Egypt, where it was increasingly at odds with the new regime under Nasser, Saudi Arabia not only bankrolled the Brothers but offered its territory as a safe haven. A series of Saudi kings were preoccupied with the threat of communism, and they saw the Muslim Brotherhood and others on the Islamic right as the leading edge of the anti-communist movement. Equally important, perhaps, Saudi Arabia saw Egypt's Nasser as a dire threat, since Nasser—ruling impoverished Egypt—coveted Saudi Arabia's oil. So for reasons of both anti-communism and anti-Arab nationalism, Saudi Arabia encouraged the growth of the Muslim Brotherhood in Egypt and throughout the Middle East.

RAMADAN AT THE WHITE HOUSE

In the late summer of 1953, the Oval Office at the White House served as the stage for a little-noticed encounter between President Dwight D. Eisenhower and a young Middle Eastern firebrand. In the muted black-and-white photograph[19] recording the event, the grandfatherly, balding Ike, then sixty-three, stands gray suited, erect, his elbows bent and his fists clenched as if to add muscle to some forceful point. To his left is a young, olive-skinned Egyptian in a dark suit, with a neatly trimmed, full beard and closely cropped hair, clutching a sheaf of papers behind his back. Staring intently at the president, he is just twenty-seven years old, but already has more than a decade of experience at the very heart of the Islamic world's violent and passionate politics. Alongside him, some dressed in Western attire and others wearing robes, shawls, and Muslim headgear, are members of a delegation of scholars, mullahs, and activists from India, Syria, Yemen, and North Africa.

The president's visitor that September day was Said Ramadan, a militant official and ideologue of the Muslim Brotherhood. The young man even had a claim to semi-royalty in Brotherhood circles, since he had married Wafa al-Banna, Hassan al-Banna's daughter, making him the son-in-law of the organization's founder. As he stood at the president's side, Ramadan appeared respectable and harmless. Yet the Brotherhood was known throughout the Middle East, since at least the late 1940s, as an organization of fanatics and terrorists. Its acolytes had murdered several Egyptian officials, including a prime minister, and just five years before Ramadan met Ike, the Muslim Brotherhood was declared illegal by the faltering regime of King Farouq of Egypt. But it didn't disappear. Over the next fifty years, the Muslim Brotherhood would stage repeated comebacks, slowly building its power and influence, spreading its ideology and building chapters in Jordan, Syria, Kuwait, and beyond. And until his death, in Switzerland, in 1995, Said Ramadan would be its chief international organizer.

Despite the fact that Ramadan was angry, violence prone, and openly intent on remaking the Middle East according to Islamic fundamentalist specifications, he wasn't regarded as a threat. In fact, based on a secret evaluation by the U.S. ambassador in Cairo, Ramadan was viewed as a potential ally. It was the very height of McCarthyism and the Cold War, and the Muslim Brotherhood was bitterly anti-communist. Not only that, but Ramadan's allies in the Muslim Brotherhood, Pakistan's Islamic Group,[20] and similar organizations across the region were vigorously opposed to Marxists, left-wing activists on campuses, trade union organizers, Arab nationalists, "Arab socialists," the Baath Party, and secularists of all kinds. In the latter category were pesky upstarts like Egypt's president Gamal Abdel Nasser, whose loyalty to the American side in the Cold War was in doubt even in 1953, just a year after his Free Officers movement had ousted the corrupt and despised monarchy.

Said Ramadan was born in 1926 at Shibin el Kom, a village about seventy miles north of Cairo in the Egyptian Nile Delta.[21] As a young teenager, he encountered Hassan al-Banna and he joined the movement immediately. After graduating from Cairo University, in 1946 Ramadan became Banna's personal secretary and right-hand man. A year later, Ramadan was named editor of *Al Shihab,* the Muslim Brotherhood weekly.

Besides helping the Brotherhood's leader with organizational tasks, the founder's son-in-law became a roving ambassador for the Muslim Brotherhood, amassing a vast network of international contacts that the more parochial, and Egypt-based, Banna didn't have. In 1945, Ramadan traveled to Jerusalem, which was then a British-controlled city under the Palestine Mandate, where the storm clouds of the war between the Arabs and Jews were beginning to gather. Over the coming years, Ramadan would spend a great deal of time traveling between Jerusalem, Amman, Damascus, and Beirut, building the Brotherhood's chapters. On October 26, 1945, Ramadan opened the Muslim Brotherhood's first office in Jerusalem,[22] founding the organization that, by the 1980s, would become known as the Islamic Resistance Movement (Hamas). By 1947, twenty-five branches of the Muslim Brotherhood existed in Palestine, with between 12,000 and 20,000 members.[23] In 1948, Ramadan helped to organize the Muslim Brotherhood's symbolically significant Islamic force that battled the Jewish forces that established Israel that year.

Ramadan also made the first of many visits to Pakistan in the late 1940s, taking part in the first meetings of the World Muslim Congress in Karachi in 1949 and 1951, where he flirted with becoming secretary-general of the organization.[24] (The congress itself was denounced by the Pakistan left as having been organized by "Anglo-American imperialism.")[25] Pakistan had achieved independence from Great Britain a year earlier, and as the first Islamic state it became a magnet for Islamist ideologues, organizers, and scholars. A young Islamist named Abul-Ala Mawdudi—who'd founded a Muslim Brotherhood–style movement in Pakistan called the Islamic Group—was transforming his movement into a political party. For the next decade, Pakistan would become a kind of second home for Ramadan. The fledgling Islamic state gave Ramadan a broadcast slot on Radio Pakistan, and he enjoyed good relations with the Western-leaning government of Pakistan, including with Prime Minister Liaquat Ali Khan, who wrote the preface to one of Ramadan's books.[26]

Ramadan's stay in Pakistan wasn't entirely voluntary. The Brotherhood had been banned in Egypt, and Hassan al-Banna assassinated. Ramadan returned to Egypt in 1950, when the Brotherhood made one of its many comebacks, but he would periodically spend long periods of time in Pakistan, where he worked closely with Mawdudi and his Islamic Group. Ramadan also worked with Pakistan's Muslim League, and with official Pakistani support he traveled and lectured throughout the Arab world. At the time, politics in Pakistan was split among radical Islamists, moderate Islamists, secular nationalists, and the left. Meanwhile, the country was being drawn into pro-Western military alliances. During several years in Karachi, Ramadan helped Mawdudi organize a muscular phalanx of fanatical Islamic students that battled Pakistan's left, especially on university campuses. The so-called Islamic Student Society, known by its Urdu initials as the IJT,[27] modeled on Mussolini's fascist *squadristi,* was a Ramadan project. "Although organized under the supervision of the [Islamic Group], IJT was greatly influenced by the Muslim Brotherhood of Egypt. Between 1952 and 1955, Ramadan helped IJT leaders formalize an administrative structure and devise an organizational strategy. The most visible marks of the brotherhood's influence are IJT's 'study circle' and all-night study sessions, both of which were means of indoctrinating new members and fostering organizational bonds," according to one expert, Vali Reza Nasr. The often-armed IJT thugs clashed repeatedly with left-wing students on campus. "Egg tossing gradually gave way to more serious clashes, especially in Karachi and Multan," wrote Nasr. "Antileftist student activism had become the IJT's calling and increasingly determined its course of action. [The IJT became] a soldiers brigade which would fight for Islam against its enemies—secularists and leftists—within the government and without."[28]

In between his trips to Pakistan, Ramadan also apparently worked with Arab fundamentalists, especially among Palestinians and Jordanians who founded the so-called Islamic Liberation Party.[29] (Later, the Liberation Party metastasized, relocating its headquarters to Germany and then spreading through Muslim Central Asia. It was increasingly supported by Saudi Arabia. By the 1990s, it had become an important violence-prone force allied to the Islamic Movement of Uzbekistan and to Al Qaeda.) While in Jordan in the 1950s, Ramadan also helped found the Jordanian branch of the Muslim Brotherhood. The leader of Jordan's Muslim Brotherhood was Abu Qurah, a wealthy Jordanian merchant with close ties to King Abdullah and the British-backed Hashemite monarchy. According to Marion Boulby,

Banna sent Ramadan to Amman for the express purpose of getting the
Muslim Brotherhood of Jordan off the ground, and the king "granted
the Brotherhood legal status as a welfare organization, hoping to
secure its support against the secular opposition," i.e., against the left.
As in Pakistan, the Brotherhood became a tool for suppressing the left
and Arab nationalists. Ramadan and Qurah "argued that in the twentieth century Egypt and the rest of the Islamic world were threatened
by the onslaught of communist and nationalist ideologies which denied
the supremacy of *sharia* in society."[30]

Ramadan's presence in the Oval Office that day in 1953 was no
accident. Officially, Ramadan was in the United States to attend the
Colloquium on Islamic Culture at Princeton University, with a side
trip to Washington. The Library of Congress joined Princeton in putting together the nine-day program. It was an august event, full of
pomp and circumstance, held under the leafy greenery shading Princeton's Nassau Hall, in the high-ceilinged Faculty Room. Among the
speakers and attendees were some of the leading Orientalists of the
era, men like Philip K. Hitti, T. Cuyler Young, and Bayly Winder of
Princeton, Wilfred Cantwell Smith of McGill University, Richard
Nelson Frye of Harvard University, Carleton Coon of the University
of Pennsylvania, and Kenneth Cragg, editor of the journal *The Muslim World,* from the Hartford Seminary Foundation. Directing the
conference was Dr. Bayard Dodge, the venerable former president of
the American University in Beirut.

According to the official record, the conference fortuitously took
advantage of the fact that a number of celebrated personages from the
Middle East were visiting. But the participants didn't just "happen"
to have crossed the Atlantic. The colloquium was organized by the
U.S. government, which funded it, tapped participants it considered
useful or promising, and bundled them off to New Jersey. Hitti, perhaps the dean of the Orientalists, visited Cairo, Bahrain, Baghdad,
Beirut, New Delhi, and other cities to scout participants, and supple-
mentary funding for the colloquium was sought from U.S. airlines,
including Pan Am and TWA, and from Aramco, the U.S. oil consortium in Saudi Arabia. Like many of the participants, Ramadan, a
hard-edged ideologue and no scholar, was visiting the conference as

an all-expenses-paid guest. And the U.S. government was not exactly in the dark about who he was.

Paying for the conference—including the expenses for transporting attendees from the Middle East—was the International Information Administration, a branch of the State Department, with roots in the U.S. intelligence community. The IIA had a brief existence, officially set up in 1952 and then incorporated, in 1953, into the CIA-connected U.S. Information Agency. Among its responsibilities, the IIA oversaw official U.S. "culture exchange programs," such as the Princeton colloquium. It's also clear that a primary purpose of the colloquium was political. A declassified IIA document labeled "Confidential—Security Information," says: "On the surface, the conference looks like an exercise in pure learning. This in effect is the impression desired." The conference, it goes on, was designed to "bring together persons exerting great influence in formulating Muslim opinion in fields such as education, science, law and philosophy and inevitably, therefore, on politics." Its goal was sweeping. "Among the various results expected from the colloquium are the impetus and direction that may be given to the Renaissance movement within Islam itself."[31]

America's ambassador in Cairo at the time was the veteran diplomat Jefferson Caffery, a Louisiana lawyer then nearing the end of a stellar foreign service career that spanned four decades. He'd been in Cairo since 1949, ultimately serving six years in the languid capital on the Nile. In July 1953 Caffery penned a classified cable suggesting that Ramadan be invited to the Princeton conclave. Caffery's dispatch provides a revealing glimpse into how much U.S. intelligence had already gathered on the Muslim Brotherhood and its leadership, reach, and activities. Caffery's dispatch provides a capsule biography of Ramadan and a thumbnail sketch of the Muslim Brotherhood. But, read in full, it is eerily sanitized, making no mention of the Brotherhood's involvement in terrorism and violence, and nowhere does Caffery cite their commitment to an Islamic state under the Koran. Caffery, a highly experienced diplomat, is not naïve, and it is clear from his account that he (and perhaps the CIA) were willing to overlook any violence tied to the Brothers and were targeting Ramadan for recruitment as either ally or agent:

Saeed Ramadhan is considered to be among the most learned scholars of Islamic culture in the Ikhwan el Muslimin (Moslem Brotherhood). A graduate of the Faculty of Law from Fouad University in Cairo in 1945, he takes but few cases and devotes most of his time to the study of Islam. Born in 1925, he is young in years but old in experience.

At present he is engaged as editor in chief of El Musliman, a monthly magazine now in its second year, which publishes articles on Islamic law and culture by scholars through the Muslim world. Its circulation is about 10,000 and subscribers reach from Tunisia to Indonesia. As General Secretary of the World Islamic Conference, he travels extensively throughout the Islamic States and has recently returned from conferences in Pakistan. When in Egypt he gives weekly radio broadcasts in Islamic culture and interpretation of the Koran.

In 1940 Ramadhan began his studies of Islam under Hassan al Banna, former Supreme Guide of the Ikhwan el Muslimin, and became editor of El Shihab, a magazine introduced by the latter in 1947. It was a monthly magazine for articles on Islamic law and culture but ceased publication after five issues under pressure from ex-King Farouk's government. Shortly thereafter the Brotherhood was outlawed and upwards of 2,000 of its members arrested. Saeed Ramadhan left for Pakistan in time to prevent possible detention. He lived there about a year during which time he had two radio broadcasts weekly which were beamed to the Arab States, including Egypt. Late in 1949 the Muslim League of Pakistan requested Ramadhan to give a series of lectures on Islamic Culture in many parts of the Middle East. Starting in Sudan, he gave talks mainly in universities through Egypt and ending in Turkey.[32]

Caffery had been contacted by an unnamed American agent, on behalf of Mohammed el Bakay of Al Azhar, the centuries-old Islamic center of learning in Cairo. Bakay, who also traveled to Princeton, described Ramadan as "a distinguished member of the Muslim Brotherhood" and suggested that he be invited to attend the Princeton gathering, adding that the Society of Muslim Brothers was willing to help pay his expenses.[33] Concluded Caffery:

The Embassy believes that Ramadhan's scholarly attainments are sufficient to make him eligible to attend the Colloquium on Islamic Culture. His position with the Muslim Brotherhood makes it important that his desire for an invitation be considered carefully in light of the possible effects of offending this important body.[34]

For the next four decades, Ramadan would turn up, Zelig-like, as a key operative in virtually every manifestation of radical, political Islam, from the Muslim Brotherhood–led terrorism in Egypt in the 1950s and 1960s to the rise of Ayatollah Khomeini in Iran in the 1970s to the civil war in Algeria in the 1990s. There's no concrete evidence to prove that Ramadan was recruited as a CIA agent in the 1950s, but it's clear that his invitation to the Princeton colloquium marked him as a potential target for recruitment, and he would later become a crucial ally of Saudi Arabia's royal family in assembling an Islamic bloc of nations and movements opposed to the spread of communism and to Soviet expansion along its southern frontier. According to declassified documents in the Swiss archives, reported by Sylvain Besson in *Le Temps* of Geneva, in the 1960s the Swiss authorities—then hosting Ramadan at his Islamic Center in Geneva—looked upon Ramadan favorably, thanks to his anti-communist views. And they added: "Said Ramadan is, among other things, an intelligence agent of the English and the Americans. What's more, I believe that he has rendered services—according to an intelligence plan—to the [Swiss federal police]." Ramadan's dossier, reported *Le Temps,* includes several documents indicating his connections to "certain Western secret services."[35]

ISLAM: BULWARK AGAINST COMMUNISM?

Were Ramadan, the Muslim Brotherhood, and the Islamic right useful allies in the Cold War struggle against communism? Was Islam itself a bulwark against a foreign, atheistic ideology? In one sense, the answer was no. Both communism and nationalism could and did easily attract adherents among the masses of Muslims. In Iraq, for instance, the Iraqi Communist Party, the Arab world's largest, won the allegiance of millions of Iraqi Shiites during the period after World War II, and by the late 1950s the party was strong enough to organize a demonstration in Baghdad that attracted more than one million Iraqis. And Egypt's Nasser, whose Cairo-based Voice of the Arabs radio broadcasts carried his nationalist message into Syria, Jordan, Lebanon, Iraq, and Saudi Arabia, gathered an enormous following and for much of the 1950s and 1960s was by far the most popular Arab political leader. Just as Christians in Europe joined the communist parties en masse, in the Islamic world Muslims unhappy with their status or their quality of life, or who were opposed to Western imperialism and Anglo-American influence in the Middle East, opted for communism or, more often, for Arab nationalism.

Yet even if Muslims were attracted to left-wing ideologies, some Orientalists and U.S. policy makers felt that there was still reason to believe that political Islam might yet be mobilized in forms that were explicitly anti-communist. In the Middle East, organized Islam took many forms, of course. First and foremost was the traditionalist, clergy-based religion, organized around mosques, religious foundations or endowments, Islamic courts, and other institutions, many of which had a powerful social impact but were not explicitly political. Next, there was "state Islam," such as existed in Saudi Arabia since its founding in the 1920s or in Pakistan since independence (and especially since the 1970s), in which entire nations were organized according to religious identity and Islamic law, and it was sometimes difficult to see the dividing line between Islam and the state. And finally, there was the emerging "New Right" in the Muslim world, including the Muslim Brotherhood and other explicitly political organizations or parties committed to the establishment of an Islamic republic. To those in the West looking for ideological forces in the Middle East that could provide an intellectual counterweight to the radical appeal of communism, all three of these forms seemed attractive at one time or another, and indeed there was overlap among them.

In the United States, there was alarm over the fact that the Arab "elite"—that is, opinion leaders, intellectuals, politicians, journalists, and the like—were increasingly drawn to left-wing movements and parties. Among the masses, there was more reluctance to abandon the Koran for *Das Kapital,* especially among ill-educated peasants, Bedouin tribesmen, and pro-capitalist merchants and bazaar leaders, making them harder to mobilize on behalf of Marxism and Arab socialism. So the question was: What sort of ideological framework might be able to attract both the Arab and Muslim masses on one hand and to capture some important segment of the Arab elite on the other? For some analysts, the "new Islam," led by intellectuals and political operatives such as Banna, Ramadan, and Mawdudi, seemed made to order. The Muslim Brotherhood was having some success on university campuses, attracting students—especially engineers, scientists, physicians, and management and business students. Could such a movement, especially with the support of the Saudi Arabian royal family, counteract the Marxist-nationalist bloc? And could U.S. propaganda, stressing America's own religious values in contrast to the atheistic Soviet Union, draw the Muslim masses into the American camp—or at least away from Moscow? It seemed worth a try.

One who seemed to think it might be worthwhile was Bernard Lewis, the inventor of the phrase "clash of civilizations." For five decades, Lewis, who is currently an emeritus professor at Princeton, has been arguably the single most influential theorist in the field of Islamic scholarship. Yet, for all that time, Lewis has been intensely controversial, largely because he has taken a highly partisan, conservative—and later, "neoconservative"—point of view, and because of his strong affinity for Israel. A 1953 essay by Professor Lewis, "Communism and Islam," is an important example of the then-current thinking on the great battle of ideologies.

Lewis made it clear that the people of the Muslim world seemed intent on creating a string of authoritarian governments and that, if the West's objective was to oppose the spread of communism, that wouldn't be so bad. "If the peoples of Islam are forced to make a straight choice, to abandon their own traditions in favour of either Communism or parliamentarianism, then we are at a great disadvantage," he wrote. "It is fortunate, both for Islam and for the Western world, that the choice is not restricted to these two simple alternatives, for the possibility still remains for the Muslim peoples of restoring, perhaps in a modified form, their own tradition; of evolving a form of government which, though authoritarian, and perhaps even autocratic, is nevertheless far removed from the cynical tyranny of European-style dictatorship."[36]

After endorsing the "fortunate" likelihood of authoritarian Muslim regimes, Lewis went on to suggest that, indeed, Islam would ultimately prove infertile ground for Marxist ideas:

> Communism is not and cannot be a religion, while Islam, for the great mass of believers, still is; and that is the core of the Islamic resistance to Communist ideas. Though their belief in liberty be too weak to sustain them, their belief in God may yet be strong enough. The Islamic peoples are still profoundly religious in the deepest and simplest meaning of the word. Islam as a religion is no more anti-Communist than Christianity; in fact, as I have suggested, rather less so. But it is more potent as a force affecting the lives and thoughts of its adherents. Pious Muslims—and most Muslims are pious—will not long tolerate an atheist creed, nor one that violates their traditional religious moral principles. . . . The present revolt of the Muslims against the immorality and opportunism of their own and of some Western leaders may temporarily favor the Communists, with their appearance of selfless devotion to an ideal, but will work against Communism when Muslims come to see the realities behind the propaganda. Let us hope that they will not take too long over it.

At the Princeton colloquium, held the same year Lewis's essay was written, a marker was laid down by a Pakistani scholar, Mazheruddin Siddiqi, a fellow at the Institute of Islamic Culture in Lahore. A former government official and prolific writer, educated at the University of Madras in India, Siddiqi was the author of *Islam and Communism, Marxism and Islam,* and *Historical Materialism and Islam.* In his address to the Princeton gathering, Siddiqi made it clear that communism could be resisted only if its opposition was faith-based and built on Islamic fundamentals. Siddiqi attacked Muslim "authoritarianism," but also unleashed a bitter salvo against the Islamic world's secularists, "the pseudo-scientists and half-baked intellectuals who surreptitiously or openly advocate the gradual annihilation of religion," and who argue that religion is "a mass of superstitions, dogmas, and supernatural doctrines which tend to belittle the power of reason." Secularists, not communists, are the greatest danger to the stability of Pakistan and, by implication, the broader Middle East:

> Communist atheism [Siddiqi said] has a power of inspiration which pure rationalism does not have. It is a faith as well as a science, a social gospel as well as a metaphysical system. It is the only real substitute for religious faith which the champions of science and technology are seeking to undermine in Pakistan.
>
> It is the socio-economic significance of Islam that makes it a standing barrier against Communism. The Muslim masses are attached to the Islamic idea, just because it offers them the promise of social and economic equality and freedom of expression.
>
> If any attempt is made to deny the socio-economic content of Islamic teachings, Communism is sure to rush into the vacuum that would be created. For, as I have pointed out, Communism offers both the emotional satisfaction of religious faith and the promise of social and economic security. . . . In the Islamic world, the choice is not between Communism and secular democracy, but between Communism and liberal Islam. . . . The greatest danger to the stability of Pakistan comes neither from reactionary theologians nor from the Communists who can offer nothing better to a Muslim, but from those who without any knowledge of the deeper aspects of Islam . . . are trying to create a spiritual vacuum in our life that would safely let in Communism.[37]

Kenneth Cragg, *The Muslim World* editor, had a similar message. Cragg's paper, "The Intellectual Impact of Communism upon Contemporary Islam," originally delivered at the colloquium, was published a few months later in the *Middle East Journal*.[38] In it, he presented a sophisticated argument for an Islamic revival. "We in religious resistance to Communism," wrote Cragg, "understand that the Muslim world must develop an intellectual response to the challenge of communism, on a level that is spiritual, metaphysical, and moral, in order to combat the Marxist 'eschatology' that 'looks forward to a Communist Heaven on earth.'" Cragg offered an antidote to this seductive

Marxism: "With Islam, as countless modern writers have explained, [the perfect society] is the true Islamic society—some would say the true Islamic State." And he concludes with a hopeful vision: "May it not be that by virtue of this common need to give a worthy answer to Communism the two faiths, Islam and Christianity, have the opportunity of a fruitful relationship with each other?" Cragg cites a comment from the Princeton gathering, in which the occasion of Turkish troops fighting in the Korean War was evoked, to conclude: "Now at last after 1,300 years of largely fruitless controversy, men of the two great monotheistic religions are struggling shoulder to shoulder against godless materialism."

Yet, in the 1950s, the idea that Islam would join the "Christian" West in a jihad-crusade against "godless materialism" was decidedly a minority point of view. On one hand, many hard-headed strategists—who might be called "realists" today—felt that Islamism was too weak or uncertain a force to be relied upon. A second pole of opposition came from some of those who believed that Islam could never serve the anti-communist cause because it was inherently too anti-Western.

Hermann Eilts recalls the idea that Islam was an ally in the struggle against Moscow as an "overstatement."

"There was a view that Islam and communism were simply antithetical," says Eilts, who began his service in Iran and Saudi Arabia in the 1940s. "Very few people in government even thought very much about Islam. . . . There were those who said, 'It's helpful to keep the communists out.' But no one really took it very seriously. The general view in the U.S. government and in the academic world was that Islam was becoming a shrinking political factor, and *sharia* law, Islamic law, was being relegated to personal status. And I remember so well American economic specialists coming out to the countries in which I served and making the point that the quicker you get rid of Islam, the more quickly you are going to develop, because Islam was seen by them as a barrier to economic development."

John C. Campbell, for decades the Council on Foreign Relations' chief Middle East strategist, led a CFR task force, launched in 1954, comprised of many of the heavyweights of the U.S. foreign policy establishment. For Campbell, Islam may or may not have been a barrier to economic growth, but it didn't appear to be a barrier against the USSR:

> Certainly Islam cannot be counted on to serve as such a barrier. The theory that communism and Soviet influence could never make inroads in the Moslem world because they are materialistic and atheistic has not been borne out. Religion does have a significant place in Middle Eastern society. It colors both popular and official attitudes. But it does not establish an absolute immunity to a political virus such as fascism or communism. Communist theory does have certain superficial parallels with Islamic dogma, and the promise of a better material life is not inconsistent with it. Above all, the impact of the modern world on Islam has produced two major trends which tend to open the door toward communist influence: first, the inability of traditional doctrines and institutions to hold the loyalty of the intellectual leaders and new generations bent on finding a way out of material backwardness; and second, the revulsion against the West, which, while often reinforcing the sense of dedication to Islam, has often created also a sense of identification with whatever theories and political forces were hostile to the West. . . . In the Arab lands and Iran, the anti-Western nationalist movement has had a strong admixture of religious feeling, even fanaticism.

The inherently anti-Western bias of political Islam, thought Campbell, ought to preclude any idea of its usefulness in U.S. strategy.[39]

Despite such warnings, the United States experimented, often clumsily, with Islamism in the years between 1945 and 1957.

Even as early as 1945, when British and American planners began thinking about how to build alliances and a system of defense against the USSR across its vast southern border, Islam was factored in. The British-inspired League of Arab States, for instance, was considered weak because it didn't include Turkey, Iran, and Pakistan. So, it was proposed at one point to convert the Arab League into a League of Islamic States, to include at least some of the Northern Tier countries.[40]

That idea fizzled, and subsequent policies focused less on Islam and more on direct Anglo-American power. Still, during the Truman and Eisenhower years, the United States carried out a series of efforts to mobilize political Islam in the Cold War, and to use Islam as a weapon against Soviet influence. Some of them were serious-minded. Others were clumsy, even hilariously misguided.

Consider the "Red Pig" program. Part of the American approach toward political Islam in the 1950s was to try to win propaganda points by emphasizing that the United States was a pious nation and that the Soviet Union persecuted religion. In 1951, the U.S. Information Service in Baghdad proudly announced the launch of a propaganda campaign designed to win the hearts and minds of Iraqi Muslims by a "comparison of the state of religion in the United States and in 'a Communist state.'" A poster was created "which showed the Communist state as a big bully maltreating a man labeled 'Religion.'" A second poster

> tells the story of the Greedy Red Pig and how he came to a bad
> end. The fact that the pig is wearing a Red Star on his armband
> and has at his rear instead of the normally piggy curl a hammer-
> and-sickle tail has not escaped the observers. . . . Others remarked
> on the suitability of making the Communist villain a pig because
> of the resistance appeal it has for Moslems. We feel that a whole
> series of cartoon-posters can be developed, using the Red Pig as
> the central figure.[41]

Edward S. Crocker, the foreign service official who helped design the campaign, helpfully included thirty-two illustrations of the Red Pig campaign with his dispatch.

The fledgling Central Intelligence Agency also experimented with creative, if half-cocked, ways of connecting with the Islamist movement. Some of them are told in the raucously funny book *The Game of Nations* by Miles Copeland, the CIA operations officer who, during the 1950s, served as a liaison to Nasser and who spent many years embroiled in Arab political skullduggery. Copeland retired early from the CIA but maintained close connections to dozens of its current and former operatives, especially to Kermit and Archie Roosevelt, grandsons of Teddy Roosevelt. A back-slapping southerner, Copeland used his good-ol'-boy charm to mask a sophisticated understanding of the Arab world. He reported that around the same time as the "Red Pig" campaign, the CIA came up with the "Moslem Billy Graham" project. In 1951, Secretary of State Dean Acheson "borrowed Kermit Roosevelt from the newly formed Central Intelligence Agency to head a highly secret committee of specialists—some from the State Department, some from the Department of Defense, and some brought in as consultants from business concerns and universities (and none from the CIA except Roosevelt himself)—to study the Arab world," said Copeland. At the gathering, an operation designed to mobilize Islamic religious sentiments was launched. "Someone advanced the idea of promoting a 'Moslem Billy Graham' to mobilize religious fervor in a great move against Communism and actually got as far as selecting a wild-eyed Iraqi holy man to send on a tour of Arab countries." The identity of the Iraqi wasn't revealed. But Copeland considered the entire effort to be a learning experience. "The project did no harm, and the managing of it taught the committee much about what was wrong with their basic planning assumptions—lessons that were put to good use later when [Saudi Arabia's] King Feisal's advisers put Feisal up to much the same kind of project, with Feisal himself as the holy man."[42]

Another, less ambitious CIA project involved some sardonic propaganda aimed at the USSR's influence in Egypt. The CIA unearthed some pre–World War I anti-Islamic tracts with titles like *Mohammed Never Existed, The Harmful Consequences of Fasting during Ramadan,* and *Against the Veil,* and reissued them, this time attributing them to the Soviet embassy in Cairo.[43]

The CIA also experimented with using Egypt as a center for reaching out to Islamic activists in the Middle East and Africa. The vehicle for the effort was none other than Anwar Sadat. Since World War II, Sadat had been close to the Muslim Brotherhood, serving as the liaison between the organization and Nasser's Free Officers movement in the 1940s and early 1950s. Sadat approached Nasser with the idea of creating an Islamic Congress and, when Nasser agreed, Sadat was appointed to lead it. According to Miles Copeland, "Religious attachés were sent to various Egyptian missions abroad and assigned the task of watching for opportunities to use common religious interests to achieve at least tactical 'union.' . . . The American Government at first gave limited encouragement to the program."[44] Later, when relations between the United States and Nasser reached the breaking point, the CIA's support for the venture was withdrawn.

More seriously, the United States began to explore with Saudi Arabia the possibility of creating an Islamic bloc, whose potential was noted by some U.S. officials and diplomats beginning in the 1940s. It was still too early for the U.S.-Saudi Islamic alliance to take concrete form as it later would. However, the question of whether Islam could serve as a barrier against communism, Marxist ideas, and radical Arab nationalism occupied the thoughts of many academics, policy makers, and foreign service officers.

In 1951, William A. Eddy, the U.S. consul general in Dhahran, Saudi Arabia, wrote a detailed account of discussions he'd had with various Muslim leaders, including the king of Saudi Arabia, the mufti of Jerusalem, an Islamic leader in Egypt, and an Arab League official suggesting a strategy for the "Christian, democratic West joining with the Muslim world in a common moral front against Communism." According to Eddy, the mufti, Haj Amin al-Husseini, the British-linked Palestinian who'd been a supporter of Nazism during the 1930s and 1940s, "spoke of Russia and Communism with the deepest hate, insisted that we were on the wrong side in the last war [World War II] and should have been allied with Germany against Russia. . . . He spoke cordially of the cooperation which would be offered by Muslims to promote a joint propaganda with Christians to make this danger clear." Regarding Saudi Arabia, Eddy explicitly noted the power of the fundamentalist Wahhabi movement:

> While in an audience with the King of Saudi Arabia, Abdul Aziz al Saud, this week, the King addressed himself strongly to the same point. He affirmed that both Christianity and Islam are threatened by Communism, their common enemy. . . . Muslims in the East, and Christians in the West, should be allies in this trouble to defend their historic faith. . . . As head of the puritanical Wahhabi movement to restore the pure faith and practices of Islam, the

King is without any doubt the most representative and influential Muslim in the world today.[45]

Eddy sent copies of the letter to three officials of Aramco, the consortium made up of Exxon, Mobil, Texaco, and Chevron, and to Brigadier General Robert A. McClure, director of psychological warfare, Department of Defense.

Eddy was more than a low-level consular official. During World War II, Eddy had been an intelligence operative for the Office of Strategic Services (OSS), where he'd gotten experience using political Islam on America's behalf. "Born in Syria of missionary parents, he spoke fluent Arabic and was a distinguished scholar and war hero who had lost a leg in the First World War." With great derring-do, Eddy conducted operations in parts of German-occupied North Africa. "Eddy formed chains of informants to gather intelligence, spread subversive propaganda, and organize a resistance movement." That resistance, however, would include a Muslim secret society, led by collaborators known only by the nicknames "Strings" and "Tassels." Strings was the "leader of a powerful Muslim brotherhood in northern Morocco."[46]

A year later, an unsigned 1952 diplomatic report entitled "Conversation with Prince Saud," labeled "Secret: Security Information," said that Aramco was paying for a print shop and a broadcasting station in Riyadh for the propagation of religious tracts. Prince Saud, who would soon become king, declared that Saudi Arabia was "a leader among the Arab states because of . . . the presence of the Holy Cities within the Kingdom." And Saud had another point to make, the U.S. diplomat added:

> Some day, he said, he was going to give tangible form to this leadership. He said that he had plans which he did not wish to discuss in detail now to spark plug a pan-Islamic movement. He said it could do a great deal of good in the Muslim countries by causing them to work together as a unit but again he repeated that he was not ready to discuss the plan in detail. . . . I told him that his information about Islamic unity was very interesting and we would be very glad to know more about it when his plans were clearly formulated. . . .

I told him that we would welcome such a movement under his leadership because we were sure that it would be friendly.[47]

While some foreign policy functionaries had their doubts, efforts to encourage Faisal in this direction were undertaken tentatively anyway, without a real grasp of either the politics or the culture of the Muslim world.

David Long, a retired foreign service officer and specialist on Saudi Arabia and the Gulf, says that in the period after World War II the United States was operating blind. "We didn't know anything," he says. "When we get up to the period after World War II, yes, there were times when Islam was used as a rallying cry for the political issue of the day." But, says Long, U.S. policy lacked an understanding of historical precedent. "We were trying a replay of what they'd tried a thousand years ago," he says, referring to the caliphates of old. "Their ideology is ancient. Well, we never heard of any of this when we jumped into this 1,300-year-old saga, simply because we were the biggest player in the game." Some Americans, said Long, had a rudimentary familiarity with the Middle East and Islamic culture. "It was usually said that the oil company kids and the missionary kids knew a little. But I've talked to them, many of them, over the years. They lived in their own little world, and what they knew was in fact very, very limited. We wanted oil, and we wanted to fight communism, but we weren't really all that interested in all that crap about Islam. We were neophytes—way, way behind the curve of what the British and French picked up after all the time they'd spent there." Asked whether the United States actively supported political Islam as an alternative to communism in those days, Long says, "We encouraged it. But we didn't create it."

Adds Long:

The deal was, the Saudis were vulnerable. We would provide security for them, and they would provide oil for us.

When it came to Nasser, Faisal reviewed the bidding and opposed pan-Arabism. He decided that they were socialists and that they were against Islam. So, while we and the Israelis were demonizing Nasser, here was Faisal opposing him. He was worried that Muslim youth would turn to socialism and abandon Islam. We didn't understand that—we didn't understand Faisal's motivations. We tried to set up an alliance between Saudi Arabia and Tunisia, forgetting that Bourguiba was a secularist. We said, 'Hey, you're all moderates.' But to Faisal, Bourguiba was an apostate.

So we were going in the same direction, but we didn't understand it. We tried to give it a different slant, that of power politics. To the Saudis, however, it was based on the idea that they are the defenders of the faith, of the Muslim holy places. But we saw it in a power politics framework.[48]

As Long suggests, the American "neophytes" stumbled into an alliance of sorts with Islamic fundamentalism almost without realizing what was happening. Very few American diplomats and scholars had studied the relationship between Islam and politics, and those who did were often muddled. In 1951, the Middle East Institute convened a two-day conference on "Islam in the Modern World," at which Philip W. Ireland, a senior State Department official who'd served as U.S. chargé d'affaires in Baghdad, delivered an address on the relationship of Islam, democracy, and communism, wondering "whether present trends will carry Islam into the camp of Communism or into that of Democracy." After noting that "Communism"—actually, he was referring to nationalism—was making gains in Syria, Iraq, and Jordan, Ireland noted:

In Saudi Arabia, the Yemen, and the Hadramaut, the primitive and austere character of Islam has indeed proven, practically as well as theoretically, a barrier to Communism.[49]

Ireland did not put much stock in the theocratic version of Islam, expressing the hope that somehow Muslims would be able to blend Islam with modern political theories. Leading U.S. strategists worried that as Islam modernized, Muslims would abandon their faith for secularism, and that such a trend would open the doors to the spread of Marxist ideas in the Middle East. Bayard Dodge, the highly influential ex-president of the American University in Beirut (1923 to 1948), told the same Middle East Institute group:

> Today nationalism of a materialistic type is becoming a strong element in Islamic thought and society. And that, of course, works directly against the old idea of Pan-Islam or the Caliphate, of Islam as a great organized brotherhood. To a large extent, nationalism has taken the place of the religious side of the Pan-Islam movement. Needless to say, it is the young Muslim, uninterested in Islam as a great system, who is particularly likely to become a Communist. . . . The reaction of the Muslims of the rising generation is an exceedingly unfortunate one, as so many of them are casting aside their religion, their morality, or their loyalty to the cult. They live licentious lives, drinking, . . . gambling, . . . amusing themselves in cabarets and houses of prostitution.
>
> If Islam is undermined, if materialism and radicalism come in, with Communist thought perhaps permeating it, the outcome will certainly be a major tragedy for the world.[50]

Loyalty to "the cult"? Living "licentious lives . . . in houses of prostitution"? Dodge, the scion of Protestant missionaries with roots in the Middle East of the nineteenth century, sounds more like a Bible-thumping revivalist than a foreign policy analyst. And, in fact, in his address, Dodge praised the Muslim Brotherhood, Turkey's anti-Ataturk religious revival, and Persians under Reza Shah who are "finding that they must go back and have more religion if they are to combat Communism."[51] Dodge here expressed almost exactly the sought-after Christian-Muslim alliance that so many U.S. policy makers dreamed of, regardless of how impractical it seemed. Worse, though, it was precisely what the Middle East didn't need, as it struggled with modernity, and as secular leaders everywhere in the region (except Saudi Arabia) sought to reduce or eliminate the role of Islam, the clergy, the Wahhabis, and the Muslim Brotherhood. What Dodge, and many others, feared is that communism, and not Western-style capitalism, would win the hearts and minds of Arabs, Turks, Persians, and Indians freed of the shackles of religious belief.

Many American diplomats, of course, equally concerned about promoting U.S. interests overseas and combating communism, took the sensible view that the United States ought to concentrate on economic development in the Middle East, and that facilitating the region's transition away from backward religious fundamentalism to modern, and Western, ideas of organizing society might not necessarily benefit the Soviet Union. Many, too, believed that Islam should not be anything more than a system of personal belief, not a political or social system.

But as the 1950s wore on, their voices were less and less influential. Nasser's nonalignment, or "positive neutralism," began to look more and more like a communist Trojan Horse to the Dulles brothers and their Cold War co-thinkers. So, too, did the nationalism of Prime Minister Mossadegh in Iran. In both cases, as the Eisenhower administration moved to confront these regimes, it reached for one of the most dangerous implements in its tool box: Islamic fundamentalism.

4

THE WAR AGAINST NASSER AND MOSSADEGH

IN THE EARLY 1950s, two nationalist leaders emerged in two of the most powerful countries of the Middle East, Egypt and Iran. In Egypt, Gamal Abdel Nasser's Free Officers ousted that country's dissolute king and threatened to spark revolution in Saudi Arabia, the heart of the world's energy supply. In Iran, a freely elected democrat and socialist-inclined leader named Mohammed Mossadegh successfully challenged the ruling shah of Iran, forced him to flee, and asserted his country's right to take over the oil industry from Britain's Anglo-Persian Oil Company.

In both cases Great Britain, the United States, and their intelligence agencies went into action, overthrowing Mossadegh and trying but failing to do the same to Nasser, and in both cases, MI6 and the CIA used the Islamic right as a cat's-paw. In Egypt, they used the Muslim Brotherhood, and in Iran they mobilized a group of ayatollahs that included the ideological godfather of Ayatollah Ruhollah Khomeini.

Perhaps the greatest twin tragedies, or lost opportunities, for the United States in the Middle East in the past half century are the American failures to embrace Gamal Abdel Nasser and Mohammed Mossadegh when they emerged, in the 1950s, as leaders of their people's aspirations. That error created a residue of resentment, bitterness, and anger in the Middle East, feeding widespread, lingering anti-Americanism to this day and even providing fuel for Al Qaeda's recruiters. Yet it was a folly compounded by yet another massive error: the U.S. decision to support Saudi Arabia as the counter pole to Arab and Persian nationalism, and to tie itself to a worldwide network of Islamists sponsored by the Saudis. It was a decision whose consequences led, indirectly, to the rise of Ayatollah Khomeini's theocracy, the destruction of Afghanistan, and Osama bin Laden's terrorist international.

THE BROTHERHOOD AGAINST NASSER

From 1954, when Nasser consolidated power over his rivals, until 1970, when he died, Nasser garnered unparalleled, even legendary, support in Egypt, and throughout the Arab world. André Malraux, the French writer, said, of Nasser: "He will enter history as representative of Egypt, the same as Napoleon of France."[1] William R. Polk, an official at the National Security Council in the 1960s, said: "He was the John Kennedy of the Arab world."[2] Five million people turned out for his funeral, and that doesn't count the tens of millions of Arabs who mourned privately, "the ones who wept in coffeehouses, at home, alone, in groups, silently, loudly, through prayer, in cars in faraway California, or who suffered the pain of his death in frozen numbness."[3] Yet over and over, in the 1950s and again in the 1960s, the United States stiff-armed Nasser, and worse. Behind the scenes, the CIA schemed to topple him.

"We were trying to overthrow Nasser," says Ed Kane, a CIA operations officer who was stationed in Cairo in the late 1950s and early 1960s. "The Agency was involved in a covert operation—a very inept one, I might add—relying on members of the ancien régime, who had absolutely no power. We were attempting to find elements who could overthrow him, mostly figures tied to the old regime—landowners, industrialists, and other old enemies of Nasser's. It was a futile project."[4]

Half a century ago, Nasser symbolized Arab revolution, self-determination, and independence. The seizure of power by the Free

Officers in Egypt came during an era when the entire Arab world, from Morocco to Iraq, was locked in the grip of a political ice age. Morocco, Algeria, and Tunisia were French colonies; Kuwait, Qatar, Bahrain, the United Arab Emirates, Oman, and Yemen were British colonies. Iraq, Jordan, and Saudi Arabia were kingdoms ruled by monarchies installed by London. And Egypt, under the wobbly King Farouq, was the political and economic center of the Arab world. By taking power in Egypt, Nasser electrified the political class in the Arab world, inspiring a host of would-be imitators, liberation-minded political parties, and army revolutionists. From 1954 onward, through agents, political support, and the powerful Voice of the Arabs radio in Cairo, and by virtue of his charismatic appeal, Nasser led the independence movement in the Arab Middle East. From 1956 to 1958, Lebanon, Jordan, and Iraq were rocked by rebellions, Iraq's king fell, and Syria united with Egypt in Nasser's United Arab Republic, a short-lived but exciting experiment in unifying the Arab world. The Algerian revolution drew moral and material support from Cairo, before winning independence in 1962, the same year that Yemen underwent a Nasser-inspired revolt, triggering a proxy war pitting Saudi Arabia against Egypt. Even as late as 1969, a year before Nasser's death, Libya's king was overthrown and Sudan's right-wing regime eliminated by military leaders loyal to Nasser.

In the Manichean, with-us-or-against-us world of the Cold War, Nasser was loathed and demonized by London, Washington, and Tel Aviv. Around the world, from Guatemala to the Congo to Indonesia—and in Iran—the CIA was busy getting rid of leaders not because they were communists, but because their independent streak made them untrustworthy interlocutors in the war between the superpowers. Nasser was no exception.

Unlike other leaders in Latin America or Africa, however, Nasser, with his revolutionary outlook, threatened the very heart of America's post–World War II strategy: the vast oil fields of Saudi Arabia. Not only was Egypt a potential military rival to Saudi Arabia, not only did Cairo clash with Riyadh in a shooting war in Yemen, not only did Nasser inspire Arabs in Saudi Arabia with republican ideals, but the Egyptian leader even won over some of Saudi Arabia's royal family, who, led by Prince Talal, formed the so-called "Free Princes," defected to Egypt, and demanded the establishment of a republic in Arabia.

As the United States built its network of alliances in the Middle East, relying more and more on non-Arab states, including Turkey, Iran, and Israel, there developed an "Arab cold war," with Egypt at one end and Saudi Arabia at the other. Superficially, it seemed as if the struggle within the Arab world pitted Soviet-leaning Arab countries against American-allied ones, but in fact the Soviet Union had no true allies and few friends in the region. The real dynamic that played out between 1954 and 1970 occurred between competing visions of the future of the Middle East. On one hand, there was Nasser's secular, modernizing, industrial Arab world of independent but cooperative Arab republics. On the other was Saudi Arabia's semi-feudal array of monarchies, with their natural resources put at the West's disposal, in which the royal families' ace-in-the-hole was the Muslim Brotherhood and the Islamic right.

A contingent of America's Arabists rejected the strategy of isolating Nasser, and some even saw him as the Arab world's savior. "In the beginning Nasser had some strong support from the Agency and from the embassy," says Kane, referring to the period from 1952 to 1954.[5] According to one widely cited account, by Miles Copeland in *The Game of Nations,* the CIA even encouraged the Free Officers in their revolution, after first trying to get King Farouq to modernize Egypt. The legendary Kermit ("Kim") Roosevelt, the man who would coordinate the 1953 CIA coup that restored the shah of Iran to his throne, secretly visited Egypt in 1952:

> His mission, specifically, was first to attempt to organize a "peaceful revolution" in Egypt wherein King Farouq himself would supervise the liquidation of the old and its replacement by the new, thereby defusing the revolutionary forces which CIA agents had identified as much as two years earlier.[6]

But, according to Copeland, Farouq was too "bird-brained"[7] and corrupt to respond, preferring to engage in orgies and troll Cairo's

Red Light district in sunglasses than to take responsibility for Egypt. Kim Roosevelt thus

> ... agreed to meet the officers whom the CIA had spotted as likely leaders of the secret military society known to be plotting a coup. This he did in March 1952, four months before Nasser's coup. ... There were three such meetings, the third attended by one of Nasser's most trusted lieutenants.[8]

Roosevelt returned to Washington to convince the U.S. government that it must accept the removal of Farouq.

There is no way to corroborate Copeland's account. Declassified archives don't provide any help, and no one else has stepped forward to endorse Copeland's specific assertions. Yet the United States initially enjoyed generally good relations with the new Egyptian government. In his excellent book, *Nasser's Blessed Movement*, Joel Gordon reports that declassified "records do substantiate charges of close links between the U.S. embassy in Cairo and the new regime." The British, on the other hand, though resigned to following the U.S. lead, seethed with anger at Washington, fearing that Nasser's rise to power threatened the Suez Canal, its bases, and its path to India.[9]

But more was at stake than the remnants of the British Empire. The emergence of Nasser was an existential threat to the oil kingdoms—to Saudi Arabia, to Iraq, and to the British-owned sheikhs in the Gulf. The British, and then the Anglo-Americans, opposed Nasser not because he was a communist, or because he was susceptible to communist influence; in fact, Nasser suppressed the Egyptian left and the various communist parties vigorously. In addition, the Egyptian communists were poorly organized and divided, with support primarily among the intelligentsia, and had no chance of taking power except as a minority stakeholder in a Wafd-led nationalist government. What was intolerable to London and Washington (and to Paris, too, until 1956) was that Nasser refused to be controlled, was adept at playing the superpowers off against each other, and inspired loyalty among Arabs outside of Egypt, including those sitting on top of the oil.

What especially worried London and Washington was the idea

that Nasser might succeed in unifying Egypt and Saudi Arabia, thus creating a major Arab power. One of the ironies of the Arab world is that Egypt, Syria, Lebanon, and Palestine, which have historically been the centers of Arab learning and political movements, have no oil. On the other hand, except for Iraq and non-Arab Iran, the oil states—Saudi Arabia, Kuwait, the United Arab Emirates, Bahrain, Qatar—have tiny populations and no intellectual tradition (except ultra-orthodox Islamic theology), and are ruled by royal kleptocracies whose legitimacy is nil and whose existence depends on outside military protection. Most Arabs are aware that both the monarchies themselves, and the artificial borders that demarcate their states, were designed by imperialists seeking to build fences around oil wells in the 1920s. From a strategic standpoint, the Arabs would gain much by marrying the sophistication and manpower of the urban Arab countries (including Iraq) with the oil wealth of the desert kingdoms. At the center of that idea lies Egypt, with its tens of millions of people, and Saudi Arabia, with 200 billion barrels of oil. Underlying the rhetoric of secular pan-Arabism is the reality that uniting Cairo and Riyadh would create a vastly important new Arab center of gravity with worldwide influence.

So, after its initial flirtation with Nasser, the United States—led by Secretary of State John Foster Dulles and his brother, CIA director Allen Dulles—lined up with London against Arab nationalism. British prime minister Anthony Eden, who had been violently anti-Nasser all along, considered a British-sponsored coup d'état in Cairo as early as 1953. The only political force in Egypt that could mount a challenge to Nasser—except for the army—was the Muslim Brotherhood, which had hundreds of thousands of followers. The Brotherhood also had the sympathy of some Egyptian officers, including Brigadier General Mohammed Naguib, a longtime Muslim Brotherhood fellow traveler who was a conservative member of Nasser's Free Officers movement. In 1952, after the officers' coup toppled the king, Naguib was named president and prime minister of Egypt, with Nasser as deputy prime minister. Behind the scenes, Nasser was the real power. "William Lakeland, the [U.S.] embassy's political officer, realized almost immediately that Naguib was only Nasser's front man," wrote

Miles Copeland. "While the Egyptian public and the outside world were cheering Naguib, the embassy, through Lakeland, had begun to deal with Nasser as the one who really made the decisions."[10] But Naguib, though less powerful than Nasser, had close ties to Hassan Ismail al-Hudaybi, the man who had succeeded Hassan al-Banna as the leader of the Muslim Brotherhood. Ultimately, a power struggle between Nasser and Naguib would develop, and Naguib—with British support—would reach out to the Brotherhood as his chief ally.

Nasser's own early relationship with the Muslim Brotherhood was tricky and nuanced.[11] On taking power in 1952, the Free Officers were very careful not to alienate the Muslim Brothers. Several members of the officers' movement were members, and most of them, including Nasser, had extensive contacts with the organization going back to the 1940s. At the start the military junta faced a diverse coalition of opponents, including the Wafd and the left, the monarchists, the fascist Young Egypt party, and the Muslim Brotherhood. Nasser, who personally oversaw the military's delicate relationship with the Brotherhood, decided at first to co-opt and neutralize the group rather than confront it. When the new Egyptian regime banned political parties in 1953, it exempted the Brotherhood.

There was, however, little chance that Nasser and the Muslim Brotherhood would ever see eye to eye. The Brotherhood wanted an Islamic society, Nasser a secular one. Perhaps even more important, Nasser wanted reforms, including land reform and educational changes, that the Muslim Brotherhood bitterly opposed. In conversations with U.S. ambassador Jefferson Caffery—the same Caffery who recommended that the Brothers' Said Ramadan visit Princeton and the White House in 1953—Hudaybi, the Brotherhood's chieftain, said that he "would be glad to see several of the [Free Officers] 'eliminated.'"[12] At around the same time, a senior British diplomat, Trefor Evans, the "oriental counselor" at the British embassy in Cairo, held at least one meeting with Hassan Ismail al-Hudaybi, the supreme guide of the Muslim Brotherhood—a meeting later cited as treason by Nasser when he cracked down on the organization. Both British and American officials maintained an ongoing relationship with the group.

Nasser's long-postponed showdown with the Muslim Brotherhood occurred in 1954. It coincided with rising British frustration with the Egyptian leader during U.K.-Egypt negotiations over the transfer of the Suez Canal and its bases to Egypt. While left-wing and Labour politicians in England seemed willing to make a deal with Nasser, the British right—led by unreconstructed imperialists such as Winston Churchill—was nearly apoplectic about the Egyptian upstart. From 1954 on, Anthony Eden, the British prime minister, was demanding Nasser's head. We are indebted to Stephen Dorril for the story of Eden's jihad against Nasser, which culminated in 1956. "MI6 had been considering a plan to assassinate President Nasser," according to Dorril, who adds that in *Cutting the Lion's Tail,* Nasser's adviser Mohammed Heikal published a copy of a telegram from CIA's James Eichelberger in London to CIA director Allen Dulles, citing discussions with MI6's George Young. "He talked openly of assassinating Nasser, instead of using a polite euphemism like 'liquidating.' He said his people had been in contact with suitable elements in Egypt and in the rest of the Arab world." Eichelberger—like Copeland, part of the CIA's shrinking pro-Nasser faction—leaked what Young said to Nasser![13] A month later, Eden ranted: "What's all this nonsense about isolating Nasser or 'neutralising' him, as you call it? I want him destroyed, can't you understand? I want him murdered. . . . And I don't give a damn if there's anarchy and chaos in Egypt."[14]

In the first months of 1954, the chaos nearly began, as the Muslim Brotherhood and Nasser went to war. It started in January, when Muslim Brotherhood thugs attacked pro-Nasser nationalist students at Cairo University. Anwar Sadat, the former Muslim Brotherhood member who had cast his lot with Nasser against his former organization, penned an article attacking groups that "traffic in religion." Two days later Nasser issued a decree outlawing the terrorist group, and he blasted the Brotherhood as a pawn of the British. The decree banning the organization said: "The revolution will never allow reactionary corruption to recur in the name of religion."[15] Declassified records show that British intelligence was carefully reporting on Muslim Brotherhood activity, noting "rumors of clashes between Brothers and the police in the Delta and covert meetings held in Ismailia."[16]

According to Robert Baer, a former CIA covert operations specialist, the CIA also endorsed the idea of using the Muslim Brotherhood against Nasser. In *Sleeping with the Devil,* Baer describes the rough outlines of a top secret U.S. effort:

> At the bottom of it all was this dirty little secret in Washington: The White House looked on the Brothers as a silent ally, a secret weapon against (what else?) communism. This covert action started in the 1950s with the Dulles brothers—Allen at the CIA and John Foster at the State Department—when they approved Saudi Arabia's funding of Egypt's Brothers against Nasser. As far as Washington was concerned, Nasser was a communist. He'd nationalized Egypt's big-business industries, including the Suez Canal. The logic of the cold war led to a clear conclusion: If Allah agreed to fight on our side, fine. If Allah decided political assassination was permissible, that was fine, too, as long as no one talked about it in polite company.
>
> Like any other truly effective covert action, this one was strictly off the books. There was no CIA finding, no memorandum notification to Congress. Not a penny came out of the Treasury to fund it. In other words, no record. All the White House had to do was give a wink and a nod to countries harboring the Muslim Brothers, like Saudi Arabia and Jordan.[17]

While both Britain and the United States were playing with fire, mobilizing assassins from the Muslim Brotherhood against Nasser, there is also evidence that the Brotherhood was cooperating with a violent, assassination-prone Islamist group from Iran, the so-called Devotees of Islam, one of whose founders was an Iranian ayatollah who worked with the CIA in toppling Mossadegh. Bernard Lewis, a former British intelligence officer and a leading Orientalist, noted that the Brothers' decision to engage in outright opposition to Nasser was tied, in part, to its connections to the Devotees. It was, reported Lewis, a visit to Cairo in 1954 by the leader of the Devotees of Islam that triggered the Muslim Brotherhood's 1954 uprising against Nasser:

> The same combination of idealism and violence, of piety and terror, can be seen in the Persian organization known as the

Fidaiyan-i Islam—the devotees of Islam, which, significantly, bor-
rows a term used by the medieval emissaries of the Old Man of the
Mountain. Though Shiites, they hold pan-Islamic opinions rather
similar to those of the Egyptian brothers, with whom they have
contacts. On March 7, 1951, one of their members shot and killed
Persian Prime Minister General Razmara. It was a visit of the
Fidai leader, Nawab Safavi, to Egypt in January, 1954, that
touched off the first serious and open clash between the Brotherhood and [Nasser's] military regime.[18]

The 1954 Brotherhood-Devotees link reveals the extent to which,
even in the 1950s, Islamic fundamentalism was truly international. It
reached across national borders in the Arab world, it connected Arab
fanatics with those in Pakistan, and it linked Sunni militants with Shiite ones in Iran and elsewhere. Even half a century later, it isn't clear
whether the CIA understood the international scope and power of the
forces they were dealing with. Did they understand that the Islamic
right in Egypt, in Saudi Arabia, in Iran and elsewhere operated a
shadowy, worldwide fraternity—or did they believe that they could
pick and choose when and where to support the Islamic right, on a
case-by-case basis? The fact is that by the 1950s the Islamists had created a transnational organism, whose existence appeared to elude the
CIA for decades. Instead, American diplomats and CIA officials preferred to see Islamic activists only in relation to the country in which
they were stationed.

During 1954, relations between Nasser and the Brothers grew
more tense. Though now officially outlawed, the Brotherhood still
maintained a powerful presence throughout the country. Nasser moved
first against Naguib. In a prolonged struggle during February and
March, Nasser marginalized Naguib, shunting him aside and deftly
neutralizing the Muslim Brotherhood in the process. In April, Nasser
brought to trial the first of several leading Brotherhood officials, and a
final confrontation with the organization seemed inevitable. The Egyptian police began watching the organization's actions, even raiding its
mosques and imposing controls on sermons by radical imams. In September, the Egyptian government stripped five Muslim Brotherhood
officials of their citizenship while they were on a mission to Syria.

Among them was Said Ramadan, the Brotherhood's chief ideologue. The five men were attending a conference in Damascus at which they organized Muslim Brotherhood members from Iraq, Jordan, and Sudan to denounce Nasser.[19] Leading members of the Brotherhood, including Hudaybi, went into hiding.

Finally, on October 26, a member of the Muslim Brotherhood fired eight shots at Nasser. The facts surrounding the assassination attempt are somewhat murky, but in most accounts the shots at Nasser were fired at point-blank range by a Brotherhood member who was immediately arrested. Was there a larger conspiracy? Were the British putting the Brothers up to killing Nasser? Certainly, the record shows, the idea wasn't beyond Eden.

During the mid-1950s, in actions that foreshadowed the attempts to kill Fidel Castro by John F. Kennedy's CIA, the British hatched innumerable schemes to murder the Egyptian leader, some of them harebrained. They funneled money into Egypt to bribe Nasser's doctor to poison him, concocted a plot to "inject lethal poison into some popular Egyptian Kropje chocolates" destined for him, created a James Bond–like "modified cigarette packet which fired a poisoned dart," and tried to "slip a poisoned pill into Nasser's coffee." (Copeland, who learned about the latter scheme, says that he joked with Nasser about it. "Turn your head, Gamal, and let me see if I can put this poison in your coffee.")[20] Yet all of this British skullduggery was not funny, and it gives credence to the notion that the British may have tried to use the Muslim Brotherhood's veteran assassins, too.

Reprisals against the Muslim Brotherhood were swift and deadly. More than a thousand Brothers were arrested; many were sentenced to long prison terms, and six were hanged. Assets of the organization were seized, and its offices and welfare centers taken over by government agencies. Naguib, with his credibility among the army fading and his Brotherhood allies scattered, was ousted from the government entirely in November, leading C. L. Sulzberger to describe him as "Kerensky with a fez" in the *New York Times*.[21]

To help round up the Muslim Brotherhood's leading lights, Nasser played a secret card, using a jujitsu-like maneuver against a clique of former Nazis who had taken roost in Egypt after World War II. During

the war, many right-wing Islamists and Brotherhood activists—
including Haj Amin al-Husseini, the mufti of Jerusalem, who had
settled in Cairo—had intimate ties to the Nazis and to German intelligence. After the war, many former Nazis who escaped the Nuremberg
trials and other dragnets fled to safe havens around the world, and
Egypt in the 1940s was particularly welcoming. By then, the CIA and
MI6 were fast recruiting former Nazis to the Cold War struggle
against the Soviet Union. Working with Reinhard Gehlen, the former
Nazi intelligence chief, the CIA and the U.S. army helped to set up the
famous Gehlen Organization, the association of ex-Nazi spies that
was used by James Critchfield of the CIA as the core of the West German intelligence system. Some of them, no doubt, infiltrated Egypt on
behalf of either U.S. or British intelligence; others were simply migrat-
ing to what they hoped was a hospitable environment.

One of the ex-Nazis who ended up in Egypt was Franz Buensch, a
German whose claim to fame was the publication of an anti-Semitic
tract called *Sexual Habits of the Jews,* and it was Buensch that Nasser
manipulated in order to ferret out Brotherhood plotters. According to
Miles Copeland, Buensch proposed an outlandish scheme to use former Nazis to organize an international Islamic underground in conjunction with the Muslim Brotherhood. Nasser feigned interest in the
gambit, then, says Copeland, had his security chief use it to round up
Muslim Brotherhood members:

> Buensch . . . did develop one project that quickly gained Egyptian
> interest: a plan to collect Nazi diehards from their various hiding
> places all over the world (Argentina, Brazil, Ireland, Spain, etc.)
> and give them Islamic names, join them to "underground assets"
> developed by Egypt during the Second World War, build a subver-
> sive intelligence org combining the best in German and Egyptian
> talent, and "put it at the disposal" of Gamal Abdel Nasser for his
> international war against communism and imperialism.
>
> The plan was presented to Saad Afraq, the General Intelli-
> gence Agency officer then responsible for administration and sur-
> veillance of the Germans. Saad, whose genial manner covered one
> of the shrewdest brains in Egypt, affected great interest in the
> plan, but insisted that he must hear much more about these

"underground assets." Buensch, who until then had been sulking at Egyptian indifference to his pet subject, began to feel that at last he was being appreciated and that perhaps he was on to something big. With Saad Afraq's encouragement, he produced all the information on the subject he could remember, then pumped other members of the German colony for what they remembered. The result was enough evidence to hang half the Moslem Brotherhood, plus enough leads to keep Egyptian security officers busy for the next two years establishing the extent of influence of the organization not only in Egypt but throughout the Arab world.[22]

In 1954, Egypt and the United Kingdom had signed an agreement over the Suez Canal and British military basing rights. It was short-lived. In 1956, Great Britain, France, and Israel concocted a plot against Egypt aimed at toppling Nasser and seizing control of the Suez Canal—a conspiracy in which they enlisted the Muslim Brotherhood. When the gathering British-Egyptian showdown erupted in 1956, the organization had been largely dismantled and its members jailed, driven into exile, or forced underground in Egypt. But that didn't stop London from reaching out to its old allies. The story of Suez has been told countless times: how Nasser sought U.S. financial help to build the Aswan Dam and was rebuffed insultingly; how the United States refused to sell arms to Egypt; how the Soviet Union stepped in to supply aid and sell Czech arms to Nasser; how the British stonewalled negotiations about handing over the canal; and how London and Paris plotted with Israel to go to war. Eden's hatred for Nasser had reached fever pitch. Less well known, however, is the fact that as the plot unfolded, the British held secret powwows with the Muslim Brotherhood in Geneva. According to Dorril, two British spooks, Col. Neil McLean and Julian Amery, helped MI6 organize a clandestine anti-Nasser opposition in the south of France and in Switzerland. "They also went so far as to make contact in Geneva, where the MI6 head of station was Norman Darbyshire, with members of the Muslim Brotherhood, informing only MI6 of this demarche which they kept secret from the rest of the Suez Group [which was planning the military operation]. Amery forwarded various names to [Selwyn] Lloyd," the British foreign secretary.[23] The exact nature of MI6's contacts with the Muslim Brotherhood in Europe during this period is not known, but it may have ranged from organizing a secret assassination effort to assembling a secret government-in-exile to replace Nasser after the Suez war.

The Anglo-French plot that unfolded in 1956 reads like a nineteenth-century imperialist scheme. London and Paris arranged for Israel to launch an unprovoked war against Egypt. According to the conspiracy, the British and French would wait a decent interval, perhaps some days, and then intervene militarily to impose a truce on Egypt and Israel, meanwhile seizing the Suez Canal in the process. Nasser, they hoped, would fall—perhaps be overthrown. And the Muslim Brotherhood, though weakened, was waiting in the wings. In the end, President Eisenhower—fearing that the Soviet Union would reap untold rewards by capitalizing on the Anglo-French-Israeli aggression—joined with other nations to foil the plot. For a time, it seemed as if the United States had an opportunity once again to build a positive relationship with Nasser. Almost immediately, however, the opportunity was lost, and the Dulles brothers went back to the usual pattern of confronting both Nasser and Arab nationalism.

There were those State Department and CIA officials who were dismayed by the administration's reflexively anti-Nasser position. One of those was Copeland, who was an unabashed admirer of Nasser. Wrote Copeland, mixing praise with tongue-in-cheek scolding, "He is one of the most courageous, most incorruptible, most unprincipled, and in his way, most humanitarian national leaders I have ever met."[24] Yet as the 1950s wore on, Copeland became more and more a minority voice, as Washington Cold Warriors turned Nasser into the devil incarnate. The State Department's Arabists were "soft on Nasser," Copeland says, but "this tendency was more than offset by the opposition of the commercial community," especially the big U.S. oil companies and banks. As the tide turned against Copeland's view of Nasser, he was pulled aside by a joking CIA colleague visiting Cairo. "I think we've finally got you Nasser lovers on the run," he said. In 1954, Copeland notes ruefully, the CIA chief in Cairo cabled Washington that it should persuade Israel to emphasize "the Brotherhood's commendable capability to overthrow Nasser."[25]

John Voll, a noted specialist on Islam, says matter-of-factly that CIA support for the Muslim Brotherhood during the Cold War was the right thing to do. "It was a smart intelligence vehicle," says Voll. "It was the only alternative to Nasser. The Communist Party in Egypt was a nonstarter. In terms of intelligence and policy planning we would have been stupid not to have had a relationship with them."[26]

In retrospect, however, it is hard to think of anything more stupid. The United States didn't need an alternative to Nasser—it ought to have embraced him, and helped him undermine the Islamic right. Instead, U.S. policy hardened against Nasser, joined the Saudi royals and their Islamic fundamentalist allies, and launched a decades-long effort to use political Islam as a cornerstone of American influence in the Middle East.

Moreover, the ideological rigidity of American foreign policy elites wasn't confined to Egypt. While the U.S. sought to undermine Nasser, it took on another regional nationalist, Prime Minister Mohammed Mossadegh of Iran. That effort would culminate in America's most famous CIA covert operation, the 1953 coup d'état in Iran—and, as in Egypt, right-wing Islamists would play a prominent role.

THE CIA AND KHOMEINI'S GODFATHER

It is one of the ironies in regard to both Nasser and Mossadegh that both men had a modicum of American support during their initial rise to power, until the exigencies of the Cold War turned U.S. policy decisively against them. At first, the United States tentatively supported the Iranian nationalists led by Mossadegh, partly out of Washington's early belief that liberal Third World nationalists might be able to modernize their nations while, at the same time, keeping them in the Western orbit. But the Eisenhower administration wasn't buying it. Its view was: You are either with us—that is, Third World leaders had to allow military bases, join alliances, and make economic concessions while implementing free-market policies—or you were against us. In a less polarized world Mossadegh, like Nasser, might have been able to reach a long-term accommodation with Washington.

As in Egypt, where the Muslim Brotherhood was mobilized against Nasser, Iran's forces of radical political Islam were cynically used against Mossadegh. The very same cleric-led, right-wing Islamists that toppled the shah in 1979 were paid by the CIA in 1953 to support him.

Mossadegh, an Iranian lawyer educated in Paris and Switzerland, was a complex figure who was a fixture in Iranian politics for decades before 1953, having served in Iran's parliament under the pre-Pahlavi Qajar dynasty in 1915 and as foreign minister in 1924. His association with the earlier line of Iranian kings set him at odds with Reza Pahlavi and his son, Mohammed Reza Pahlavi. In 1944, he was elected to parliament again, as a strong advocate of nationalizing Iran's oil industry, then under the grip of what is today British Petroleum. Mossadegh became chairman of the parliament's oil commission, and he created a coalition political movement, called the National Front. After the assassination of General Ali Razmara in 1951, the shah felt compelled to name Mossadegh to succeed Razmara as prime minister. But Mossadegh pushed through the nationalization of the Anglo-Persian Oil Company (APOC). It was a catastrophic blow to England; APOC, later Anglo-Iranian Oil Company and then British Petroleum, was the pride and joy of Britain's imperial assets, having gotten its start during World War I as the special project of Winston Churchill, who saw Persian oil as a source of fuel for the worldwide British navy. Mossadegh instantly became a hated man in London, and he clashed bitterly with the shah, whose own nationalist impulses were subordinate to his desire to maintain his throne and to have good relations with London and Washington. At first, many of Iran's most political ayatollahs participated in the National Front, but they left it and joined the CIA-sponsored campaign against Mossadegh, which resulted in a military coup d'état in August 1953. The shah, who had fled the country, was restored to the Peacock Throne—and the nationalization of Iran's oil industry was annulled. In the process, the United States muscled in on Iranian oil: 40 percent of the share in the new consortium was given to five big American oil companies, and BP's share was reduced.

The story of the coup, run jointly by the CIA and MI6, has been told many times. Almost never reported, however, is the fact that the two intelligence agencies worked closely with Iran's clergy, the ulema, to weaken and ultimately to overthrow Mossadegh. A critical role was played by street mobs, bought and paid for by the CIA and mobilized by rabble rousers tied to the ulema, who demanded the ouster of the prime minister and the return of the shah. Ayatollah Seyyed Abolqassem Kashani, the chief representative of the Muslim Brotherhood in Iran and Ayatollah Ruhollah Khomeini's mentor and predecessor as Iran's leading Islamist cleric, was a central figure in the campaign.

According to former Iranian government officials, Khomeini himself, then no more than an obscure, middle-aged mullah and a follower of Kashani's, took part in the CIA-organized, pro-shah demonstrations against Mossadegh.[27] It is a supreme irony. Twenty-five years later, in 1978, that same Khomeini would once again lead a religious mob, this time to unseat the shah and create the Islamic Republic of Iran.

Ayatollah Abolqassem Kashani (1882–1962) was Khomeini's godfather. He was quintessentially political, having started his political career in the 1920s by serving in the Iranian parliament. In Iran, the clergy had a reputation for stopping at nothing to protect their status. In the 1920s, that meant that the establishment ulema would vociferously veto the creation of an Iranian republic. Reza Pahlavi, the military strongman who took control of Iran in the early 1920s, admired Kemal Ataturk, the secular Turkish republican leader, and wanted to declare Iran a republic on the Turkish model. But the mullahs, including Kashani, feared that a secular republic would fatally undermine their power, and so they demanded a monarchy. Princess Ashraf Pahlavi, the shah's twin sister, wrote in her memoirs about the clergy's resistance to republicanism: "My father favored a republic like that of Turkey, and he proposed this idea to the leading Shiite mullahs. But at a meeting in the holy city of Qom, the clergy—staunch supporters of the feudal system, the monarchy, and all tradition representing the status quo—told my father they would oppose any plan for a republic."[28] Not ready to challenge the powerful religious establishment, Reza abandoned the idea of a republic and proclaimed himself king. The young Kashani was one of the kingmakers.

Over the next twenty years, Kashani would have two enemies: the communists and the shah. Like Islamists everywhere, the ulema feared and hated the communists and their Tudeh Party, and used their religious muscle against the left. But for the mullahs, the real threat to their power in Iran came from the shah, who disdained the clergy as medieval-minded relics opposed to his efforts to modernize the country. Beginning in the 1930s, following the Ataturk model, the shah acted forcefully against the clergy. He brought the backward sharia courts under state control and nationalized some of the clergy's religious endowments, reducing the clergy's financial power and removing an important source of their income. He instituted a Western form of dress, banning Islamic garb, took control of marriage and divorce proceedings, and battled the Islamists over the emancipation of women. The shah ordered that public places be open to women and outlawed the veil and the oppressive chador. In 1939, the shah banned the horrific practice of self-flagellation, a mutilating ritual practiced by some fundamentalist Shiites.[29] The measures were welcomed by Iran's modernists, but the clergy fumed. Often outflanked by the shah, Kashani quietly built up political power.

Just as the Muslim Brotherhood in Egypt in the late 1940s carried out acts of terrorism, in Iran, Kashani and his ilk fomented terrorist violence against the shah. In 1945, Kashani helped found the unofficial Iranian branch of the Muslim Brotherhood, the Devotees of Islam, led by a radical mullah named Navab Safavi. A series of terrorist attacks by Kashani's movement included a 1949 assassination attempt against the shah, carried out by a member of the Islamist underground affiliated to a publication called *The Flag of Islam*. In 1950, one of the Devotees of Islam assassinated Abdul Hussein Hajir, the shah's minister of court, and in 1951 another Devotee murdered the prime minister, General Ali Razmara, just as Iran was renegotiating the rights to its oil resources with London. Razmara, said the shah in his memoirs, "had the agreement with the Anglo-Iranian Oil Company in his pocket when he died."[30] Most educated Iranians, from the shah on down, suspected the British of having ties to Iran's clergy and to the Islamist movement, if not to the actual acts of terrorism.

"The British wanted to keep up their empire, and the best way to do that was to divide and rule," says Fereydoun Hoveyda, who served as

Iran's ambassador to the United Nations until the 1979 revolution, and whose brother, Amir Abbas Hoveyda, Iran's prime minister in the 1970s, was executed by the Khomeini regime. "The British were playing all sides. They were dealing with the Muslim Brotherhood in Egypt and the mullahs in Iran, but at the same time they were dealing with the army and the royal families." He says that the British saw the Islamists as just another tool through which their power could be extended:

> They had financial deals with the mullahs. They would find the most important ones and they would help them. And the mullahs were smart: they knew that the British were the most important power in the world. It was also about money. The British would bring suitcases full of cash and give it to these people. For example, people in the bazaar, the wealthy merchants, would each have their own ayatollah that they would finance. And that's what the British were doing.[31]

Ashraf, in her memoirs, wrote about Britain's unholy ties to the clergy in Iran:

> Many influential clergymen formed alliances with representatives of foreign powers, most often the British, and there was in fact a standing joke in Persia that said if you picked up a clergyman's beard, you would see the words "Made in England" stamped on the other side. These Shiite mullahs exercised a powerful influence over the minds of the masses. At times the voice of God seemed to be speaking with a British or Russian accent. It was difficult for the peasant to decipher where religion left off and politics began.[32]

Ashraf added that after World War II, London bolstered the Islamic right as part of its Cold War strategy for the region. "With the encouragement of the British, who saw the mullahs as an effective counterforce to the Communists, the elements of the extreme religious right were starting to surface again, after years of being suppressed."[33]

The shah himself, in memoirs written just before his death in exile, notes that the man who killed his minister of court in 1950, Fakhr Arai, had ties both to the Devotees of Islam and to the British. "Arai was involved with an ultraconservative religious group that was comprised of the most backward religious fanatics," he wrote, adding that he may also have had indirect ties to the British embassy in Teheran. "The British had their fingers in strange pies. The British had ties to the most reactionary clergy in the country."[34]

By the early 1950s, Britain's stake in Iran was threatened. Since World War I, the British had enjoyed exclusive rights to Iran's oil. So it wasn't surprising when the United States at first viewed Mossadegh favorably. Mossadegh was seeking to renegotiate the Iran-U.K. oil agreement on terms more favorable to Teheran, and the British were rattling swords and making threats. Washington, at odds with London over Middle East oil, provided aid and sold arms to Mossadegh's government and, in 1951, Mossadegh visited Washington. "President Truman sent a note imploring the British not to invade Iran," wrote a leading historian.[35] But when Mossadegh rejected an American plan to allow U.S. oil companies into Iran, the United States switched course, and turned against Mossadegh. Suddenly, the fledgling CIA and Britain's MI6 joined together in a plot to topple Mossadegh.

Enter Kashani.

Until 1952, Kashani posed as an ally of Mossadegh's in the National Front, the nationalist coalition that governed Iran under the shah. But as the United States and the British moved against Mossadegh, Kashani abandoned him and moved into opposition. Kashani maintained covert ties to the Islamist-terrorist underground, but in public he adroitly distanced himself from the Devotees of Islam and their ilk. The CIA was well aware of Kashani's power. In a report in October 1952, "Prospects for Survival of Mossadeq Regime in Iran," the CIA noted:

> Since Mossadeq returned to power in July 1952 there have been continuous reports of plots to overthrow him. Kashani and army officers are frequently mentioned as leaders. . . . A contest in the streets between the forces supporting Mossadeq and Kashani would be bitter and destructive.[36]

Among the forces that could be mobilized by Kashani, the CIA included "the Bazaar mobs and the bands organized by his son" and "the Fedayan terrorist organization of Moslem extremists." Even as that report was being written by the CIA's analysts, the CIA's covert-operations unit was already working with Kashani to mobilize his forces and to provoke exactly that "contest in the streets." In a 1952 State Department memo, one of Kashani's allies is quoted predicting violence, saying that it "might be necessary . . . to punish the communists physically."[37]

In 1952–53, the CIA and MI6 approached Kashani and half a dozen other key Iranian religious leaders, offering money and other inducements to break with Mossadegh and support the shah. "Religious leaders were encouraged with funding to adopt a more fundamentalist line and break with Mossadeq," according to Dorril.[38] The British took the lead, using its vast intelligence network in Iran, including the resources of the Anglo-Iranian Oil Company, which maintained its own, private secret service, the Central Information Bureau. The British, of course, were active in covert operations against Mossadegh long before the United States came on board, but the Americans reportedly had the chief pipeline to Kashani. Ann Lambton, a professor at Oxford's School of Oriental and African Studies and a former British intelligence officer, played a behind-the-scenes role in the action to undermine Mossadegh and, in a report at the time, she noted that "Kashani has received large sums of money from somewhere" and noted that it may have been coming from the CIA.[39]

From 1946 to 1953, the man who ran U.S. covert operations in Iran was John Waller, a veteran of the American clandestine service who joined the Office of Strategic Services (OSS) during World War II and then served with the CIA until the 1970s. He spent much of World War II in Cairo and Teheran and as a very young man was given a leading responsibility. "Here I was," Waller recalls, "head of counterespionage for the Middle East at age nineteen." In 1946, barely into his twenties, he opened the first American intelligence station in postwar Iran, recruiting former German spies to assist the United States in the Cold War and working with Iran's tribal chieftains, including the Qashqai, the Bakhtiari, and the Kurds.

"We, in the field, liked Mossadegh," says Waller, now in his eighties. "In fact, his niece married a [CIA] case officer." But soon the

Americans began to side with the British, who despised Mossadegh. "We had an obligation to our old ally, the British, and oil was an issue." According to Waller, one of the main props holding up Mossadegh were the mullahs and the bazaar. "The bazaar and the mullahs were very, very close. And the mullahs had control of the people, especially the lower classes," he says.[40]

Of all of the religious leaders, the most important was Kashani, says Waller, who as the CIA station chief, developed a warm relationship with the fiery ayatollah during the seven years that he was stationed in Iran. "I did a portrait of Mullah Kashani, in pastels," Waller recalls, with a smile. "Or, I should say, Ayatollah Kashani. He sat for me for a bit, and I finished it from photographs." Waller insists that Kashani never became a full-fledged CIA "agent"—"you don't make an ayatollah your agent," he says—but adds that the United States and the British had several important agents in the anti-Mossadegh coalition, "some of whom were extremely adroit at handling both the bazaar and the mullahs." And Waller says:

> It was obvious that the clergy were important. . . . Kashani told me why he was dropping out of the Mossadegh coalition. Because the Tudeh Party was being tolerated by Mossadegh. They were synonymous with the Russians, and religious men don't like communism.
>
> Kashani was the head man of his god, which gave him political power. It's like the Christian right here. He was the ayatollah, the Khomeini of the day. He had power over the church. He had power over the poor people, which was most of the people in the southern part of the city. And, from time immemorial, the mullahs were close to the bazaaris.

Did the CIA fund Kashani directly? "Yes," according to Waller. "It was money both to Kashani and to his chosen instruments, money to finance his communication channels, pamphleteering, and so on to the people in south Teheran." Waller adds, with a wry grin, that even ayatollahs are, well, corruptible. Choosing his words carefully, he says, "I think he was truly religious, but forgive me for being a cynic. Being religious doesn't distract you from political or commercial reality, or from sex."

With Kashani on board, the CIA and MI6 found it easier to stage street riots and demonstrations against Mossadegh and against the communists. Kashani's power among the masses of Teheran's slums and in the mosques was considerable. The military coup that ousted Mossadegh was coupled with demonstrations financed by the CIA, using the crowds loyal to Kashani and organized by the clergy and by gangs of thugs in the pay of mobsters. Waller returned to Washington to oversee the coup d'état from headquarters, and in the field the legendary Kermit Roosevelt ran the operation on the ground. Two Iranian brothers, the "Boscoes," under CIA control, and three other Iranian brothers, the Rashidians, under MI6 control, joined with Shaaban Jaafari, a famous Iranian athlete and performer, to work with Kashani in assembling the mobs. "One of our agents was a man called 'the Brainless One,' " recalls Waller. "He was a sports hero, a juggler—getting him to work with us was like getting Babe Ruth. He could get a mob together fast. We paid for those."

"Through the Rashidians," wrote Dorril, the CIA and MI6 "established contact with conservative clerics such as Ayatollahs Borujerdi and Behbehani, who feared that Mossadeq's 'leftist advances were endangering national security,' and dissident mullahs from the National Front, Kashani and Makki, who claimed that the ministries were full of 'Kremlin-controlled atheists.' "[41] Recalls Waller, "At the time Islam hadn't raised its head in an organized way. But communism and Islam have never been compatible."[42]

An important part of the CIA's work in Iran in the early 1950s involved efforts to mobilize Iranian religious sentiment against the USSR. It came during a time when the United States was experimenting with Islamist anti-communist fervor in Egypt, Pakistan, and elsewhere. In Iran, much of the CIA's focus was directed against the communist Tudeh Party, although the Tudeh was never really a serious threat. Mossadegh was no communist, having come to power in part with U.S. support. But once he was placed on Washington's enemies list, the CIA went all-out to discredit him by portraying him as communist-controlled, especially in propaganda aimed at the mullahs. The propaganda effort was coordinated by two CIA officers whom we shall meet later, Donald Wilber and Richard Cottam.

At times, the propaganda was heavy-handed:

> The next move was to bring out the psychological warfare assets.
> "In a lurid effort to totally discredit the left," Ayatollah Behbehani,
> who received money from the Americans, sent out letters bearing
> the insignia of the Tudeh Party, and containing "grisly threats"
> written in red ink "to hang all the mullahs from the lampposts of
> various Iranian cities."[43]

According to Dorril, the CIA used journalists Kenneth Love of the
New York Times and Don Schwind of the Associated Press as agents
to circulate their propaganda.[44] Not only did the CIA use ayatollahs
such as Behbehani to spread falsified threats from the Tudeh about
hanging mullahs, but it paid violent agents provocateurs to rile up
Iran's religious community. The CIA and MI6 paid thugs and rabble-
rousers to pose as Tudeh followers in violent street demonstrations
attacking Iran's Shiite establishment:

> The mobs came out onto the streets. . . . A key aspect of the plot
> was to portray the mobs as supporters of the Tudeh Party in order
> to provide a suitable pretext for the coup and the resumption of
> power by the shah. [MI6 agents] hired a fake Tudeh crowd, com-
> prising an unusual mixture of pan-Iranians and Tudeh members,
> paid for with fifty thousand dollars given to them by a CIA officer.
> Richard Cottam observed that agents working on behalf of the
> British "saw the opportunity and sent the people we had under our
> control into the streets to act as if they were Tudeh. They were more
> than just provocateurs, they were shock troops, who acted as if they
> were Tudeh people throwing rocks at mosques and [mullahs]."
> "The purpose" [another writer said], "was to frighten a majority of
> Iranians into believing that a victory for Mossadeq would be a vic-
> tory for the Tudeh, the Soviet Union, and irreligion."[45]

After the restoration of the shah, efforts were made to put the
Islamist genie back in the bottle. But the force of political Islam,
repressed in Iran since the 1920s, had now revived, thanks in part to
the assistance of the CIA and MI6. It would not be so easy to quiet it
down again, and in a very literal sense the forces that toppled the shah

in 1979 were exactly those unleashed to return him to power in 1953. In the 1950s, the shah and his SAVAK secret service strove mightily to keep the Islamists in check and to buy off, corrupt, or otherwise neutralize the medieval mullahs, including Khomeini. "During the shah's reign, the government paid the clergy, too," says Fereydoun Hoveyda, the former Iranian UN ambassador, whose brother served as the shah's prime minister for many years. "Some of the money came from my brother, and some of it came from SAVAK," he says. "And SAVAK had its own people in the clergy."[46] Yet the shah preferred to dismiss Islam as a relic of the past. And so when the movement against the shah began in earnest in the mid-1970s, neither the shah nor most of his sycophantic aides would recognize it for what it was.

After 1953, Kashani gradually faded from view. But his acolyte would introduce a virulent new strain of political Islam. He was just beginning his rise to power.

The 1940s and 1950s were still formative years for Khomeini. His political views were in flux, although Khomeini's writings during World War II reflected distaste for the "dark dictatorship" of Reza Shah, whose reign ended when he was deposed in 1941.[47] By instinct, Khomeini was prone to denounce the compliant, Shiite clerical establishment in Iran. He gravitated toward Kashani, Navab Safavi, and the Devotees of Islam, and began to refine his radical views. "Khomeini's own political position during this period was somewhere between that of the clerical establishment and the *Fedaiyan*," wrote Khomeini's biographer, Baqer Moin. He supported the fairly conservative Ayatollah Borujerdi, but

> he was radically opposed to secularism, believed adamantly in the rule of the *sharia*, and had activist tendencies. He had absorbed, in other words, some of the ideas of the Fedaiyan perhaps in the course of conversations with Navvab Safavi who, according to the latter's widow, was a frequent visitor to Khomeini's home.[48]

Kashani began to act as Khomeini's mentor at this point.

> Another indication of the Khomeini's political ideas at the time was his admiration for Ayatollah Abolqassem Kashani (1882–1962), who from 1945 was closely linked to the Fedaiyan-e

Islam. . . . Khomeini was a frequent visitor to Kashani's home and admired his courage and stamina. He shared his views on many issues such as anti-colonialism, Islamic universalism, political activism, and populism.[49]

During the 1953 coup, Khomeini was involved with the terrorist-inclined Devotees of Islam, even after Kashani decided to keep his distance. Yet Khomeini and Kashani remained close, and Khomeini followed Kashani's advice to break with Mossadegh and support the return of the shah. Still, Khomeini maintained ties to the Devotees, and he intervened in a vain effort to prevent the execution of Navab Safavi in the mid-1950s. But the calculating ayatollah learned a great deal from his experience in 1953. Kashani and the Devotees, he felt, were too political, and lost the all-important connection with the establishment ulema in the holy city of Qom. Borujerdi, on the other hand, though admired by Khomeini for his religious scholarship, was too distant from politics. Repairing to Qom, Khomeini spent the next ten years seeking to unite the political and the religious elements of Iran's Shiite movement. He would next explode onto the scene in 1963–64, mounting a frontal challenge to the shah.

The United States, meanwhile, would forget all about Islam in Iran. The shah was reinstalled, and secure. Washington had won a healthy chunk of the Iranian oil industry for U.S. oil companies, and the United States was busily helping the shah build his army, his police force, and his much-feared intelligence service, the SAVAK. Despite the help of some of the mullahs in toppling Mossadegh, the imperial shah was in no mood to share power with anyone—liberals, businessmen, or clergy. So the Islamists seethed and simmered beneath him, unnoticed.

The story of political Islam and its burgeoning alliance with the United States now shifted to the Arab world. Nasser, victorious after the Suez War of 1956 and unbowed, was presenting an ever more serious challenge to the Cold War ideologues of the Eisenhower administration. Egypt's Muslim Brotherhood was crushed and forced into exile. To stop Nasser, and to support anti-communist and anti-nationalist forces across the entire Arab world, the United States turned to Saudi Arabia.

5

THE KING OF ALL ISLAM

"The genius of you Americans is that you never make clear cut stupid moves, only *complicated* stupid moves which make us wonder at the possibility that there may be something we are missing."

—Gamal Abdel Nasser, 1957

DWIGHT DAVID EISENHOWER was a good general, a modest president, and a poor student of Islam.

In the immediate aftermath of Suez in 1956, after Ike had intervened to force Israel out of the Sinai and to undo the Anglo-French conspiracy against Gamal Abdel Nasser's Egypt, the United States had a chance to improve relations with Nasser and Arab nationalism. Instead, Eisenhower opted for an alliance with Saudi Arabia, making the reactionary bastion of Islamic fundamentalism into America's chief ally in the Arab world. Until Nasser's untimely death in 1970, Saudi Arabia would serve as the bulwark of American influence in the region. Like Franklin Roosevelt before him, who had announced America's claim to a strategic stake in Saudi oil, Eisenhower premised friendly relations with Saudi Arabia on the importance of that country's petroleum wealth. But he expanded that relationship to include a utilitarian alliance with Saudi Arabia's benighted version of Islam. He set a course that continued under the Kennedy, Johnson, and Nixon administrations.

The cornerstone of the administration's Middle East policy was the Eisenhower Doctrine. Echoing FDR, Ike proclaimed America's imperial goal of incorporating the Middle East into its permanent sphere of influence. "The existing vacuum in the Middle East must be filled by the United States before it is filled by Russia," proclaimed Ike.[1] In a message to Congress in January 1957, the president promised that the United States would provide military and financial aid to any Middle East countries "requesting such aid against overt aggression from any nation controlled by international Communism."[2] To support the doctrine, Eisenhower invited King Saud to make an official state visit to Washington, emphasizing the importance of Saudi Arabia by personally going out to the airport to meet the arriving monarch. Ever grateful, the king endorsed the Eisenhower Doctrine.

It made sense to Eisenhower to view Saudi Arabia as the ultimate prize, since one-fourth of the world's oil lay beneath its sands. But Eisenhower saw Saudi Arabia as more than a treasure to be protected. Its role as the worldwide center of Islam suggested to Washington that Islam—and Islamism—could be wielded as a sword against the Soviet Union and against left-leaning nationalists like Nasser.

Eisenhower, CIA Director Allen Dulles, and Secretary of State John Foster Dulles also sought to build an alliance with Saudi Arabia's Wahhabi pan-Islamic movement, and Allen Dulles's CIA secretly encouraged Saudi Arabia to rebuild the Muslim Brotherhood against Nasser. The president feared that the Soviet Union was trying to use Egyptian president Nasser as the "head of an enormous Moslem confederation." Eisenhower recalled:

> To check any movement in this direction we wanted to explore the possibilities of building up King Saud as a counterweight to Nasser. The king was a logical choice in this regard; he at least professed anti-Communism, and he enjoyed, on religious grounds, a high standing among all Arab nations.[3]

It was a flawed idea.

First, Eisenhower's fear that the Soviet Union was on the verge of making major gains in the Middle East was greatly exaggerated, and the notion the USSR might try to embrace Islam was wildly off the mark. True, Moscow was trying to leapfrog the anti-communist Northern Tier states of Turkey, Iran, and Pakistan. It did so by seeking influence in the Arab world, especially by cultivating ties to Nasser and, after 1958, hoping that the revolutionary government of Iraq would form a pan-Arab alliance with Egypt. But neither the Egyptian nor the Iraqi government was pro-communist, and an Egypt-Iraq alliance never emerged.[4] In addition, although the Soviet Union may have looked with favor on pan-Arabism, with its emphasis on nationalism, Moscow feared the rise of Islam within its own borders in Central Asia and had no intention of fostering pan-Islam in the Middle East. Yet none of this deterred Ike from pursuing a fateful alliance with Riyadh.

Moreover, the notion of a U.S.-Saudi alliance built on Islam ignored the fact that King Saud did not exactly enjoy much prestige among Muslims. "Saud was weak, stupid, and corrupt, and he was surrounded by Levantine courtiers," says James Akins, a veteran U.S. diplomat who served as ambassador to Saudi Arabia in the 1970s.[5] Besides the fact that he was hopelessly ignorant, with only the foggiest understanding of the modern world, Saud was also widely seen as dissolute, a sex addict, a drunk, and an all-around seeker of pleasure, served by pimps and procurers of alcohol in ten lavish palaces. With more than a hundred children[6] from an endless series of wives and concubines, he was also, quite literally, the father of his country. All in all, Saud was a less-than-solid foundation upon which to build a Middle East empire, and especially not if one wished to appeal to the conservatives in the Muslim world.

Yet as king of Saudi Arabia, whose territory included Mecca and Medina, the holiest cities in Islam, Saud did embody worldwide prestige as custodian of Islam's two shrines. As the Cold War matured, Saudi Arabia's role as the center of worldwide Islam would loom ever larger in U.S. strategic thinking. Saud—cynically, some might say—sought to portray himself as King of All Islam, and that was enough for Eisenhower. "Arabia," wrote Eisenhower, "is a country that contains the holy places of the Moslem world," and he reasoned that "the King could be built up as a spiritual leader."[7] According to Nathan Citino, the effort to build up King Saud as the leader of Islam was part of a joint strategy with Great Britain called "Omega." Eisenhower insisted that "our efforts should be toward separating the Saudi Arabians from the Egyptians."[8] The president and the Dulles brothers were even more encouraged when King Saud requested an Islamic legal ruling from the Wahhabi clergy forbidding Muslims from accepting aid from the Soviet bloc.

An effort to cobble together an "Islam strategy" emerged early in 1957. "Following the Saud-Eisenhower summit, the administration continued to cultivate Islam as a bulwark against communism, and as part of this policy it sought opportunities to overcome the social fragmentation that afflicted the Middle East," wrote Citino, who conducted a study of U.S.-Saudi relations during the Eisenhower years. "In late January, the National Security Council staff established a working committee on Islamic organizations that compiled a list of Middle Eastern and North African social, cultural, and religious groups, such as Sufi brotherhoods, which the United States Information Agency could target with propaganda."[9]

The CIA's chief specialist on Islam at the time was none other than Donald Wilber, the operative who had helped organize the 1953 coup d'état in Iran. "Wilber knew a lot about Islam," says John Waller, a retired CIA official who oversaw the coup from CIA headquarters.[10] But in his memoirs, *Adventures in the Middle East,* Wilber rather modestly describes his work on Islam at the time:

> One subject on which I was continually active was Islam and the Muslims of the Middle East. For lack of anyone better qualified, I became the Agency's specialist on Islam. In the spring of 1957 I was the CIA member of an inter-agency working group on Islam, and then the co-author of the group study. In the field and at headquarters I reviewed files and also collected publications and information on trips, and I authored several studies: "Islam in Iran," "Islam in Pakistan," "Islam in Afghanistan," [etc.]. More exhaustive than any published material, these were to serve as guidelines for working with Muslim groups.[11]

Wilber also included in his surveys research into the extent to which the Central Asian Muslim population inside the Soviet Union could be mobilized against the USSR, and he coordinated propaganda efforts in the late 1950s "exposing the Soviet Communist attitude toward Islam."[12]

Eisenhower also sought input from non-CIA specialists on Islam, including those within academia. Leading Orientalists, some of whom had highlighted the Princeton colloquium in which the Muslim Brotherhood's Said Ramadan took part, were tapped for their expertise. Wrote Citino:

> The Eisenhower administration sponsored a conference in Washington of leading historians of the Middle East, including, among many others, the prominent Ottoman historian and later University of Chicago professor Halil Inalcik. National Security Council staffers routinely attended academic conferences and collected scholarly papers on the contemporary Middle East. In one notable example of Middle Eastern scholarship with Cold War ramifications, filed away in the NSC staff papers at the Eisenhower Library, Bernard Lewis explains how Naqshbandi Sufis living in the Caucasus region might be used as a fifth column inside the Soviet empire.[13]

Two close advisers of King Saud—Yusuf Yassin and Mohammed Sorour Sabhan—conducted the negotiations with Secretary of State John Foster Dulles.[14] Yassin, a Syrian from Latakia, on the coast of the Mediterranean, was a sly, well-connected member of the king's entourage who had first come to Saudi Arabia on the recommendation of right-wing Syrian politicians. He represented Ibn Saud's financial interests in Damascus. Making use of Saudi money and his Syrian connections, Yassin plotted to subvert or destabilize that country. Beginning in 1956–57, the CIA, too, launched a covert operation aimed at toppling the Syrian government.[15] In 1958, Yassin was implicated in a Saudi conspiracy to assassinate Egypt's President Nasser, who was flying into Damascus. The existence of the plot was announced by the Syrian army's chief of intelligence, who revealed that Saudi Arabia had offered him a bribe of £1.9 million to help carry it out. It would not be the last U.S.-Saudi conspiracy against Arab nationalist leaders.

More interesting, for our story, is the role of Mohammed Sorour Sabhan. Sorour was the freed slave who, while serving as Saudi Arabia's deputy finance minister in the late 1940s, was the Saudi paymaster for the Muslim Brotherhood in Egypt. In the 1950s, Sorour had become minister of finance and one of King Saud's closest advisers. In the 1960s, he would assume a powerful position overseeing Saudi Arabia's worldwide effort to promote the Muslim Brotherhood and other radical Muslim fundamentalist groups, from Africa to Indonesia. It isn't known if at all, or to what extent, Sorour and Dulles discussed the Brotherhood. But in supporting an alliance with Saudi Arabia, then the Brotherhood's chief financial supporter, the United States was in fact enlisting the Brothers in the Cold War.

Asked about America's decision to support Saudi Arabia's Islamic bloc against Nasser, a former senior CIA official who served in the Middle East summarized the Cold War rationale: "What other pole was there? King Hussein?" he asks. "The optic was the Cold War. The Cold War was the defining clarity of the time. We saw Nasser as socialist, anti-Western, anti–Baghdad Pact, and we were looking for some sort of counterfoil. Saudi efforts to Islamicize the region were seen as powerful and effective and likely to be successful. We loved that. We had an ally against communism."[16]

One consequence of Eisenhower's efforts in the 1950s to build up Saudi Arabia as a bulwark against communism was the rise of the bin Laden family. Seeking to enhance Saudi prestige as custodians of the Muslim holy places in Mecca and Medina, Ike authorized half a million dollars for Saudi Arabia to study the construction of a railroad to carry pilgrims to Mecca, part of an effort to refurbish Mecca as the center of Islamic culture. King Saud hired Sheikh Mohammed bin Laden to undertake the reconstruction of the Great Mosque in Mecca. It was through this plum contract that the bin Ladens began to accumulate their vast wealth.

THE BROTHERHOOD'S SAUDI REFUGE

Initially Saudi Arabia supplied the Muslim Brotherhood with money only. After 1954, however, the country itself became a chief base of its operations. When Nasser cracked down on the Muslim Brotherhood in Egypt, Saudi Arabia provided an important refuge for the organization, and many of its members flocked to the desert kingdom. This migration occurred just as the United States was giving up on Nasser and turning to Saudi Arabia. The Brothers settled in Jeddah, where they went into business, and in Riyadh, Mecca, and Medina, where they radicalized the Wahhabi movement. For the next half century, Saudi Arabia would be the Brothers' ultimate redoubt, providing succor and support, along with virtually unlimited financing.

"One of the stupidest things Faisal ever did was to invite the Ikhwanis into Saudi Arabia," says David Long, who'd served in the State Department's Bureau of Intelligence and Research. "But it seemed innocuous at the time. At the time, everybody was fighting Communism, and so were we. And so was Faisal."[17] Faisal, the crown prince, wouldn't become king of Saudi Arabia until the 1960s, when he ousted Saud in a palace coup, but he was widely seen as more sophisticated, more enlightened, and far shrewder than the dissolute Saud.

The Muslim Brotherhood, a highly political organization dedicated to creating a worldwide caliphate-based Islamic state, was both an ally and a threat to Saudi Arabia. "The Saudis weren't terribly happy with the Muslim Brotherhood, but if you—and the Saudis were—scared to death of Nasser, the Muslim Brotherhood was still the only game in town," says John Voll, a Georgetown University professor.[18] In its foreign policy, Saudi Arabia utilized the Brotherhood against Egypt, Syria, and Iraq, built its power in Sudan, encouraged it in Afghanistan and Pakistan—where it allied with Abul-Ala Mawdudi's Islamic Group—and even toyed with supporting it in Soviet Central Asia. But internally, the royal family did not tolerate Muslim Brotherhood action. "The Saudis were very tolerant of the Muslim Brotherhood, and they encouraged it in Egypt, Sudan, and elsewhere, but they were adamantly opposed to [Brotherhood] activity inside Saudi Arabia," says Ray Close, who served as the CIA's chief of station in Saudi Arabia from 1970 to 1977.[19]

"The Saudis, as you know, oppose all political parties," says Hermann Eilts, one of America's most experienced Arabists, who served as ambassador to Saudi Arabia. "And the Saudi regime had the experience in the late 1920s with the Ikhwan, not exactly the Muslim Brotherhood but the tribesmen who were becoming rather fanatical. Now what Hassan al-Banna and the Muslim Brotherhood were doing in Egypt, and in Syria, was something that was generally in line with Saudi thinking on the importance of Islam, as opposed to nationalism, as a uniting factor. Nevertheless, they were not eager to have the Muslim Brotherhood, or any other political force, organize themselves in Saudi Arabia. They were unwilling to allow any political parties, including Muslim political parties."[20] In fact, in 1946, when Hassan al-Banna tried to open a Muslim Brotherhood branch in Mecca, the Saudi authorities bluntly refused.[21]

Though the Saudis took strong measures to prevent the Muslim Brotherhood from becoming a force inside Saudi Arabia, the Brothers operated there in a semi-underground fashion. Many of them went into business, establishing Islamic banks and corporations that made them wealthy. Others became influential in the mass media. Close, the CIA station chief, recalls that Richard Mitchell, the author of the definitive book, *The Society of the Muslim Brothers*, introduced him to one key personality. "It was through Dick Mitchell that I met the only member of the Ikhwan that I ever knew, Mohammed Salahuddin," says Close. "He was the editor of *Al Medina* newspaper. He was born in Sudan, and spent some time in Egypt, knew all the Ikhwanis. His presence was tolerated as long as he wrote things against communism." And still others went into academia, infiltrating Saudi Arabia's network of Islamic universities. Yet they operated as a secret society, kept their membership hidden, and maintained a clandestine presence in many Saudi institutions.

It was in the university system that the Muslim Brotherhood would find its most secure perch. Saudi Arabia had never had much of a system of higher education, and what it did have was overwhelmingly dedicated to training clerics and inculcating Wahhabi values among the country's youth. In the 1960s, Saudi Arabia created a pair of institutions, the Islamic University of Medina (1961) and King Abdel Aziz University (1967), which became intellectual centers for the Islamic right. The Islamic University of Medina began with Pakistan's Mawdudi, a militant Islamist, as one of its trustees, who wanted to make it into the fundamentalist alternative to Cairo's Al Azhar, the thousand-year-old repository of the mainstream Islamic tradition.[22] The Muslim Brotherhood and its Wahhabi allies convinced the royal family that Al Azhar was too close to Nasser, so they lavishly funded the Islamic University of Medina. Dozens of Egyptian Islamic scholars affiliated with or sympathetic to the Muslim Brotherhood took up posts at the university.

The vice president of the university was a man who would figure in hard-right Islamic politics in Saudi Arabia for the next several decades: Sheikh Abdel Aziz bin Baz. Blind since youth, bin Baz was a fanatical Wahhabi who would resist modernization in Saudi Arabia and flirt with violence and terrorism. In 1966, bin Baz insisted that the Copernican view of the universe was heresy, that the sun revolved around the earth, and that the earth itself was flat. Anyone who disagreed, said bin Baz, was guilty of "falsehood toward God, the Koran, and the Prophet."[23] His views angered King Faisal, but in 1974 bin Baz would be appointed president of the official Directorate of Religious Research, Islamic Legal Rulings, Islamic Propagation, and Guidance.[24]

The Islamic University of Medina was controlled by Saudi Arabia's Grand Mufti Mohammed ibn Ibrahim Al Shaikh, a chief of the Wahhabi Al Shaikh clan. Fully 85 percent of its students were non-Saudi, coming from virtually every Islamic country in the world. Through this institution and its sister universities in Saudi Arabia, the Muslim Brotherhood was able to spread its ideology everywhere.[25] In addition, tens of thousands of young Saudis were indoctrinated through the Saudi system of higher education. The Saudi university system expanded exponentially, from 3,625 students in 1965 to more than 113,000 students by 1986. Half of its six universities were religious in nature and, according to one study, nearly one-third of all

Saudi students majored in Islamic studies; for the other 70 percent, a third of their course work was religious in nature.[26]

James Akins, who served as U.S. ambassador to Saudi Arabia in the early 1970s, was troubled by the emphasis on religion, but the royal family told him to keep out of it. "They told me, 'It's not your business,'" says Akins. "There wasn't much we could do about it." Akins, along with more progressive Saudis, was upset that the Saudi university system wasn't training administrators, managers, scientists, and engineers. "I talked to them about training more doctors, chemists, engineers, and fewer mullahs," recalls Akins. "But I was let to know that I was beyond my competence, and that I was meddling where I wasn't wanted. I thought it was rank stupidity. It was an absolute catastrophe, training all those mullahs. A number of the princes urged me to talk to the power structure." To no avail. The Saudi ministry of education was controlled by the Al Shaikh, and its hold over that part of government was unshakable.

The relationship between the Al Saud, the Al Shaikh, and the Muslim Brothers was a complex one. Some members of the royal family were pious and orthodox, and saw Wahhabism as the righteous Islamic path. Others, of course—King Saud and King Fahd, and hundreds of pleasure-seeking lesser princes—were libertines, whose relationship to Wahhabi ideology was tenuous at best. The Al Shaikh, usually a distinct bloodline, also began marrying the Al Saud, creating family bonds that pulled parts of both clans in two directions, the royal and the religious. (King Faisal's mother, for instance, was from the Al Shaikh family, giving Faisal an aura of piety that other sons of Abdel Aziz couldn't as easily claim.) According to Eilts, there was a "constant tug of war" between the royal family and the religious family:

> Over time, one also found that among the Al Shaikh, more and more were leaving, and were not going into the religious leadership, but into the army and things of that nature. So the sacral nature of the Al Shaikh family came to be diluted, so much so that Faisal, in 1971, when the Grand Mufti died, eliminated the post for a period and established a ministry of justice, which was seen as a weakening of this long-standing, two-century-old relationship

between the Saudis and the religious leadership. The ministry of justice remained, but the king later reestablished the muftiate, and named a member of the Al Shaikh family to it.

The ulema [clergy] were powerful, and the Al Shaikh family could control the ulema. But as the Al Shaikh family weakened in its influence, with only some members going into the clergy, and younger people coming up and many of them becoming ulema, the relationship between the Saudi family and the Al Shaikh family cracked somewhat. So you get to the current situation, where a large number of younger people object to their elders, to the ulema, and to the Saudi royal family and are seeking to go their own way, and rather militantly.[27]

As strains between the Al Saud and Al Shaikh began to show, the Al Shaikh began to exhibit the effects of prolonged exposure to the Muslim Brotherhood. Whereas the Al Shaikh were establishment-oriented, more religious than political, and above all committed to stability (especially for the Saudi throne), the Muslim Brotherhood's members were often brash, highly political, and as often as not, revolution-minded. After 1954, as more and more Brothers settled in Saudi Arabia, the Al Shaikh naturally become more militant. If the Al Shaikh had interests that diverged from those of the Al Saud, the Muslim Brotherhood did so even more strongly.

According to Martha Kessler, a former CIA Middle East analyst who has studied the Muslim Brotherhood, the loyalty of the Wahhabi establishment in Saudi Arabia to the royal family went only so far, and that was even truer for the Brotherhood members in the kingdom. "The Egyptian Brothers in Saudi Arabia were even further removed [than the Al Shaikh] from any sense of loyalty to the House of Saud," she says. "It's not clear that they wanted to overthrow the regime, but inside the Brotherhood, there was always a debate between those who wanted to overthrow what they saw as the corrupt regimes and those who wanted to spend their time organizing, developing a base in the community."[28]

The delicate relationship among the Saudi royal family, its Wahhabi establishment, the Muslim Brotherhood, and the even more radical Islamic terrorist groups would continue to evolve. The balance would shift, depending on their relative strengths, power struggles within the royal family, and regional politics. This balance was made even more complex, thanks to the role of Islamic charities, often connected to one or more Saudi princes, that wittingly or unwittingly acted as conduits for money to terrorist groups. The situation was exacerbated by the fact that individual princes often acted independently of the king, the government, and other members of the family. "The Saudi royal family is not a monolith by any means," says Ray Close. "There is always somebody ready to give money to someone. There is a lot of free enterprise going on in royal family politics."

As the Muslim Brotherhood gained influence in Saudi Arabia, King Saud and then King Faisal skillfully incorporated the organization into the kingdom's official foreign policy. In the 1960s, two landmark events marked that grand design: the creation of the Muslim World League in 1962 and the establishment of the Organization of the Islamic Conference in 1969. Under Faisal, Saudi Arabia vigorously worked to set up an "Islamic bloc," complete with American support, which ultimately succeeded in eclipsing Egypt's Nasser.

King Faisal's Islamic Bloc

What Eisenhower had helped set in motion in the 1950s continued apace in the decade that followed.

Faisal, king from 1964 to 1975, was a more modern monarch than King Saud (1953–1964), and had a clear vision of Saudi Arabia's foreign policy. "Faisal," says Charles Freeman, a veteran U.S. foreign service officer who served as U.S. ambassador to Saudi Arabia, "made a deliberate decision that Islam was the antidote to Nasser."[29] It was a development that Washington viewed enthusiastically. Although some secular-minded U.S. diplomats and intelligence officers registered objections from time to time, the U.S.-Saudi alliance was set in stone, and so Saudi Arabia's Islam-based foreign policy worried few. Even advocates of the U.S.-Israeli alliance, who gained momentum in the 1960s, were far more worried about Nasser than about Saudi Arabia.

The foundation of the Muslim World League in 1962 marks the

formal beginning of the resurgence of radical-right political Islam. Founded in Mecca in 1962, the Muslim World League was a *Who's Who* of the Islamic right. For the first time the movement had a central nervous system more organized than the clandestine Muslim Brotherhood. The virtually unlimited ability of Saudi Arabia to fund the organization gave it enormous clout. Among the founding members and officers of the League[30] were virtually all of the leaders of the Islamic resurgence, including:

Said Ramadan, the son-in-law of Hassan al-Banna, the founder of the Muslim Brotherhood, and the Brotherhood's chief international organizer, who'd spent years in Syria, Jordan, Pakistan and elsewhere before opening the Islamic Center of Geneva in 1961, with Saudi support.

Abul-Ala Mawdudi, the founder of Pakistan's radical-right Islamic Society (*Jamaat-e Islami*), who is the single most important architect of the notion of an Islamic Republic, and who played a crucial role in battering Pakistan's left-secular opposition movement and in pushing Pakistan into the hard-right Islamic camp under Zia ul-Haq, the dictator who seized power in 1977.

Hajj Amin al-Husseini, the pro-Nazi mufti of Jerusalem, who'd been an agent of British intelligence since the 1920s and who, after World War II, became a Saudi-funded anti-Nasser propagandist.

Muhammad Sadiq al-Mujaddidi of Afghanistan, who maintained CIA contacts in that unfortunate country in the 1960s and whose direct heirs would form the core of the 1979–89 anti-Soviet Afghan jihad backed by the CIA, Saudi Arabia, Egypt, and Pakistan.

Muhammad ibn Ibrahim al-Shaikh, the government-appointed Grand Mufti of Saudi Arabia and the titular head of the Wahhabi movement, who had enormous clout within the Saudi royal family.

Abdel Rahman al-Iryani, the militant Muslim fundamentalist who would take power in Yemen in 1967 and lead that formerly pro-Nasser republic into the Saudi camp after a long civil war.

In all, a couple of dozen of the world's leading Islamists came together in the League.[31]

"The Wahhabi vision went international in the 1960s in response to the threat posed by Arab nationalism and socialism," wrote Georgetown University's John Esposito. "Saudi Arabia and other monarchies were threatened in particular by Nasserism and in general by radical Arab socialist governments. . . . The Saudis championed a pan-Islamic policy against Nasser's 'secular, socialist' pan-Arabism with its ties to 'atheistic communism.' . . . The Saudi government also developed close ties with the Muslim Brotherhood and the Jamaat-e Islami. Despite significant differences, they shared [an] antipathy to common enemies—Nasserism, secularism, communism."[32]

The Muslim World League sent out missionaries, printed propaganda, and doled out funds for the building of Wahhabi-oriented mosques and Islamic associations:

> The league identified worthy beneficiaries, invited them to Saudi Arabia, and gave them the recommendation (*tazkiya*) that would later provide them with largesse from a generous private donor, a member of the royal family, a prince, or an ordinary businessman. The league was managed by members of the Saudi religious establishment, working with other Arabs who either belonged to the Muslim Brothers or were close to them, along with ulemas from the Indian subcontinent connected to the Deoband Schools or to the party founded by Mawdudi.[33]

The CIA was only vaguely aware of the Muslim World League's importance, and official Washington—committed to winning the Cold War regardless of how unsavory its allies—didn't ask the CIA to investigate it. "We saw it all in a short-term perspective," says a CIA officer who served in Saudi Arabia. "We weren't looking at long-term consequences." According to this officer, in the early 1970s the CIA tried to place an agent inside the Muslim World League. "I ran a penetration of Rabitat," he says, using the Arabic name for the organization. "It was considered, in Washington, as one of the least important things I'd done." Headquarters was interested in wars, coups, and gunrunning in the Persian Gulf, not in the activities of the League. "I found it fascinating, and important," he says. "I didn't see Rabitat as an effort to expand Saudi Arabia's own influence internationally, but as a way to expand Islam's influence in the Arab world and beyond. It wasn't Saudi Arabia so much as, well, kind of a 'Vatican'-type organism. It's almost as if it were an operation being run in spite of the Saudis." Yet, he says, it certainly wasn't seen as a threat, or something of geopolitical concern, and Washington wasn't interested. "The sound of snoring," he says, "was deafening." The covert operation was dropped.[34]

Charles Waterman, a CIA Arabist who spent many years in the Middle East and ultimately became the agency's chief of station in Saudi Arabia, says that to the CIA the Muslim World League looked innocent enough in the 1960s and 1970s. "It looked like another Muslim organization worth monitoring, but not something to worry about," says Waterman. "If they ended up supporting Islamic student movements somewhere, and they got involved in some conflict with left-wing students, our reaction was, 'Okay, fine, another benign action intended to control the left.'" Was the CIA wrong at the time for not focusing on these groups and these characters? "They seemed like they were just Islamic charitable organizations, and so what?"[35]

Ray Close, the former CIA chief, agrees. Asked whether the CIA had any worries about ties between Muslim Brotherhood and Wahhabi clergy, he says: "We didn't follow it. If anyone is at fault, it was me. We just didn't see them as a threat. They weren't a target of ours. I'd get target lists—but no one in Washington was asking me to look at them. . . . It didn't enter into our consciousness."

Ninety-nine percent of the funding for the Muslim World League came from the government of Saudi Arabia. Its ties to the Saudi establishment were manifold. One of the League's secretary-generals, Muhammad Ali al-Harkan, was a leading Wahhabi and ex–Saudi minister of justice, who would later serve as de facto grand mufti of Saudi Arabia. Besides the ministry of justice, the Wahhabis and the League interlocked with the Saudi ministry of education and the powerful ministry of pilgrimage and religious endowments, which controlled the enormous annual Muslim pilgrimages to Mecca and the vast funds available for charities and proselytizing. All that, in turn, meshed with the university system, especially the Islamic universities. The League worked closely with the militant World Assembly of Muslim Youth (WAMY), established in 1972, which would later be accused of sustaining terrorist activities overseas.[36]

During the 1960s, the struggle between Egypt and Saudi Arabia—in effect, a proxy fight in which the United States took the Saudi side—unfolded in two directions: first, in yet another flare-up of the Muslim Brotherhood in Egypt; and second, in a shooting war that pitted Nasser against Faisal in Yemen, a tiny nation at the southwestern corner of the Arabian Peninsula. In both cases, the ties linking the Muslim Brotherhood, the Muslim World League, and the Arab world's conservative monarchies provided Riyadh with a powerful regional apparatus to wield against Nasser.

Ramadan and the Return of the Brothers

A central organizer of the Saudi Islamic bloc was the man whom Ike had encountered in the Oval Office in 1953: Said Ramadan. According to a Swiss report, during this period Ramadan was believed to have been an American agent. He also got help from West Germany, was backed financially by Saudi Arabia and Qatar, and served as Jordan's representative to the United Nations in Geneva. At the same time, Ramadan served as the international mastermind of the Muslim Brotherhood, and in 1965 he was allegedly involved in a second assassination attempt against Nasser. The action against Nasser occurred in the midst of yet another revolt by the Brotherhood in Egypt, this time aided by Ramadan's well-organized apparatus of exiles. Part of his machine was based in Saudi Arabia, and part in Geneva, where Ramadan had settled.

Compared to its pre-1954 strength, the organization in Egypt was a shadow of its former self. It had been forced to operate deep underground since the 1950s. It tried to establish front organizations and political salons to maintain its organizational presence, but Nasser's security services were effective in repressing it. By the mid-1960s, however, many of the political prisoners who had been arrested in the post-1954 crackdown on the movement had been released. Once again they tried to organize against Nasser.

From Geneva, Ramadan was pulling many of the organization's strings. In 1954, Nasser had stripped him of his Egyptian citizenship, and he went into exile. With help from the West German government, which was angry at Egypt for having recognized East Germany, and traveling on a West German diplomatic passport, he went to Munich, West Germany, before going to Switzerland. There, bankrolled by the king of Saudi Arabia, Ramadan established the Islamic Center of Geneva in 1961, which would serve as a headquarters for the Muslim Brotherhood. Ramadan would live there for the next thirty-four years, until his death in 1995.

The Center became an organizational nerve center, publishing house, and meeting place for the Islamic right and Muslim Brotherhood activists from across the Muslim world. According to Richard Labeviere, a journalist who has written about the Muslim Brotherhood's ties to terrorism, Ramadan not only managed the organization's funds but, along with Youssef Nada, a Brotherhood financier, helped to establish the group's bank, Al Taqwa.[37]

In 1962, Ramadan helped Saudi Arabia establish the Muslim World League. "My father wasn't just one of the leaders of the founding group of the league," says Hani Ramadan, Said's son and the current director of the Islamic Center in Geneva. "He had the original idea for the creation of an Islamic league, which eventually became a parallel channel though which he could communicate his thoughts." According to Hani Ramadan, the Islamic Center was well received in Switzerland when it was first established. "There was nothing like today's Islamophobia," he says. "The first reactions to my father's activity and to the presence of an Islamic Center in Geneva were positive, both within Switzerland and more generally with the European public." But Hani Ramadan admits that the whole purpose of the venture was to promote the Muslim Brotherhood. "The creation of the Islamic Center was supposed to realize my father's desire of creating a center from which he could spread the teachings of Hassan al-Banna, a place where students coming from various Arab countries could meet and be trained in the message of Islam."[38]

Scattered in exile, and underground in Egypt, the Muslim Brother-hood grew ever more radical in the early 1960s. In Cairo, the Brother-hood was gathering strength for another showdown with Nasser. Elsewhere, political Islam was growing. Saudi Arabia was increasingly making an aggressive bid to act as leader of the Arab and Islamic blocs; Ayatollah Khomeini was beginning to stir in Iran; Iraqi fundamentalist Shiites had created a conspiratorial political party, the Call;[39] and Mawdudi's movement in Pakistan was gaining momentum. When the 1965 crisis over the Brotherhood exploded in Egypt, Ramadan and the Brotherhood's chief ideologue, the militant leader Sayyid Qutb, both of whom were allegedly behind an attempt to kill Nasser, were at the center of the crisis. This time, Nasser was better prepared, and he called on friends and supporters within Egypt's Muslim clergy to back him, while painting Ramadan and the Muslim Brotherhood as U.S. agents. "On 30 August Egyptian public opinion learned, through a speech Nasser delivered from Moscow, that the Society of Muslim Brethren was the force behind a gigantic plot exposed by the intelligence services. Their accomplices, said the president, included Mustapha Amin, a leading liberal journalist arrested on 2 September on charges of 'spying for the United States.' After the raids, the regime's religious functionaries, spokesmen, and writers were mobilized to denounce seditious elements, . . . condemning the Muslim Brethren as 'medieval terrorists,' " writes Gilles Kepel, one the world's foremost analysts of political Islam. "The newspapers exposed the foreign links of the 'religious fanatics': Said Ramadan, al-Banna's son-in-law, was said to be pulling the strings from Amman, Jordan, on orders from CENTO."[40] Ramadan may or may not have been a U.S. agent, but there is no doubt that he had aligned himself closely with the axis of nations—including Pakistan, a CENTO member, Jordan, and Saudi Arabia—that the United States was supporting against Nasser.

According to *Le Temps,* Egypt wasn't the only government that considered Said Ramadan to be an American agent. The government of Switzerland, too, believed that Ramadan was working for the United States. In 1966, at the height of crisis in Egypt, a high-level meeting of Swiss officials, including diplomats, the Swiss federal police, and the security services, met to discuss Ramadan's case. Documents now in the Swiss archives reveal that the Swiss authorities concluded that Ramadan represented a "conservative tendency, pro-Western and not hostile" to the interests of Switzerland. The Swiss archives also reveal that the Swiss, at least, believed that Ramadan was an agent of the CIA and MI6. "He was more than a simple propagandist appreciated for his anti-communism," according to *Le Temps*. A Swiss government analyst concluded: "Said Ramadan is, among other things, an intelligence agent of the English and the Americans." *Le Temps* noted that Ramadan's ties "to certain Western secret services are suggested in several documents in his dossier."[41]

Nasser's 1965–66 crackdown on the Brotherhood decimated the organization once again. Many of its underground leaders were arrested and others fled. Nasser ordered the execution by hanging of the organization's chief ideologue and theoretician, Sayyid Qutb, who had earlier been granted exile in Saudi Arabia.[42] According to Hermann Eilts, King Faisal vigorously intervened with Nasser on Qutb's behalf, to no avail.[43]

Kennedy, Nasser, and Yemen

The struggle between Nasser and Faisal erupted into open warfare from 1962 to 1970, when Egypt and Saudi Arabia fought a bitter and bloody proxy war in Yemen. The two protagonists were at the height of their powers in the 1960s. Nasser was an Arab icon with followers in every Arab country, and Faisal—who edged out King Saud in the early 1960s—was using Saudi money, the Muslim World League, and the Wahhabi movement to bolster the conservative coalition. The Egyptian leader, wielding his typically colorful rhetoric, blasted the desert kingdom for acting on behalf of U.S. imperialism, while Faisal equated Nasser's Arab socialism with "atheistic communism."

Although the war was by and large invisible to the American public, it had a very significant impact on U.S. policy in the Middle East, strengthening American ties to the conservative Arab states and above all to Saudi Arabia and its Islamic bloc. The story of the Yemen war's impact on U.S. Middle East policy is told in some detail in Warren Bass's *Support Any Friend,* an account of the Kennedy administration's flirtation with Nasser. With the departure of Eisenhower and his uncompromising attitude toward nonalignment, the Kennedy administration offered an olive branch to Egypt. Under Kennedy, some U.S. officials accepted that Nasser was independent, not a Soviet pawn, and that Washington would have to reach an accommodation with him. Optimists believed that Nasser, who was no communist—in fact, he ruthlessly locked up members of the Egyptian Communist Party and other leftists—might be convinced to abandon his ties to the USSR. More realistic analysts felt that Nasser could at least be persuaded to reach a modus vivendi with the United States. And, of course, still others, especially partisans of Israel, saw Nasser much as Saudi Arabia did, as the devil incarnate.

"Our relations with Nasser were difficult," recalls Talcott Seelye, who headed the State Department's Arabian Peninsula desk during the Kennedy years. "We saw that his movement constituted a threat to the Saudi regime, and there was a reaction in Saudi Arabia, too. Prince Talal [one of the so-called Saudi 'Free Princes'] defected [to Egypt], and two Saudi pilots did, too. So we were very worried about the survival of the Saudi regime."[44] The CIA prepared a National Intelligence Estimate (NIE) called "Nasser and the Future of Arab Nationalism," which told the White House: "Militant nationalism will continue to be the most dynamic force in Arab political affairs, and Nasser is very likely to remain its foremost leader and symbol for the foreseeable future." It went on to warn the young president that "the long-term outlook for the conservative and Western-aligned regimes is bleak," and that the Saudi regime was likely to be swept away.[45]

Kennedy thought it worthwhile to explore an opening to Nasser, to the chagrin of both Israel and Saudi Arabia, and he began a series of exchanges with the Egyptian leader, through diplomatic contacts, letters, and personal meetings. To Kennedy, Nasser wrote: "Why does the United States, a country established on foundations of freedom and by means of a revolution, oppose the call of freedom and revolutionary movements, and line up with reactionary forces and enemies of progress?"[46] By reactionary forces, of course, Nasser meant above all Saudi Arabia, and his question was a good one. Unlike Ike, who reflexively saw independent-minded Third World countries as communist stooges, JFK was willing to explore the possibility that such movements were not necessarily incompatible with U.S. interests. In fact, as a senator in the 1950s, Kennedy "blasted the Eisenhower administration's 'head-in-the-sand' attitude toward Arab nationalism."[47]

But the Kennedy-Nasser duet faltered, and ultimately failed. In September 1962, pro-Nasser forces overthrew the medieval government of Yemen, which occupied a crucial piece of real estate strategically positioned on the southern flank of Saudi Arabia astride the Red Sea and the Indian Ocean. At the time, Kennedy said, "I don't even know where it is."[48] The leader of Yemen in 1962 was Imam Ahmad, a decrepit, 300-pound autocrat with a reputation for brutality. He thought of himself as the "protector of God's religion," and he denounced Nasser's economic program as "un-Islamic."[49] When he died, rebels backed by Nasser overthrew his equally reactionary son, Mohammed al-Badr. According to Seelye, Nasser "was behind the overthrow of the regime, and Saudi Arabia was very, very upset."[50] The revolution in Yemen, soon backed by the arrival of thousands of Egyptian troops, posed a threat to the very existence of Saudi Arabia. Robert Komer, the White House aide for Middle East policy, warned Kennedy, "The House of Saud well knows it could be next."[51] Saudi Arabia, alarmed, lent arms and money to the Yemeni monarchists. The subsequent war left 200,000 dead in nearly a decade of fighting.

Kennedy had already been warned, by the CIA and others, that Saudi Arabia's regime might not last long, and that Nasser was likely the Arab world's future. Initially, he tried to be even-handed, recognizing the new government of Yemen and sending Ellsworth Bunker to mediate a settlement between Egypt and Saudi Arabia. But pressure mounted on Kennedy from all directions. The British, still clinging to their precarious perch in the Arab Gulf and Aden, were again (as during the Suez Crisis) apoplectic about Nasser. Prime Minister Harold Macmillan, who'd been in the British government during Suez, wanted to "tear Nasser's scalp off with his fingernails."[52] They immediately devised a scheme with Israel's secret service, the Mossad, to aid the anti-Nasser forces in Yemen by supplying them with arms and financial help. "MI6's former vice-chief, George Young, who was now a banker with Kleinwort Benson, was approached by Mossad to find an Englishman acceptable to the Saudis to run a guerrilla war against the [Yemeni] republicans and their Egyptian backers," wrote Dorril. "'I can find you a Scotsman,' replied Young. He then introduced McLean to Brigadier Dan Hiram, the Israeli defense attaché, who promised to supply weapons, funds, and instructors who could pass themselves off as Arabs, a strategy that the Saudis eagerly grasped."[53] Israel drew on its population of Yemeni Jews, who had immigrated to Israel and who could pass themselves off as Yemeni Arabs, and dispatched them to the war zone where they served as military instructors. According to Dorril: "The CIA helped the Israelis infiltrate back into Yemen some of these Jews to train the guerrillas in the use of modern weapons. The trainers, naturally, took care to disguise their true nationality." Both Iran's SAVAK secret service and Saudi Arabian intelligence were witting members of the anti-Nasser front in Yemen. Israel also contributed arms to the rebels, including Soviet-made weapons it had seized in conflicts with the Arab states. "The CIA and MI6 relied on . . . 'practical-minded members of the Saudi royal family' to develop a covert alliance between Israel, Saudi Arabia, Iran, and Jordan."[54] According to Howard Teicher, a pro-Israeli U.S. official, the Israeli air force also intervened on behalf of Saudi Arabia against Egypt, during the war in Yemen. "Israeli warplanes," wrote Teicher, "flew south over the Red Sea to signal unambiguously to the Egyptians to keep their distance from Saudi Arabia."[55]

In Washington, the British urged Kennedy to take a stand against Nasser. Further pressure on Kennedy came, of course, from Israel. During the war in Yemen, the Israelis tried to reinforce those in Washington who saw Nasser as a tool in a Soviet scheme to control the Persian Gulf, and Israel cast itself as America's most reliable anti-communist ally in the region.

Yet more pressure came from the big U.S. oil companies, who were alarmed over the threat that Nasser posed to their cash cow, Saudi

Arabia. Aides to Kennedy were swamped with lobbying from the Aramco partners and Gulf Oil. The latter company was represented by Kermit Roosevelt, who told the White House that U.S. interests and Nasser's "are simply incompatible." JFK sent a former Aramco executive, Terry Duce, to meet with King Faisal on his behalf.[56] And Kennedy began to run operations against Egypt in and around Yemen. "Kennedy," says former ambassador Charles Freeman, "was screwing around with all sorts of covert operations and the Green Berets in Arabia."[57]

Kennedy's overture to Nasser was over. More important, the United States had squarely set itself against a central goal of Arab nationalists: to unite Egypt and other oil-poor Arab nations with Saudi Arabia's vast wealth. "The Saudi kingdom has always been wary of any Arab unification scheme," wrote Shireen Hunter. "The Arab nationalists believed, for example, that the oil of Saudi Arabia and other oil-rich Arab states belonged to the Arab nation and not only to the oil producers and should be used for Arab economic development and be at the service of achieving its other goals. . . . Thus the Arab radicals posed an existential threat to Saudi Arabia."[58] In retrospect, it is possible to ask: What might have happened if the United States had supported or tolerated Nasser, and had allowed Saudi Arabia to fall to Nasser? In the 1960s, in the midst of the Cold War, it was an unthinkable option.

The Johnson administration vigorously reinforced the U.S.-Saudi alliance. King Faisal was lionized by LBJ, who offered military assistance and technical help to the Saudi ruler, who'd replaced the discredited King Saud at the start of the Yemen war. A $400 million Anglo-American air defense program was launched in Saudi Arabia, along with a massive scheme to build military bases and other infrastructure and a $100 million U.S. program to supply Saudi Arabia with trucks and military transport vehicles.[59]

The U.S. support for Saudi Arabia tacitly backed a vast international effort by King Faisal to rally Muslim support in the Cold War. In 1965, Faisal began a frenetic tour of Muslim countries to find allies, describing Marxism as "a subversive creed originated by a vile Jew."[60] He was ever more determined to stamp it out. He joined the shah in calling for a grand Islamic alliance, and visited Jordan, Sudan,

Pakistan, Turkey, Morocco, Guinea, and Mali in 1966 to drum up support.

In Jordan, he wailed that "the powers of evil have planned to fight Islam and Muslims wherever they are" and are "trying to kill every sign of Islamic influence."[61] In Sudan, he proclaimed: "As for the communists, they are attacking us because the Islamic movement is going to destroy all that communism stands for, in particular, disbelief in the Almighty God." Noting that the USSR contained Muslim territories, he added: "The Communists fear the expansion of our movement because it will reach the Islamic territories that have fallen under their oppressive domination."[62] In Pakistan, he issued a clarion call for an Islamic bloc despite the fact that Islam "is facing many undercurrents that are pulling Moslems left and right."[63] Pakistan, a right-wing Islamic state that was part of two formal alliances with the West, sent troops to stabilize Saudi Arabia from both internal and external threats. Beginning in the early 1960s, Pakistani army officers had taken up posts in Saudi Arabia's armed forces, as trainers and commanders. One of them was General Zia ul-Haq, who in 1977 would mount an Islamist coup d'état against Zulfiqar Ali Bhutto.[64]

Though Faisal's campaign for Islamic solidarity drew support among right-wing Islamic states—even the shah, no fan of Islamic fundamentalism, favored it—it was seen by Egypt, Syria, and Iraq as threatening. But Faisal's Islamic bloc was viewed favorably by London and Washington. In 1966, a political officer in the British embassy in Saudi Arabia explicitly endorsed Faisal's efforts, adding that the United States was in accord, too:

> I take the relaxed view of Faisal's activities. . . . The American embassy here, with whom we have discussed the subject at several levels, share this view. That is to say that the concept of Islam as an aggressive force has completely disappeared except among some older Saudis.[65]

After all, he wrote approvingly, the Saudi enmity was directed only against communism, Zionism, and a handful of Christian missionaries.

As Faisal's star rose, Nasser's fell. The crushing end to Nasser's appeal came in 1967, when, in six devastating days of war, Israel defeated Egypt, Syria, Jordan, and their allies, occupying Jerusalem and parts of all three countries, including the Sinai peninsula. Nasser would live for another three years, but the 1967 war sapped Arab nationalism's vitality. "Nasser was able to retool anti-colonialism and excite people, but the 1967 war blew that myth totally, because he lost, and not only lost, but lost miserably," says David Long. "I was in Jeddah, and my boss, the political counselor, said to me: 'That's the end of Nasser.' "[66]

Faisal, now with clear American backing, redoubled his efforts to organize a bloc of Islamic states, touring as far afield as Indonesia, Algeria, Afghanistan, and Malaysia. "Faisal," wrote the authors of *The House of Saud*, "had become more demented than ever about the 'Zionist-Bolshevist' conspiracy."[67] His efforts came to fruition in 1969, in part thanks to the actions of a mentally unbalanced Australian who attempted to set fire to Jerusalem's Al Aqsa mosque. Whether this was a convenient provocation or deliberately staged as an excuse to mobilize Islamic militancy, King Faisal eagerly seized on it, summoning leaders of the Islamic world to Rabat, Morocco, for what would be the world's first Islamic summit conference. Because the imagery of Al Aqsa was so strong, even Egypt felt compelled to attend Faisal's triumphant gathering.[68] Although Syria and Iraq boycotted the meeting, twenty-five nations attended. The summit resolved to create the Organization of the Islamic Conference, an ever-expanding mini–United Nations for the Islamic world, which rapidly moved Islamism to the center of the agenda in country after country: in Pakistan, in Afghanistan, in Turkey, and among the Arabs.

Nominally anti-Israel, Faisal's real goal was to forge a broad Islamic front against the Soviet Union. "By the late 1960s we're still fighting communism, so we reinforced Faisal's support for the Muslim Brotherhood and pan-Islam," says David Long. "We needed them against any allies that Moscow could conjure up. If Saudi Arabia could help create an institutionalized Islamic consensus, so much the better."

Long, a perceptive analyst with a strong sense of irony, says that despite the fact that it was glaringly obvious, most U.S. policy makers and analysts had little or no appreciation of the potentially explosive nature of the Islamic resurgence. "We didn't see Islam. We saw Saudi Arabia," he says. "Pan-Islam was not, to us, seen as a strategic threat. There were bad guys doing bad things to people on the left, to Nasser. They were fighting the pinkos. So we didn't see pan-Islam as a threat."

In 1970, working as an analyst at the State Department's Bureau of Intelligence and Research, Long had an inkling that the energy of pan-Islam might be channeled into anti-Americanism one day, but no one was listening:

> I was at INR in 1970, and I tried to write about Islam. But there was no market for it. I felt that there was still a body of disenchanted, disaffected people who were still focused on anti-colonialism, even though the 1967 war had shattered the myth of Nasser. I saw increasing disillusionment with Arab nationalism, but most people didn't see it. Sooner or later, I felt that these guys would latch on to something, and that that something might be Islam, since they were still disaffected. I just felt that Islam would be the new paradigm, but the higher-ups were still following the old script. I was sensing that disillusionment with Arab nationalism and Nasserism was setting in. I became profoundly suspicious that there would not be a follow-on to Nasser, to create the transnational movement that would appeal to the malcontents. I didn't see anyone coming along, except Islam.[69]

The Arab defeat in the 1967 war encouraged an Islamic resurgence. The Arabs' crushing loss raised critical questions about the future of the Arab world. It provoked inchoate anger among the population of the countries involved, and it led to enormous turmoil in Arab politics. On the one hand, between 1967 and 1970, several Arab regimes fell to left-leaning nationalists. Hafez Assad took over Syria, Muammar Qaddafi ousted Libya's king, Jaafar Numeiri seized power in Sudan, the Arab Baath Socialist Party rose to power in Iraq, and the Palestinians came close to toppling Jordan's King Hussein in the uprising culminating in Black September 1970. Some of these leaders cited Nasser as a hero and role model.

But another ideology was seeking to replace Nasser-style national-ism: Islamism.

The seeming inability of the Arabs to compete with Israel and the loss of more Arab territory (the Sinai peninsula, Gaza, the Golan Heights, and the West Bank) were stinging blows. Nasser's enemies, including the Muslim Brotherhood, used them against him, charging that Nasserism and Arab socialism had failed. They began preaching about a return to Islam as the solution to the Arab world's ills. It was a timeless message, delivered in the past by Jamal Eddine al-Afghani and Hassan al-Banna. But in the wake of the 1967 debacle, it res-onated with millions of angry Arabs.

Watching Iraq, Libya, and Sudan fall to rebels, both Saudi Arabia and the United States were desperate to contain the spiraling changes in the Arab world, not least to deflect the growing strength of the Palestinian movement and the Palestine Liberation Organization. Saudi Arabia bet on conservative Islam as the antidote to Nasserism, and the United States went along.

Three years later, in the midst of the Black September civil war in Jordan, Nasser died. He was replaced by Anwar Sadat. Sadat's eleven-year career as president of Egypt was, from the standpoint of Washing-ton and Riyadh, a real blessing. The wily ex–Muslim Brotherhood member and longtime Nasser aide struck up an alliance with Saudi Arabia, suppressed Egypt's left, brought the Muslim Brotherhood tri-umphantly back to Cairo, and finally realigned Egypt with the United States and Israel. Sadat would change the course of history. And for all that, he would die at the hands of Islamist assassins.

6

THE SORCERER'S APPRENTICE

IN THE 1970S, guided by Kamal Adham, Saudi Arabia's chief of intelligence, Anwar Sadat brought the Muslim Brotherhood back to Egypt. The United States, accustomed to working with Saudi Arabia, was untroubled by the rise of Islamism in Egypt. In fact, Washington was so eager to work with Anwar Sadat to bring Egypt over to the U.S. side in the Cold War that policy makers, diplomats, and intelligence officers viewed Sadat's restoration of the Islamic right benignly or tacitly encouraged it.

But Sadat had opened a Pandora's box. Once freed, the Brotherhood knew no bounds. Back in their ancestral home, the Brothers worked feverishly to spread their influence worldwide. The consequences were profound, and deadly—not least for the Egyptian president himself.

Concurrent with the growth of the Islamic right in Egypt, Sadat helped engineer a dramatic expansion of America's power in the Middle East. Under Nasser, Egypt was a nation at odds with the United States. Twenty thousand Soviet troops, technicians, and advisers backed Egypt's armed forces; a war of attrition was under way along the Egypt-Israel border; and Egypt and the United States lacked even normal diplomatic ties. But Sadat established a covert relationship with Adham, the CIA, and Henry Kissinger, the U.S. national security adviser. In 1971, within a year of assuming control, Sadat ousted the Egyptian left from the government, and in 1972 he stunned Moscow by expelling the Soviet forces. After the 1973 Ramadan War—waged in concert with Saudi Arabia and organized around Islamic themes rather than Arab nationalism—Egypt and the United States reestablished ties. In 1977, Sadat flew to Jerusalem, splitting the Arab world and opening negotiations with Israel that led to the Camp David Egypt-Israel agreement. By 1980, Egypt was America's leading Arab ally, engaged in supporting the U.S. jihad in Afghanistan and providing a base for U.S. influence in the oil-rich Persian Gulf. For even the most cynical U.S. Middle East specialists, the change in Egypt, from foe to ally, was dizzying.

At the beginning, few expected very much from Sadat. For thirty years, he had operated in Nasser's shadow. He'd been a member of the Muslim Brotherhood and played the role of intermediary in the intrigue between the palace, the Brotherhood, and the Free Officers movement. After Nasser's coup, Sadat served as the Egyptian leader's liaison to the Brotherhood, then functioned as Egypt's unofficial ambassador to Islamists worldwide. But to Egyptians and to U.S. officials, Sadat never seemed to be more than a second banana. After Nasser's death, in October 1970, Sadat was widely seen as a placeholder who would be ousted after a behind-the-scenes struggle for power in Cairo. "In the United States, expectations of Sadat were zip," says David Long, a former U.S. foreign service officer. "He was the bumbling vice president."[1]

In his autobiography, *In Search of Identity,* Sadat wrote that when American envoy Elliott Richardson returned home to Washington after visiting Cairo to offer condolences on Nasser's death, he predicted that Sadat "wouldn't survive in power for more than four or six weeks."[2] Inside Egypt, Sadat faced formidable opponents, including Nasser-style nationalists, who were deeply suspicious of Sadat, and communist-leaning or pro-Soviet officials. Sadat himself had no real political base or constituency. Yet not only did Sadat survive, he succeeded in engineering a complete about-face in Egypt's foreign and domestic policies. Where Nasser had forged ties to Syria, Iraq, and

Algeria, Sadat embraced the conservative monarchies of Saudi Arabia and the Gulf. Where Nasser relied on the Soviet Union for arms and maintained a nonaligned posture internationally, Sadat broke Egypt's ties to the USSR and enrolled Egypt in America's Cold War bloc. And where Nasser promoted Egypt as a Third World leader along with Yugoslavia, India, and African and Latin American nations, Sadat implemented an Egypt-centered, go-it-alone foreign policy.

Sadat consolidated his shaky rule by unleashing the power of the Islamic right as a hammer against the left, with the generous financial assistance of Saudi Arabia. Though Nasser had suppressed the Muslim Brotherhood and fought to reduce the power of right-wing Islamism in Egypt, Sadat welcomed the exiled Muslim Brotherhood back to Egypt, reinvigorated the organization, and built its institutional presence within the universities, professional associations, and the media. Before Sadat, the Islamists were for the most part fringe-dwelling, marginalized radicals; after Sadat, the Muslim Brotherhood and its even more radical youth wing were part of mainstream political discourse in Egypt.

People who traveled even casually to Egypt during the 1970s were struck by this thorough transformation. In the schools, in the streets, in the mosques, in the press, there were manifestations of the growing presence of Islamic fundamentalism. Michael Dunn, editor of the *Middle East Journal,* says that he could not help but be amazed by the shift during the mid-1970s. "In Egypt things changed dramatically," he says. "People were wearing beards everywhere. There were things called Muslim Brotherhood magazines or newspapers. People were wearing white *djellabas.* The mosques were overflowing, with people spilling out into the streets."[3] Students flocked to join Islamist groups, and thousands of new mosques were constructed. Muslim Brotherhood–linked banks and businesses sprouted, and phalanxes of Islamist thugs emerged to intimidate political opponents.

But for Sadat, it was a fatal embrace.

Initially, the Islamic right served as Sadat's allies. Gradually, however, more and more of them turned against him, especially after the Egyptian-Israeli accord. In Egypt, Sadat underestimated the depth and virulence of the growing Islamist opposition, especially among its terrorist factions. In the United States, the State Department and the CIA failed to pay sufficient attention to the danger from the Islamic right in Egypt, relying instead on assurances from the Egyptians that it was under control. By the time Sadat was assassinated in 1981 by members of a militant Muslim Brotherhood offshoot, a violent Islamist underground was flourishing. Other Egyptian officials were assassinated, tourists massacred, Christians attacked, and secular Egyptian intellectuals murdered or silenced.

Once again, Egypt would be the Muslim Brotherhood's chief base of operations.

SADAT UNCAGES THE BROTHERS

No one was more closely connected to Anwar Sadat's reconstruction of Egyptian politics than Kamal Adham, the chief of Saudi intelligence. Adham, secretly working the back channels to Henry Kissinger, U.S. secretary of state and national security adviser, was busily setting the stage for America's Cold War empire in the Middle East.

Even before Nasser's death, Saudi Arabia, Kuwait, and other wealthy Gulf states had stepped in after Egypt's defeat in 1967, offering promises of financial aid to the battered country as a way of strengthening political ties. Saudi Arabia quietly began to back the Brotherhood in Egypt. The Muslim Brotherhood blamed Nasser's alleged lack of piety and suppression of Islam for the reverses suffered in the war, and they began agitating against Nasser. "The Saudi campaign made itself felt at a time of student unrest in Cairo in the summer of 1969," wrote Reinhard Schulze. "For the first time in years, oppositionists openly appeared as 'Muslim Brothers' and demanded a more definite fight against left-wing and communist activities."[4]

After Nasser died, Faisal maintained a lingering suspicion of Sadat, but Adham worked hard to convince the king, ever on the lookout for Zionist-Bolshevik conspiracies, that Sadat was not another Nasser. Adham had close ties to both Faisal and Sadat. As the brother of Faisal's wife Iffat, the spy chief led a group of senior advisers who argued that Sadat's membership in the Muslim Brotherhood indicated, at the very least, a "right-wing temperament."[5] At the same time, the wily Adham had business ties to Sadat, recognizing that the Egyptian president had a taste for the finer things in life and letting Sadat know that Saudi Arabia could provide them. In the 1960s, the Saudi intelligence chief had formed a series of profitable joint business ventures with Anwar Sadat's wife, Jihan, giving the new Egyptian leader a personal stake in better ties between Cairo and Riyadh.[6] King Faisal designated Adham as his go-between, and less than a month after Nasser died, Faisal sent Adham to Cairo. Apparently, Adham arrived not only with promises of Saudi aid, but also with a secret American assurance that Washington would help Egypt get its land back from Israel, if Sadat would only break with Moscow and order the withdrawal of the Soviet forces from Egypt.[7]

By early 1971, Adham had become a ubiquitous presence in the Egyptian capital. Mohammed Heikal, the pro-Nasser journalist and editor of *Al Ahram,* who was appointed minister of information in 1970 but resigned from government in 1974 over differences with Sadat, observed, "This was not something to reassure the Russians."[8] Not only was Adham acting as an intermediary for Faisal, but he was also secretly working as a conduit for communications between Sadat and Kissinger.[9] In his memoirs, Kissinger describes the connection, noting that the Saudi role allowed Sadat and Nixon to stay in touch while "bypassing both foreign ministries."[10] At the time, the United States had no embassy in Cairo; Egypt, like most Arab countries, had broken diplomatic relations with the United States after the 1967 war. Saudi Arabia had not. So in effect, Saudi Arabia was the broker for U.S.-Egyptian relations in the early 1970s.

In May 1971, Sadat took the first step in consolidating power and purging the government of its Nasserists. Claiming to have evidence of a plot to assassinate him by Nasser-era officials, whom Sadat called "Soviet agents," Sadat struck. Joined by Ashraf Marwan, a wily Egyptian bureaucrat who was a close friend of Adham's, Sadat arrested the speaker of the National Assembly, the war minister, the information minister, the minister of presidential affairs, members of the Central Committee, and other senior officials, whose "inane socialist slogans" were "at variance . . . with our religious faith."[11]

Sadat called it "the Second Revolution." A year later, coordinating with Adham, Sadat ordered the expulsion of Soviet forces.

"Kamal Adham persuaded Sadat to kick the Russians out of Egypt," says the CIA's Raymond Close, who worked closely with Adham.[12] Sadat, of course, was already predisposed to do so. But Adham offered cash and Islamist backing.

On Sadat's invitation, and with Kamal Adham's and King Faisal's support, key members of the exiled Muslim Brotherhood leadership began returning to Egypt. In addition, after 1971 Sadat freed large numbers of Brotherhood prisoners. Many of them were angry and even more committed to violence and secretive underground organizing, and immediately disappeared to build their movement. Others, particularly those of the older generation, sought to establish themselves as overt allies of the new Egyptian president. Omar Telmassani, freed in 1971, was a lawyer and future editor of *The Call*, the Muslim Brotherhood's journal, who would eventually become the organization's supreme guide. Upon his release, he went directly to Sadat's presidential palace to inscribe his thanks, along with those of other members of the Muslim Brotherhood, in the public registry.[13]

The Islamic Community

Throughout the decade, the Muslim Brotherhood metastasized and divided into various factions and competing currents. On the surface at least, the old guard appeared to put a premium on moderation. Many of the older Muslim Brotherhood officials who'd fled to Saudi Arabia returned to Egypt as prosperous and well-connected businessmen. In contrast, fiery younger members, especially those on campuses, spun off mini–Muslim Brotherhood clubs and organizations. These groups, with the full support of Sadat and the Egyptian security and intelligence services, proliferated rapidly. Soon they became known as the Islamic Community.[14] Because Sadat did not formally legalize the Muslim Brotherhood organization, the movement spread willy-nilly, with no central leadership.

For the Egyptian leader, supporting the growth of these proto–Islamic Community groups on campuses was merely one more way of using Islam to consolidate his power. "To escape living in Nasser's shadow, Sadat shifted gears and made strong appeals to Islam," according to John Esposito. He added:

> Sadat assumed the title of the Believer-President, an allusion to the Islamic caliph's titled Commander of the Faithful. He began and ended his speeches with verses from the Quran. TV broadcasts frequently featured him in a mosque, cameras zeroing in on his prominent prayer mark, a callus caused by touching the forehead to the ground in prayer.[15]

Islamic Community student gangs received behind-the-scenes support from Sadat's secret police. "After December 1972 the fortunes of the Islamist students took a turn for the better," wrote Kepel. "They finally found the key to success: discreet, tactical collaboration with the regime to break the left's domination of the campuses."[16] Like Islamist groups everywhere, they used heavy-handed tactics, violence, and intimidation against their opponents, and they often had significant financial backing from Saudi Arabia and from right-wing Egyptian businessmen. "The *jama'at islamiyya* [Islamic Community] were Islamist student associations that became the dominant force on Egyptian university campuses during Sadat's presidency," wrote Kepel. "They constituted the Islamist movement's only genuine mass organizations." Soon chants of "Democracy!" clashed with "*Allahu Akbar!*" in student demonstrations. A few years later, the Islamic Community groups had virtually seized control of universities in Egypt and forced the left-wing groups into hiding.[17]

One of Sadat's aides played a critical role in getting the Islamic Community up and running. Mohammed Uthman Ismail, a former lawyer, had in 1971 worked closely with the Egyptian president as he outmaneuvered and then locked up his opponents on the left. Ismail is "considered to have acted as the godfather of the *jama'at islamiyya*, in Cairo from late 1971 and throughout Middle Egypt beginning in 1973."[18] In 1973, Ismail was appointed governor of Asyut, long a stronghold of the Islamists, from which post he continued to urge the Islamic Community groups to "fight against the communists." Reminiscent of the early days of the Muslim Brotherhood, when the muscular Rovers and the terrorist Secret Apparatus grew out of athletic camps for boys and young men, the 1970s-era Islamic Community organized government-sponsored summer camps. The first one was held at Cairo University in 1973, where Sadat sent a high government official to signal the regime's support. The camps were held with increasing frequency over the next several years. In 1974 Sadat reorganized the rules governing the Egyptian Student Union, to allow the Islamic Community to take over that important institution. One government decree declared that henceforth the chief purpose of the Student Union would be "to deepen religious values among the students." The takeover of the Student Union would be only the first of many: professional associations of doctors, lawyers, engineers, and other guilds would soon fall, too, and, of course, the redoubt of Al Azhar would be captured by the right once again, ending the role it had been developing as a more balanced, and non-fundamentalist, Islamic center. In 1973, the Muslim World League, that powerful instrument of Saudi Islamization efforts, concluded a pact with Al Azhar, pulling that venerable institution into the orbit of the Wahhabis.[19] That same year, Sadat also created the post of deputy prime minister for religious affairs and established a Supreme Committee for Introducing Legislation According to the Sharia. Islamists introduced bills in the National Assembly to prohibit alcohol, to use sharia-based punishments, and for mandatory teaching of religion in schools.[20]

An astute observer of that period, Abdel Moneim Said, director of Egypt's Al Ahram Center for Political and Strategic Studies, says that the influence of Saudi Arabia in Egypt during the early 1970s was pervasive. Many Egyptians went to work in Saudi Arabia, and returned having imbibed conservative, Wahhabi theology, he says. Saudi Arabia also lavishly funded Egyptian institutions, desperate for funding. "It moved Al Azhar to the right, and to publish extremely conservative views. Many Saudi Arabian NGOs donated money to Egyptian mosques, and that was also moving them to the right," says Said. "And many Egyptian journalists were on the Saudi payroll, secretly, of course."

According to Said, the Saudi influence also had an effect on Egyptian law. "Egyptian judicial thinking changed—from the 1920s to the 1960s it was so moderate, enlightened," he says. "But by the 1970s, those who'd been to the Gulf started coming back and brought with them a narrow-minded interpretation of the law. Egyptian perceptions of Saudi Arabia were changing, too. Saudi Arabia always feared the impact of Egypt on Saudi Arabia, but now it was working in reverse. Habits began to change, ways of thinking about life, about separation of males and females," he says.[21]

The Ramadan War

In October 1973, Anwar Sadat launched a surprise attack, coordinated with Syria, on Israeli-occupied Egyptian and Syrian territory. It turned out to be an abject military failure, but a resounding political success. And, because it was laden with Muslim themes and begun during Ramadan, the holiest month in the Islamic calendar, the war ratcheted up the level of Islamist fervor in Egypt.

After some initial battlefield victories, during which Egyptian troops crossed the Suez Canal and advanced against Israeli forces in the Sinai peninsula, Egypt suffered massive reverses when Israel's Ariel Sharon struck back. The Israelis surrounded and cut off an entire Egyptian army on the western side of the canal, precipitating a U.S.-USSR confrontation, a worldwide nuclear alert, and a crisis that was perhaps the closest the world came to Armageddon during the Cold War.

But for Sadat the war had important consequences. First, it led to an engagement with the United States to arrange the cease-fire and then the disengagement agreements, which cemented the U.S.-Egyptian alliance of the 1970s. Second, it confirmed the ties between Egypt and Saudi Arabia, which led to the Arab oil embargo of 1973–74. With its newfound, Croesus-like riches from the OPEC price increases of those years, Saudi Arabia suddenly found itself with virtually unlimited resources to advance the cause of Wahhabi fundamentalism. And third, the 1973 Arab-Israeli war burnished Sadat's Islamic credentials and bolstered the ability of the believer-president to cloak himself in the garb of a Muslim holy man fighting a holy war.

In many ways, the 1973 war marks the rebirth of the Islamist movement. Egypt referred to the October war as the "War of Ramadan," the Muslim holy month. Its troops were indoctrinated for the battle with Islamic pep talks about liberating the Al Aqsa Mosque in Jerusalem. "When Egyptian troops crossed the canal," says Hermann Eilts, the U.S. ambassador, "they were shouting '*Allahu Akbar.*'"[22]

Symbolically, the 1973 war was designed to avenge the 1967 defeat. That war, implied Sadat's propagandists, marked the failure of Nasserism and Arab socialism. The imams had long decried the 1967 defeat as one brought on by Nasser's lack of piety and his disparagement of Islam. In contrast, and to rally the support of the Islamic right, Sadat portrayed the mythical triumph of the 1973 war as a sign of Islam's power. Despite the fact that the Ramadan War had not defeated Israel, and despite the fact that Egypt nearly suffered the catastrophic loss of an entire army, the Egyptian crossing of the Suez Canal was touted as a landmark event. Desperate for a victory, conservative Muslims worldwide compared the Ramadan War to the great military victories of Islam's first centuries, when Muslim rule was extended to Central Asia and Spain and its armies hammered at the gates of France and Austria. It's safe to say that Sadat didn't expect to conquer Israel, or even to liberate the Sinai. Sadat's war was planned as a "limited" war, with strictly political motivations. To this day, it's unknown whether or not some U.S. officials deliberately plotted with Sadat, or at least tolerated his saber-rattling, in order to complete the Cold War reorientation of Egypt—at Israel's expense. What is certain, however, is that the CIA was fully aware of Sadat's war plans, and so was Kamal Adham, the Saudi intelligence chief. Indeed, months before the war was launched, Adham and the Saudi intelligence service outlined for the CIA the plan for the Ramadan War, including Saudi Arabia's decision to use the so-called oil weapon, and the CIA station in Saudi Arabia dutifully reported all this to Washington.[23]

Martha Kessler, one of the CIA's most perceptive analysts of political Islam, says that the war marked a turning point. "The 1973 Arab-Israeli war was fought under the banner of Islam, and that period marks the serious disillusionment in the Arab world with European ideas, including communism, Baathism, and Nasserism," she says.

"None of these ideas were very inspired in the first place, and more important, weren't working. So the idea to base that war on Islam was very intentional: units were renamed, call signals changed, and so on, all to reflect Islamic themes. I mark the rise of political Islam, at least for this cycle, with the war."[24]

But the return of political Islam to Egypt proved double-edged. Underneath the piety, conservative dress, and sharia-style juridical rulings, unbeknownst either to Sadat or to the CIA, dangerous new forces were gathering momentum.

The Qutb Factor

Toward the end of the 1970s, and especially after Sadat made his trip to Jerusalem and began talking to Israel, the Islamic right became increasingly radicalized and many of them moved into outright opposition to Sadat—or plotted secretly. While backing the Islamists might have seemed like a clever idea to Sadat at the time, it was too clever by half. Even as the militants of Egypt's Islamic Community battered Sadat's political rivals on the left, they fell increasingly under the spell of radical, independent new imams who preached not only an anti-communist message, but an anti-Western one.

The first inkling that something might be wrong came as early as 1974, when a gang of Islamists, mostly Egyptians but led by a Palestinian, sparked a bloody uprising at the military's Technical College, an event that was supposed to have led to the assassination of Sadat. Many were killed, and more arrested, and Sadat officially blamed the revolt on Libya. Its leader, Salih Sirriya, was from a small town near Haifa, Israel, which was the birthplace of the founder of the Islamic Liberation Party, a far-right group dedicated to restoring the Islamic caliphate, and which had close ties to Said Ramadan and the Muslim Brotherhood. Sirriya was, most likely, an adherent of the Liberation Party.[25] According to Gilles Kepel,

> Sirriya lived in Jordan until 1970. He then spent a year in Iraq, but finally had to flee Baghdad, where he was sentenced in absentia in 1972 for membership in the party. He then moved to Cairo. When

he arrived in Cairo Sirriya began frequenting the Muslim Brethren, especially Supreme Guide Hudaybi and Zaynab al-Ghazali, the movement's *passionaria*. He won her confidence and had regular discussions with her.[26]

According to Said, when Egyptian investigators examined the events at the college, they found disturbing signs of profound, underlying shifts among the cadets. "When they did a review," he says, "they found things had been changing at the Technical College: much more praying, separation of groups, signs of extremism." But so intent was Sadat on mobilizing Islamic fervor that neither Egypt's intelligence service nor the CIA picked up on the trend.[27] "The leader of the Muslim Brotherhood at the time was a man named Telmassani, who had been in jail, whom Sadat had freed, and freed on the understanding that they would—well, let me use the term 'behave,'" says Eilts. "And they did. Occasionally there would be an article in one of the Muslim Brotherhood publications that would criticize the government, and it would be closed for a month, and Sadat felt that the question of controlling the reemergence of the Muslim Brotherhood organization was no great problem."[28]

But while the official Muslim Brotherhood remained ostensibly docile, the underground and student-based Islamic Community groups and offshoots were preparing for war. Over the next years, these militants would patiently build their forces in Egypt, occasionally engaging in spectacular violence or assassinations. "Many Islamists began to live alone, to go out to the desert, to build their movement," says Said. "Egyptian intelligence missed it."[29] In 1977, Islamic terrorists assassinated the Egyptian minister of religious endowments, and began to face repression and arrest, yet they continued to proliferate. When Sadat stunned Egypt by going to Jerusalem in 1977 to seek a deal with Menachem Begin, the Israeli prime minister, Egypt's Islamists—including the Brothers and the Islamic Community gangs—would move toward even more militant opposition.

Many of Egypt's Islamic radicals were followers of Sayyid Qutb, who was hanged by Nasser in 1966. During the 1960s, Qutb had developed a radical theory that compared Muslims who did not follow the ultra-orthodox views he espoused to the barbarian nomads of Arabia who existed in a state of "ignorance" before the arrival of the prophet. Qutb and his followers used this theory as a justification for assassination of Arab leaders who were less than devout. Although Qutb's theories were confused and inconsistent, some Western Orientalists hailed him as a thoughtful critic of secularism in the Middle East. It was Qutb, and his book, *Signposts,* that inspired the most radical (and the most violent) Egyptian Islamists, mostly outside the purview of both Egyptian intelligence and the CIA.

According to Eilts, Sadat failed to see any danger in encouraging radical-right Islamic groups, but some others in his immediate circle did, including his wife, Jihan. "Sadat, who had been, after all, a Muslim Brother earlier, took the view that the growing influence of Islam and the Muslim Brotherhood, especially in the universities, was no more than young people expressing their views," says Eilts. But he adds: "I remember many people, including his wife, saying, 'You have to watch these people,' and saying that they are dangerous, and he would just wave his hand and say, 'Oh, they are just young people.' He simply did not believe that their interest in religion and the Muslim Brotherhood represented a threat, and he could not be persuaded by some of his ministers that they were."[30]

So, too, few U.S. diplomats or CIA officers truly understood the depth of the Muslim Brotherhood's penetration of Egyptian society in the late 1970s, nor did they grasp the fuzzy relationship among the official Muslim Brotherhood, the Islamic Community, and the underground groups and followers of Qutb. Eilts, along with U.S. intelligence officers in Egypt, observed the Islamicization of Egypt, but found it hard to read. After all, Sadat was encouraging it, and the Egyptian leader seemed to believe that it was both useful and ultimately harmless. "There was an awareness that some elements of the religious movement were troublesome," says Eilts. "I took the view that it was something that had to be watched carefully." But Eilts believed that the Egyptian government could control the phenomenon, and that the more established, conservative leaders of the Muslim Brotherhood, such as Telmassani, were averse to violent tactics and militant actions. "Telmassani denounced [the radicals], but did he mean it?" asks Eilts, rhetorically. The ambassador believed that there was an overlap between the Muslim Brotherhood leadership and the militants, but he couldn't be sure. "It was hard to tell," he says. "So one had to rely to some extent on the judgment of the president, and the ministers."[31]

The CIA hardly fared better. A senior CIA official who spent many years in the Middle East, including several years in Cairo in the 1970s, says that some of Egypt's own intelligence people warned him not to underestimate the danger from the Islamists. "I had a good friend, a senior Egyptian intelligence officer, who once told me: 'You people have got to understand the power of the mosque. We are going to lose control, and people will believe only in the mosque.'"[32] Kathy Christison, who joined the CIA in 1971 and headed the CIA's Egypt desk from 1973 to 1977, says that the potential danger of Islamism in Egypt during those years wasn't something that the agency worried about. "I'd heard about the Muslim Brotherhood, of course, but there was very little emphasis on Islam," she says. "It was very easy to ignore Islam at the time."[33] There is no question that a major reason why the Islamic right in Egypt was ignored is because American intelligence and policy officials had for decades seen fit to view Islamism as an anti-Soviet force.

Eilts says that during his tenure as ambassador, from 1974—when Egypt and the United States reestablished diplomatic ties—until 1979, it was difficult for the embassy and the CIA to meet with or otherwise contact the Islamists, especially those who were now starting to adopt explicitly anti-government positions. "The government took a dim view of open contacts between the United States and opposition forces, on the grounds that it would encourage the opposition forces to believe that they were supported by the United States," says Eilts. "So one had to handle these things very carefully, meeting these people at receptions given by others." During Kissinger's shuttle diplomacy in the wake of the 1973 Arab-Israeli War, Eilts says, the United States promised Sadat that the CIA would not act clandestinely against Egypt. "So that limited the intelligence that we could get," he adds. "You can talk about covert contacts [with Islamists], but it's a little hard to get them arranged."[34]

Besides, the CIA wasn't exactly well equipped to go hobnobbing with bearded, radical Egyptian imams and violence-oriented Islamic Community activists. Reflecting a problem that has plagued the CIA for decades, the agency lacked the requisite skills: few non-Western case officers, few fluent Arabic speakers, few people with credentials in Islamic history and culture. One CIA officer who served in the Middle East, and who did not want his name used, tells an illustrative story of one doomed effort to grapple with Islamism. "I remember seeing this little office, run by this red-headed officer, who told me that his office was in charge of 'penetrating fundamentalist Islam,'" he says, laughing. "And I remember thinking, Don't give me a red-headed Irishman to go out and 'penetrate' Islam. It requires a great deal of planning and strategy and understanding. I don't think there is a tougher intelligence problem to deal with, unless you're a Muslim and you can go to the mosque and talk to these people and get your hands around the problem. And we didn't do it."[35]

For the Islamic right, the 1970s was a decade of transition. The sort of Islamic fundamentalism that the United States had known since the end of World War II still existed—and still exists today. But alongside it, a new and more virulent strain was taking shape. In Egypt, it took the form of the Islamic Community's radicals, who later formed the core of Islamic Jihad, led by Ayman al-Zawahiri, Al Qaeda's number two leader. In Iran, it was represented by the ultra-militant Shiite fundamentalists who formed the radical wing of Ayatollah Khomeini's movement. And in Saudi Arabia, the austere desert home of the Wahhabi, it gave rise to Osama bin Laden and his followers, who considered even Saudi Arabia's orthodox clergy false and impious Muslim pretenders.

The State Department and the CIA failed to pick up on the transubstantiation of the Islamic right in the 1970s. Instead, they saw what they wanted to see: a political Islam that was conservative, anti-communist, and content to busy itself with the finer points of sharia as interpreted by its bearded scholars. A handful of American specialists on Islam and the Middle East argued that the Islamic right was not only anti-communist but anti-democratic, anti-Western, and prone to violence, but in the late 1970s that was a minority view.

Even after the stunning events of the next several years—the revolution in Iran, the seizure of the Grand Mosque in Mecca, Sadat's assassination, Hezbollah's truck bomb in Lebanon that killed 241 U.S. Marines—the Islamic right was still viewed as an ally, above all during the Afghan jihad.

Part of the reason why Islamism continued to have appeal in the West was the rise of Islamic economics in the 1970s. Many of the very same militants whose acolytes engaged in terrorism also wore suits, built businesses, founded banks, and appeared to all the world to be nothing more than prosperous, if pious, citizens. Yet the businesses and banks generated both profits and extremist followers of the prophet.

The Brotherhood's Bank

Besides politics, economics played a critical role in the spread of Islamism in Egypt in the 1970s. When Sadat came to power in 1970, the clamorous vested interests of the pre-Nasser ancien régime—the very same forces that the CIA had tried and failed to mobilize against Nasser in the late 1950s—saw an opportunity to restore their wealth and political connections. Many of them, especially the semi-feudal landowning families, whose power had been reduced but not eliminated, maintained close ties to the Islamic right. Indeed, across the Middle East, from Pakistan and Iran to Turkey and Egypt, the big landowning families and the *bazaar,* the wealthy merchant families, had intimate ties to Islamists. In many cases, they were family ties: a wealthy landowner, or *bazaari,* might have a brother or cousin who was an imam, mullah, or ayatollah. And they worked hand in hand.

The Brotherhood became big supporters of Sadat's plan to expand free enterprise in Egypt, and they enthusiastically joined in support of Sadat's new economic policy of openness, or *infitah.* From the outside, the *infitah* was driven by the austerity-minded demands of the International Monetary Fund. During the 1960s and 1970s, the IMF forced brutal changes in many Third World economies, as a condition for receiving international loans. These so-called conditionalities led to severe economic pain in country after country, as subsidies were eliminated, jobs lost, and industries privatized. Often, IMF policies led regimes into confrontations with the left and with labor unions. Egypt was no exception. The IMF's strict demands for austerity and cutbacks were the direct result of vigorous U.S. efforts to encourage free-enterprise economics in the Third World and to combat socialism. In Egypt, right-wing Islamists and conservative business owners quickly found common cause.

The Call, the magazine of the newly liberated Muslim Brotherhood, received substantial financial support from wealthy Egyptian rightists. Businesses capitalizing on Sadat's *infitah* policy provided the bulk of the magazine's advertising. "Out of the total of nearly 180 pages of color advertising in *al-Dawa* [*The Call*], 49 were bought by real-estate promoters and entrepreneurs, 52 by chemical and plastics companies, 20 by automobile importers, 12 by 'Islamic' banks and investment companies, and 45 by food companies," according to Gilles Kepel. Forty percent of the magazine's ads came from just three companies controlled by Muslim Brotherhood members who'd made fortunes in Saudi Arabia.[36]

Interviewed in an Egyptian weekly, the Muslim Brotherhood's Telmassani was forced to admit that "most of the commanding levers of the policy of economic opening (*infitah*) are now in the hands of former Muslim Brethren who were in exile and have now returned to Egypt."[37]

In 1974, the Muslim Brotherhood formally issued a declaration commanding its members to support Sadat's pro-IMF *infitah*. Such an action was true to form for political Islam. Throughout their history, Islamists have always been militantly pro-capitalist, opposing class-struggle politics on principle. Rarely did they rally support for the poor, the disenfranchised, or the downtrodden. In Egypt, especially, the Islamists did not make common cause with aggrieved workers or farmers who failed to benefit from Sadat's economic policies or whose livelihoods were thrown into turmoil by the *infitah*; instead, they engaged in strikebreaking, enthusiastically opposing trade unions and intellectuals allied to the left.

The rise of so-called Islamic banks was central to the Islamization of Egypt's economy. Organized on the questionable principle that ordinary commercial banks do not operate according to Islamic law, especially because that law supposedly does not allow interest to be charged on loans, Islamic banks often disparaged their non-Islamic competitors for being irreligious, and even, most offensively, for being "Jewish." They used an insidious tactic to market their services, warning that users of conventional banks were anti-Islam and were thus "destined to go directly to hell."[38]

The development of an "Islamic economy" in Egypt further encouraged the spread of political Islam. Members of the Muslim Brotherhood drew on the financial and business resources of its wealthy supporters to strengthen its social and political organizing. Wealthy members of the Islamic right and Muslim Brotherhood operatives in financial institutions directed funds to mosques, small businesses, friendly media outlets, and other ventures that bolstered the community. Because the Brotherhood operates as a clandestine fraternity, some of this could be done secretly, with a wink and a nod. Egypt's Islamic right still drew on Saudi support, but it was becoming financially independent. Says a leading Egyptian analyst, "They created many businesses and banks, and they had solidarity with each other. A Muslim Brotherhood member is happy to give half his income to the Muslim Brotherhood."[39]

The creation of the Faisal Islamic Bank of Egypt (FIBE) in 1976 reenergized the Muslim Brotherhood in that country, in tandem with Sadat's efforts to mobilize the Islamic right. The bank was the cornerstone of an empire of Islamic banks run by Prince Mohammed al-Faisal of Saudi Arabia, a son of King Faisal, and it played a decisive role in the Islamization of Egypt and the region.

By all accounts, Prince Mohammad was not a member of the Brotherhood, in keeping with the policy of the Saudi royal family to use the organization as an arm of its foreign policy, but to avoid getting too close to it. The prince tended to rely more on establishment figures, including Egypt's grand mufti, to gain legitimacy for the bank. And he won Sadat's support for a special law to charter the FIBE.[40] Among the founders of FIBE were former Egyptian prime minister Abdel Aziz Hijazi, who would move on to become a leader of the Islamic economic movement, and Uthman Ahmed Uthman, an ultra-wealthy industrialist known as "the Egyptian Rockefeller" who played a key part in bankrolling the Muslim Brotherhood's resurgence in the 1970s.[41] Influential Muslim Brotherhood members, including Yusuf al-Qaradawi, Abdel-Latif al-Sharif, and Youssef Nada all joined FIBE's early board of directors.[42] Each one of these men would play a critical role in the growth of Islamism not only in Egypt but throughout the region. And each one, in later years, would hover on the fringes of the most extreme wing of the Islamist movement. The most notorious of FIBE's founders was the blind Islamic scholar and rabble-rouser Omar Abdul Rahman. Abdul Rahman was "spiritual adviser" to Islamic Jihad, the fundamentalist group whose members would murder Sadat. Later, Abdul Rahman would help the CIA recruit martyrdom-seeking holy warriors for the anti-Soviet Afghanistan jihad. He would then immigrate to the United States, where he would be arrested and convicted for his role in the 1993 bombing of New York's World Trade Center.

The Faisal Islamic Bank was given unprecedented state assistance at its founding. The special law that authorized it guaranteed that the bank could not be nationalized, that it would not be subject to standard state banking regulations, that it would be exempt from many taxes, and that it could operate in total secrecy.[43] The official who presented the law to the Egyptian parliament was not the economics minister but the minister of religious endowments. The passage of the law sailed though parliament because even left-wing deputies were afraid to appear to be "voting against Allah."[44]

Al-Sharif, who would be jailed by Egypt in the 1990s, was a notorious wheeler-dealer who traded on his connections to militant Islamists. From his position at FIBE, he became involved with the fast-and-loose Islamic Money Management Companies, which emerged in the 1980s as go-go, free-market investment firms, offering rates of return to investors that were significantly higher than those proffered by traditional banks. An IMMC typically offered a 25 percent return, double the usual rate at a bank. One of the first, and most important, was the Al-Sharif Group, which "had ties to the Muslim Brothers."[45] The IMMCs were highly political, and covertly intervened to support Muslim Brotherhood–linked candidates in Egypt's parliamentary elections, especially in 1987. The high-flying IMMC system shattered in the late 1980s, threatening the very foundation of the Islamic banking network, and Faisal's FIBE in particular. "It was rumored that

Prince Mohammed al-Faisal loaded planes with billions of U.S. dollars, with orders that they be sent directly from Cairo airport to Faisal Bank branches in order to meet the withdrawal demands of depositors," wrote Soliman.[46] In 1993, Saleh Kamel of Al-Baraka bought the Al-Sharif Group for $170 million.

Yusuf al-Qaradawi, the Egyptian Muslim Brotherhood activist in Qatar, was another FIBE founder. Qaradawi is widely known in the Arab world for his militant, table-thumping speeches, which circulate on cassettes. He is a vocal supporter of suicide bombers against Israel and, after the U.S. invasion of Iraq, he issued proclamations to justify the murder of U.S. civilians there. But Qaradawi tones down his extremist rhetoric when talking to Western audiences. In 2004 he was invited to attend a Brookings Institution–organized international forum on Islam.

Perhaps the most important of the FIBE Muslim Brotherhood founders is Youssef Nada. Nada, one of the original, pre-Nasser members of the Brotherhood, was implicated in a 1954 assassination attempt against the Egyptian leader, and like Said Ramadan, Nada escaped Egypt, fleeing to Germany and then to Italy. Along with other Muslim Brotherhood veterans, Nada helped found the Bank Al Taqwa ("Fear of God"), with centers in the Bahamas, Italy, and Switzerland. Al Taqwa is seen as the Muslim Brotherhood's semi-official bank. Abdelkader Shoheib, an Egyptian journalist who spent years following Nada, observes, "Initially, A.T. Bank was conceived as a central economic instrument of the Muslim Brotherhood, in particular its international branch." The international branch was long associated with Said Ramadan, who is the son-in-law of Hassan al-Banna, founder of the Muslim Brotherhood in Geneva, and who founded the Islamic Center in Geneva, Switzerland. Al Taqwa was "directed by Youssef Nada," said Shoheib.[47] A confidential list of Bank Al Taqwa's founders included leaders of the Muslim Brotherhood in Syria and Tunisia, along with Yusuf al-Qaradawi, who served as "president of A.T.'s office of religious affairs."[48] Many of those connected to the FIBE-Taqwa circles would later turn up in the investigation of Al Qaeda and its allies. In 2001, Nada was designated by the U.S. Department of the Treasury as a terrorist financier.[49]

FIBE's connection to radical Islamists wasn't the only thing that helped bring it down in the 1980s. The bank also enjoyed an intimate relationship with the infamous Bank of Credit and Commerce International (BCCI), otherwise known as the "Bank of Crooks and Criminals International." BCCI, owned by Pakistani and Gulf investors, was notoriously involved in helping to finance terrorism, gunrunning, drug trafficking, and unadulterated financial chicanery until its spectacular collapse in 1988. The CIA was a frequent BCCI customer, using the bank to deposit U.S. and Saudi funds to finance the Afghanistan war—funds that supplied extremist Islamic militants tied to the mujahideen there. BCCI, though not officially an Islamic bank, made extensive use of Islamic bank credentials, language, and symbolism. When it crashed, investigators found that BCCI had $589 million in "unrecorded deposits," of which $245 million "belonged to the Faisal Islamic Bank of Egypt."[50]

After Sadat's assassination, many of the radicals who'd been placed in senior positions at FIBE were ousted, including Nada, Qaradawi, and Al-Sharif. Egypt's State Security Office specifically asked Prince Mohammed that they be removed.[51] Yet the damage was done. Prince Mohammed's bank had helped institutionalize the Islamic revival in Egypt, which fostered a violent underground of terrorists. During the 1980s and 1990s, this network would resist all efforts by the government of Husni Mubarak to dismantle it.

Sadat's death was the end of the road for the believer-president. But by then, Iran was under the sway of Khomeini's version of Islam, the U.S.-backed jihad in Afghanistan was in full swing, and Islamism had become the defining ideology of activists from North Africa to deep in Soviet Central Asia. This extraordinary series of developments were made possible in part by Sadat's and America's favorite ally, Saudi Arabia. Now awash in tens of billions of petrodollars, thanks to the 1970s oil-price increases imposed by the Organization of Petroleum Exporting Countries, the Saudis used cold, hard cash to build a pro-American empire of Islamic banks and financial institutions in Egypt, Sudan, Kuwait, Turkey, Pakistan, and elsewhere. It was the marriage between the Muslim Brotherhood's ideology and the power of Islamic banking that finally catapulted right-wing Islamism to worldwide power.

7

THE RISE OF ECONOMIC ISLAM

IN THE 1970s, political Islam was bolstered by the explosion of a parallel force: economic Islam. Part of the vast wealth pouring into the Arab oil-exporting countries found its way into a network of banks and investment companies controlled by the Islamic right and the Muslim Brotherhood. In country after country, these Islamic banks did much more than serve as money-changers. Sometimes openly, sometimes secretly, they supported sympathetic politicians and army officers and funded activists and political parties, Islamist-run media companies, and businesses controlled by the Brotherhood. From 1974 onward, the Islamic banking system served as the financial backbone for the Islamic right.

And throughout it all, the Islamic banking system—which went from zero to global powerhouse in the two decades after 1974—depended heavily on the advice and technological assistance it received from a host of American and European institutions, including such major banks as Citibank.

To Western bank executives, International Monetary Fund officials, and free-market ideologues, the Islamic banks seemed ideal. The Islamic right had long made clear that it preferred capitalism to atheistic communism. None of the important Islamist movements, from the Muslim Brotherhood in Egypt to Pakistan's Islamic Group to the Shiite fundamentalists in Iraq, preached social and economic justice. Instead, they opposed state ownership, land reform, and social welfare programs.

Like the Muslim Brotherhood itself, Islamic banking was born in Egypt, financed by Saudi Arabia, and then spread to the far corners of the Muslim world. At first it seemed innocuous, a free-market-oriented system of financial power that professed fealty to the Koran but delivered cold, hard cash to its many supporters; soon enough, the Islamist political dimension of Islamic banking made itself felt. Eventually, the Islamic banking movement became a vehicle not only for exporting political Islam, but for sponsoring violence. Often the Islamic banks had direct or tacit support from Western banks and governments.

At the beginning, the growth of economic Islam seemed to fit perfectly with Washington's Cold War design for the Middle East. It emerged as a marriage between militant economic theoreticians of the Islamic right in the Arab world and the technology and know-how of several leading Western banks, financial institutions, and universities. It began slowly in the 1950s, as Muslim Brotherhood economists and two leading Iraqi clergymen developed the early prototypes for an Islamic economy. It gathered momentum in the 1960s, when a Muslim Brotherhood financier founded the first Islamic bank. And it took off in the 1970s, with the full support of Saudi, Kuwaiti, and Arab Gulf potentates, especially after oil prices quadrupled in 1973–74. Prince Mohammed al-Faisal, the brother of the Saudi foreign minister, finally brought it all together, creating the first multibillion-dollar network of Islamic banks and building a reputation as Islam's "prince of tithes." Throughout these years, the Islamic banking network was organized, staffed, and often controlled by wealthy Muslim Brotherhood activists, who used the banks to finance right-wing political transformations in Egypt, Sudan, Kuwait, Pakistan, Turkey, and Jordan.

Economic Islam operated on two levels in the 1970s. First, Saudi Arabia itself, wielding huge dollar surpluses, dangled these riches in front of poverty-stricken Muslim nations such as Egypt, Turkey, Pakistan, and Afghanistan, offering aid in exchange for a pronounced political shift to the right. Second, a tightly disciplined network of Islamic banks set up shop in Cairo, Karachi, Khartoum, and Istanbul, where they not only became important financial players but quietly funded the growth of the Islamic right.

In Egypt, Islamic bankers joined Sadat to support that country's transition from Arab socialism to Sadat's *infitah* (economic opening) to restore free-market policies, and in the process they helped build the political momentum of the Islamic right. In Kuwait, the royal family invited Muslim Brotherhood–linked bankers to fund a political force against nationalists and Palestinians in that tiny oil emirate. In Sudan, Jordan, and Turkey, the Muslim Brotherhood and right-wing politicians built financial empires on the foundation of Islamic banks and used their wealth and connections to advance the cause of the Islamic right. Often, as in Egypt, they identified their economic policies with economic reforms demanded by the International Monetary Fund and by inviting in multinational corporations and foreign lenders.

Thanks to economic Islam, there was now a direct line from ultra-wealthy Saudi, Kuwaiti, and Qatari sheikhs, princes, and emirs to Muslim Brotherhood businessmen and bankers to street-level thugs of the Islamic right—all of it fueled by petrodollars. It was a force that transformed the Middle East.

ISLAMIC BANKS AND THE WEST

Big banks, oil companies, and U.S. government institutions eagerly encouraged the Islamic bankers in the 1970s. The 1973 OPEC price increases made the Gulf important not just because of its oil wells, but for its financial clout as well. Vast quantities of U.S. military goods poured into Saudi Arabia, Iran, and other Gulf countries. Egypt joined traditional U.S. allies such as Israel and Turkey as outposts of Western influence. And the United States and Great Britain began constructing and expanding air and naval bases and bolstering fleets in the Indian Ocean, the Horn of Africa, southern Arabia, and the eastern Mediterranean.

Islamic clerics and medieval-minded Muslim Brotherhood scribblers didn't get the Islamic banking movement off the ground on their own. Western bankers, salivating at the prospect of tapping into the vast stores of petrodollars that were accumulating after OPEC's 1973–74 price increases, did more than play along. The big banks were already major players with Saudi and Arab Gulf conventional bankers, so when the Islamic banking movement emerged it seemed too good an opportunity to miss. Major Western banks and financial institutions pitched in to provide expertise, training, and the latest banking technology to facilitate the explosion of Islamic-right banking power. Reassured by Orientalists and academics who asserted that Islam's commitment to capitalism went back to Mohammed, the big money center banks plunged in.

Major participants included Citibank; the Hong Kong and Shanghai Banking Corporation; Bankers Trust; Chase Manhattan; the disciples of the University of Chicago's Milton Friedman; the International Monetary Fund; Price Waterhouse; U.S., British, and Swiss technicians; the major oil companies; Harvard University; and the University of Southern California; among others. Creating a banking system that didn't charge interest, and yet still could function both legally and efficiently in the world of global finance, was no mean trick. It is beyond the scope of this book to discuss the theory of Islamic finance, and the mechanisms that allowed non-interest "lenders" to recoup their "loans" and still make a profit. Suffice it to say that a complex and multilayered theory of exactly how to do just that developed in the 1970s.[1] More important, for our story, is how these banks propelled the growth of political Islam, with the connivance of Western bankers.

Ibrahim Warde, one of the keenest observers of the world of Islamic finance concludes:

> The international banking system was . . . instrumental in the very creation of Islamic banks. The fledgling Islamic banks, lacking experience and resources, had little choice but to rely on the expertise of their international counterparts. And as Islamic banks gained experience, the world of finance was undergoing major

transformations. So rather than being phased out, the cooperation with Western banks—in the form of joint ventures, management agreements, technical cooperation and correspondent banking—was stepped up, leading to increased convergence and fusion between conventional and Islamic finance."[2]

Some of the groundbreaking work on the development of a theory of Islamic banking, including how to organize a modern bank using non-interest-bearing securities, was being done in Pakistan, in London, and, in the 1960s, at the University of Chicago, by the economist Lloyd Metzler.[3] By the 1970s, when petro-Islam took off, they were ready.

"Citibank, Bankers Trust, Chase Manhattan, all the American banks at the time were doing a lot of work for the Saudis, so when this Islamic banking phenomenon started, it was seen as an opportunity to do business," says Warde. "Goldman Sachs was active in creating certain types of commodity-based products for Islamic banks."[4] Between 1975 and 2000, U.S. institutions such as Fannie Mae and Freddie Mac did pilot projects for Islamic mortgages, the U.S. Federal Reserve started Islamic banking programs, the World Bank's International Finance Corporation got involved, and even Big Oil used Islamic financial instruments for project financing. "The large Western multinationals . . . opened Islamic windows for receiving deposits from their wealthy Gulf clients," wrote Clement Henry. "The French, led by Banque Nationale de Paris . . . joined the many American and British presences, headed by Citibank and Kleinworth Benson."[5]

In fact, Islamic banks set up headquarters in Europe and other worldwide money centers. Islamic banking "operates more out of London, Geneva or the Bahamas than it does out of Jeddah, Karachi or Cairo," according to Warde. It hewed closely to an alliance with neoliberal economists. "Ideologically, both liberalism and economic Islam were driven by their common opposition to socialism and economic *dirigisme*."[6]

Islamic finance repeatedly relied on right-wing economists and Islamist politicians who advocated the privatizing, free-market views of the Chicago School. "Even Islamic Republics have on occasion openly embraced neo-liberalism," wrote Warde. "In Sudan, between 1992 and the end of 1993, Economics Minister Abdul Rahim Hamdi—a disciple of Milton Friedman and incidentally a former Islamic banker in London—did not hesitate to implement the harshest free-market remedies dictated by the International Monetary Fund. He said he was committed to transforming the heretofore statist economy 'according to free-market rules, because this is how an Islamic economy should function.'"[7] Similarly, the radical Algerian Islamist movement, which would force that nation into a protracted civil war in the 1990s, openly backed the International Monetary Fund's harsh prescription for Algeria. "When founded in 1989," wrote Clement Henry, an astute observer of Islamic finance, "the Algerian Front Islamique du Salut (FIS) advocated market reforms in its party program—including aligning the dinar [Algeria's currency] at international market rates as the IMF was insisting at the time— and Islamic banking."[8]

Citibank was a pioneer. "Citibank became the first Western bank to set up an Islamic window," says Warde.[9] It would continue to pay dividends. Shaukut Aziz, who served on the board of directors of Citi Islamic Bank and the Citibank-connected Saudi American Bank, and who spent thirty years as an Islamic banker, set up Citibank's Islamic banking program in Bahrain.[10] Aziz would eventually rise to become minister of finance and economic affairs in Pakistan and, in 2004, Aziz would be named Pakistan's prime minister by President Pervez Musharraf.

What excited Western free-market gurus was the notion that by its nature Islam was a capitalist religion. Mohammed, the Prophet, was a capitalist and profit-seeking trader who believed in free markets, low taxes, private enterprise, and the absence of regulations, and his early Islamic regime in Mecca obeyed rules that would make a neo-liberal economist smile—or at least that is the portrait painted by Islamic fundamentalists and by free-market ideologues from the West. It was a portrait that not only justified Western support for the economic projects of the Islamic right but provided yet another means to attack Arab socialism, state-run enterprises, and dirigisme as "anti-Islamic." Though the idea of drawing upon seventh-century religious tracts and

fourteenth-century Islamic economic theories to build a modern economic system might seem laughable, Western bankers and secular-
minded Middle East politicians couldn't resist the lure of the money
flaunted by Muslim Brotherhood financiers.

The Islamic Free Market Institute, a conservative foundation in
Virginia, issued a paper called "Islam and the Free Market," which
captures the outlook perfectly. Citing scores of Koranic verses, IFMI
proclaimed that being a true Muslim means opposing socialism,
resisting taxes, respecting private property rights, and obeying the
unalterable law of supply and demand:

> The Qur'an explicitly requires a free market of open trade based on
> consensual, voluntary transactions. . . . Indeed, Islam commands
> its followers to go out into the market and earn their livelihood and
> profit, to support their families and enjoy prosperity. . . .
>
> Islam specifically provides for private property rights. In con-
> trast to socialism, Islam enshrines private property in a sacred
> Trust. Islam recognizes contract rights as well and the Qur'an
> commands followers to fulfill their contractual promises.
> Muhammad's teachings also provided that prices should be deter-
> mined by supply and demand in the open marketplace and not set
> arbitrarily by intervening officials. This reflected the long-
> established merchant background of his tribe, as well as his own
> merchant trading activities. . . . In his rule of the city of al-Madinah,
> Muhammad explicitly chose not to impose any taxes on trade,
> making the city an effective free-trade zone. . . .
>
> Islam's thoroughly free-market economic policies produced
> an enormous economic boom in the lands it governed, as has
> always been true everywhere such policies have been tried. As a
> result, while Europe remained mired in the anti-market feudalism
> of the Dark Ages, the Islamic World would become the dominant
> economic power on earth for almost 500 years.[11]

The idea that the Koran somehow provides guidance that might be
used to outlaw socialism and to insist upon unfettered private enterprise is unfounded, since its strictures are far from explicit and certainly cannot be applied to modern economic systems. Yet that didn't

stop conservative Western economists from saying it did, and it didn't stop Muslim clergy, including well-known Iraqi and Iranian ayatollahs, from issuing legal rulings (or fatwas) to codify such narrow-minded interpretation.

Graham Fuller, a former CIA officer who headed the Middle East desk at the CIA National Intelligence Council in the early 1980s, later argued that America's interests are not incompatible with the rise of fundamentalist Islam. In the mid-1980s, as a CIA official, he authored a controversial national intelligence estimate (NIE) that proposed that the United States seek closer relations with Iran's ayatollah-led regime in order to prevent Soviet gains, a paper that contributed to the initiative by the Reagan administration's Oliver North and William Casey that became known as "Iran-contra." Fuller, now a prolific author, has also written extensively that the economic vision of the Islamic right is friendly to free-market advocates. "There is," he wrote, "no mainstream Islamist organization . . . with radical social views."[12] Continued Fuller:

> Islam does not favor, in principle, heavy state intervention in the marketplace or in the economic profile of society. . . . Strangely, Islamists remain quite ambivalent about or even hostile to social revolution.[13]
>
> Islamists strongly oppose Marxist interpretations of society.[14] . . . Islamists are ambivalent on the role of the state in the economy—a disparity between theory and practice. . . . Classical Islamic theory envisages the role of the state as limited to facilitating the well-being of markets and merchants rather than controlling them. Islamists have always powerfully objected to socialism and communism. . . . Islam has never had problems with the idea that wealth is unevenly distributed.[15]

Islamic banking grew astronomically. According to the General Council of Islamic Banks and Financial Institutions, by 2004 there were more than 270 Islamic banks with assets of $260 billion and deposits of $200 billion.[16] Chief credit belongs to an Iraqi clergyman, an Egyptian banker, a Saudi prince, and a cluster of Kuwaiti royals. Their stories follow.

THE AYATOLLAH AND THE PRINCE

The man who laid the cornerstone for "economic Islam" was an Iraqi Shiite clergyman named Mohammed Bakr al-Sadr, the patriarch of the Sadr family and a close relative of Iraqi rebel cleric Muqtada al-Sadr, whose Mahdi Army emerged as a powerful force in Iraq in 2003. Ayatollah Sadr's ideas provided the theoretical justification for an Islamist economic policy.

In 1960, Sadr wrote *Our Economy,* which became the Holy Bible of Islamic fundamentalism's economic theories. His *Nonusurious Banks in Islam* (1973) was one of the first tomes explicating the basis of Islamic banking.[17] Both works would be among the founding documents for a pro-capitalist, and militantly anti-socialist, Islamist political economy. It is not surprising that Muhammad Bakr al-Sadr also helped found an underground, terrorist Islamist party, the Islamic Call (Al Dawa) in the 1950s. The Call was established as an anticommunist force in Baghdad, organizing conservative Iraqi students against Marxists on campus; later, it reportedly received covert support from Iran's SAVAK secret service in order to undermine the Baath Party in Iraq, carrying out assassinations and bombings for decades against Iraqi leaders.

Sadr's partner in creating the Call was Ayatollah Muhsin al-Hakim, founder of another long-lasting Iraqi fundamentalist political dynasty, whose scions would also take part in the U.S.-installed regime in 2003 through the Supreme Council for the Islamic Revolution in Iraq (SCIRI). Sadr and Hakim were the co-organizers of right-wing political Islam in Iraq in the late 1950s. What propelled them to organize their movement was the growth of left-wing activism in Iraq and the strength of the Iraqi Communist Party. The communists and the left were strongest among the disenfranchised Shiites of Iraq, especially in the sprawling, Shiite-dominated slums of Baghdad. According to a former CIA official, "Membership in the leftist organizations during the period was so strong that one author on the period describes the Communist Party in Iraq as the only political party that represented the Shi'a."[18] What frightened Sadr and Hakim was that hundreds of young Shiites, especially on university campuses, were abandoning their allegiance to Islam and joining the socialists, the communists, the Baath, or the pro-Nasser forces. Led by Ayatollah Hakim's son, Mahdi al-Hakim, the Call "was organized along strict party lines.... The party functioned in secrecy, with small cells, anonymity, and a strict hierarchy."[19]

Many of Iraq's leading clerics had long-established ties to British intelligence. For more than a century, London had maintained ties to the Shiite clergy of Iraq and Iran, especially those based in the holy city of Najaf, Iraq. From 1852 until the early 1950s, through a clever financial mechanism called the Oudh Bequest, imperial England and its intelligence service kept hundreds of Iraqi Shiite clergy in Najaf and Karbala on the British payroll.[20] After the overthrow of England's Iraqi king in 1958, many of those ayatollahs began organizing against the Iraqi left and the Iraqi Communist Party, and it was during this period that the Islamic Call was founded, with direct ties to the Muslim Brotherhood in Egypt (despite the fact that the Brothers were Sunni and the Iraqis were Shiites).[21] In 1960 a joint Sunni-Shiite declaration representing something called the Islamic Party issued a strong attack on the Iraqi government and its communist allies, an attack that was endorsed by Ayatollah Hakim. Concluded Yitzhak Nakash, the author of *The Shi'is of Iraq*, "Hakim not only supported the memorandum, but himself issued a *fatwa* attacking communism by name and asserting that it was incompatible with Islam."[22]

The anti-communist organizing and economic theorizing of the two Iraqi Shiite ayatollahs inspired an iconoclastic young Saudi to build the first Islamic banking empire: Prince Mohammed al-Faisal, son of the late King Faisal and brother of Prince Saud al-Faisal, the Saudi foreign minister. Prince Mohammed, the "prince of tithes" and founder of the Faisal Group, the worldwide network of Islamic banks, along with Saleh Kamel, the brother-in-law of then-Saudi Crown Prince Fahd and a billionaire who created the Al Baraka banking empire, pioneered the rapid expansion of economic Islam.

Prince Mohammed, Saleh Kamel, and their allies not only launched the Islamic banking movement, but changed the face of the Middle East. Not all Islamic bankers were political, and even fewer gravitated toward the violent Islamic-right fringe, but in practice it was hard to tell them apart. Some Islamic banking circles were run by non-activist, pious Muslims who simply spied an opportunity to make some money. Many more were activists, who saw Islamic banking as a means to advance the cause of militant, political Islam, and who used their banks to support the Brotherhood and its allies. And still others either founded Islamic banks, or utilized existing ones, as innocent-looking fronts for terrorism, arms trade, and other skullduggery. Unfortunately for the CIA, and for Citibank, knowing which was which was all but impossible—and often, all three worked together cheek by jowl: the pious, the political, and the perpetrators.

Many of the leading Islamist activists of the last four decades were involved with Islamic banking both in theory and practice, often under the wing of Prince Mohammed al-Faisal. Many were connected to the Brotherhood. Sayyid Qutb, the extremist from Egypt who was hanged in 1966, wrote *Social Justice in Islam,* purporting to be a blueprint for how fundamentalist Muslims ought to look at economic theory. Yusuf al-Qaradawi, an Egyptian scholar of Islamic law, who settled in the Wahhabi Gulf sheikhdom of Qatar, parlayed his religious credentials into seats on the board of several Islamic banks. Mohammed al-Ghazali, another Egyptian Muslim Brotherhood leader who found a haven in the Gulf, wrote tracts on Islamic economics, including *Islam and Economic Questions.*

In Egypt, the man who got it all started was Ahmed al-Najjar, a German-trained Egyptian banker who, in 1963, created the Mit Ghamr Bank, described as "the first Islamic bank in Egypt and the world."[23] Mit Ghamr was begun with German banking assistance and, through Najjar's family, with the support of forces within the Egyptian intelligence service. It was done covertly. Neither the public nor the Egyptian government were told that it was intended to be an Islamic bank.[24] At the time, in Egypt, the Muslim Brotherhood was Nasser's nemesis, and Najjar took steps to distance himself, at least publicly, from the violent underground movement. But Najjar was certainly connected. The foreword to a book that he wrote describing his experience as the pioneer of Islamic banking was written by Jamal al-Banna, the brother of Hassan al-Banna, the Muslim Brotherhood's founder. "The main distinction between Dr. Najjar and [other] economists . . . is that he does not consider Islamic economics as a science or a study, but as a cause for awakening the Muslims, and a method for their renaissance. Therefore, he considers 'Islamic banks' only as a base for his mission."[25] Najjar himself wrote that the reason he started the first Islamic bank was to "save the Islamic identity which was starting to fade away in our society . . . in preparation to shift to Marxism." He bitterly attacked Nasser and bemoaned the fact that Egyptians were "ashamed of Islam and proud of socialism or nationalism." Yet in public, says Najjar, "I could not declare my true goals."[26]

The Muslim Brotherhood was deeply involved in Najjar's work, and many of its members invested in his early ventures.[27] By 1967, it was clear that the Muslim Brotherhood had essentially taken over Mit Ghamr, and the bank was closed. Egypt's experiment with Islamic banking in the 1960s was "liquidated," says Monzer Kahf, when "Islamic revivalists and former Muslim Brotherhood members infiltrated [it] as clients, depositors, and probably employees."[28] At its peak, Mit Ghamr had nine branches and 250,000 depositors. Najjar, in his memoirs, blames Nasser for the undoing of his bank. Undeterred, he went to Sudan, where he was welcomed by the Muslim Brotherhood there. "The Society [of the Muslim Brothers] in the Sudan was a harmonious Islamic and democratic civilian one," he wrote, specifically citing as his interlocutor there Hassan Turabi, the leader of the Muslim Brotherhood in Sudan, who would rise to power in the late 1970s.[29] When the Sudanese government was overthrown by Jaafar Numeiri, who pledged loyalty to Nasser, Najjar fled.

Najjar traveled to Germany, Saudi Arabia, the United Arab Emirates, and Malaysia, spreading the gospel of Islamic banking. He would turn up over the next three decades virtually everywhere an Islamic bank opened its doors. "He was a promoter of the idea of Islamic banking to anyone who would listen to him," says Abdelkader Thomas, the founder of the *American Journal of Islamic Finance,* who worked with Citibank on Islamic finance in Bahrain. When the Saudi-backed Organization of the Islamic Conference created the Islamic Development Bank (IDB) in Jeddah in 1975, Najjar was there. The IDB was the granddaddy of Islamic banks, generously supported by Saudi Arabia, Libya, Kuwait, and the UAE. It was quickly followed by the Dubai Islamic Bank (1975), the Kuwait Finance House (1977), the Islamic Bank of Sudan (1977), the Jordan Islamic Bank for Finance and Investment (1978), and the Bahrain Islamic Bank (1978).

Najjar recruited his most important acolytes when he convinced Prince Mohammed al-Faisal and Saleh Kamel to get into Islamic banking. "It was the same guy," says Thomas. "It was his meetings they attended in the 1970s. Their ideas are similar because the same person inspired them. They started at the same time, and many of the same people worked with them."[30] According to Najjar, he first encountered Prince Mohammed at a meeting of the Islamic Development Bank in the early 1970s.[31]

Mohammed al-Faisal's Islamic banking empire started with the creation of the Faisal Islamic Bank of Egypt (FIBE) in 1976. Of all the Islamic banks, FIBE was the most formal and carefully structured, establishing a sharia board made up of carefully screened Egyptian clergy. Prince Mohammed also founded the International Association of Islamic Banks, created the *Handbook of Islamic Banking,* and set up the global network called the "Faisal Group." That group included all or part of the Jordan Islamic Bank, the Faisal Islamic Bank of Sudan (1978), and Faisal Finance House in Turkey (1985). In 1981, at an Islamic summit meeting in Taif, in Saudi Arabia, Prince Mohammed put together the House of Islamic Funds (in Arabic, Dar al-Maal al-Islami, or DMI), a huge holding company that served as the nerve center of his empire. DMI, based in the Bahamas and with its operations center in Geneva, at one point had subsidiaries in ten countries, including Bahrain, Pakistan, Turkey, Denmark, Luxembourg, Guinea, Senegal, and Niger.[32]

Saleh Kamel, meanwhile, was setting up his own empire, the Al-Baraka Group. Kamel, a Saudi billionaire related to the royal family by marriage, "sponsors an annual seminar at which scores of economists and bankers meet with *sharia* scholars."[33] At Al Azhar, the thousand-year-old Cairo center of Islamic learning, he established the Saleh Kamel Center for Islamic Economic Studies. The managing director of Al-Baraka Investment and Development Company was a leading Muslim Brotherhood member,[34] and its branches in Sudan, Turkey, and elsewhere worked closely with the Brotherhood.

Throughout the 1970s and 1980s, both DMI and Al-Baraka found strong allies in London, New York, Hong Kong, Switzerland, and off-shore money centers in such places as the Bahamas and the Cayman Islands. Ibrahim Kamel, DMI's vice chairman and CEO, told an Islamic banking conference in Baden-Baden, West Germany, that the very existence of DMI's Geneva operations center could not have occurred but for the assistance DMI received from Price Waterhouse: "The people who explained [Islamic banking] to the Swiss Banking Commission are Price Waterhouse, who have been auditing us for over three years." Literally dozens of conferences took place in Western money centers on Islamic banking, and prestigious academic institutions got into the act. Eventually, even Harvard University would join in, with its Harvard Islamic Finance Information Program, supported financially by Western and Islamic banking circles.

Islamic banking provided a mechanism to bring together wealthy conservatives, Islamist activists, and right-wing Islamic law scholars in an environment that empowered all three. Islamic banking provided the engine that made Islamic revivalism go. During the Cold War, no thought was given to the notion that Islamic banking might have a deleterious impact on Middle East societies, and that it might boomerang against the West. Timur Quran, the Turkish author of *Islam and Mammon*, points out now that Islamic economics "has promoted the spread of anti-modern and in some respects deliberately anti-Western currents of thought all across the Islamic world."[35]

The most vivid description of how Islamic banking fostered the expansion of political Islam appears in the writing of Monzer Kahf, a radical Islamist from Syria. Kahf, who received a Ph.D. in economics from the University of Utah, graduated from the University of Damascus and studied Islamic jurisprudence (*fiqh*). From 1975 to 1981, Kahf ran the financial affairs of the Islamic Society of North America, a militant Muslim fundamentalist organization based in Indiana with close ties to the Muslim Brotherhood. After a stint as a banker in New York, Kahf went to work for the Islamic Research and Training Institute of the Islamic Development Bank (IDB) in Jeddah, from 1985 to

1999. Since then, Kahf has been a consultant and lecturer on Islamic finance in California, and has written widely on the subject.

In a paper presented to the 2002 Harvard Forum on Islamic Finance and Banking, Kahf describes how the big Islamic banks forged a political-economic alliance with the Muslim clergy, the ulema.

> The formal systematic contact between bankers and sharia scholars came during the almost concurrent preparation for the establishment of Islamic banks in Egypt and Jordan in the second half of the 1970s.
>
> When the new species of international Islamic Investment Funds emerged, though managed by Western bankers, brokers, and houses of finance, they had to get sharia scholars on board, too, in order to gain acceptance and legitimacy. The many seminars, meetings, conferences, and symposia that ensued since the mid-1970s in the four corners of the world have further enhanced this new alliance between Islamic bankers and sharia scholars and developed mutually rewarding working relationships.
>
> From the point of view of the ulema, this new alliance brings them back to the forefront of the political scene at a time when they needed this boost very much. . . . This alliance also gives the ulema a new source of income and a window to a new lifestyle that includes air travel, sometimes in private jets, staying in five-star hotels, being under the focus of media attention, providing their opinions to people of high social and economic rank, who come running for listening, being commissioned to undertake paid-for *fiqh* research. . . . They in fact became celebrities in their respective countries, and even outside their borders.
>
> The alliance creates an atmosphere of fresh political rapprochement by the Islamic movement and the governments in the Muslim, and especially the Arab, countries.[36]

By rapprochement, Kahf means the Islamization of social and political society in the Islamic world. Kahf adds that the sharia scholars who were picked for the advisory boards and other posts were carefully selected. Those who were too radical, and who wouldn't be accepted by moderate government officials and Western bankers, were avoided; at the same time, the "government-cheering ulema" were similarly excluded.[37] The process created an entire new class of wealthy, right-wing Islamists, with access to money and media.

THE DESERTIZATION OF KUWAIT

The experience of Kuwait provides a classic case in point of how the Islamic banks changed the Middle East.

There is a distinctive pattern to the political evolution of Islamic banking. One or more Islamic banks establish a beachhead in a particular capital. The bank serves as an economic headquarters for Muslim Brotherhood businessmen and other Islamist activists. The bank builds a base of devout followers, while establishing lucrative alliances with politicians, both religious and secular. Islamist organizations then draw strength from the bank's economic power, and Islamist institutions—including mosques, charities, and businesses—prosper as a result. And a new class of wealthy Islamists emerges to help finance the Muslim Brotherhood and Islamist political fronts.

Unlike Saudi Arabia, which is strongly influenced by the Wahhabi sect, the tiny, wealthy statelet of Kuwait is traditionally more liberal and freewheeling. But in the 1970s, the Kuwaiti royal family, the Islamic right, and Islamic banking groups joined hands to do battle with a rising nationalist movement. As a result, the Persian Gulf emirate was fundamentally transformed. The centerpiece of the effort was an Islamic bank called the Kuwait Finance House.

Kuwait was never especially a haven for the devout. The Wahhabi militancy that seized Arabia for the Saudis and had influence in Qatar and parts of the United Arab Emirates never found a foothold there. Its playboy-dominated royal family, maintained in power by force of British arms, seemed mostly content with its lot. Yet it was a shaky, artificial nation, carved out of Iraq's southern provinces and the Ottoman Empire, created strictly as a British outpost in the Gulf that doubled as an oil field for British Petroleum and Gulf Oil. A series of Iraqi governments laid claim to it, and its fragile existence was preserved against Iraqi irredentism at least twice, by British forces in 1961—when it first achieved independence—and by an American-led coalition in 1991. Even after 1961, Kuwait was dependent on British civil servants, army officers, and Anglo-American oil experts, and the arrangement was satisfying to both sides: the Anglo-Americans would have exclusive access to Kuwait's oil, and its royal family would gratefully accept their protection and a healthy cut of the proceeds. Still, it was a largely secular society, and in the Gulf, Kuwait was known for its relatively liberal tradition, with an on-again, off-again parliament, a mostly free media, and a modestly flourishing political debate. Because the tiny population of Kuwait preferred not to work if they didn't have to, Kuwait imported hundreds of thousands of workers from the Arab world and Asia, especially Palestinians. And that was the rub.

"Kuwait was a listening post for Arab nationalism," says Talcott Seelye, who was a U.S. foreign service officer in Kuwait in the late 1950s. "Nasserism, secular Nasserism, was the predominant political force then, and it overshadowed Islam." The revolution in Iraq in 1958, led by communists and nationalists, found widespread sympathy in Kuwait, even among a minority in the royal family, the Al Sabah. "I remember sitting with Sheikh Jabr al-Sabah, who is now the ruler," recalls Seelye. "I mentioned the king of Iraq, he went like this"—drawing his finger across throat—"to indicate, 'He has to go.' " Seelye says that even then, a lot of Palestinians had gathered in Kuwait. "It was very much a secular society," he says. "But the British were in control."[38]

During the 1960s, Kuwait's government, though it wouldn't be mistaken for a Greek city-state, was among the least authoritarian in the Middle East. Palestinians, who made up a great part of Kuwait's working and professional classes, along with students, were an important force. The Islamists, represented by the Muslim Brotherhood, had only marginal impact then. "I used to attend the National Assembly in those days," says a former CIA official who served in Kuwait, "and I was always amused by listening to the conservative Islamists, who were always criticizing the Sabahs." Yet they were not a significant factor, nor were they organized. "There was always the Muslim Brotherhood, coming out of Egypt," says the CIA veteran. "But I never thought that the Islamic side was significant."[39]

Many of the most progressive Palestinians in Kuwait had emerged from the ranks of the Arab Nationalist Movement, founded in the 1940s by George Habash, who would later create the Popular Front for the Liberation of Palestine (PFLP). The ANM, which was liberal and secular, received some backing from Nasser and from the Arab Baath Socialist Party, and it built a significant following among Palestinians in Beirut, Amman, and Kuwait. "In 1968, when the PFLP was formed, they were all ANM," says another CIA official, who often dealt with Palestinian leaders. "I talked to a lot of the ANM people back then."[40] The ANM was only one expression of Arab nationalism and pan-Arabism, which began to gain adherents in Kuwait during the 1950s and 1960s, first among expatriate Arabs working in Kuwait, then spreading to privileged Kuwaiti nationals, and even gaining support among some members of the oligarchic Kuwaiti ruling family. By the mid-1970s, the strength of Arab nationalists in Kuwait alarmed the dominant branch of the Al Sabah clan, and like Sadat in Egypt, they reached out to the Islamists.

For the story of how an Islamic bank helped change Kuwait, we are indebted to Kristin Smith, author of a brilliant and instructive case study of how right-wing Islamist money and a threatened oligarchy joined forces.[41] "The Kuwaiti government, alarmed over the volatile mix of the opposition's rhetoric and the large Palestinian expatriate community working in Kuwait, dissolved the parliament [in 1976] for the first time since liberation and began casting about for new allies to counter the Arab nationalists," wrote Smith. "It found them in the Islamic forces."[42]

In reaching out to the Islamists, the Kuwaitis had Jordan in mind, where the Muslim Brotherhood had helped King Hussein crush a Palestinian insurgency. That small state, whose monarch was descended from the Hashemite dynasty installed in Amman by T. E. Lawrence, Churchill, and the British Arab Bureau, hosted a huge population of Palestinian refugees. After years of tension, a civil war erupted there in 1970. In a massacre remembered as "Black September," King Hussein mobilized Jordan's Bedouin military to defeat the Palestinian uprising. The Muslim Brotherhood of Jordan, which had long supported the

Jordanian monarchy, threw its weight into the battle against the Palestine Liberation Organization in support of the king. So, the Kuwaiti rulers must have reasoned, the Islamic right might also provide important leverage against the Arab and Palestinian nationalists in the Gulf sheikhdom.

At the time virtually no Kuwaiti women wore veils. In mosques, mostly the elderly prayed. In Kuwaiti universities, men and women attended classes together. Most Kuwaitis believed that religion was important in private life and in cultural activities, but not in politics. Political Islam in Kuwait had only a tenuous foothold, although the small Muslim Brotherhood was efficiently organized through the Social Reform Society, which had been formed in 1962.

But beginning in the mid-1970s, the Al Sabah and Islamists joined hands. As the political pressure mounted from nationalists, PLO supporters, and restive Kuwaitis excluded from power by the royal family, the Al Sabah clamped down, eliminating the noisy legislature. The dissolution of the parliament by the ruler was applauded by the Muslim Brotherhood and the Social Reform Society, whose chairman was brought into the government as minister of religious endowments. That minister, in turn, encouraged and helped create an interest-free banking institution, the Kuwait Finance House (KFH) in 1977. Based on discredited theories that the Koran prohibits interest on loans, a thesis that modern Islamic scholars ridicule, Islamists in Kuwait—backed by the Muslim Brotherhood in Egypt—had been lobbying for the establishment of such a bank since the early 1970s. Almost overnight, KFH grew into Kuwait's second largest bank, under the patronage of the Al Sabah.

> KFH was established with a 49 percent government share in the capital, and it has enjoyed perks not afforded other banks, most significantly freedom from Central Bank regulation and protected monopoly status as Kuwait's only Islamic bank. . . . KFH is a concrete expression of the de facto alliance between the ruling family and the Islamic movement. . . . Islamic finance in Kuwait, then, embodies the growing Islamization of public life in Kuwait under the benign gaze of the Kuwaiti government.[43]

KFH had another effect, too. It bypassed Kuwait's merchant elite, the private traders who resented the Al Sabah's dominance of the mininnation. Many in the merchant class had gravitated toward the Arab nationalists in opposition to the Al Sabah. But they were barred from involvement in KFH; instead, the Kuwaiti government mobilized the desert-based Bedouins against the merchants. The tribal Bedouins were the force that King Hussein used against the PLO, and they provided the core of the most reactionary forces in Saudi Arabia.

A leading Kuwaiti professor, Shafeeq N. Ghabra, called the rising influence of the Bedouin in Kuwait "desertization":

> The marriage between Bedouin conservative values and the [Islamic] movement matured. . . . The majority of the relatively deprived Bedouin tribes have moved from the sidelines to the forefront in demanding societal recognition and equality, the basis for which is found in Islam. Several influential populist Islamists have risen from their ranks. . . . This process of "desertization," as the Bahraini thinker Muhammad Ansari labels it, is among the most destructive processes in the Middle East. It undermines modern society by bringing into urban society the ultraconservative values of the desert and mixing them with Islamic populism.[44]

The Al Sabah were prepared to risk everything to encourage Islamism against the left. It worked. When the Al Sabah decided it was safe to restore parliament, Islamists quickly took advantage, winning two seats in 1981 and steadily gaining after that. Wrote Ghabra, "In the elections [of 1981], the secular pan-Arabist forces were defeated by the Islamists, who became the only organized political group in Parliament."[45] None of this, of course, was the result of some native, legitimate Islamist upsurge; rather, it was the direct result of a conscious decision taken by the Kuwaiti rulers, and it was backed by the Kuwait Finance House.

The deep pockets of KFH bankrolled the growth of the Islamists in Kuwait from 1977 forward. It was widely reported in Kuwait that KFH "repays Islamist politicians in kind, putting its considerable resources behind their election campaigns." KFH, Kristin Smith wrote, used "money, real estate, jobs . . . to influence elections."[46] Its real estate was reportedly used for rallies and demonstrations, and its huge workforce enlisted in Islamist campaigns. KFH also became home to more than a hundred Islamic charities, usually tied to Islamist groups. Some of the KFH-based money was diverted to support radical Islamist groups in Egypt, Afghanistan, and Algeria. Islamist cash from KFH also directly supported Kuwaiti charities and social groups run by Islamists, and at least one of the KFH-linked charities was reportedly tied to Al Qaeda.[47] Inside the bank, KFH imposed strict segregation of the sexes, and outside it created "Islamically run" buildings, shopping malls, and schools organized according to ultraconservative principles. Its tentacles were everywhere:

> KFH has been especially interested in education, sponsoring field trips to KFH, scholarships encouraging students to study Islamic economics, Islamic competitions (Koranic memorization and the like), and the establishment of private Islamic schools. . . . KFH reaches out to society at large through its monthly magazine, *Al Noor*, which has a circulation of over 10,000.[48]

The presence of the KFH, which became a $1 billion institution, accelerated the spread of right-wing Islamism in previously secular Kuwait. The teachers' association and the ministry of education were taken over by Islamists, and curricula were changed to reflect the new religiosity. The ministry of information also fell under the influence of Islamists, and television broadcasts became more conservative and subject to censorship. Books, too, were censored, while pamphlets and audiotapes reflecting Islamist views and revivalist-style preachers flooded the country.[49]

The desertization of Kuwait is just one example of how the moneyed power of the new Islamic right extended the movement's influence. But what appeared businesslike on the surface—to the CIA and even to many rulers in the Middle East—had a dark side, in the surreptitious growth of an Islamist underground whose wrath was directed not solely against the left and the nationalists but against the United States, the West, and its Arab and Middle Eastern allies. The institutions of economic Islam—banks, finance houses, and charities established by the Muslim Brotherhood and its allies in the Gulf— quietly helped to spawn this new generation of Islamists, including the forerunners of Al Qaeda.

Yet the United States, Saudi Arabia, and Pakistan continued blithely to make use of the Islamic right in their foreign policy calculations, and other countries joined in. In the late 1970s, as the United States laid the groundwork for the jihad against the USSR in Afghanistan, two key U.S. allies, Israel and Jordan, launched a mini-jihad of their own, mobilizing the Islamic right against Syria and the Palestine Liberation Organization.

8

ISRAEL'S ISLAMISTS

AMERICA'S POSITION IN the Middle East never seemed more secure than during the late 1970s. Only a handful of so-called rejectionist states—Iraq, Syria, Libya, and the Palestine Liberation Organization—stood outside America's nascent empire. And the United States was on the offensive. Along with its allies, including Israel, Egypt, Jordan, and the Gulf monarchies, Washington sought to weaken and isolate the remaining rejectionists, minimizing their role in the region and even seeking regime changes, using a combination of threats, persuasion, and bribes. Two members of the anti-U.S. bloc, Syria and the PLO, found themselves facing simultaneous civil wars against forces led by the Muslim Brotherhood and the Islamic right. In turn, the Muslim Brotherhood was supported by two U.S. allies, Israel and Jordan. And the United States tacitly backed its allies in promoting Islamist unrest against Damascus and the PLO's Yasser Arafat.

The Israeli-Jordanian effort in support of the Muslim Brotherhood took off in the late 1970s, and it continued well into the 1980s. During that time, the Islamic right would begin to exhibit the radical and anti-American characteristics that would later mark its Osama bin

Laden–linked terrorist phase. A hostile Islamist takeover in Iran, a major Islamist revolt in Saudi Arabia, and the murder of Sadat by Muslim Brotherhood–linked terrorists all erupted in 1979–81. But before, during, and after these events, Amman and Jerusalem would continue their reckless policy in support of Brotherhood-allied groups in Syria and Palestine. Although there is no evidence that the United States was directly involved in the Israeli-Jordanian efforts, according to U.S. officials who served in the Middle East during this period, the CIA reported on these developments and U.S. officials were aware of what Israel and Jordan were doing. At no time did the United States dissuade them.

It might seem surprising that a Jewish state and a secular Arab monarchy would join forces with Islamic fundamentalism. But both in Amman and in Jerusalem, the Muslim Brotherhood was seen, cynically, as a weapon against Syria and the PLO. In Syria, the Brothers carried out systematic attacks, terrorism, and uprisings in a civil war that left thousands dead. And beginning in 1967 through the late 1980s, Israel helped the Muslim Brotherhood establish itself in the occupied territories. It assisted Ahmed Yassin, the leader of the Brotherhood, in creating Hamas, betting that its Islamist character would weaken the PLO. It did, though it backfired in a way that the Israeli supporters of Hamas didn't count on, evolving into a terrorist group that in the 1990s carried out suicide bombings that killed hundreds of Israeli Jews. Together, Israel and Jordan unleashed a monster.

ISRAEL'S TRAINED ZEAL

"Israel started Hamas," says Charles Freeman, the veteran U.S. diplomat and former U.S. ambassador to Saudi Arabia. "It was a project of Shin Bet [the Israeli domestic intelligence agency], which had a feeling that they could use it to hem in the PLO."[1]

In Arabic, Hamas—an acronym for the Islamic Resistance Movement—means "zeal." Though it was formally established in 1987, the founders of Hamas were all members of the Muslim Brotherhood, especially in the Gaza Strip. In the wake of the 1967 war, and Israel's occupation of Gaza and the West Bank, the Islamists flourished with support from both Israel and Jordan. Officially, the Brotherhood in the occupied territories fell under the supervision of the Muslim Brotherhood of Jordan, and Hamas was a wholly owned subsidiary of the organization.

The roots of Hamas go back to the 1930s. Beginning with the activities of the pro-Nazi (and pro-British) mufti of Jerusalem, Haj Amin al-Husseini, Palestinian activism has all along had a minority Islamist component. The mufti met Hassan al-Banna's emissaries in 1935. A forerunner of the Muslim Brotherhood in Palestine, the Makarem Society of Jerusalem, was set up in 1943.[2] Many Palestinian nationalists who would go on to become leaders of the secular, non-Islamist movement for a Palestinian state were attracted to the Brotherhood at the time, as branches began to proliferate in Amman, in the Syrian cities of Aleppo, Hama, and Damascus, and in Gaza, Jerusalem, Ramallah, Haifa, and elsewhere. The Muslim Brotherhood's first office in Jerusalem was opened in 1945 by Said Ramadan, and by 1947 there were twenty-five Muslim Brotherhood branches in Palestine with as many as 25,000 members.[3] In October 1946, and again in 1947, the Muslim Brotherhood held a regional convention in Haifa, with delegates from Lebanon and Transjordan, calling for the "spread of Muslim Brotherhood chapters throughout Palestine."[4]

In the early days, the movement was bifurcated. In Gaza, the Muslim Brotherhood was affiliated with the organization's headquarters branch in Cairo. On the West Bank, the area of Palestine that came under Jordanian administration after 1948, the Brotherhood was attached to the Jordanian branch. In 1950, the West Bank and Jordanian branches of the Muslim Brotherhood united to form the Muslim Brotherhood of Jordan. It was a docile, conservative group that developed increasingly close ties to the monarchy, and which was scorned by nationalists.[5] The Hashemites, in turn, encouraged the activities of the Brotherhood, seeing it as a force to counterbalance communist, leftist, and, later, Nasserist and Baathist sentiments. The founder and organizational leader of the Brotherhood in Jordan was Abu Qurah, a wealthy merchant with no interest in upsetting any apple carts. Qurah had close ties to Syrian businessmen in Amman and to Banna and Ramadan in Egypt. King Abdullah "granted the Brotherhood legal status as a welfare organization, hoping to secure its support against the secular opposition."[6] The king regarded the Brothers with some suspicion, but he hoped that by coopting them he could enhance his legitimacy as an Islamic leader. His father, T. E. Lawrence's Sharif Hussein of Mecca, maintained a well-publicized but spurious claim to be a direct descendant of the Prophet Mohammed, and although the aura was dimming, Abdullah and his grandson, the future King Hussein, would do what they could to keep it alive.

The Brotherhood, like the Islamic right everywhere, was strongly anti-communist, arguing "that in the twentieth century Egypt and the rest of the Islamic world were threatened by the onslaught of communist and nationalist ideologies which denied the supremacy of *sharia*."[7] The Muslim Brotherhood was a loyal force in support of King Hussein, and bitterly opposed to pan-Arabism. Its social base in Jordan was rooted in the wealthy, East Bank landowning families who saw socialism and land reform as existential threats. When Jordan's left-leaning prime minister Suleiman al-Nabulsi, who was influenced by Nasser, challenged the monarchy in a showdown in 1957 that came close to toppling it, the Brotherhood sided with the king and saved his throne. "From this point on," wrote Boulby, "there existed an unwritten understanding of coexistence between King Hussein and the Brotherhood."[8] Yusaf al-Azm, a leader of the Brothers in Jordan, said: "We agreed with the king because Nasser was irrational in his attacks against him, [and] to protect ourselves, because if Nasser's followers had risen to power in Jordan, the Muslim Brotherhood would have been liquidated, as they were in Egypt."[9] The Brotherhood's support for the king came at a critical moment. Nasser and his allies were ascendant, the king of Iraq (a fellow Hashemite) was overthrown, and U.S. policy had shifted decisively against Egypt. In 1958, U.S. troops were sent to Lebanon and the British army to Jordan and Kuwait, to halt the nationalist upsurge, and the Brotherhood joined in. While communist, Baathist, and Nasserist parties were suppressed by the king, the Muslim Brotherhood was encouraged to run candidates in elections for Jordan's sham parliament, winning seats in Hebron, Nablus, and other West Bank cities. The Jordanian army also provided military training to Brotherhood paramilitary forces.[10]

In Gaza, later a stronghold of Hamas, the Muslim Brotherhood took root among Palestinian students coming from Cairo and Kuwait. The Brothers created the League of Palestinian Students, many of whose leaders would later abandon the Islamists and form the core of the PLO, including Yasser Arafat, Salah Khalaf, and the Hassan brothers.[11] In Gaza, then under Egyptian administration, the Brotherhood found itself feeling the heat when President Nasser of Egypt crushed the organization in Cairo. In July 1957, Khalil al-Wazir, a future PLO leader, wrote a paper proposing that "the Palestinian Brotherhood establish a special organization alongside their own which has no visible Islamic coloration or agenda but which has the stated goal of liberating Palestine." From this moment on, the Palestinian movement was divided. On one side were the nationalists, those who agreed with Wazir, who went on to form the Palestine National Liberation Movement, or Fatah, in 1958–59. On the other side were the Islamists, those who preferred to remain loyal to the Muslim Brotherhood, who did not join Fatah and, in 1960, explicitly opposed the new organization.[12]

Fatah—which began guerrilla attacks against Israel in 1965—would embody Palestinian nationalism and ally itself, sometimes uncomfortably, with Nasser's vision of Arab nationalism. The Brotherhood, on the other hand, remained in the camp of the Arab conservatives, allied to the Jordanian king, and supported by Saudi Arabia, Kuwait, and the soon-to-be-independent Gulf sheikhdoms. The Brotherhood's membership among Palestinians, which had reached many thousands in the 1940s, declined sharply as Arab nationalism became the rallying cry in the Middle East. Pro-Nasser parties, the Baath, communists, and Fatah all gained. The Muslim Brotherhood had a membership of less than a thousand on the West Bank, and a thousand in Gaza, before the 1967 war with Israel. In the West Bank, the Brotherhood was tolerated by the Jordanian authorities, while in Gaza it was repressed by Nasser's Egypt.

It is during this period that Ahmed Yassin first emerged as the fundamentalist firebrand who would win Israeli backing in the 1970s and 1980s and who would found Hamas in 1987.[13] In 1965, Yassin was arrested by Egyptian intelligence in one of Nasser's crackdowns. After 1967, with Israel in control of the West Bank and Gaza, things changed. Yassin was freed. According to Shaul Mishal and Avraham Sela, Israeli scholars who wrote *The Palestinian Hamas:*

> Israel was more permissive regarding social and cultural Islamic activity, and the very fact that the West Bank and the Gaza Strip were under one government enabled a renewed encounter between Islamic activists of both regions. This in turn paved the way for the development of joint organizational endeavors. . . . In the late 1960s, a joint organization of Islamic activity for the Gaza Strip and the West Bank—the United Palestinian [Muslim] Brotherhood Organization—was founded. . . . The 1970s witnessed growing links between the Muslim Brotherhood in the Israeli-occupied territories and Israel's Arab citizens. Thus leading Muslim Brotherhood figures from the West Bank and Gaza, like Sheikh Yassin, visited Israeli Muslim communities from the Galilee to the Negev to preach and lead Friday prayers.[14]

Soon Israel would begin to see Yassin, and the Muslim Brotherhood, as valuable allies against the PLO. In 1967 the Muslim Brotherhood began to create its infrastructure, under the tolerant eye of the now all-powerful Israeli authorities. Charity organizations proliferated. The religious endowments (*waqfs*) grew richer, controlling 10 percent of all the real estate in Gaza, hundreds of businesses, and thousands of acres of agricultural land. And, like Egypt, Sudan, and other countries after 1967, the Palestinians were being Islamized. From 1967 to 1987 the numbers of mosques in Gaza grew from 200 to 600, and on the West Bank, from 400 to 750.[15]

In 1970, the PLO was expelled from Jordan after being defeated in the civil war that erupted in September. The Muslim Brotherhood in Jordan supported the king and his Bedouin army against the PLO, and Israel helped King Hussein, threatening action if the Syrian army moved to help the PLO. That same year, Ahmed Yassin, leader of the Muslim Brotherhood in Gaza, asked the Israeli military administration for permission to establish an organization. His appeal was rejected, but three years later, under the watchful eye of the Shin Bet, Yassin founded the Islamic Center, an Islamist group that was only thinly disguised as a religious institution. Yassin began to establish effective control over hundreds of mosques. Many of these mosques, along with charities and schools, served as recruiting vehicles and political organizing centers for Islamists. In 1976, Yassin's Islamic Center spun off the Islamic Association, a membership group with branches throughout the Gaza Strip, and the movement grew.

Israel's formal support for the Islamists occurred after 1977, when Menachem Begin's Herut Party and the Likud bloc stunned the Israeli Labor Party in national elections. In 1978, Begin's new government formally licensed Ahmed Yassin's Islamic Association. It was part of a full-court press against the PLO. Civil war was raging in Lebanon, where Israeli-backed Maronite Christian militias were battling the Palestinians. In the West Bank and Gaza, Begin tried to undermine the PLO's powerful influence in two ways: by fostering the Islamist movement, and by the creation of so-called Village Leagues, local councils run by anti-PLO Palestinians who were carefully vetted by the Israeli military authorities. Yassin and the Brotherhood won significant influence over the Village Leagues. Up to 200 members of the Leagues were given paramilitary training by Israel, and Shin Bet recruited many paid informers through the network.[16] The leagues themselves, run by quislings, were destined to fail, scorned and ridiculed by Palestinians in the occupied territories. But the Brotherhood would continue to gain, at the expense of both Fatah and the more left-wing Palestinian groups, such as the Popular Front for the Liberation of Palestine.

David Shipler, a former reporter for the *New York Times*, cites the Israeli military governor of Gaza as boasting that Israel expressly financed the Islamists against the PLO:

> Politically speaking, Islamic fundamentalists were sometimes regarded as useful to Israel, because they had conflicts with the secular supporters of the PLO. Violence between the two groups erupted occasionally on West Bank university campuses, and the

Israeli military governor of the Gaza Strip, Brigadier General Yitzhak Segev, once told me how he had financed the Islamic movement as a counterweight to the PLO and the Communists. "The Israeli Government gave me a budget and the military government gives to the mosques," he said. In 1980, when fundamentalist protestors set fire to the office of the Red Crescent Society in Gaza, headed by Dr. Haider Abdel-Shafi, a Communist and PLO supporter, the Israeli army did nothing, intervening only when the mob marched to his home and seemed to threaten him personally.[17]

Israel was not the only supporter of Yassin and the Muslim Brotherhood. Religious elements in Saudi Arabia, too, wanted to undermine the secular PLO, and wealthy Saudi business leaders helped finance Yassin, although his ability to operate in Gaza depended on the goodwill of the Israeli authorities. Yassin's "ties with the Muslim Brotherhood in Jordan were instrumental in enabling them to forge close relations with Islamic institutions in Saudi Arabia, which in the 1970s and 1980s provided generous financial aid to Islamic associations."[18] Still, the government of Saudi Arabia remained suspicious of Yassin, and eventually it would seek to halt even private Saudi aid to the Yassin-led movement. Perhaps to curry favor with conservative Saudi Islamists and Wahhabi-influenced members of the royal family, the Brotherhood attacked the PLO for its irreligious outlook. The Brotherhood said that the PLO "does not serve God," and Yassin declared: "The PLO is secularist. It cannot be accepted as a representative unless it becomes Islamic."[19]

At the time, it seemed unlikely that the Muslim Brotherhood would gain much of a foothold among Palestinians. First of all, many Palestinians were Christian, and would have no truck with an organization pledged to create an Islamic state. Palestinians were also among the Arab world's most modern, educated, and Westernized populations, and as a diaspora they were well traveled and well connected throughout the Arab world, the United States, and Europe, not to mention the USSR. Above all, they were nationalists. On the other hand, the very nature of the Palestinian Islamists was to oppose nationalism, and to oppose the creation of a state of Palestine, instead focusing on the necessity of first Islamizing Palestine and the Arab world. But among Palestinians the appeal of Islamism grew as Israel's relentless repression of the PLO caused people in the West Bank and Gaza to look for alternatives.

U.S. diplomats and CIA officials were aware that Israel was fostering Islamism in the occupied territories. "We saw Israel cultivate Islam as a counterweight to Palestinian nationalism," says Martha Kessler, a senior analyst for the CIA who early on was alert to the importance of the Islamist movement and the threat it could pose to U.S. interests in the region.[20] But neither the CIA nor the State Department tried to stop it. Throughout the foreign service and the national security bureaucracy in Washington, there was division as to the significance of Palestinian Islamism. Some saw it as benign or useful, some as possibly harmful, and some simply believed it wouldn't catch on, that Islamism wouldn't attract a following among Palestinians. Says Kessler:

> Radical Islam and extremism didn't come into play as much with the Palestinians as elsewhere, at least early on. Many among the Palestinian diaspora were educated, sophisticated, and secular. Their move toward Islamic radicalism didn't take place until later. The Israelis encouraged it quite a bit. Although they weren't responsible for it completely, they didn't crack down on it. They allowed them to flourish. Where they could fiddle around with events to elevate Islamists to the detriment of Fatah, they would. They'd treat religious figures with deference.[21]

"I thought they were playing with fire," says David Long, a former Middle East expert at the State Department's Bureau of Intelligence and Research. "I didn't realize they'd end up creating a monster. But I don't think you ought to mess around with potential fanatics."[22]

Meanwhile, in Syria, Israel and Jordan were doing just that.

TARGET: DAMASCUS

In the 1970s, Israel and Jordan were technically at war with each other, but they had a complex and cooperative relationship behind the scenes. King Hussein was on the CIA payroll, and Israel's and Jordan's intelligence services had a relationship that, while it couldn't be characterized as warm, was at least professionally correct. "There is a long tradition of complex covert relations between the Hashemites and the Zionists, over many years," according to Philip Wilcox, an experienced U.S. foreign service officer.[23] Israel and Jordan also had a common enemy: Syria.

The Syrian ruler, Hafez Assad, was vulnerable on Islamic grounds. He was, of course, a secular leader and a Baathist. But Assad was also a member of a religious minority in Syria, the Alawites, a quasi-Shiite sect that was viewed with disdain by the ultra-orthodox Muslim Brotherhood and which was considered un-Islamic by Wahhabi clerics. Perhaps more than in other Arab countries, the Muslim Brotherhood in Syria was highly factionalized, with kaleidoscopically shifting power centers both in Syrian Sunni strongholds such as Aleppo, Homs, and Hama and among Muslim Brotherhood leaders in exile in Germany, Switzerland, and London.

The Syrian Muslim Brotherhood was also an early offshoot of Hassan al-Banna's movement in Egypt. The Brotherhood in Syria drew its members from the ranks of Syrian students returning from Al Azhar in Cairo in the mid-1930s, and it formed branches in Syria's major cities under the name Shabab Muhammed (Young Men of Muhammed). Aleppo, in northern Syria, served as the headquarters of the Muslim Brotherhood beginning in 1935.[24] In 1944, its headquarters moved to Damascus, and it was led by Mustafa Sibai, a graduate of Al Azhar and friend of Hassan al-Banna. In the 1950s, as Nasser cracked down on the movement, a significant number of Brotherhood members took refuge in Syria. But as Syria moved into the nationalist camp, first joining Nasser as part of the United Arab Republic and then under the Baath in the 1960s, the Muslim Brotherhood found Syria less hospitable. In 1964, the Brothers led anti-Baath riots in Syria, under the slogan "Islam or Baath." In 1967, during and after Syria's defeat in the war with Israel, the Brotherhood's most militant faction declared a jihad against the Syrian government. Their animosity only intensified after 1973, when Assad proclaimed a new secular constitution for Syria that described the country as a "democratic, popular, socialist state." Violent Islamist demonstrations followed.[25]

In the mid-1970s, as Lebanon's agonizing civil war began, drawing in Israel and Syria, the Muslim Brotherhood launched an all-out assault against the government of Syria.

Beginning in 1976, the Muslim Brotherhood in Syria carried out assassinations, bomb attacks, and other violent actions in numerous cities, including Damascus. Next door, in Lebanon, Syria was engaged in a proxy war with Israel in the midst of Lebanon's civil war, and the Brothers proved to be a formidable anti-Assad force. Accusing the Syrian regime of being run by "false Muslims," the Brotherhood declared jihad, its campaign led by Adnan Saad al-Din, a former member of the Egyptian Muslim Brotherhood. The Combat Vanguard of Fighters, an underground paramilitary arm, assassinated Baath officials and prominent Alawites, security agents, and informers, along with Soviet military advisers in Syria. Gradually the crisis escalated into violent demonstrations and strikes, and then to major terrorist attacks. In June 1979, a gang of Brotherhood terrorists attacked a Syrian military school in Aleppo, killing eighty-three cadets by locking them into a building and attacking it with automatic weapons and firebombs. The following year, the Muslim Brotherhood attempted to assassinate Assad, and the government retaliated in an unrestrained counterattack. In October 1980, the so-called Islamic Front of Syria was established, uniting the Islamic Liberation Party, both factions of the Muslim Brotherhood, and other fundamentalist groups. Fighting intensified in 1981, and in November a massive car bomb in Damascus killed two hundred people.[26]

To carry out such sophisticated operations against a state known for its security apparatus, the Muslim Brotherhood depended on support from both Jordan and Israel. The two nations did not try very hard to keep their support secret, establishing training camps for Muslim Brotherhood fighters in Lebanon and in northern Jordan, near the Syrian border. Israel funneled support for the Muslim Brotherhood through Lebanon, part of which went to the Free Lebanon Forces, a private army of mostly Christian, but partly Shiite, militiamen in southern Lebanon run by a charismatic rebel military officer, Major Saad Haddad. In 1978, in the midst of the Lebanese civil war, Israel sent 20,000 troops into Lebanon, and in withdrawing, left part of Lebanon under the control of Major Haddad's FLF, which remained allied with Israel until the mid-1980s. In a series of communiqués in the early 1980s, Haddad boasted of training the Muslim Brotherhood. For example:

> Yesterday the Free Lebanon commander, Maj. Sa'd Haddad, opened the seventh training camp for the Muslim Brotherhood somewhere in Free Lebanon. About 200 persons, most of them Syrians and including some Lebanese, are attending this course. In a speech, Maj. Haddad urged the trainees to train on commando operations so that they and their colleagues liberate Syria from the factional Alawi regime. . . . The Major said: "The training you will receive, which is of high standards and includes the art of surprising the enemy, is not available anywhere else in the region or even in the whole world."[27]

Actually, the training that the Israeli-backed Haddad provided the Brotherhood was available in at least two other places at that exact moment: northern Jordan, and the Maronite Christian enclave in Lebanon, where the Phalangists, a fascist-like militia run by the pro-Nazi Gemayel clan and supported by Israel, ran Brotherhood camps for war in Syria.

The camps in Jordan operated more or less openly. In 1981, Syria's foreign minister denounced King Hussein: "The king's policy has driven him to transform Jordan into a base for the gang of murder and crime, the Muslim Brotherhood, in order to exert pressure on and confuse Syria."[28] Two weeks later, Assad delivered a lengthy speech in which he bitterly criticized Jordan for supporting the Muslim Brotherhood insurrection in Syria:

> Problems created by the Muslim Brotherhood [have begun] to emerge increasingly in Syria. Of course, the Muslim Brotherhood is an essential historical link in the chain of reactionary-imperialist relations in the region. . . . It was natural for the Jordanian regime and the Muslim Brothers to exchange support. . . . It was natural

for the Muslim Brotherhood gang to implement the orders and for that gang to find all the necessary arms, training, and financial facilities in the Jordanian arena.... We arrested criminals belonging to the Muslim Brotherhood gang in Syria and at the Jordanian-Syrian border who told us they had been in Jordan, [where they received] sums of money, weapons, and forged identity cards.[29]

And a month later, Abdullah Omar, a leading Baath Party official in Syria, said that Syria had evidence that the Muslim Brotherhood was backed by Jordan and by the "Phalangist gangs in Lebanon, supported by Israel and U.S. imperialism."[30] After the explosion in Damascus in 1981 that killed hundreds, Syria accused the Muslim Brotherhood of acting as "agents of Israel."[31]

All of Assad's and Omar's charges were true.

The scale of the attacks in Syria was barely reported in the United States. A rare exception appeared in *Newsweek*. "Over the past five years the Brotherhood has assassinated hundreds of Alawite members of Assad's ruling Baath Party, along with their relatives, Assad's personal doctor, and a number of Soviet advisers," *Newsweek* reported. "Assad has accused Jordan of providing shelter and training for Syrian Brothers."[32] But for the most part, the Brotherhood terror campaign in Syria was invisible to Americans. Not so to U.S. intelligence, however. "We knew about the Muslim Brotherhood there, a lot more than what was in the papers," says David Long. "I was the division chief for Near East at INR [the Bureau of Intelligence and Research]. We looked benignly upon it. We knew it was risky, but life is risky."[33]

For Assad, the Muslim Brotherhood presented an existential threat. Martha Kessler, the former CIA analyst, says that Israel and Jordan

...were playing with fire, and I don't think they realized how dangerous it would become. But for Assad it was critical. He spent nearly five years trying to deal with the Muslim Brotherhood, to accommodate them or co-opt them. In the end, he'd virtually lost control of the northern third of the country. He was going down at the time. He was really in trouble."[34]

U.S. diplomats were aware of Jordanian support, at least, for the Muslim Brotherhood in Syria, but claimed that the United States had a hands-off policy. Talcott Seelye, the U.S. ambassador to Syria at the time, says:

> I was ambassador to Syria from 1978 to 1981, and that's when I became aware of an underground movement in Syria, because there was a campaign of bombing and assassinations of Baathist officials. By 1979 we sensed the Islamic movement in Syria. In 1980, while I was out of the country, someone got into Assad's office and threw a bomb, and killed one of Assad's bodyguards but missed him. The Soviets, who had a lot of people there, would ride around in heavily protected vehicles.

Seelye says that Assad summoned him to complain about the Muslim Brotherhood violence.

> King Hussein had propitiated the [Muslim Brotherhood], which had established camps in north Jordan. I went to see Assad, and he told me: "I know the United States is behind this." I said, "I'd like to see the evidence. I can tell you 100 percent that we are not." Whether King Hussein was actively involved, I don't know.

But Seelye adds: "I don't think it bothered us too much that they were causing problems for Assad."[35]

Actually, King Hussein was involved. Four years later, Jordan admitted its role in support of the Muslim Brotherhood and apologized to Syria. "It turns out that some who did have a connection with the bloody events in Syria were present in our quarters," wrote the king, in a letter to Assad.[36] In what was called an "extraordinary admission," Hussein said that his country had permitted the Brotherhood to wage war on Syria from the kingdom but, in seeking a reconciliation with Assad, he now believed that the Muslim Brotherhood were "outlaws committing crimes and sowing seeds of dissension among people." King Hussein's prime minister visited Damascus, and the king declared that he wanted to warn "against the evil designs of this rotten group."[37] A few days later, hundreds of anti-Syrian Muslim Brotherhood members were rounded up in Jordan.[38]

Robert Baer, a CIA operations officer who worked in the Middle East and India, has written about his encounters with the Muslim Brotherhood, criticizing the agency for its willingness to play along with the Brothers. "Syria," wrote Baer, in *Sleeping with the Devil,* "seemed to be the real problem." That country was critical to the prospects of Middle East peace and, officially, Washington wanted Assad gone. "But," wrote Baer, "if he were replaced by the Brothers, you could count on things getting a lot worse." Baer asked his boss, Tom Twetten, about the Muslim Brotherhood:

> He shrugged. "The Jordanians give them money and refuge, but only because they hate the Syrians—my enemy's enemy is my friend sort of deal." "What do the Jordanians say about them?" I asked. "We don't press the Jordanians for details. And they don't volunteer anything. The Muslim Brotherhood isn't a target for us." What Twetten was telling me was that he had no instructions to spy on the Muslim Brotherhood. . . . Since the Muslim Brotherhood wasn't a target, [the CIA in] Amman wasn't supposed to waste money on them.[39]

Did the United States support the Muslim Brotherhood directly? According to Baer, the answer is highly classified. "People said there were code-word files on this," he says, meaning that only those who were directly involved could access those ultra-secret reports. "I don't know. It was supported by Saudi Arabia, which was supported by us. What happened was, you simply went to governments and said: Here's some money—do your dirty work. Or, we'd give them supplies and equipment."

According to Baer, the Muslim Brotherhood wasn't getting support only from Haddad, the Israeli-backed militiaman in southern Lebanon. "It wasn't just Major Haddad, it was the Lebanese Front," he says, meaning the right-wing Lebanese Christian bloc that had close ties to Israel. "The Lebanese Front was protecting the Brotherhood in Beirut, in Christian East Beirut." Baer says that the CIA failed to take the organization seriously as a potential threat. "We missed the Muslim Brotherhood. It was seen as 'their' problem," he says. "Our approach to the Middle East was defined by the Cold War, and if these guys were going after Assad, well, so what? We certainly didn't confront King Hussein on this."[40] Nor did we confront or challenge the Israelis.

HAMA AND HAMAS

In different ways, Israeli and Jordanian support for the Muslim Brotherhood came to a head in the 1980s.

In Syria, the final showdown between Assad's government and the Brotherhood took place in Hama, a Syrian city of 200,000 which had always been a stronghold of Sunni fundamentalism. It began, recalls former U.S. ambassador Seelye, with a rumor. "The events in Hama started with a false report that Assad had been overthrown," Seelye says. Excited by the news, the Muslim Brotherhood went on a murder spree in the city, slaughtering hundreds of soldiers and Syrian officials. "The Islamists killed all of the Baathist officials in the city," says Seelye.[41] For Assad, it was an intolerable provocation. He assembled his army special forces, under the command of his brother, Rifaat Assad, a notoriously heavy-handed enforcer. Thousands of troops—12,000, according to Amnesty International, with the Brotherhood claiming there were upwards of 50,000[42]—entered Hama, ruthlessly suppressing the insurrection and leaving many dead. Again, figures vary. An early report in *Time* said that 1,000 were killed. Most observers estimated that 5,000 people died. Israeli sources, and the Muslim Brotherhood, both charged that the death toll passed 20,000. Over time, the legend of Hama grew. It was used by Syria's critics to portray Assad as a ruthless, Stalin-like killer, a depiction that Assad did little to discourage because it intimidated Muslim Brotherhood troublemakers. Reported *Time,* weeks after the crisis, "There were no signs last week that the trouble in Hama was spreading elsewhere."[43]

"That," says Seelye, "was the end of the Islamic movement in Syria."[44]

But in Israel's occupied territories, the Brotherhood was still gaining momentum. In the early 1980s Israel supported the Islamists on several fronts. It was, of course, supporting the Gaza and West Bank Islamists that, in 1987, would found Hamas. It was, with Jordan, backing the Muslim Brotherhood war against Syria. In Afghanistan, Israel quietly supported the jihad against the USSR, backing the Muslim Brotherhood–linked fundamentalists who led the mujahideen. And Israel backed Iran, the militant heart of the Islamist movement, during its long war with Iraq.

Not everyone in Israel was happy with the policy of collaborating with Islamists. From all accounts, it was primarily Israel's far right— Begin, Prime Minister Yitzhak Shamir, and Defense Minister Ariel Sharon—who pursued this policy most aggressively. The Labor Party in Israel tended to see the PLO as a viable partner for negotiations on a final settlement. But the Israeli right opposed a settlement on principle and wanted to hold on to the occupied West Bank, citing biblical reasons for wanting control over Judea and Samaria, the ancient names for that disputed real estate.

"The fact is that Israel's policy was a mistake in the long run," says Patrick Lang, the former Middle East director for the Defense Intelligence Agency. Lang says that the not everyone in the Mossad, Israel's intelligence service, agreed that supporting Ahmed Yassin's Muslim Brotherhood was a good idea. Especially those in the Mossad who were most knowledgeable about Arab and Islamic culture were opposed. "The Arabists in Israeli security services didn't like it. But the Israeli leaders figured they would kill off the PLO terrorists, and then they could deal with Hamas. They misunderstood the phenomenon. The Israelis, most of them, were secularists, too, and they thought these religious terrorists were a flash in the pan. They were trying to defeat Arab nationalism using Muslim zealots."[45]

Victor Ostrovsky, a former Mossad officer who left the agency and became a strong critic, is the author of two books on the Israeli secret service.[46] According to Ostrovsky, "right-wing elements in the Mossad" feared that the popularity of Egypt's president Anwar Sadat might force Israel to give up territories that it wanted to hold on to, so they backed fundamentalist Egyptian groups "under false flags," that is, by disguising the fact that the aid was coming from Israel.[47] And

Ostrovsky leveled charges that the Israeli right deliberately fostered Islamic fundamentalism among Palestinians.

> Supporting the radical elements of Muslim fundamentalism sat well with Mossad's general plan for the region. An Arab world run by fundamentalists would not be a party to any negotiations with the West, thus leaving Israel again as the only democratic, rational country in the region. And if the Mossad could arrange for Hamas . . . to take over the Palestinian streets from the PLO, then the picture would be complete.[48]

During most of the 1980s, the Muslim Brotherhood in Gaza and the West Bank did not support resistance to the Israeli occupation. Most of its energy went into fighting the PLO, especially its more left-wing factions, on university campuses. Yassin's followers used clubs, chains, and even guns in violent clashes with pro-PLO Palestinian nationalists. The Islamic University in Gaza was the site of numerous battles, with PLO supporters seeking to secularize the university and the Muslim Brotherhood trying to preserve its Islamist character. In one clash alone, on June 4, 1983, more than 200 students were injured. Similar confrontations occurred at Birzeit University and Najah University in the West Bank.[49] Fatah, the main component of the PLO, tried to co-opt the Muslim Brotherhood, seeking to arrange a workable compromise. The Muslim Brotherhood, however, demanded nothing less than the complete Islamization of the PLO, including the elimination of the PLO's left wing. "The Muslim Brotherhood leadership urged Fatah to purge its ranks of Marxist elements, to be aware of the futility of secularism, and to cooperate closely with the Islamic groups."[50]

In 1983, there occurred a curious and still unexplained incident which has led some of Ahmed Yassin's critics to suspect that he had secret ties to the Shin Bet. Early in the year, Yassin was arrested by Israeli authorities after he "ordered members of [the Islamic Center] to secretly gather firearms, which were then distributed among selected operatives."[51] Some of the weapons were stored in Yassin's own house, and he was jailed. At the time, Palestinian resistance to Israel was far more subdued than during the two uprisings, or intifadas, of later years, when armed Palestinian fighters were common. In 1983, however, a collection of deadly weaponry would have been seen as a very serious offense. Although Yassin was sentenced to thirteen years in prison, he was released after only a year. Compounding PLO suspicions, Yassin claimed that the weapons were being gathered not to attack Israeli forces but to combat other Palestinian factions.

In 1986–87, Yassin founded Hamas. Even then, as the intifada began to develop, there were reports that Israel was backing Hamas. "There were persistent rumors that the Israeli secret service gave covert support to Hamas, because they were seen as a rival to the PLO," says Philip Wilcox, a former U.S. ambassador and counterterrorism expert, who headed the U.S. consulate in Jerusalem at the time. "I have never seen an intelligence document to that effect, but I wouldn't be surprised if it were true." Wilcox says that U.S. officials in Jerusalem dealt "regularly and intensively" with Hamas in the late 1980s, calling it a "complex organization with different strains. . . . There is a more moderate element, which we've always thought might be amenable to negotiations, and then there are the fanatics and the militants."[52]

Although Hamas won support from Kuwait and from some wealthy Saudis, the Saudi government was suspicious of Hamas. "Saudi Arabia didn't want money going to an Israeli front organization," says Charles Freeman, who was U.S. ambassador to Saudi Arabia. "So they pulled in Prince Salman, the governor of Riyadh, and made him the head of a committee to stop the collection of money in the mosques that might go to Hamas." Eventually, however, as Hamas seemed to grow more independent of Israel, and as the intifada gathered momentum, the committee stopped functioning and Saudi Arabia began to look the other way. "Probably there are members of the Saudi royal family who give money to Hamas," says Freeman.[53]

Not everyone in the U.S. government was happy about the emergence of Hamas, particularly the Arabists and the more anti-Israel centers of power in the Pentagon. The Defense Intelligence Agency, alarmed at the strength of the Palestinian Islamists, began collecting data for an analysis of the phenomenon in the mid- to late 1980s. "For us, at the beginning, the Palestinian Islamic movement was way below the radar," says Lang. "We tried to write an NIE [National Intelligence Estimate] at the end of the 1980s, since nothing had been written. But the friends of Israel in the Reagan administration stopped us."[54]

Even after the Palestinian uprising began in 1987, the PLO accused Hamas and Ahmed Yassin of acting "with the direct support of reactionary Arab regimes . . . in collusion with the Israeli occupation." Yasser Arafat, the chairman of the PLO and president of the Palestinian Authority, told an Italian newspaper: "Hamas is a creature of Israel, which, at the time of Prime Minister Shamir, gave them money and more than 700 institutions, among them schools, universities, and mosques."[55] Arafat told the paper that former Israeli prime minister Yitzhak Rabin admitted Israeli support for Hamas to him, in the presence of Egyptian president Husni Mubarak. Arafat said that Rabin described it as a "fatal error."

The establishment of Hamas roughly coincided with the start of the first intifada (1987–93). It was the first major, coordinated Palestinian uprising in the occupied territories, and virtually all Palestinian factions supported it, including Hamas and the PLO. The uprising, which included both violent and nonviolent tactics, had several important effects. It once again brought the Palestinian-Israeli conflict to world attention, and it propelled moderate Israelis, such as Yitzhak Rabin, Shimon Peres, and Ehud Barak, toward negotiations with the PLO. The inauguration of the peace talks in Oslo, Norway, which began the so-called Oslo process, raised the first realistic hope for an Israeli-PLO settlement since 1967.

Hamas, which had previously used violence only against other Palestinian groups, took up arms against Israel during the intifada, leading to an Israeli crackdown. Many Hamas leaders were arrested, including Yassin, in 1989. Despite the support of Hamas for the intifada, however, the PLO and Hamas were engaged in a constant tug-of-war. Whenever the PLO and the Israeli Labor Party moved toward an accord, Hamas would unleash a violent wave of attacks to disrupt the talks. "Undermining the peace process has always been the real target of Hamas and has played into the political ambitions of

Likud," wrote one analyst. "Every time Israeli and Palestinian negotiators appeared ready to take a major step toward achieving peace, an act of Hamas terrorism has scuttled the peace process and pushed the two sides apart."[56]

Hamas sought to gain advantage over the PLO by promoting itself as the most militant force. Reports Ray Hanania:

> The more the Labor-Arafat peace process advanced, the more Hamas turned to violence. When . . . PLO officials denounced the murder of tourists in Egypt in February 1990, Hamas countered by sending vehicles with loudspeakers through the streets of major Palestinian cities, praising the attacks and denouncing the PLO for its criticism.[57]

Besides Hamas, which joined other Islamist organizations such as Palestinian Islamic Jihad and Hezbollah (Party of God) in adopting a rejectionist stance, the Israeli right, led by Benjamin Netanyahu and Ariel Sharon of the Likud, were fundamentally opposed to the kinds of concessions Rabin, Peres, and Barak were willing to offer. From 1993 onward, Likud and Hamas would reinforce each other's opposition to peace talks, often taking advantage of high-profile provocations from one side or the other.

Initially, Hamas found itself outflanked by Oslo. "During the years of the Oslo peace process (from September 1993 to September 2000) the political and military sectors of the Islamic movement in which Hamas predominated were substantively weakened by a number of factors."[58] The Israeli Labor government and the PLO combined to undermine Hamas. In addition to arrests and executions of leaders of Hamas, secular Palestinians were mobilized to support the peace talks. Popular opposition to terrorism was widespread. But the Israeli right, including its terrorist far right, would fatally undermine Oslo. In February 1994, an Israeli terrorist named Baruch Goldstein, a member of the extremist Kach movement, entered a mosque in Hebron, in the West Bank, and murdered dozens of unarmed worshipers. The massacre invigorated Hamas, which portrayed the attack as an assault on Islam requiring an armed jihad in response. A wave of suicide bombings followed. Then, in November 1995, another

Israeli Likud-inspired terrorist murdered Prime Minister Rabin. The death of Rabin left a vacuum in Israeli politics, and the continuing suicide attacks by Hamas panicked the Israeli electorate, leading to the election of Netanyahu's Likud in 1996. The tough-talking Netanyahu launched an unsparing campaign of repression aimed at all Palestinian groups, and in 1997 he ordered a botched attempt to kill a top Hamas official in Jordan. But Yassin proved to be a survivor. In the aftermath of that debacle, Israel and Jordan reached an accord that freed Sheikh Ahmed Yassin from prison, where he'd languished since his 1989 arrest. Suddenly Yassin was back in action in Gaza, thundering against Oslo and building opposition to the PLO.

The pattern repeated itself in 2000. Netanyahu fell in 1999, and was replaced by Barak, who reengaged the PLO in negotiations and, with President Clinton's help, came close to reaching a comprehensive deal. Once again, however, the Israeli right provoked the Islamists. In September 2000, Sharon made a heavy-handed, provocative visit to an Islamic holy site, the Haram al-Sharif/Temple Mount, an action calculated to provoke the Muslim Brotherhood fundamentalists, and it did. The result was the second intifada (2000–2004). Suicide attacks in Israel murdered scores of Jews, and stampeded security-minded Israeli voters into Sharon's camp. Sharon was overwhelmingly elected prime minister, dooming any chance of a PLO-Israel deal. Longtime observers of Israeli politics were stunned that Israel would be led by a man who conducted terrorist attacks against Palestinians in the 1950s, as head of the infamous Unit 101, and who bore responsibility for the massacre of hundreds of Palestinian refugees in the Sabra and Shatila camps near Beirut by Israel's Phalangist allies, during the 1982 Israeli invasion of Lebanon. Called "the Bulldozer," General Sharon launched an all-out effort to destroy both the PLO and the Palestinian Authority. Arafat was caught between Hamas and Sharon: the Islamists would carry out an atrocity, and Sharon would hold Arafat responsible, retaliating against the PLO.

Both Sharon and the Bush administration refused to talk to Arafat, marginalizing the PLO leader and creating further room for Hamas to grow. The result was predictable. Polls show that in 1996, only 15 percent of Palestinians backed the Islamists; by 2000, it was still only

17 percent. By 2001, however, 27 percent of Palestinians supported Hamas, and by 2002, a Birzeit University poll revealed that 42 percent of Palestinians supported the Hamas idea of an Islamic state. This was, Roy says, "totally unprecedented."[59]

At times it seemed as if Sharon was intent on demolishing any possibility of a PLO-Hamas agreement, even though the Israeli government ostensibly was demanding that the PLO end Hamas's campaign of suicide attacks. In 2001, when the PLO secured a Hamas pledge to halt its terrorist attacks, Sharon ordered the assassination of a top Hamas official. "Whoever gave the green light to this act of liquidation knew full well that he was thereby shattering in one blow the gentlemen's agreement between Hamas and the Palestinian Authority," wrote Alex Fishman in the Israeli newspaper *Yediot Achronot*. Again, in 2002, only ninety minutes before Hamas's Yassin was to announce a cease-fire, Israel bombed a Hamas headquarters in Gaza, killing seventeen people, including eleven children. Wrote Roy: "Some analysts maintain that while Hamas leaders are being targeted, Israeli is simultaneously pursuing its old strategy of promoting Hamas over the secular nationalist factions as a way of ensuring the ultimate demise of the [Palestinian Authority], and as an effort to extinguish Palestinian nationalism once and for all."[60]

Yassin, and several other top Hamas officials, were assassinated by the Israeli military and secret services in 2004. Yet Hamas continues to grow. In 2004, Sharon announced plans to withdraw unilaterally from the Gaza Strip. After years of violence there, Hamas is reportedly the most powerful presence on the ground, and if Israel does withdraw, Hamas will make a play to emerge as the leading force in Gaza, especially in the vacuum left by the death of Yasser Arafat.

The story of Hamas—from an Israeli experimental pet project to the PLO's chief nemesis to the main source of anti-Israeli violence in Gaza and the West Bank—ran the gamut of Islamist political expansion from the 1960s to the 1990s and beyond. From an Israeli standpoint, the growth and transformation of Hamas over these decades was an earthquake, and it signaled to many in Israel that political Islam was not a force to be trifled with. But the radicalization of the Palestinian Islamist movement was really not an earthquake so much as an aftershock. The original earthquake was the one that shook Iran in 1979, toppling the shah and leading to the establishment of the Islamic Republic of Iran. That event transformed Islamism from being a non-state actor to the government of one of the region's most powerful states, and it excited the Islamic right throughout the region.

For the United States, perhaps, the forces of Islamism being used against Syria and the PLO were small potatoes. But Iran, one of America's twin pillars of the Persian Gulf, was at the heart of U.S. interests in the region. For the first time, after the Shiite revolution in Iran, the United States was moved to take a serious look at whether the Islamic right was a double-edged sword that could pose a serious threat to the West.

9

HELL'S AYATOLLAH

NEVER DID A REVOLUTION catch the United States more by
surprise than did the one that swamped Iran in 1978–79. For a
moment, it seemed as if the entire U.S. position in the Middle East
might crumble, that Saudi Arabia and the Gulf would fall to a revolution like that in Iran, that no Arab monarchy—from Jordan to
Morocco—was safe. Panicky U.S. officials ordered the CIA to determine if Iran's Islamic revolution might spread, and the U.S. government hired a steady stream of experts on Islam to provide insights and
predictions. National security experts worried that the line of defense
along the Soviet Union's southern flank had been breached and that
the USSR would take advantage of the collapse of Iran to swoop into
the region and supplant the United States.

For the first time, political Islam moved to center stage, and the
consequences would be profound. In Iran, in Afghanistan, in Pakistan, in widening, concentric circles, the Islamic right was no longer a
marginal force but the driving energy behind a potentially region-
wide transformation. For analysts of the big picture, it was no longer
unthinkable to envisage a string of Islamist regimes from North
Africa through Egypt and Sudan to Syria, Iraq, and Saudi Arabia and
into Pakistan and Afghanistan.

Yet when the dust cleared, the American position held. Iran—or so it appeared—was lost to American influence, but the rest of the empire seemed secure. With the exception of marginal Sudan, where the Islamic right seized power in the 1980s, the Iranian virus seemed to have been contained. So for many policy makers, spooks, and specialists in the Middle East, it was back to business as usual. The revolution in Iran was dismissed as a special case, and while Iran itself was regarded as a regional threat, the United States did not begin to regard the Islamic right as a significant foe. The United States maintained close ties—including covert ones, through intelligence liaisons—with Saudi Arabia and Pakistan, the two bastions of Sunni Islamic fundamentalism. The Islamist insurrections against Syria and the PLO crested in the 1980s, and neither one caused any alarm in U.S. policy circles. And in the 1980s the United States spent more than $3 billion supporting the Afghan mujahideen, whose political objectives were difficult to distinguish from those of Iran's ayatollahs. The American alliance with the Islamic right rolled on.

In various ways, too, the United States tried to connect with the Islamic Republic of Iran. The Carter administration's liberals tried to befriend the seemingly moderate, American- and European-educated Islamists around Khomeini, who wore suits instead of clerical garb, while many U.S. neoconservatives, including officials in President Reagan's administration, reached out instead to the hard-core clergy and the Qom-based ayatollahs who were the real power in Teheran. Neither of these initiatives bore fruit, however, and Iran for the next quarter-century would bedevil U.S. policy.

The revolution in Iran stunned and confounded the United States. A confused, bumbling, and often contradictory policy toward Iran's revolutionaries marked U.S. policy from 1977, when the first stirring of the revolt occurred, through the uprising, the fall of the shah, the near-civil war that gripped Iran until 1981, and the consolidation of the clerical regime in the 1980s.

First, Washington exhibited an inertial reliance on its nearly unlimited confidence in the shah. Throughout the 1970s, U.S. intelligence reports repeatedly concluded that the shah's regime was secure, and these optimistic assessments continued up to the very eve of the revolution, leading many U.S. policy makers to believe that the shah was not seriously threatened. In these reports, Iran's Islamic movement was usually ignored or relegated to a footnote. The CIA's aid to Iran's Islamists in 1953 was ancient history, and in the decades that followed the shah marginalized the ayatollahs, exiling some—including Khomeini—and buying off others. The State Department and the CIA complacently ignored Islam in Iran, which suited the shah just fine: the shah vigorously opposed U.S. contacts with Iran's clergy, even with the more docile, pro-regime ayatollahs on the shah's payroll.

But after the Carter administration got its national security team in place in 1977, the United States began pressing the Iranian monarch for reforms and established a pattern of intensive, sub rosa consultations with Iranian opposition groups, including key religious leaders. This had the effect of weakening the shah's resolve, confusing his regime, and buoying the religious right. The U.S. goal in making these contacts was not revolution, but what many hoped would be a more stable, pro-U.S. constitutional monarchy. Part of what was driving this effort were persistent rumors—apparently backed by solid U.S. intelligence reports—that the shah had cancer. (He did, and he died in exile in 1980.) Those who pursued this policy apparently believed that the shah was strong enough to weather a transition peacefully, and that it would result in more power for Iran's intellectual elite, the aging heirs of Mohammed Mossadegh's National Front, the technocrats, and a smattering of moderate Shiite religious elements. What they didn't realize was that the anti-shah movement would be driven increasingly by the religious right, above all by the steely, Lenin-like figure of Ayatollah Khomeini.

Then, however, during the revolution itself—especially from November 1978 to the capture of Teheran by Khomeini in February 1979—the Carter administration fell into bitter internal warfare, with some arguing that the United States ought to abandon the shah and others urging that the United States support a bloody military putsch against the revolution. During those crucial four months the United States had no policy at all, and in any case it was too late to change the course of events. The shah fled, his government collapsed, and the Islamic Republic of Iran was born. Those who had argued for abandoning the shah had clearly underestimated the Islamist revolutionaries, and now they counted on the emergence of a democratic successor regime with a slight Islamist tinge, not a dictatorship. Those who had argued for a coup, which would have led to tens of thousands of deaths, had also underestimated the depth and power of the Khomeini movement. Their view was often colored by the insistent, though absurd, belief that the USSR was behind the trouble in Iran. How could so powerful an American ally as the shah of Iran be toppled if it weren't Moscow's doing?

American policy wasn't any clearer after the revolution. The United States had precious few experts on Iran's Islamist movement. The U.S. diplomats who went to Iran after the revolution were mostly not Iran specialists, and they knew little about Islam or about Khomeini and his ilk. Many of them worked hard to implement the official policy of trying to work out a modus vivendi with the Islamic republic, but that policy came crashing down when the U.S. embassy was invaded by a mob in November 1979. The Western-educated, suit-wearing aides to Khomeini—men like Ibrahim Yazdi, Sadegh Ghotbzadeh, and Abolhassan Bani-Sadr—were swept away in the "second revolution" that followed the embassy takeover, and the Qom-based clergy and Khomeini asserted near-dictatorial control.

Meanwhile, U.S. hard-liners were not ready to give up on Iran. Some saw Iran's Islamic orientation as a threat to the Soviet Union. They counted on Iran's fear of its Russian neighbor to the north and on the Islamists' hostility to communism to move Iran back into accord with the United States. Supporters of Israel—and, of course, Israel itself—saw even the militant mullahs as potential allies. Even during the U.S. embassy crisis, Reagan and the neoconservatives made overtures to the mullahs. By the mid-1980s, the neoconservatives, Israeli intelligence, and Col. Oliver North of the National Security Council joined Bill Casey of the CIA in a secret initiative reaching out to the strongman of Iran, Ali Akbar Hashemi-Rafsanjani.

The religious revolution in Iran did more than kick the props out from underneath America's most important outpost in the region. It crystallized a fundamental change in the character of the Islamic right, one that had been taking shape since the rise of the Muslim

Brotherhood decades earlier. As it gained strength in the 1970s, the Islamic right grew more assertive, and parts of it were radicalized. Violence-prone offshoots, typified by the emergence of an Islamist terrorist underground in Egypt, emerged to challenge Western-oriented regimes, and the terrorist Hezbollah movement gained force in Lebanon. Even the more mainstream Islamist groups were inspired by the example of Iran, and many Muslim Brotherhood–linked organizations took on a more pronounced political character.

The errors that the United States committed during and after the revolution in Iran were almost Shakespearean in their tragic scope. An enormous part of the blame falls on the U.S. intelligence system. The fall of the shah was the most significant failure of U.S. intelligence between Pearl Harbor and the attacks of September 11, 2001. As the United States eagerly lent support to the Afghan jihadists and reached out to supposedly moderate mullahs in Teheran, almost no one in the intelligence community was looking at the big picture. To the American public, the dark-eyed, scowling visage of Ayatollah Khomeini symbolized the emergence of a threatening new force on the world scene. But for U.S. diplomats and intelligence officers, right-wing political Islam continued to be profoundly misunderstood. Even as Islamism's power made itself felt—in the violence in Mecca, civil war in Syria, Sadat's assassination—the United States failed to grasp its implications. Even after Iran, Islamism was not seen as a worldwide movement linked by fraternal bonds and secret societies, but as a fragmented, country-by-country ideological movement. The naïve argued that Iran was a unique case, a conservative dictatorship that had fallen to a peculiar form of Shiite militancy that would have no resonance among the Sunni Muslim majority. Others, naïve in a different and more dangerous way, were seized with the notion that Iranian-style Islamism and the Muslim Brotherhood could be mobilized in Afghanistan and Central Asia as a tool for dismantling the Soviet Union. Despite the pronounced anti-American feeling at the heart of Islamism, key officials—from Jimmy Carter's national security adviser, Zbigniew Brzezinski, to Ronald Reagan's CIA director, Bill Casey— would aggressively pursue the idea that political Islam was just another pawn on what Brzezinski called "the Grand Chessboard."

THE RETURN OF THE AYATOLLAH

On February 2, 1979, just a day after Ayatollah Khomeini made his triumphant return to Iran, George Lambrakis, a senior U.S. embassy officer in Teheran, dispatched a long missive to Washington. In it, he mused about the implications of the takeover of Iran by Khomeini and his ilk. And he wasn't too worried. His assessment is worth quoting at length, because it shows how profoundly the United States underestimated the Khomeini movement only days before the ayatollah took control of Iran:

> Our best assessment to date is that the Shia Islamic movement is far better organized, enlightened, and able to resist communism than its detractors would lead us to believe. It is rooted in the Iranian people more than any Western ideology, including communism. However, its governing procedures are not clear, and probably have not totally been worked out. It is possible that the process of governing might produce accommodations with anti-clerical, intellectual strains which exist in the opposition to produce something more closely approaching Westernized democratic processes than might at first be apparent. . . .
>
> The Islamic establishment is neither as weak nor as ignorant as the shah's government and some Western observers would portray it. It has a far better grip on the emotions of the people and on the money of the bazaar than any other group. In many ways it supports a reformist/traditionalist view of Iran which is far more attractive to most Iranians at this time than the models of communism represented by the Soviet Union or mainland China.
>
> On the other hand, it is not guaranteed to operate in a parliamentary democratic fashion as we understand it in the West. . . . A good deal of authority is likely to be exercised by an Islamic Council. Though the make-up of such a council is still not clear, under the movement's program, political leaders rather than mullahs would appear destined to play the preponderant role in making and executing government policy. . . . We suspect that the Moslem establishment would probably not be able to avoid making some accommodations with Westernized ideas of government held by many in the opposition movement.[1]

Khomeini had returned to Iran, from Paris, on February 1, just a day before Lambrakis's memo was written. Nine days later, the interim government of Iran collapsed and the mullahs created the dictatorship that has lasted more than a quarter of a century. President Carter welcomed the new Iranian government and optimistically reached out to its leaders, but ominously, on February 14, a Khomeini-inspired mob seized control of the U.S. embassy in Iran, only to withdraw after tense negotiations. Nine months later, a similar mob invaded the embassy and held scores of American personnel hostage for more than a year, precipitating one of the greatest diplomatic crises in American history. By the end of it, Khomeini reigned unchallenged as Iran's dictator.

How could Lambrakis have been so wrong? Why did a senior U.S. government official—and he was not alone—believe that Khomeini and his clerical mafia would cede power to "political leaders rather than mullahs"? Why would he describe the Khomeini movement as "enlightened"? Why would he expect that something "closely approaching Westernized democratic processes" would emerge?

There is plenty of blame to go around. Neither the State Department, nor the CIA, nor the vaunted community of foreign policy think tanks, nor academia got Iran right. Most of the blame must go to the U.S. government, for mixing blind ignorance of Iran with sheer incompetence. But the blindness extended to many leading U.S. academic specialists on Iran. Several—the University of Texas's James Bill, the University of Texas's Marvin Zonis, and the University of Pittsburgh's Richard Cottam, the former CIA officer—acted as semi-official consultants to the White House and the State Department in 1978–79. Bill, whose book, *The Eagle and the Lion,* is often cited as a definitive work on U.S.-Iran relations, authored a major piece in *Foreign Affairs,* the journal of the Council on Foreign Relations, in late 1978 that, like Lambrakis's missive, also completely missed the mark. Even as Khomeini thundered against the shah from Iraq and then from France, and mobs carried photos of the ayatollah down the streets of every major Iranian city, in "Iran and the Crisis of 1978" Bill concluded that

> . . . the most probable alternative if the Pahlavi dynasty should be destroyed by force and violence is that a left-wing, progressive

group of middle-ranking army officers would take charge.... Other future possibilities include a right-wing military junta, a liberal democratic system based on Western models, and a communist government.[2]

Nowhere in the piece does Bill even mention the possibility of an Islamic republic, even though by then Ayatollah Khomeini was the clearly acknowledged leader of the revolution. Bill, one of the United States' few experts on Iran, was not the only one to misread Iran's future. As the wave of Iran's revolution crested in November 1978, a high-level meeting at the State Department was called to analyze the unfolding crisis. Henry Precht, the department's Iran desk officer, recalls how—despite all the intelligence available to him—he got his analysis from a handful of Iranian students he met the night before:

> Late in November 1978, we called in all the experts on Iran, officers who'd served there, others, and we had this big confab to discuss what to do about Iran and what was going to happen there. Well, the night before I'd guest-lectured at a class at American University, and it turned out there were a lot of Iranian students there. And when I asked what they thought was going to happen in Iran, they all said: Islamic government. The next day, at our conference, we went around the room all saying what we thought would happen, and people were saying things like, "There will be a liberal government, with the National Front, and Khomeini will go to Qom." When my turn came I said, "Islamic government." I was the only one.[3]

The fact the U.S. government got Iran so wrong cannot be seen as anything but a massive intelligence failure. But the failure was not due to a lack of information, for the revolution was unfolding in the streets, and Khomeini was not an invisible actor. Yet the United States, which initially had supreme confidence in the shah of Iran, was convinced that Iran was stable and not susceptible to revolution. Even as the revolution gained momentum, and it seemed increasingly clear that the shah could not survive, the United States refused to believe that Khomeini and the clergy would seize power for themselves, preferring to believe that some sort of religious-secular hybrid democracy would emerge in the chaos that followed the fall of the shah. Thomas Ahern, the CIA station chief in Iran in 1979, arrived months after the revolution and was taken hostage by the Khomeini-directed mob that seized the embassy on November 4, spending 444 days as a captive. According to Ahern, the revolution should have been plain to see, for anyone who cared to look out the window in 1978. He recalls that when he returned to CIA headquarters in 1981, after being freed, the agency was bemoaning its failure to anticipate the revolution. "After I got back, there was a senior person in the Near East Division lamenting the intelligence failure about the fall of the shah," recalls Ahern. "And I looked at him and asked him if he hadn't been looking at what was going on in the streets!" The CIA, Ahern said, treated the problem of pre-revolutionary Iran in traditional spy-versus-spy fashion, trying to discover secrets about the Khomeini movement and the stability of the shah. But, he says, the CIA failed to draw obvious inferences from what was going on in day-to-day affairs, and so it stuck with its seemingly safe prediction that the shah was going to survive. "We joined the rest of the government apparatus in telling the White House what it wanted to hear, which is that this was just a nuisance and that the shah was just fine, and that with unlimited support from the United States he would weather the storm. There was a failure at the working level to speak truth to power."[4]

In the 1970s, that power rested with three factions in U.S. policy circles, each of which approached Iran in different ways, and—each in its own way—didn't see Khomeini's victory coming. For each, Ayatollah Khomeini was like a Rorschach test, a dark figure in whom specialists on Iran and senior policy makers could see what they wanted to see. All made mistakes, and in doing so helped Khomeini succeed.

First were the Kissinger-led realists, who guided U.S. policy toward Iran in the first half of the decade. For them, Khomeini was nearly invisible. They'd spent the 1970s building Iran into a regional power, the policeman of the Gulf, and America's bulwark against the USSR and Arab nationalism. Their allies included the CIA, from Richard Helms, the CIA director appointed as ambassador to Iran in 1973 who as a boy had gone to school with the shah in Switzerland in the

1930s, to the veterans of 1953, including the Roosevelt brothers: Kermit, the covert operator extraordinaire, and Archie, another CIA veteran who was a senior official at David Rockefeller's Chase Manhattan Bank. Kissinger, Helms, the Roosevelts, Rockefeller, and the big oil and defense firms had spent years turning Iran into a virtual American colony, especially under President Richard Nixon. They grumbled at the shah's occasional efforts to assert independence as Iran grew stronger, and they were annoyed at the shah's extravagance and seeming megalomania. They bristled at the shah's readiness to make business deals with the Soviet Union from time to time. But more important was the bottom line: Iran was hosting tens of thousands of U.S. military advisers. It was the number-one market for expensive weapons systems, and could be counted as an ally in the Cold War everywhere. And it was a very profitable place to do business. Iran was an American outpost at the heart of the world's oil supply. During the Carter administration, Zbigniew Brzezinski, the national security adviser, most closely approximated the Nixon-Kissinger view of Iran.

Second were the Carter administration liberals. For them, Khomeini was not invisible, but he was a vague force in the background, seemingly less important than a diverse collection of intellectuals, left-liberals, reformers, and former National Front activists. The Carter liberals in Washington were wary of the shah and concerned about the arms buildup in Iran. Not as hawkish as Brzezinski, they were troubled by the Nixon-Kissinger willingness to allow the shah a blank check in building up his military. They were also unhappy with the shah's record on human rights and with the authoritarian nature of the regime. In keeping with Carter's oft-spoken desire to promote human rights abroad, they pressed the shah to liberalize the regime. Some clearly felt that wholesale reform, and even the end of the shah's regime, was an important goal of U.S. foreign policy. In that connection, Khomeini's forces were seen not as a threat, but as a suitably anti-communist junior partner in a broad Iranian national reform movement. During the administration, the liberals were represented by the State Department, particularly the Iran desk and the human rights team.

Third were the hard-right advocates of Cold War supremacy and American might. Today, they would be called the "neoconservatives." During the Carter administration, the right was mostly in opposition, and it gradually coalesced around candidate Ronald Reagan in the late 1970s. Closely allied with Israel—which, in turn, was joined with Iran in an axis against the Arabs—the neoconservatives weren't fazed by Khomeini. Though they supported the shah, they didn't hesitate to develop close, though covert, connections with the Khomeini regime after 1979. In 1980, Reagan's team engaged in secret talks on arms and hostages with Teheran's ayatollahs in a calculated effort to undermine Carter, in what has come to be known as the "October Surprise" scandal. Besides arms, Israel also provided Iran with intelligence throughout its war with Iraq. And, together, Israel and the neoconservatives, along with Bill Casey, inaugurated the Iran-contra scandal, involving yet additional arms sales to Khomeini's regime, from both Israel and the United States.

Carter and the Shah

The inauguration of Jimmy Carter as president alarmed the shah and encouraged the Iranian opposition, from the intellectuals in the National Front to the ayatollahs of the Islamic right. Carter's inauguration in 1977, for many Iranians, triggered memories of an earlier period in U.S.-Iran relations—not the CIA's 1953 coup d'état, which restored the shah to power, but the early 1960s, when the Kennedy administration toyed with the idea of unseating the shah and replacing him with a less authoritarian regime. The Carter White House placed great emphasis on human rights, and many administration officials objected to the old policy of building up the shah's power.

Both the monarchy and the mullahs remembered the Kennedy administration, and they saw it as a precedent. During the Kennedy years, John Bowling, the Iran specialist at the State Department, wrote a paper analyzing Iran's opposition forces and "discussing the advantages of a Western policy shift of support for a nationalist, more popularly based, Mosaddiqist coup."[5] But the doubts about the shah didn't start with Kennedy, according to a former high-ranking CIA official who was involved in the discussions:

> There was a big debate, in the U.S. government and in the embassy: Should we support the shah, or a nationalist government? This had been going on since about 1958, when the National Front reconstituted itself. The question was: Do we want to supplant the shah or support the nationalists? There was talk about something like a British-style monarchy, with real power resting in an elected government. In the end, Kennedy made the decision to support the shah, but on condition that there would be real reforms, and that the shah would accept [the reformist] Ali Amini as prime minister.[6]

In his book, James Bill noted: "Kennedy's doubts about the shah were so strong that he even considered forcing his abdication in favor of rule by regency until his young son came of age."[7] In principle, Kennedy's concern about the shah wasn't misplaced, but the problem in the early 1960s, as in the late 1970s, was that no alternative existed outside of the clergy to replace the shah. The National Front had lost nearly all of its support in the years since Mossadegh, and increasingly it was confined to salons in Teheran, with allies among intellectuals in Western Europe.

Pressed by the United States, the shah made halfhearted efforts at reform, in what he called the White Revolution. Sensing blood, the clergy had begun to stir, and in the outlying districts the religious right—which had close ties to the wealthy landed families—began to mobilize the population against land reform. Violent incidents took place in many provinces and the prime movers were the mullahs, increasingly led by Ruhollah Khomeini. Not yet an ayatollah, he came to prominence after making a demagogic speech in 1963 denouncing the shah. To create his political organization, Khomeini established the Coalition of Islamic Societies, led by twenty-one wealthy *bazaari* merchants from three major Teheran mosques. Many of the participants in Khomeini's coalition would later become the leaders of the regime in 1979 and serve as top officials of the Islamic Republican Party, including Mohammed Hosseini Beheshti.[8]

The shah had nothing but disdain for the clergy. In a January 1963 speech, he sputtered with rage at the Khomeini-led mullahs:

> They were always a stupid and reactionary bunch whose brains have not moved [for] a thousand years. Who is opposing [the White Revolution]? Black reaction, stupid men who don't understand it and are ill intentioned. . . . It was they who formed a small and ludicrous gathering from a handful of bearded, stupid bazaaris to make noises. They don't want this country to develop.[9]

Such talk didn't endear the shah to the clergy. In 1963, Khomeini was arrested by SAVAK. Rumors circulated that he was to be tried and executed. But it was unprecedented to impose the death penalty on an ayatollah. In 1964, Khomeini was expelled from Iran, first to Turkey and then to Iraq, settling in the holy city of Najaf, where he would remain until 1978.

In 1977, recalling the Kennedy years, the shah and the clergy both anticipated that the new U.S. regime might begin to put pressure on the monarchy, creating room for the clergy to organize. Indeed, it did. According to the Iranian ambassador in London, the shah feared "that Jimmy Carter might have 'Kennedy-type pretensions.'"[10] The shah had cracked down on his clerical opposition once again in the early 1970s, arresting many of Khomeini's allies, including Ali Akbar Hashemi-Rafsanjani, the future strongman of the Khomeini regime. But the election of Carter, whose commitment to human rights resonated in Iran, stirred the clergy once again. In May 1977, Cyrus Vance, the U.S. secretary of state, visited Teheran to see the shah. "After Vance's visit, the word spread quickly through the extensive Iranian grapevine that the shah had just been given his orders from Washington: liberalize or be removed," wrote Bill. "It soon became accepted fact in Teheran. . . . The opposition . . . concluded that they could now operate under an American protective umbrella that had been raised by Cyrus Vance."[11]

According to Charles Cogan, a former CIA official who headed the agency's Near East Division, Vance foresaw a peaceful revolution in Iran leading to a regime that might even include Khomeini:

Vance and, shall we say, the State Department in general looked forward towards the possibility of a smooth transition whereby the monarchy would cede some power to the dissidents who were considered to be not just Khomeini but moderates around him, and there were some, and this could be a successful transition to the parliamentary constitutional monarchy.[12]

Slowly at first, and then accelerating as the rebellion against the shah gathered momentum, U.S. embassy officers, visiting American officials, the CIA, and semi-official envoys from Washington began making contacts with the opposition. "The shah was very angry in the late 1970s over the fact that opposition figures and members of the clergy were going in and out of the U.S. embassy," says Juan Cole, a University of Michigan professor and expert on Islam.[13] That view is confirmed by Charles Naas, a senior political officer at the U.S. embassy in Teheran, who worked under Ambassador Bill Sullivan. Sullivan, a tough-talking Irishman who served in some rough-and-tumble posts, including Laos during the CIA's covert war in that country, arrived in Iran in 1977, replacing Helms. According to Naas, Sullivan aggressively sought contacts with the anti-shah opposition: "When Bill Sullivan went out, I told him that I'd never worked on a country where I knew less about the politics there," says Naas. "When he got there, he started encouraging the political section to go out and meet more people, and they talked to young technocrats and National Front people, including a few people who had a good feel for the religious leaders."[14]

The shah, says Naas, "was aware that we had changed our m.o. and had started encouraging the opposition." In his memoirs, the shah put it this way: "The Americans wanted me out. . . . I was never told about the split in the Carter administration [nor] about the hopes some U.S. officials put in the viability of an 'Islamic Republic' as a bulwark against communism."[15]

The key player in bridging the divide between the secular National Front and the clergy was Mehdi Bazargan, the founder of the Liberation Movement, a religious, pro-clerical party. Destined to become the first prime minister of Iran after the revolution, Bazargan had a long history of working with the mullahs, but he also maintained a long-running dialogue with U.S. State Department and CIA officers. In fact, Bazargan himself was a quasi-mullah. "Bazargan," says an ex-CIA operations officer who served in Iran, "was basically an ayatollah, or what they called an 'ayatollah without a turban.'"[16] Inevitably, the U.S. effort to reach out to the opposition not only dismayed the shah but emboldened the opposition, especially its religious component. "These signals were mistaken by Bazargan and others," says Naas. "After the revolution, Bazargan told me, 'You have no idea how encouraged we were by President Carter.' This is one of those signals that goes wrong."

From his post at the United Nations, Fereydoun Hoveyda, Iran's ambassador, watched as the Carter administration undermined the shah. A coalition was emerging between the opposition liberals, Bazargan's religious movement, and the Khomeini-led clergy. "The Americans were in constant contact with the liberals in Iran after 1977," he says. "They told these liberals, especially Bazargan and the National Front, that the time had come to come out with dissent and protest. That I know for sure. Some of them told me at the time: the Americans are telling us, 'It's time to protest.' . . . I told [Americans] that it was like playing with fire. You are bringing in the worst possible enemy of the West." A top official in the State Department recalls a meeting in 1977 during which he used the very same words. "Jessica Tuchman and some of the other people on the National Security Council staff were arguing against supporting the shah, arguing against supplying him with tear gas to use against the demonstrators," he says. "And I told them: 'You don't know what you are talking about. You have no idea of the political dynamics of Iran, because nobody does. You're playing with fire.'"[17]

U.S. Intelligence and Iran

Ayatollah Khomeini's revolution unfolded in slow motion, over several years. Only the most obtuse could be surprised at its outcome.

A string of U.S. intelligence reports on Iran were wildly off the mark. A State Department analysis written in May 1972 suggests that even then some diplomats saw Khomeini as embodying "liberal values," albeit with diminishing appeal:

> The Shah of Iran maintains a posture of public piety and champions Islamic causes even though Iranians . . . are not greatly attracted by pan-Islamic sentiments. The Iranian clergy no longer have major political influence. . . . They have been, for the past decade, fighting a rear-guard and losing action against the growing tide of a secular state. . . . Ayatollah Khomeini, arrested and exiled to Iraq in 1964 as a result of his anti-government activities, aspires to lead Iranian Muslims, but his close cooperation with the Government of Iraq in anti-Shah propaganda and activity have ruled out any chance of reconciliation with the present shah and reduced his appeal to many Iranian Muslims who might otherwise share some of his basically liberal values.[18]

Charles Naas, who served as the State Department's director of Iran affairs from 1974 to 1978, and then served as deputy chief of mission in Teheran during the revolution, says that throughout the period leading up to 1979, U.S. government analysis of Iran was poor, especially when it came to so-called National Intelligence Estimates (NIEs), prepared by the CIA's National Intelligence Council. "In doing NIEs at the time, the general view was that the religious right didn't represent a threat to the regime," Naas says. "There was practically no reporting on the Islamic groups in the country, so we were caught relatively flat-footed." In the August 1977 National Intelligence Estimate on Iran, "Iran in the 1980s," the CIA concluded that "the shah will be an active participant in Iranian life well into the 1980s" and that "there will be no radical change in Iranian political behavior in the near future." A year later, in August 1978, a second CIA report concluded that Iran seemed to be headed for a smooth transition of power if and when the shah left the scene. The CIA went on to say: "Iran is not in a revolutionary or even a 'pre-revolutionary' situation."[19] By 1978, President Carter, who was watching Iran disintegrate on television, complained in writing to the national security bureaucracy, saying that he was "dissatisfied with the quality of political intelligence" he was getting on Iran.[20] Yet the CIA, lacking Iran specialists, Farsi speakers, and experts on Islamism, could not do better.

Admiral Stansfield Turner was Carter's CIA director. "In 1977, Islam as a political force was not on our radar scope," he says. "The intelligence community was not adequately prepared to understand it. We underestimated Khomeini's potential by a large margin."[21] But it was worse than that. Outside of a handful of Iran specialists, virtually no one in the Carter administration had any idea of who Khomeini was until it was too late. Henry Precht, who served as the Iran desk officer in 1978, recalls getting a dispatch from Teheran at the height of the revolutionary fervor. "The department received a cable from the embassy in Teheran, mentioning Khomeini and identifying him as 'an Iranian religious leader,'" says Precht. "To have identified him like that to your readers back in Washington told me that there wasn't a great awareness of who he was."

Although thousands of Americans, including hundreds of U.S. officials and a major CIA station were based in Iran, few if any of them had any familiarity with Iran's subcultures, religious underground, and opposition forces. Virtually all U.S. officials who have written memoirs about the Iranian revolution recall that the United States relied on the shah and his inner circle for information about Iran's internal politics. Partly that was because Washington trusted the shah implicitly and believed that his intelligence and security system were infallible, and partly it was because the shah strongly objected to any efforts by the United States to contact the clergy and the opposition. Walter Cutler, a veteran U.S. diplomat who served in Tabriz, Iran's second largest city, in the 1960s, says that even then it was difficult to establish contact with the clergy. "In Tabriz, when I was there, I was instructed to talk to the mullahs," he recalls. "But it was clear with the shah: Don't mess around the religious elements. There was a healthy presence by SAVAK."[22] By the 1970s, when Nixon and Kissinger established the U.S. partnership with the shah, U.S. officials were discouraged by Washington, too, to stay away from the opposition and the religious elements. The huge CIA station in Iran was focused primarily on Cold War objectives, keeping track of Soviet bloc personnel in Iran and overseeing the U.S. surveillance apparatus aimed at the USSR in northern Iran.

A senior CIA official who served in Iran said that because the shah was an ally who didn't want U.S. spies meddling with the clergy, the religious opposition was off-limits.[23] Precht indicates that U.S. contacts with the clergy were being carefully tracked by Iran's intelligence service. "At one point, the embassy political officer had arranged to go talk to a mullah," says Precht. "And the ambassador got a call from the minister of the court, saying, 'Your political officer has an appointment with so-and-so.' We don't think that's a good idea.'"[24]

Beginning in the mid-1970s, however, rumblings were picked up, remotely at first, by the U.S. intelligence community. According to several U.S. officials, the first to sense trouble were the British, who were able to draw on their centuries-long presence in the country, and the Israelis, whose secret service, the Mossad, was plugged into the bazaar. "The best sources I had were the British," says Precht. "They were much more informed, much more insightful. And their reporting, their assessments were not upbeat." Israel, too, sensed that the shah was finished long before the United States did. Around 1976, says Precht, while he was escorting a U.S. senator on a tour of Iran, they began with a briefing from Ambassador Helms, who told the senator that Iran was secure. "Well, we went to see Uri Lubrani, the man in charge of representing Israel in Iran, and he said that the shah was facing a serious problem from his religious opposition. That was the first time I'd heard that. No one in the embassy was saying that." Two years later, according to Precht, the warnings from Israel were more urgent. "In 1978, an Israeli foreign service officer came to see us at the Department, and he said: 'We are already in the post-shah era.' He told us, we should prepare ourselves."[25] At the time, most U.S. government officials believed that the shah would weather the storm.

Starting in the mid-1970s, it began to dawn on policy makers and U.S. intelligence officials that the shah would fall. "You could take a calendar of 1977 and 1978," says Harold Saunders, who was then the assistant secretary of state for Near East and South Asian affairs, "and put people on the calendar as to when they decided that the shah's regime could not endure."

A critical, but previously unexamined aspect of U.S. decision making on Iran in the 1970s is related to the shah's fatal illness. It is important because if it were known that the shah was fatally stricken, it would drastically affect all calculations about Iran's future; were the shah to die in office, with no clear mode of transferring power, a very real danger would exist that Iran could plunge into chaos. The shah's illness was diagnosed as early as 1969, according to Hoveyda, whose brother was Iran's prime minister. "It was only in the mid-1970s that I heard that he had cancer," he says, though it was a closely guarded secret. But he insists: "The United States must have known, because secrets like that cannot be kept, especially because the shah got second and third opinions, and he was consulting with American physicians, too."[26] Carter administration policy makers and intelligence officials provide conflicting testimony about how much the United States knew about the shah's cancer, and when it learned about it. Harold Saunders, the Middle East chief at the State Department, says that the United States did not know that the shah was sick until after he'd left Iran. But Charles Cogan, the ex-CIA official, said that the Iran crisis in fact began "when the shah's illness became apparent, not to us but to the French, very early in '72. And I think that we finally became aware of the gravity of it in '76."[27] According to Cogan, Richard Helms, who was U.S. ambassador to Teheran, suspected that the shah had cancer and told Washington so. "I think it was '75 that Helms wrote something to that effect back to Washington, but it seemed to escape people's attention," says Cogan. "The French were aware of this as far back as 1972, because one of the doctors that was treating the shah was in some way affiliated with the French intelligence service."[28] Another senior CIA official with enormous experience in Iran says flatly: "We knew the shah was ill. We had reports from—well, from a very good source."[29] By the late 1970s, it wasn't hard for U.S. intelligence to put two and two together, and to conclude that the shah was nearing the end of the road. David Long, who worked in the State Department's intelligence bureau, says that it was enough to make actionable judgments: "The fact that the shah was ill, that he had cancer, was known. But it was very closely held. But we knew enough, the worker-bees, to know that this guy was in heavy doo-doo. It was our job to handicap this."[30]

Among the very last to come to the conclusion that the shah was finished were Brzezinski and the Rockefeller-Kissinger pro-shah partisans, who clung to the belief late into 1978 that the shah would survive. The U.S. embassy in Teheran was slow to realize the extent of the threat to the shah, but U.S. consulates outside the capital were more in tune with the pulse of the country, and their reporting back to Washington was somewhat more perceptive. Individual CIA experts, some of whom had spent years in Iran, were among the first to understand that Iran was collapsing. "I left Iran in 1976, and I told four close friends to get their money out of the country, that Iran was going down the tubes," says one CIA officer.[31] But that pessimism didn't find its way into the rosy-scenario intelligence estimates prepared for the U.S. government.

Ambassador Sullivan, in Teheran, held on to the belief in the summer of 1978 that the shah's regime would continue. In his memoirs, *Mission to Iran*, he noted that some diplomats felt that the shah would fall, citing in particular a French embassy official who "expected the shah to be overthrown within a year." Yet, said Sullivan: "We felt that the shah was in trouble . . . but we did not see the beginnings of a revolution."[32] A year earlier, in a dispatch to Washington entitled "Straws in the Wind," Sullivan had taken note of growing religious unrest in Iran, adding: "There are hints that despite their right-wing fanaticism, some of the more pragmatic conservative Islamic imams and ayatollahs are willing to ride the human rights horse into alliance with those on the left [i.e., the National Front] where mutual interests can be made to coincide." Obliquely, Sullivan mentioned that religious "restiveness" had been reinforced by a parallel revival of Islamism in Pakistan, Saudi Arabia, and Turkey, but concluded that the shah's government would keep the religious movement "under control."[33] In his memoirs, Sullivan admits that he was mystified about Islam and that neither his staff nor the CIA could help him:

My efforts to penetrate further into the mysteries of Shiism were constantly frustrated. . . . Neither our political officers nor our intelligence officers were able to satisfy my interest in obtaining further insights into the workings of the Shia mind.[34]

Richard Cottam and the "Americans"

One former U.S. official who purported to understand the "Shia mind" was Richard Cottam. In the early and mid-1950s, Cottam served in Iran as part of the CIA's covert operations team. "He was a case officer of mine," says John Waller, the station chief in Iran in the late 1940s and early 1950s.[35] Cottam became a University of Pittsburgh professor in 1958, but didn't leave either the CIA or skullduggery far behind. During the 1960s and 1970s, Cottam maintained close ties to Iranian dissidents, from the National Front to leading religious figures. He was especially close to two men who would serve, in 1978, as Khomeini's closest aides during his exile in Paris, while the revolution in Iran was unfolding: Ibrahim Yazdi and Sadegh Ghotbzadeh—nicknamed "the Americans." Both men spent many years living in or visiting the United States, and both worked with the Muslim Brotherhood–linked Muslim Students Association, which Yazdi helped to found in 1963. Cottam had first met Yazdi in Iran in the 1950s, while working as a CIA officer, and the two men became close friends. During the 1960s, Yazdi traveled back and forth between Iran, Paris, and the United States, working with Ghotbzadeh and many other religious-minded Iranian activists who supported Ayatollah Khomeini. In 1967, Yazdi settled in Houston, Texas, taking up a research and teaching post at Baylor Medical College.

Early in 1978, Cottam's name began to show up in secret or confidential State Department and CIA dispatches from Iran. In May, John Stempel from the U.S. embassy in Iran met with a leader of the pro-Khomeini movement, Mohammad Tavakoli, who "asked if Stempel knew Professor Richard Cottam." According to a dispatch from Stempel, Tavakoli asked "if Stempel had some way of proving that he was a State Department officer and whether he would mind his name being checked with Professor Cottam."[36] A few weeks later, Stempel met Tavakoli with Bazargan, the leader of what was now called the

National Liberation Movement, and Tavakoli—obviously referring to Cottam—curiously asked if the Carter administration has a "separate channel" into the embassy outside State Department channels. "He noted that the Movement had supplied much information to Richard Cottam when he was a State Department officer and continued to do so," wrote Stempel.[37] Cottam continued to make back-and-forth visits to Teheran and Paris, where he met Khomeini, Yazdi, and Ghotbzadeh. In June 1978, Charles Naas of the U.S. embassy wrote to Henry Precht, the Iran desk officer: "We find it fascinating that Richard Cottam, as several of us had thought, is still a principal contact for the [Liberation Movement] in the U.S., and they were willing to confirm this."[38] By December, when the revolution was clearly about to succeed, a confidential State Department dispatch from the embassy noted rumors that Cottam had secretly traveled to Teheran. "To the best of our knowledge, Cottam is not here. Would appreciate it if Department could discreetly confirm his presence in Pittsburgh."

But by then Cottam was seeking to establish overt connections between Yazdi, Ghotbzadeh, and others in the Khomeini circle with official Washington, outside State Department channels. Precht says that Cottam repeatedly tried to open a dialogue between Khomeini's circle and the U.S. government. In late 1978, says Precht, Cottam "said that Ibrahim Yazdi was coming to Washington, and that we ought to meet him. And he called Gary Sick at the NSC with the same idea. But Cottam was persona non grata at the State Department, because he had all those contacts with Iranian dissidents. . . . Sometimes, the people in the human rights office, under Steve Cohen, dealt with them." Eventually Precht and other State Department officials did open a dialogue with the revolutionaries, including Yazdi and Shahriar Rouhani, Yazdi's son-in-law. The meetings continued in Paris, and in Teheran Cottam introduced U.S. embassy officials to Ayatollah Beheshti, who was Khomeini's official representative in Iran in the months before the revolution. The Iranians assured the U.S. officials that Khomeini was not to be feared, and that he did not have political ambitions for himself.[39]

A few months later, Khomeini had seized power, and he began to construct the institutions that would guarantee that power would remain in the hands of the clergy for the next quarter-century: the *komitehs,* or Islamic committees; the *pasdaran,* the guard; various bodies of Islamic "experts" and jurists; the Islamic courts; the revolutionary council. Hundreds, perhaps thousands of officials from the shah's era were summarily executed, and countless others were murdered by Khomeini's followers.

AFTER THE REVOLUTION

The United States struggled to recover from the shock of the January–February 1979 revolution in Iran.

A major effort was made to establish something resembling normal diplomatic relations with the new regime in Teheran, but they got off to a bad start. "We wanted to establish a dialogue," says Walter Cutler, the veteran U.S. diplomat assigned to be America's ambassador to the Islamic Republic in the middle of 1979. "I was to go out there and try to establish some sort of rapport with the new regime, from Khomeini on down."[40] Cutler had served in Iran as consul in Tabriz in the mid-1960s, and spent much of the 1980s as U.S. ambassador to Saudi Arabia. Named to succeed Bill Sullivan, the outgoing U.S. ambassador who was fatally tainted by his association with the shah, Cutler was asked to assemble an Iran team quickly. "My appointment was pretty rushed, and I had to put together a whole new team fast. [Secretary of State Cyrus] Vance said, 'Pick anyone you want, and I will break their assignment,'" meaning that Vance would reassign to Iran anyone Cutler wanted. What Cutler didn't know, of course, is that many of the people assigned to his team would be taken hostage in November and held for fifteen months under brutal conditions.

"We had to prove to the Iranians that we were not the Great Satan," says Cutler. The fact that the Iranian revolution was based on Islam, not left-wing nationalism, was something that encouraged many U.S. policy makers, diplomats, and CIA officials, from Zbigniew Brzezinski at the NSC on down. "We were in the Cold War," says Cutler, "and here was an Islamic revolution, and I'd been there long enough to know what suspicion existed about the Russians. I thought that we could handle the possibility that the Soviet Union might try to increase its influence, because of the strength of Islam. . . . If you're looking for common interests, our shared concern about Soviet penetration of that part of the world was one."

But Cutler never reached Iran. A congressional resolution condemning Khomeini in 1979 infuriated the ayatollah, and, according to Cutler, Yazdi later told him that Khomeini wanted to break relations with the United States entirely. Instead Yazdi persuaded Khomeini to take just a "half step" and to refuse the ambassador. Cutler's appointment was withdrawn.[41] But other U.S. officials, most of them fated to be taken captive in November, began arriving. Some, but not all, had served in Iran before but virtually none had any experience with or knowledge of Islamism.

Bruce Laingen, who headed the embassy in the absence of an ambassador, had two brief stints in Iran before but says frankly, "I am no expert on the subject of Islam." He was plucked from an assignment that would have taken him to Japan and hustled to Iran, because the State Department was "casting around for available, dispensable, transferable FSOs [foreign service officers]." Did he get a lot of preparation to deal with Islam and Khomeini's ideology? "No," he says. "Almost none."[42] Thomas Ahern, the new CIA station chief, calls his appointment a "bureaucratic accident," and says that he received no help from the U.S. government that enabled him to understand the dynamic of Khomeini's Islamic movement. "You can quote me as saying that there was no instruction of an academic sort on the politics, culture, and economics of Iran," he says. "It was strictly a trade-school type of thing, preparing me to take over certain functions and certain contacts."[43] John Limbert, another veteran U.S. diplomat who spoke fluent Farsi, responded to a "volunteer cable, saying something like, 'We need people to go to Iran to help rebuild, or salvage something out of these events.' Naïve as I was, I and many of my colleagues felt that now we could finally establish a healthy relationship with Iran." But did Limbert, Laingen, and their fellow officers understand Islam, or the nature of Khomeini's religious-right following? "We didn't know it," says Limbert. "We didn't understand it."[44] By

November, Laingen, Ahern, Limbert, and scores of colleagues would be prisoners of a mob secretly directed by Khomeini.

The new Iranian government was a two-headed creature. There was the "official" government: Prime Minister Bazargan, Yazdi, Ghotbzadeh, and the man who would eventually be elected as the first president of the Islamic Republic, Abolhassan Bani-Sadr. Then there was the unofficial, parallel government, consisting of Khomeini, a handful of key ayatollahs, the *komitehs,* the *pasdaran,* and the hard-core set of Islamist institutions that were taking shape to implement Khomeini's theocracy. The new U.S. embassy team and visiting CIA and State Department officials were confined, for the most part, to interaction with the ever-less-powerful official government, while Khomeini kept the United States at arm's length. Khomeini embarked on a plan to isolate and destroy, one by one, all of the secular, left-wing, and moderate religious forces that had joined the anti-shah revolution in the 1970s. His ultimate goal was the consolidation of virtually all power under his personal control and in the Revolutionary Council, the shadowy body that was made up primarily of pro-Khomeini ayatollahs.

According to Laingen:

> We had very little contact with the clergy. I never saw Khomeini. And we never really talked to the Revolutionary Council. We sensed they were there. We knew they were there. But we didn't appreciate how much power they really had. We saw our mission as to reiterate our acceptance of the Islamic revolution, and to communicate that we were a spiritual-minded country. That it was feasible for the United States to come to an understanding with political Islam, and that the shah had no future. We recognized that Khomeini would not be disestablished. But we were caught up in the belief that the secular side of the revolution would prevail. Bazargan, Yazdi, and Ghotbzadeh believed that they would be able to cope, that they would manage to contain Khomeini's influence.[45]

Embassy officials did talk to a limited number of mostly more moderate Shiite clergy, but it didn't do much to open doors to Khomeini's inner circle. Many of the more cooperative Islamist mullahs were pushed aside, assassinated, or forced into exile as Khomeini consolidated power.

The embassy wasn't getting much help from the CIA, either, which failed to produce any intelligence estimates about the future of Iran in 1979. Says Ahern:

> I don't recall any estimate or forecast of what would happen. What Washington wanted from the embassy as a whole was to be encouraging, supporting the Yazdis, the Bazargans, in hope of moderating, or helping them moderate the regressive tendencies of the regime. As I recall, this was all on the level of wistful hope, not on the level of serious planning or based on indications from Iranians that this was going to work.[46]

But if the CIA wasn't producing many conclusions about the future of Iran, it was asked to pass on to Iran crucial intelligence about Iran's neighbor, Iraq. Yet less than a year later the two countries would be engaged in a bloody, decade-long conflict that reportedly left more than a million dead. Besides the CIA station chief, other senior CIA officials, including Robert Ames and George Cave, made visits to Iran in 1979, before the embassy takeover. On at least one occasion, Ames—who headed the CIA's Near East Division—met with Ayatollah Beheshti, and other agency officials met Yazdi, Amir Abbas Entezam, and other non-clergy Iranian officials. A system of intelligence sharing was established, particularly in connection with Iraq. "Once the Bazargan government was established, we tried to do business with them," recalls a CIA official involved with Iran at the time, adding that the CIA warned Iran in 1979 about Iraqi war intentions.[47] Laingen confirms reports that the United States passed on intelligence to Iran about Iraq:

> We had concern over Iraq. Relations between Iran and Iraq were close to their lowest point, and Khomeini had enormous distaste for Saddam Hussein. He had a desire to export the revolution to Iraq. Iraq was certainly a major target. I recall briefing the Iranians on American intelligence on Iraq. We gave them information about Iraq's military capacity, troop emplacements, intentions. It

was a new experience for me, suddenly being involved in the intelligence side of diplomacy.[48]

While the United States passed on intelligence to the mullahs, including Beheshti, it gradually became clear that the Bazargans, Yazdis, and Ghotbzadehs had virtually no power, and that the Shiite clergy controlled everything. That was especially true in connection with the military. "There was no coordination between Bazargan and the military. I know this for a fact," says a former CIA official. "The military was under the ironclad control of the mullahs. And the mullahs divided Iran into seventeen villages, and assigned people to run each one, through the *komitehs*."[49]

Even so, a handful of U.S. policy makers began to see Iran's Islamist orientation as threatening to the USSR. One of the most surprising to reach that conclusion was Brzezinski, the hard-line national security adviser who'd been an advocate for using a military coup in Iran to stop Khomeini's revolution. Gradually, Brzezinski changed his mind, envisioning what he called an "arc of crisis" stretching from northeast Africa to central Asia. It was a high-stakes zone of conflict between the two superpowers, and it subsumed a region entirely imbued with the Islamic resurgence. Henry Precht, who had been one of the U.S. officials most opposed to the shah and who favored trying to establish good relations with the Islamic Republic, recalls the situation in the middle of 1979:

> After the revolution, we still considered Iran to be terribly important to U.S. interests. At one point Hal Saunders [assistant secretary of state for Near East affairs] went to the White House for a meeting, and when he came back he told me, "You'll be very pleased. We're going to try to develop new relations with Iran." There was this idea that the Islamic forces could be used against the Soviet Union. The theory was, there was an arc of crisis, and so an arc of Islam could be mobilized to contain the Soviets. It was a Brzezinski concept.[50]

Brzezinski, in his memoirs, says that he began to press for an all-encompassing U.S. security policy along the arc of crisis even before the Iranian revolution had run its course. By that, he meant strong U.S. military ties to Egypt, Saudi Arabia, Pakistan, and Turkey, four Muslim countries inside the arc, flanking U.S. support in Oman, Somalia, and Kenya, and U.S. bases in several countries and in the Indian Ocean. "By late 1978," wrote Brzezinski, "I began to press the 'arc of crisis' thesis, [arguing] for a new 'security framework' to reassert U.S. power and influence in the region."[51]

Brzezinski saw the loss of the shah as "catastrophic," according to Cottam. At first Brzezinski wanted an Iranian Pinochet, a military dictator who would suppress the Islamic revolution at any cost, but when that became impossible Brzezinski opted for a "de facto alliance with the forces of Islamic resurgence and with the regime of the Islamic Republic of Iran," wrote Cottam. "Stability was not even implicitly his objective. His primary concern was to form an effective anti-Soviet alliance in the region he described as an 'arc of crisis.' By the summer of 1979 Brzezinski was convinced of the sincerity of Khomeini's fierce anti-communism."[52]

A few months later, in pursuit of that dream, Brzezinski met in Algiers with Prime Minister Bazargan, Foreign Minister Yazdi, and Defense Minister Mustafa Chamran. The timing, however, could not have been worse. Weeks earlier, the Carter administration had allowed the dying shah, stricken with cancer, to come to New York for medical care. It was a move that inflamed Khomeini's most radical followers, and Khomeini seized on it to move against the Bazargan-Yazdi faction in the Iranian government, just three days after the Brzezinski-Bazargan encounter in Algiers. What seemed at the time to be a spontaneously assembled mob of students invaded the grounds of U.S. embassy in Teheran, and one of the most significant diplomatic crises in U.S. history was launched. With its diplomats captive, there was no possibility for dialogue between the United States and Iran. The Iranian government maintained the polite fiction that the hostage takers were simply militant "students," but there is no doubt that the entire action was carefully orchestrated by Khomeini and his inner circle as a means of consolidating the political power of the unofficial, parallel government that had been growing in strength alongside the official one. Vladimir Kuzichkin, the KGB station chief in Teheran who defected to the West a few years later, had direct information on who organized the terrorist operation. "We knew from our sources who it was who sanctioned and then carried out the seizure of the embassy," wrote Kuzichkin. "The seizure was sanctioned at the very summit of the Iranian leadership, and was carried out by a trained team that consisted exclusively of members of the Corps of Revolutionary Guards."[53]

The Carter administration had not the slightest clue about how to deal with Khomeini after the embassy takeover. Countless books, memoirs, and scholarly papers have been written about the hostage crisis. But nothing sums up the futility of Carter's efforts better than a passage from the memoir of Hamilton Jordan, the president's chief of staff, who had a lead responsibility for resolving the standoff. Jordan describes seeing Carter at his desk, writing:

> "See me later if you don't mind—I'm writing a letter to Khomeini."
> I was amused at the idea of the Southern Baptist writing to the Moslem fanatic. What will he say to the man? I thought. Maybe he'll sign the letter "The Great Satan." . . .
> "If Khomeini is the religious leader he purports to be," Carter said, "I don't see how he can condone the holding of our people."[54]

It was the beginning of the end of the Carter administration, too. The seizure of the U.S. embassy created a sustained crisis that President Carter could not extricate himself from—not by negotiations, not by threats, not by a bungled military rescue mission. Although Teheran engaged several times, often using dubious middlemen, in talks with Washington, it was clear that Khomeini had an internal political agenda that precluded the release of the hostages until he was ready. "In January 1980," says Harold Saunders, "a prominent Islamic states-man said: 'You won't get the hostages back until Khomeini puts in place all the elements of his Islamic republic.' "

That proved to be the case.

The revolution in Iran changed everything. For Washington, it eliminated a reliable ally, listening post, and base of operations. For the other big player in the Cold War, the revolution in Iran was perhaps even more alarming. Despite the shah's open alliance with the United States, the Soviet Union had grown comfortable dealing with Iran on terms that, more often than not, were marked by the kind of respect that two neighboring powers give each other. In economic relations, in particular, the USSR and Iran got along well. More important, Iran's stability meant that Moscow did not have to worry about instability or irredentism on its flank in southwest Asia. Now, all bets were off. For the first time since the 1920s, the Soviet Union started to worry about Islam. And the United States was planning to make sure it had something to worry about.

10

JIHAD I: THE "ARC OF ISLAM"

THE REVOLUTION IN Iran collapsed the more important of the two pillars holding up the American edifice in the Persian Gulf—the other being Saudi Arabia—and sent Pentagon planners and Central Intelligence Agency analysts scrambling to calculate its impact on other U.S. allies, on the region, and on the overall American presence in the Middle East. From Saudi Arabia to Morocco, American experts frantically scanned the horizon to determine if, or when, the Khomeini phenomenon might replicate itself in other Middle East monarchies.

But along with the threat from Khomeinism, some U.S. policy makers also saw opportunity.

The emergence of hard-core Islamic fundamentalism as a governing force in Iran worried all of Iran's neighbors—including its biggest, the Soviet Union. The Khomeini regime was a volatile, unpredictable new factor in the region, and some analysts believed that the Islamic resurgence led by the Iranian ayatollah could inspire sympathies inside the Soviet Union's Muslim republics. That idea gave new impetus to long-held ideas about using the Islamic right to undermine the Soviet Union in its own empire, deep in Central Asia. At the same time, plans were under way to use Muslim Brotherhood–linked organizations in neighboring Afghanistan to undermine the Soviet stake in that country, which for decades was seen as part of Moscow's sphere of influence. The twin Islamic movements, in Iran and Afghanistan, inspired Zbigniew Brzezinski, President Carter's national security adviser, and Bill Casey, President Reagan's CIA director, to pursue the Islam-in-Asia theme aggressively—most emphatically during the holy war in Afghanistan.

The U.S. proxy war in Afghanistan, which cost $3 billion and several hundred thousand lives, took America's decades-long alliance with ultra-conservative political Islam to a new, more aggressive level. Until Afghanistan, the dominant idea was Islam-as-bulwark, that is, that political Islam was a barrier against Soviet expansion. But in Afghanistan the paradigm was Islam-as-sword. The Islamic right became an offensive weapon, signaling a significant escalation in the policy of cooperating with the Muslim Brotherhood in Egypt, the Saudi Arabia–led Islamic bloc, and other elements of political Islam. Although the war in Afghanistan was sometimes portrayed as a broad-based coalition effort, the mujahideen were overwhelmingly Islamists, and two-thirds of the U.S. support for the mujahideen fighters in Afghanistan went to Islamic fundamentalist parties, channeled through Pakistan and Saudi Arabia.

The Afghan jihad also brought about a significant transformation of the Islamist movement itself. First of all, the Afghan jihad empowered its most radical fringe, which took credit for battling toe to toe with a superpower in Afghanistan. Second, the Afghan war created a new cadre of Islamists skilled in guerrilla warfare, intelligence tradecraft, assassination skills, and the making of car bombs. And third, it vastly strengthened the international bonds that tied together Islamists in North Africa, Egypt, the Gulf, Central Asia and Pakistan. In one sense, the movement had already reached its takeoff point in the 1970s, buoyed by the newfound power of Saudi Arabia's oil wealth, the emergence of the highly political Islamic banking system, and the establishment of powerful new Islamist institutions in Egypt and other conservative Muslim countries. But after Afghanistan, the movement—radicalized, and feeling its power as never before—flexed its muscle. In the late 1980s, Islamists seized control of Afghanistan and Sudan, held significant power in Saudi Arabia and Pakistan, and threatened to capture Egypt and Algeria. The foundation for Al Qaeda and its terrorist underground was laid in these years.

Some of this, perhaps most of it, was ignored by or invisible to U.S. intelligence and policy makers, who were starry-eyed about the prospect of dealing a body blow to the Soviet Union in Afghanistan. Not only that, but the more radical among U.S. officials saw Central Asia as the soft Muslim "underbelly" of the Soviet Union, and pictured the disintegration of the USSR beginning in its Central Asian republics.

Finally, in the broadest strategic terms, the Afghan jihad energized what until the 1980s had been merely a neoconservative pipe dream: the military occupation of the Persian Gulf and its oil fields. There is a direct line between the war in Afghanistan and the current U.S. military presence deep into Kazakhstan, Uzbekistan, and other parts of oil-rich Central Asia. It was a conflict that brought the United States into a part of the world which, until the 1980s, lay outside the U.S. sphere of influence. That began in the 1980s, when Afghan jihadists took U.S., Chinese, Israeli, and other weapons to fight the Red Army. It continued into the 1990s, when the United States cooperated with the rise of the militant Taliban movement. It lasted on into the present, when yet another Afghan war has facilitated a massive U.S. entanglement in the newly independent Muslim Central Asian republics. The United States has seamlessly linked its Middle East and Persian Gulf empire, complete with an archipelago of military bases in the Gulf, the Indian Ocean, and points west, with a new necklace of bases encircling Iraq, Afghanistan, and Central Asia. If the conflicts of the twenty-first century pit the United States against either Russia or China, or both, in a struggle for control of the oil and gas resources of southwest Asia, the United States already has the upper hand. For, beginning with the Afghan jihad, the U.S. military began to assemble a proto-occupation force for the Gulf and surrounding real estate.

None of this existed at the time of the Iranian revolution and the start of the jihad in Afghanistan. But the war in that country allowed the United States, for the first time, to begin to project U.S. military forces directly into southwest Asia and the Gulf. It led to new military relationships with Egypt, Saudi Arabia, and Pakistan, the creation of the Rapid Deployment Force and the U.S. Central Command, and the establishment of new bases surrounding the region. The process began just weeks after the Soviet Union moved troops into Afghanistan, when, in January 1980, President Carter proclaimed what has come to be called "the Carter Doctrine," a forceful restatement of earlier U.S. claims to the Persian Gulf that had been enunciated by Franklin Delano Roosevelt (1943) and Dwight D. Eisenhower (1957). "Let our position be absolutely clear," said Carter. "An attempt by any outside force to gain control of the Persian Gulf region will be regarded as an assault on the vital interests of the United States." Aimed mostly at the Soviet Union, Carter's announcement was, for the most part, bravado. In 1980, the United States did not have even token forces in the Gulf to repel an attack by the USSR, and it lacked the ability to airlift and sealift the U.S. military to the Gulf in an emergency. Of course, the Soviet Union had no intention of invading or occupying the Gulf. Its reluctant move into Afghanistan in 1979 was taken as a last-ditch defensive action against a carefully calculated threat from Afghan Islamist provocateurs backed by the United States and Pakistan. If there existed any threat to U.S. interests in the Gulf, it was entirely internal, but even in this arena U.S. capacities were suspect. Should Iran or Iraq go to war against the Arab Gulf states or should a military coup in Saudi Arabia unseat the royal family, America's ability to react effectively was far from certain.

Long before the crisis in Afghanistan, there had been talk in the United States about a U.S. invasion of Saudi Arabia and the occupation of its oil fields. This began in the mid-1970s, after the Arab oil embargo and fourfold increase in the price of oil imposed by the Organization of Petroleum Exporting Countries in 1973–74. Strategic thinking about a U.S. military move into the Gulf originated with Secretary of State Henry Kissinger. In 1975, an article headlined "Seizing Arab Oil" appeared in *Harper's*. The author, who used the pseudonym Miles Ignotus, was identified by the magazine as "a Washington-based professor and defense consultant with intimate links to high-level U.S. policy makers." Reputedly, the author was Edward Luttwak, a neoconservative military analyst at the Johns Hopkins School of Advanced International Studies (though Luttwak denies being its author). At around the same time, another Hopkins professor, Robert W. Tucker, wrote a similar piece for the American Jewish Committee's *Commentary* magazine, and other articles advocating the seizure of the Saudi oil fields began popping up elsewhere. According to James Akins, the U.S. ambassador to Saudi Arabia in the mid-1970s, the *Harper's* article outlined "how we could solve all of our economic and political problems by taking over the Arab oil fields [and] bringing in Texans and Oklahomans to operate them," says Akins, who took note of the sudden epidemic of such articles: "I knew that it had to have been the result of a deep background briefing. You don't have eight people coming up with the same screwy idea at the same time, independently."[1]

Then Akins made what he calls his "fatal mistake," and it eventually got him fired as U.S. ambassador. "I said on television that anyone who would propose that is either a madman, a criminal, or an agent of the Soviet Union." Soon afterward, he learned that the background briefing had been conducted by his boss, Henry Kissinger. Akins was fired later that year. Kissinger has never acknowledged his role in encouraging these articles. But in an interview with *Business Week* that same year, he delivered a thinly veiled threat to the Saudis, musing about bringing oil prices down through "massive political warfare against countries like Saudi Arabia and Iran to make them risk their political stability and maybe their security if they did not cooperate." Something of the flavor of Kissinger's attitude toward Saudi Arabia and the Gulf states is also captured in a story told by a former senior CIA official who served in the Persian Gulf in the 1970s. Determined to make a show of force in order to intimidate Saudi Arabia, Kissinger summoned a CIA executive who was heading out to the Middle East on an unrelated mission. "We have to teach Saudi Arabia a lesson," Kissinger told the CIA man. "Pick one of those sheikhdoms, any of them, and overthrow the government there, as a lesson to the Saudis." According to the CIA official: "The idea was to do it in Abu Dhabi or Dubai. But when my boss got out to the Gulf, and met with all the CIA station chiefs from the region, not one of them thought it was a good idea. So it was dropped. And Kissinger never brought it up again."[2]

Until Afghanistan's war, U.S. military planners knew that the United States didn't have the capability to rapidly dispatch tens or hundreds of thousands of U.S. forces to the Gulf in the 1970s, and America's naval presence there was only a token force, despite the bravado about occupying Arab oil fields. Along with announcing the Carter Doctrine, President Carter took steps that began to give the United States the ability to intervene directly into the Persian Gulf, if only in rudimentary form. Carter ordered the creation of the Rapid Deployment Force (RDF), an "over-the-horizon" military unit capable of rushing at least several thousand U.S. troops to the Gulf in a crisis. Under President Ronald Reagan, the RDF would be expanded, transforming itself into the Central Command, a brand-new U.S. military structure with authority for the Persian Gulf and the surrounding region, from East Africa to Central Asia and Afghanistan. It was the Central Command, or Centcom, that fought the first Persian Gulf war, the 2001 war in Afghanistan, and the 2003 Iraq war.

But in 1979, a massive U.S. military presence in the Middle East, the Gulf, and Central Asia was just a gleam in the eye of Zbigniew Brzezinski. For the national security adviser, the solution to the seething "arc of crisis" was the "arc of Islam."

EYEING MOSCOW'S ISLAMIC "UNDERBELLY"

The idea of mobilizing Islam against the USSR had a long history during the Cold War. For the most part, it was viewed skeptically by mainstream U.S. strategists, especially during the 1950s and 1960s. Working against the notion that Soviet Muslims might be induced or encouraged to revolt against rule by Moscow was the fact that the Soviets seemed to have succeeded in pacifying its Central Asian republics, colonizing Russian settlers there, forcibly relocating Muslim ethnic populations, and suppressing Muslim religious movements. In addition, it was a remote region, limiting United States access to the population. But in the 1970s several factors combined to provide stronger arguments to those who, for many years, had sought to play the Islam card against Moscow. In 1970, a census taken in the Soviet

Union showed that the Muslim population of Soviet Central Asia was growing far more rapidly than the populations of the other Soviet republics, particularly the Russians. Then revolution in Iran catapulted militant Islam to the forefront of regional politics, in Afghanistan and in Azerbaijan and other Soviet republics. And suddenly, the Soviet-leaning regime in Kabul seemed vulnerable to a ragtag coalition of Islamist forces, and Afghanistan itself emerged as a potential battleground.

At least that's how it looked to a small fraternity of U.S. officials assembled by Brzezinski and the CIA. Within the Carter administration the Nationalities Working Group was the organizational center of this strategic planning. The NWG was a rump organization, an interagency task force created with the express approval of Brzezinski's NSC and including officials from the CIA, State Department, Pentagon, and other agencies. The chairman of the NWG was Paul Henze, a Brzezinski aide and a former CIA official, who worked with a close-knit group of outside players and consultants who'd long believed that restive Soviet minorities would be the undoing of the USSR. Many of them had been associated since the 1950s with the creation of Radio Liberty, a CIA-supported broadcasting system—parallel to Radio Free Europe—that beamed propaganda into the Soviet bloc during the Cold War.

Radio Liberty's focus on Central Asia got off to a modest start in the 1950s. According to James Critchlow, a longtime Radio Free Europe/Radio Liberty (RFE/RL) executive and author of *Nationalism in Uzbekistan,* Radio Liberty began its first broadcasts into Central Asia through the Turkestan desk in Uzbek, Turkmen, Kazakh, Tajik, and Kyrgyz, along with other broadcasts through its Caucasus desk in Georgian, Azerbaijani, and Chechen. The broadcasts were limited to half an hour a day in each language, and they contained a mix of news and editorials. "Commentaries criticizing the Soviet regime, including especially its repressive policies toward Islam and other religions, were a major component," says Critchlow. But, he says, in keeping with the program's modest goals in the 1950s, the broadcasts contained an explicit ban on secessionist agitation, a prohibition that was "resented by some of the staff."[3]

From time to time, hard-line Cold Warriors would call for an intensification of the U.S. propaganda and even subversion aimed at the Central Asian republics. For example, in 1958, Charles W. Hostler, a former U.S. intelligence officer, wrote in the *Middle East Journal* that "the Soviets actively fear combined anti-Soviet action by the Turkish peoples" in Asia, that NATO-linked Turkey could inspire these Muslims to "political independence from the Soviets," and that "the West must interest itself more in these peoples and their aspirations." He called for an expansion of U.S. radio broadcasts in Central Asian languages and an expansion of U.S. government funding for "research in the Central Asian and Caucasian peoples, areas, and languages."[4]

In the 1960s, Brzezinski himself joined the ranks of those calling for stronger U.S. support for Central Asian Muslims. Gene Sosin, former director of program planning for RFE/RL, noted:

> Zbigniew Brzezinski was a consistent supporter of Radio Free Europe and Radio Liberty. But he did not always agree with some of our policies. This became evident in early 1966, when our CIA sponsors asked him to join [in] a confidential analysis of both radios. . . . Professors Brzezinski and [MIT's William] Griffith criticized Radio Liberty's nationality policy, which they felt was too passive. They argued for adopting a more militant line in the non-Russian broadcasts, which would stimulate anti-Russian antagonism.[5]

As a scion of a Polish elite family, Brzezinski was a militant anticommunist who saw the Soviet Union as a powerful but fragile mosaic of seething ethnic and religious minorities. At the NSC, he assembled a team of aides and consultants who wanted to exacerbate conflicts inside the Soviet Union in order to hasten its fall. According to Robert Gates, a senior CIA official who later became the CIA's director, the State Department was cautious about getting involved in supporting dissident minorities in Soviet Central Asia. "Brzezinski, on the other hand, was deeply interested in exploiting the Soviets' nationalities problem," wrote Gates, in his memoirs. "He wanted to pursue covert action."[6]

The core of the Brzezinski-Henze NWG were acolytes of Alexandre

Bennigsen, a count and European academic who was a prolific writer and the guru of the school that viewed Islam as a powerful threat to Soviet authority. Bennigsen's family background gave him a natural affinity for Brzezinski. He was born in St. Petersburg, Russia, the son of a Russian count who fought on the side of the anti-Bolshevik Whites in the civil war that followed the Russian revolution. In the 1950s Bennigsen established himself first at the Ecole des Hautes Etudes en Sciences Sociales in Paris, and later at the University of Chicago. His many books and articles on Islam in Central Asia fostered a movement of scholars and public officials who believed in the viability of the Islamic card, and who took up residence at the University of Chicago, the RAND Corporation, in think tanks, and in parts of the national security bureaucracy.[7] Among those influenced by Bennigsen were Brzezinski, Paul Henze, and S. Enders Wimbush, who later served as a RAND Soviet specialist and as a Radio Liberty official in Munich.

From the late 1950s on, Bennigsen produced a steady stream of books, articles, and research papers advancing the notion that an underground movement of Islamists was gaining strength inside the USSR. In *The Islamic Threat to the Soviet State,* Bennigsen said that the movement harked back to "armed religious resistance [that] began in the late eighteenth century . . . spearheaded by mystical Sufi brotherhoods (*tariqa*) fighting to establish the reign of God on earth" and opposed to the Russian imperial presence.[8] Despite tremendous Soviet efforts to fracture and suppress Islam, says Bennigsen, it thrived. Even during the 1950s, when Nikita Khrushchev cracked down on Islam, "far from destroying forever the religious feelings of the Muslim population, it only gave a new impulse to the fundamentalist, conservative trend represented by the 'parallel,' underground Sufi Islam."[9] Bennigsen claimed that these secret Sufi brotherhoods led the resistance to the Soviet authority in broad swaths of Central Asia:

> Since the victory of the Bolsheviks up to the present day, the only serious, organized resistance encountered by the Soviets in the Muslim territories has come from the Sufi *tariqa,* what Soviet sources call the "parallel," "nonofficial," or "sectarian" Islam. "Parallel Islam" is more powerful and more deeply rooted than

official Islam. The Sufi brotherhoods are closed, but not wholly secret, societies. . . . Soviet sources present Sufi brotherhoods as "dangerous, fanatical, anti-Soviet, anti-Socialist, anti-Russian reactionary forces," but they recognize their efficiency and dynamism.[10]

According to Bennigsen, the most significant of the Sufi brotherhoods was a secret society called the Naqshbandiya, a Freemason-style fraternity closely tied to the elite of Turkey, which had long-standing connections in Central Asia. The Naqshbandiya were especially strong in Chechnya, Dagestan, and parts of Central Asia, including southern Uzbekistan. "The Naqshbandiya adepts have a long tradition of 'Holy War' against the Russians," wrote Bennigsen. His conclusion was that nationalism in Central Asia was inextricably bound up with radical political Islam:

> Since [World War II] some orders have become more and more infused with nationalism, with the result that any nationalist movement—even progressive—which is bound to emerge will be strongly influenced by the traditionalist conservative idea of Sufism. That such a movement will emerge is beyond doubt.[11]

Bennigsen, and others in his circle, urged a stronger U.S. effort to encourage political Islam in the Soviet republics to revolt, even though, as Bennigsen wrote, the most likely outcome would be "probably, a conservative Islamic radicalism comparable to that of the present-day 'Islamic Revolution' in Iran."[12] Bennigsen's rather cavalier attitude toward the emergence of radical-Islamist governments in Central Asia precisely paralleled Brzezinski's belief that the United States ought to foster the spread of Islamism in Afghanistan without worrying about the consequences.

"In the 1970s, Bennigsen and I taught a seminar on Soviet nationality affairs," says Jeremy Azrael, author of *Emergent Nationality Problems in the USSR* (1977). The University of Chicago program produced a cohort of experts on Soviet Central Asia and Islam, mostly followers of Bennigsen's controversial theories, and some, including Paul Goble, became noted CIA analysts on the topic. Azrael himself joined the CIA in 1978 as a guest analyst. "Once I was on board there, I became a charter member of the Soviet Nationalities Working Group." During the Brzezinski era, efforts were at first restricted to small gestures, such as the distribution of Korans in Central Asian languages and stepped-up efforts, in coordination with Saudi Arabia's intelligence service, to contact Soviet Muslims visiting Mecca for the hajj, according to Azrael.[13] But the revolution in Iran stimulated the imagination of everyone involved.

"I brought Bennigsen to the CIA to give a lecture at the time of the overthrow of the shah," recalls Azrael. It was an exciting and challenging moment. By toppling the shah, Khomeini had rewritten the rules of what Islam might accomplish, and Cold War analysts in the United States were alive with the possibilities. The neoconservatives, in particular, along with other Cold War hard-liners, saw an opening for an anti-Soviet jihad, not just in Afghanistan, but throughout the region. After the Soviet invasion of Afghanistan in December 1979, Zalmay Khalilzad—a neoconservative analyst, RAND strategist, and future U.S. ambassador to Afghanistan—wrote a paper in which he suggested the problems that Khomeini's regime had created for the USSR. "The Khomeini regime also poses risks to the Soviets," he wrote. "The change of regime has encouraged similar movements in Iraq and Afghanistan, and might even affect Soviet Muslim Central Asia."[14] He added:

> The cost for the Soviet Union could include . . . possible domestic unrest in those regions of the USSR referred to by the Soviets as their "internal colony"—the Islamic population of Soviet Central Asia, which might reach 100 million by the year 2000—where despite official attempts at assimilation, Islamic consciousness forms a kind of counterculture and may be susceptible to Muslim agitation if the Soviets continue to make war on their ethnic and religious counterparts across the border. . . . Hostility to the Soviets may increase generally in Muslim countries and groups.[15]

It was, of course, straight out of Bennigsen.

Henze, the chairman of Brzezinski's Nationalities Working Group, was himself a longtime advocate of the Bennigsen view. Henze, whose career included a stint as CIA station chief in Turkey in the mid-1970s, held radical and offbeat views. He earned renown in the 1980s as one of the leading advocates for the discredited notion that the USSR and Bulgarian intelligence were behind the attempted assassination of Pope John Paul II by a Turkish fascist.[16] As early as 1958, Henze wrote an article on the Soviet Union's "Shamil problem," referring to a nineteenth-century Muslim resistance leader who opposed Russian expansion in Asia. Henze, like Bennigsen, was inspired by Shamil and believed that eventually the collapse of the Soviet Union could begin in Central Asia. In his 1958 article, Henze wrote:

> It will be extremely difficult for Soviet Communists, however, to continue their active pro-Arab "anti-colonial" policy for several years without running the risk of provoking unrest among their own Caucasian and Central Asian peoples. The Shamil debate shows that an alert, proud, nationalistically inclined intelligentsia has again developed among these peoples. . . . The Soviet Union is not immune from Algerian situations of its own, though the day when issues which are still in an incipient stage might reach such proportions is still far off.[17]

By the late 1970s, it no longer seemed so far off to Bennigsen, Brzezinski, and Henze. They joined forces with Richard Pipes, another advocate of the Islamic card, who had been writing about Central Asian Muslims and the threat to the Soviet Union since the 1950s, including a two-part analysis published in the *Middle East Journal* in 1955 entitled: "Muslims of Soviet Central Asia: Trends and Prospects." In it, Pipes wrote: "The entire area of Central Asia, including Chinese Turkestan with which Russian Central Asia has always been closely connected, may well tend to move with time in the direction of independent statehood. It is not inconceivable that this vast territory may some day be encompassed in a new Turkic, Muslim state oriented toward the Middle East."[18] Pipes, who once wrote that Soviet Muslims would "explode into genocidal fury" against Moscow,[19] also wrote extensively on the nationalities problem in Soviet Central Asia, and when President Reagan replaced Carter in 1981, Pipes assumed chairmanship of the Nationalities Working Group.

Many other scholars and experts on the Soviet Union disagreed with Bennigsen and his followers, and in any case no such anti-Soviet Muslim revolt emerged. Radical political Islam was not a factor in the dissolution of the USSR after perestroika, the collapse of the Berlin Wall, and the establishment of Central Asia's republics. The Central Asian regimes that emerged in the 1990s were not tinged with Islamism. Instead they found themselves battling militant Islamists from Al Qaeda to the Islamic Liberation Party, and a case can be made that, if anything, America's support for political Islam in Asia has aided the growth of a terrorist Islamist underground in Chechnya, Uzbekistan, and other countries in the region.

THE CIA IN AFGHANISTAN BEFORE 1979

In 1979, the theory that Islam might undermine the USSR in Asia became practice. The United States, Pakistan, and Saudi Arabia officially launched the Islamist jihad that threatened the government in Kabul, provoked the Soviet Union into invading Afghanistan, and spawned the ten-year civil war. The Afghan war, for Brzezinski, tied two concepts together. The first was his idea of an "arc of Islam" in southwest Asia, as a barrier against the USSR. As Fawaz Gerges, author of *America and Political Islam,* wrote:

> Containing Soviet Communism, said Brzezinski, dictated an avoidance of anything that might split Islamic opposition to the Soviets, especially a U.S.-Iranian military confrontation: "It now seemed to me more important to forge an anti-Soviet Islamic coalition." As in the 1950s and 1960s, the United States hoped to use Islam against radical, secular forces and their atheist ally, the Soviet Union. Carter administration officials now recognized the new possibilities for cooperation with Islamic resurgence and hoped to harness its ideological and material resources against Communist expansionism. Uppermost in U.S. officials' minds were the lessons of the 1950s and 1960s, when Islam was employed as an ideological weapon in the fight against secular, pan-Arab nationalism.[20]

The Bennigsen-Brzezinski notion of mobilizing Islam as a weapon against Moscow's Asian "underbelly" was the second salient of this strategic plan.

Yet the Afghan Islamists didn't emerge fully developed, out of nowhere, when they began receiving official CIA support. Long before 1979, the Islamic right had emerged as a potent force inside Afghanistan, where, from the 1950s on, it did battle with progressive, left, and secular forces in Kabul. America's connection to the Muslim Brotherhood–linked Islamic fundamentalists in Afghanistan began at least as early as the 1950s, and U.S. support for the Islamic right's political movement in the country began as far back as 1973.

Although the CIA did not have a great presence in Afghanistan in the early decades of the Cold War, it did dispatch a team there through the offices of the Asia Foundation, a CIA front organization. During the 1950s and 1960s, the Asia Foundation provided significant support to Kabul University and had several modest projects that dealt with Afghanistan's organized Muslim community. According to John and Rose Bannigan, longtime Asia Foundation officials who worked for the foundation in both Pakistan and Afghanistan in the 1960s, the organization helped the Islamic Research Institute in Lahore, Pakistan, to publish the Urdu Encyclopedia of Islam. "We were also involved with the major universities, through the departments of Islamic theology," John Bannigan says. In both Pakistan and Afghanistan, the Bannigans worked with student groups to combat pro-Soviet student organizations. "The students were target number one," he says. In Afghanistan, according to Rose Bannigan, the Asia foundation established relations with the Mujaddidi family, that country's leading Islamic clerical family, and with the ministry of justice, which was headed for a time by a Mujaddidi. The foundation also sent Shafiq Kamawi, the deputy minister of justice, to Henry Kissinger's seminar on international affairs at Harvard, she says. "A lot of people in the ministry of justice were mullahs, including the legal adviser to the Asia Foundation."

It is not clear to what extent the CIA maintained regular contacts with Afghan Islamists in the 1960s, since Afghanistan was not a priority for U.S. policy until well into the following decade. "When I was there in 1957, Afghanistan was already a Soviet client state," says a former senior CIA official. "They wanted me to find out everything I could about the Soviet presence in Afghanistan, because President Eisenhower wanted a study of the importance of the country to U.S. strategy and its relevance in Washington." But the study proved only that Afghanistan was not very important. "We concluded that there wasn't any relevance," he says. "Even if the Soviets took it over, there was no great risk to the United States."[21] Still, in the 1960s, the Asia Foundation maintained a presence in Afghanistan, with two or three permanent U.S. staffers and perhaps a dozen or more U.S. advisers and consultants.[22]

During the 1960s, the Islamist movement in Afghanistan underwent a slow but steady politicization. Although Afghanistan society had always been a conservative, traditional one in which Islam played a central role, the version of Islam that prevailed in the country, at least until the 1960s, was pious but not political. Islam in Afghanistan was a faith and not a sociopolitical credo. But under the influence of outside religious and intellectual forces—especially Egypt's Muslim Brotherhood, Pakistan's Islamic Group, and the international organization of the Brotherhood based in Geneva and led by Said Ramadan—Afghan Islam underwent a critical transformation, becoming politicized and more militantly anti-communist. Leading Afghan Islamist organizers and scholars began to return to Afghanistan from Egypt, where they had come into contact with the heirs of Hassan al-Banna's movement. According to Olivier Roy, a leading French Orientalist and expert on Afghanistan and Islam, the origin of political Islam in Afghanistan began with a semi-secret clique called "the professors," who came to prominence in Afghanistan after studying at Cairo's Al Azhar mosque, where they hobnobbed with the Muslim Brotherhood. The movement in Afghanistan coalesced in 1958, when a leading Afghan religious scholar clashed with Muhammad Daoud, the king's cousin and future leader of the Afghan republic. Many Islamists were arrested, and the nascent organization was forced to operate underground. It called itself the Islamic Society.[23]

By the mid-1960s, the Islamic Society and its offshoots were following in the mode of Islamist organizations in Egypt, Pakistan, Iraq, and elsewhere, physically assaulting left-wing and communist students and threatening violence against their political opponents. Led by many of the same men who would, in 1979, become the beneficiaries of the CIA's largesse, they also began open political agitation. Wrote Roy:

> The "professors" greatly influenced their pupils and in 1965, the year of the foundation of the communist party, the Islamist students demonstrated openly by distributing a leaflet entitled . . . the "tract of the holy war." The period from 1965 to 1972 was one of political turmoil on the campus at Kabul. . . . They were very much opposed to communism, and a great number of violent fights broke out on Kabul campus between them and the Maoists. Although at the beginning they were outnumbered by the communists, the Islamists' influence steadily increased and they gained a majority in the student elections of 1970.[24]

As early as June 1970, a confidential State Department dispatch from the U.S. embassy in Kabul identified Afghanistan's religious leadership, in particular the clerical family of the Mujadiddis, as a strong and active force. It concluded that agitation by the mullahs "set back the leftist cause, at least in the countryside" and that "religious conservatism, for the first time in many years, vividly demonstrated that it remains a force with which the government must contend." "The mullahs are reliably reported to have agreed to continue the good fight in the provinces," wrote the embassy's political officer. "Here, in Kabul, there have been some efforts to keep the flame of religious fervor burning in the bazaar." He added, with some irony given future developments: "It will probably not be known for some time how much staying power the clerical militancy has."[25]

Among the leaders of the Afghan Islamist movement in the early 1970s were Abdul Rasul Sayyaf, whose organization was affiliated with the Muslim Brotherhood and Saudi Arabia; Burhanuddin Rabbani; and Gulbuddin Hekmatyar, all of whom led major components of the jihad forces in the 1980s. According to Roy, "The movement functioned on an open level, the Muslim Youth, and a more secret level, centered upon the 'professors.'" The leader of "the professors," and the man who led the semi-secret Organization of Muslim Youth, was Professor Gholam Muhammad Niyazi of the faculty of theology at Kabul University, a major beneficiary of CIA support through the Asia Foundation. In 1972, Rabbani, Sayyaf, and later Hekmatyar formed a guiding council for the movement, and Hekmatyar supervised its secret military wing. The entire organization operated in small cells of five members, and in the early 1970s—again, following the pattern set by the Brotherhood in Egypt and Pakistan—they began to infiltrate the armed forces.[26] In 1972, declassified U.S. embassy documents reveal, a member of the Muslim Youth met a U.S. official several times to request assistance, "describing in some detail the anti-communist activities of his group" (including the murder of "four leftists") and requesting covert U.S. aid to buy a printing press. But it was too early for direct CIA help, and the embassy official turned down the request, while expressing sympathy for the group's goals.[27]

Beginning about this time, the CIA began to take a more active role on behalf of the Afghan Islamists. Previously, the CIA's assistance was modest, much of it funneled through the Asia Foundation to Kabul University and more establishment Islamic forces. But then in 1973, Prince Muhammad Daoud—with the assistance of the communists—toppled the king and established an Afghan republic. Caught off guard, bitterly divided into factions based on ego and ideology, the Islamic right in Afghanistan nevertheless moved into open opposition to Daoud. They soon found a plethora of friends abroad.

The CIA, Pakistan—first under Zulfikar Ali Bhutto, and then under the Islamist General Zia ul-Haq—and the shah of Iran began urgent efforts to undermine the new Afghan government. It was years before the Soviet invasion of Afghanistan, long before the 1980s jihad, but the momentum for an Islamist holy war in the landlocked Asian nation was already gathering—with the full complicity of the CIA. Years later a Pakistani government official working for Bhutto's daughter, who was then prime minister, admitted that the CIA's support for the Islamists in Afghanistan began immediately after Daoud's 1973 coup. "Prime Minister Benazir Bhutto's Special Assistant Nasirullah Babar reportedly stated in a press interview in April 1989 that the United

States had been financing Afghan dissidents since 1973 and that it had taken [Islamic Party] chieftain Gulbuddin Hekmatyar 'under its umbrella' months prior to Soviet military intervention," according to one account.[28]

Diego Cordovez and Selig Harrison, drawing heavily on recently released Soviet archives, described in detail the effort by the United States, Iran, Saudi Arabia, and Pakistan to mobilize the Islamic right inside Afghanistan:

> It was in the early 1970s, with oil prices rising, that Shah Mohammed Reza Pahlavi of Iran embarked on his ambitious effort to roll back Soviet influence in neighboring countries and create a modern version of the ancient Persian empire. . . . Beginning in 1974, the Shah launched a determined effort to draw Kabul into a Western-tilted, Teheran-centered regional economic and security sphere embracing India, Pakistan and the Persian Gulf states. . . . The United States actively encouraged this roll-back policy as part of its broad partnership with the Shah in the economic and security spheres as well as in covert action throughout southwest Asia.[29]

The goal of the U.S.-Iranian effort, which was also supported by Saudi Arabia and Pakistan, was to strengthen right-wing and conservative forces in Daoud's moderate government, in order to pull Afghanistan out of the Soviet orbit. According to Cordovez and Harrison:

> Savak and the CIA worked hand in hand, sometimes in loose collaboration with underground Afghan Islamic fundamentalist groups that shared their anti-Soviet objectives but had their own agendas as well. The Afghan fundamentalists were closely linked, in turn, to the Cairo-based Ikhwan al-Muslimeen (Muslim Brotherhood) and the Rabitat al Alam al Islami (Muslim World League), a leading exponent of Saudi Wahhabi orthodoxy. As oil profits skyrocketed, emissaries from these newly affluent Arab fundamentalist groups arrived on the Afghan scene with bulging bankrolls. Like Savak, they hired informers who attempted to identify Communist sympathizers throughout the Afghan government and armed forces.

The authors added that Iran's intelligence service fed weapons and other assistance to underground groups in Afghanistan tied to the Islamic right, while Pakistan's Interservices Intelligence Directorate (ISI) helped coordinate raids on Afghan targets. "Savak, the CIA, and Pakistani agents were also involved in the abortive, fundamentalist-backed coup attempts against Daoud in September and December 1973 and June 1974."[30]

In 1975, Afghan's Islamists felt that they had enough power to launch an all-out rebellion against Daoud, who, though wavering, was still allied to Afghan's communists. But the uprising was crushed, many of the rebels were arrested and executed, and others—such as Hekmatyar and Rabbani—fled into exile, mostly to Pakistan, where they began to get significant support from the Pakistani military intelligence service. For the next four years, the ISI developed an increasingly close relationship to the motley coalition of Afghanistan rebels, especially its Islamist core. A confidential State Department analysis of the crisis in Afghanistan in 1975 specifically linked the Muslim Brotherhood and ISI:

> What went almost unnoticed in the excitement of alleged Pakistani involvement was the fact that Daoud was putting down a manifestation of "international" Islam. Afghan nationals who were ringleaders in the insurgency, in addition to being persons allegedly subverted by Pakistani aims, were reportedly members of . . . the Muslim Brotherhood, and it was the Brotherhood as part of a larger group that was said to have entered an agreement with Pakistan's chief of intelligence, General Jailani.[31]

Inside Afghanistan, however, the vacillating Daoud began to tilt right, under pressure from the United States, the shah of Iran, and Pakistan. Between 1975 and 1978, Daoud switched sides, breaking decisively with his left-wing supporters and embracing the army and Afghanistan's conservative establishment. In 1976, Daoud met with the shah and Prime Minister Bhutto, and in response he began to install right-wing officers and other pro-Western leaders in key posts. By 1978, Afghan government death squads started assassinating leftist and communist leaders, and the communists and the left were purged from the Kabul regime. Increasingly, Daoud's power base was reduced to a small, ultraconservative clique and the armed forces, and, according to Cordovez and Harrison, behind-the-scenes power was wielded by SAVAK, the allies of Saudi Arabia's Muslim World League, and the Muslim Brotherhood.[32] The crisis raged until April 1978, when Nur Mohammed Taraki, a communist, staged a pro-Soviet coup d'état and signed a friendship treaty with the Soviet Union. The Islamic right, supported by the ISI, carried out a countrywide campaign of terrorism, assassinating hundreds of teachers and civil servants in a Pol Pot–style attack against secular and educated Afghanis.

The United States was well aware that the organizations in Afghanistan carrying out anti-Soviet terrorism were affiliated with the Muslim Brotherhood, according to numerous State Department and embassy dispatches. One, from a CENTO meeting in 1978, says flatly that the "main threat to new regime could come from tribes and such groups as the Muslim Brotherhood."[33] Another analysis noted in April 1979 that "some of the clerical opposition could eventually coalesce around the *Ikhwan-i Muslimin* Muslim Brotherhood."[34] In June 1979 in a lengthy document entitled "Current Status of the Insurrection in Afghanistan," an embassy officer noted that "entire provinces in the central, eastern, and western portions of Afghanistan have slid under rebel control." It said that the rebels are "known by many names—such as mujahideen ('holy warriors') [and] *Ikhwan-i-Muslimin* ('Muslim Brotherhood')." It noted without comment that the Afghan government referred to the opposition as "made-in-London mullahs."[35]

During this period, even as the 1978–79 revolution in Iran unfolded, Pakistan's ties to the Afghan Islamists grew stronger, and so did Pakistan's own Islamist leanings. General Zia instituted a regime based on Islamic law and encouraged the growth of Pakistan's Islamic Group, led by Abul-Ala Mawdudi. As Ayatollah Khomeini was busily creating his Islamic Republic of Iran, Zbigniew Brzezinski and the CIA launched their Islamic-right army in Afghanistan. But it was more than just an Afghanistan strategy. Brzezinski's effort was designed to implement the cataclysmic view of the Bennigsen school, to use the Islamic right as a sword against the USSR itself.

ZBIG AND BILL'S MUSLIM ARMY

In his oft-quoted 1998 interview with *Le Nouvel Observateur*, Zbigniew Brzezinski revealed a secret behind a secret, that the CIA's assistance to the mujahideen in Afghanistan began before, not after, the Soviet invasion:

> According to the official version of history [said Brzezinski], CIA aid to the mujahideen began during 1980, that is to say, after the Soviet army invaded Afghanistan, on December 24, 1979. But the reality, secretly guarded until now, is completely otherwise: Indeed, it was July 3, 1979, that President Carter signed the first directive for secret aid to the opponents of the pro-Soviet regime in Kabul. And that very day I wrote a note to the president in which I explained to him in my opinion this aid was going to induce a Soviet military intervention.[36]

But behind that secret, of course, was yet another: that the United States had been involved with the Islamic right in Afghanistan and the Middle East throughout the 1970s. In addition, the Afghan holy war began in earnest not in 1980, after Soviet troops crossed the border, and not in 1979, when CIA aid officially began to flow, but in 1978, when the Afghan Islamic right began a coordinated uprising with ISI support, starting in northeast Afghanistan. In March 1979, the western half of the country exploded, especially Herat, a major provincial capital in the west, close to Iran. A hard-core Islamist organization, linked to warlord Ismail Khan and supported by the Islamic Republic of Iran, rose up and slaughtered numerous Afghan government officials. More than a dozen Soviet advisers were hacked to death, along with their wives and children. During this period, the United States maintained relations with Iran's military and intelligence apparatus and with the new Iranian government of Prime Minister Bazargan, and the CIA was providing Iran with intelligence about the USSR, Iraq, and Afghanistan—a secret collaboration that continued until the seizure of the U.S. embassy in Teheran by Khomeini's agents in December 1979.

In March 1979, the CIA completed its first formal proposal for direct aid to the Afghan Islamists, coinciding with the revolt in Herat. According to Gates, some in the CIA believed that Soviet involvement in Afghanistan would "encourage a polarization of Muslim and Arab sentiment against the USSR." Not only that, but there was a practical side, too: the CIA had surveyed Afghanistan as a possible site to replace the listening posts that U.S. intelligence had in Iran until 1979, according to Gates.[37] At the beginning of 1979, the United States began to consider active, covert assistance to the jihadis, and both Pakistan and Saudi Arabia were asking the United States to get more involved. "In Saudi Arabia, a senior official . . . had raised the prospect of a Soviet setback in Afghanistan and said that his government was considering officially proposing that the United States aid the rebels."[38] Even though some U.S. analysts, including some CIA officials, believed that direct U.S. support for the Afghan rebels could lead to a Soviet attack on Pakistan and a worldwide showdown between the United States and the USSR, the U.S. government went ahead. The CIA contacted Saudi Arabia and Pakistan about providing aid to Afghan rebels and, as Brzezinski asserted, in July 1979 President Carter signed the first presidential decision, or "finding," to have the CIA supply "nonlethal" aid, including communications equipment, to the Islamic right in Afghanistan.

In the *Nouvel Observateur* interview, Brzezinski admitted that his intention all along was to provoke a Soviet invasion of Afghanistan—even though, after the Soviet action occurred, U.S. officials expressed shock and surprise. "We didn't push the Russians to intervene, but we knowingly increased the probability that they would," said Brzezinski. When he was asked if, in retrospect, he regretted supporting the rise of Islamic fundamentalism and providing arms and training to future terrorists, he answered:

> What is more important to the history of the world? The Taliban or the collapse of the Soviet empire? Some stirred-up Muslims or the liberation of Central Europe and the end of the cold war?

"Now," he told President Carter in 1979, "we can give the USSR its Vietnam war."[39]

By the end of 1979, more than three-fourths of Afghanistan was in open revolt. Just before Christmas, the Red Army invaded Afghanistan to shore up the beleaguered Afghan government.

One of the quirks of the American jihad in Afghanistan was that from the start the United States allowed Pakistan's ISI and General Zia to control the distribution of aid to the Afghan mujahideen. "Zia," wrote Steve Coll, a journalist whose book *Ghost Wars* is a definitive account of the Afghan jihad, "sought and obtained political control over the CIA's weapons and money. He insisted that every gun and every dollar allocated for the mujahideen pass through Pakistani hands. He would decide which guerrillas benefited. . . . The CIA accepted ISI's approach with little dissent."[40] Prince Turki al-Faisal, then the head of the General Intelligence Department of Saudi Arabia, visited Washington, met Brzezinski and the CIA, and agreed to match U.S. contributions to the Afghan jihad dollar for dollar.

What unfolded, in the years after 1980, was an alliance between Pakistan's ISI, General Zia, and the Islamists in Pakistan, on the one hand, and a nexus of Saudi Arabian government and private networks, from Saudi intelligence to the Muslim World League to Osama bin Laden, on the other. Saudi Arabia and Pakistan had been close for years; this included close military ties, with Pakistani troops and mercenaries being dispatched to help protect the Saudi royal family and train Saudi forces. "Pakistan's relations with Saudi Arabia, and with other Gulf Arab states, dated to the early 1960s," wrote Shireen Hunter. "Pakistani military officers, for example, had trained the Saudi and Gulf militaries. One such officer was General Zia ul-Haq."[41] In addition, in the 1970s first Bhutto and then Zia depended on Saudi aid, especially since the OPEC oil price increases of 1973–74 drained the Pakistan treasury of hard currency to pay for oil. The Saudi aid came with political strings attached. The growth of Islamism in Pakistan was directly tied to Saudi aid to Islamabad.

For the United States, the Saudi-Pakistani alliance was made to order, since both countries were staunch U.S. allies that could be counted on to join in a crusade against the USSR. The fact that both Saudi Arabia and Pakistan had ulterior motives and their own grand designs was ignored or overlooked by the Carter and Reagan administrations, who were eager to bloody the Soviet Union in Afghanistan whatever the cost. Pakistan, always concerned with its main foe, India, saw Afghanistan as strategic depth and an ally in the subcontinent against New Delhi, and General Zia envisioned a kind of "Greater Pakistan." Saudi Arabia had its own interests, too, and saw the conflict in Afghanistan as part of its broader competition with Iran, whose Shiite fundamentalist regime was threatening Iraq and the Gulf states. Saudi Arabia saw Afghanistan and Central Asia as a flank in the struggle with Iran, and Riyadh wanted to strengthen the orthodox Sunni Wahhabi forces in Afghanistan and beyond, to weaken Iran.

Brzezinski, and then Casey, embraced the Pakistan-Saudi axis. But both Pakistan and Saudi Arabia had their favored clients in Afghanistan.

For Pakistan, it was Gulbuddin Hekmatyar, the militant Islamist whose group was called the Islamic Party (Hizb-i Islami). Hekmatyar had a well-earned reputation for being a brutal fanatic:

> Gulbuddin was the darling of Zia and the Pakistan intelligence service. Like other mujahideen leaders, he had been working with the ISI since the early 1970s, when Pakistan had begun secretly backing fundamentalist students at the University of Kabul who were rebelling against Soviet influence in the Afghan government. Back then Gulbuddin was very much a part of the emerging global wave of Islamic radicalism. By all accounts, he was responsible for the practice of throwing acid in the faces of Afghan women who failed to cover themselves properly.[42]

Hekmatyar's specialty was skinning prisoners alive.[43] Sigbhatullah Mujaddidi, an Islamist of somewhat less radical stripes, called Hekmatyar a "true monster."[44] But Representative Charles Wilson, a Texas Republican who was the leading congressional advocate for the Afghan jihad, approvingly noted that Zia was "totally committed to Hekmatyar, because Zia saw the world as a conflict between Muslims and Hindus, and he thought he could count on Hekmatyar to work for a pan-Islamic entity that could stand up to India."[45]

Hekmatyar's Islamic Party was one of the six to eight Afghan parties that made up the anti-Soviet resistance. It was the largest, and it also was reputed to have the fiercest fighters, which increased its appeal to the CIA. "We didn't think, at the beginning, that we would defeat the Soviets," says a CIA official who helped oversee the jihad. "But we did want to kill as many Russians as we could, and Hekmatyar seemed like the guy who could do that."[46] His bone-chilling ruthlessness was a plus. "The CIA officers in the Near East Division who were running the Afghan program also embraced Hekmatyar as their most dependable and effective ally," according to Coll. "At least Hekmatyar knew who the enemy was, the CIA's officers reassured themselves."[47] For those, like Casey and Brzezinski, who envisioned Afghanistan as the key to weakening the Soviet Union among its Muslim republics, Hekmatyar had appeal, too, since he wanted to expand the war beyond Afghanistan. Hekmatyar, according to Dilip Hiro, "talked of carrying the guerrilla raids beyond the Oxus River into Soviet Central Asia and rolling back communism by freeing the Muslim lands of Bukhara, Tashkent, and Dushanbe."[48]

Saudi Arabia's favored client was Abdul Rasul Sayyaf, the Afghan Muslim Brotherhood leader. As the war evolved, both Hekmatyar and Sayyaf would emerge as the Afghan leaders closest to the legions of foreign, mostly Arab, fighters who flocked to Afghanistan to join the jihad. By the end of the 1980s, it would be these so-called Arab Afghans who would graduate to become leaders of the militant and terrorist Islamists in Egypt, Algeria, Saudi Arabia, Iraq, and elsewhere— including Chechnya and Uzbekistan. Hekmatyar and Sayyaf, though not allies, were also close to Osama bin Laden, whose rise to prominence began as early as 1979–80, when he enlisted in the Afghan jihad. "Once in Pakistani exile, [Hekmatyar] gathered around him the most radical, anti-Western, transnational Islamists fighting in the jihad— including bin Laden and other Arabs who arrived as volunteers."[49]

So the stage was set for a climactic showdown between the United States and the Soviet Union in Afghanistan. In the wake of the Iranian revolution, the United States continued to pursue the chimera of an Islamic bloc against the USSR, leading Pakistan, Saudi Arabia, and Egypt into battle in the remote mountains of Central Asia. Hundreds of thousands of jihadis, electrified by the holy war, flocked to war camps along the Pakistan-Afghanistan border from all over the world. The United States had little comprehension of the forces that it was unleashing. But that did not prevent the Reagan administration from pushing the war in Afghanistan into the Soviet Union itself and trying to enlist even Khomeini's Iran in the jihad.

11

JIHAD II: INTO CENTRAL ASIA

WHEN THE AMERICAN-SPONSORED jihad in Afghanistan began in 1979, it took place during a critical transformation in the history of political Islam.

From 1945 until 1979, the Islamic right seemed firmly attached to the Western, and anti-communist, camp in the Cold War. During this period, it was understandable for many analysts to have seen political Islam as docile and, if not pro-American, then at least sympathetic to American political and economic goals in the region. In the Afghan mountains, fierce mullahs expressed their hatred of communism; in the Saudi desert, the Wahhabi establishment thundered against leftist and nationalist forces in North Africa, the Middle East, and Pakistan; and on campuses from Kabul and Islamabad to Baghdad and Cairo, the Muslim Brotherhood battled secularists and preached against Marxism.

Starting in 1979, however, things changed. Ayatollah Khomeini's revolution in Iran was a frontal challenge to U.S. interests. Moreover, the Islamic right had begun to spawn deadly terrorist offshoots that attacked U.S. interests and pro-Western leaders, from the Grand Mosque in Mecca to Anwar Sadat to Hezbollah's predatory terror in Lebanon. The United States was exceedingly slow to grasp the lessons of these developments. First, it failed to concentrate resources on Islamist terrorism after 1979, despite pleas from Arab leaders like Egypt's President Mubarak to do so. More important, the United States failed to understand the larger lesson: that the Islamic right was not just anti-communist, but fundamentally opposed to the West and to its most reliable long-term partners in the Middle East, namely, the secular, democratic nationalists.

Despite the mounting evidence that the Islamic right was a devilishly dangerous ally, the Reagan administration joined their jihad.

The scope of the U.S.-Islamist alliance then is hard to imagine now, in the midst of what the Bush administration calls a global war on terrorism against Al Qaeda and its ilk. But, just as in 1953, when Said Ramadan of the Muslim Brotherhood was ushered into the Oval Office to see President Eisenhower, in 1981 Reagan's tough-minded— and often neoconservative—national security officials and intelligence professionals pursued the Afghan jihad with a vengeance. In fact, the same neoconservatives who today lead the charge for a "clash of civilizations"–style war on terror then pressed the hardest for an alliance with the Afghan Islamists and, at the same time, repeatedly reached out for a deal with the ayatollahs in Teheran.

The U.S.-Islamist alliance of the 1980s was undertaken with all deliberateness. From 1979 to 1982, the Carter and Reagan administrations considered the existence of a threat from right-wing Islam, and decided to ignore it.

Following the Iranian revolution, Carter administration officials convened a government-wide meeting to analyze political Islam. It included State Department experts, intelligence analysts, and ambassadors from the Middle East. "There was a big analytical effort," says Harold Saunders, who was assistant secretary of state for Near East affairs, and it centered on the conservative Arab states and monarchies. "The main focus was to gain an understanding of whether it could happen in Jordan, in Egypt, in Saudi Arabia, or perhaps this was sui generis to Iran." According to Saunders, and to other U.S. officials and intelligence officers, the conclusion of this reevaluation was that political Islam was not threatening. "We realized there would be a ratcheting up of political Islam," says Saunders. "The question was, could the existing governments deal with it? I pushed pretty hard on Saudi Arabia, and I couldn't get anyone to say that Saudi Arabia would fall. In Egypt, at the time, we thought Sadat could handle it."[1]

Certainly, no effort was made to discourage Saudi Arabia from pursuing its long-held notion of a foreign policy based on right-wing Islamism. No effort was made to discourage Sadat from cozying up to the Muslim Brotherhood. No effort was made to discourage Israel and Jordan from supporting the Muslim Brotherhood's campaign of terrorism against Syria and the Palestine Liberation Organization. And, of course, in Pakistan the United States jumped into bed with General Zia ul-Haq, whose Muslim Brotherhood–linked regime and ISI intelligence service were organizing the Afghan jihad.

In the end, the Islamist movement was seen as a force that could be contained by existing governments. No real effort was made to understand how those governments might be changed, how it might affect the societies these governments presided over, and how the Islamists were organized across international borders. Policy makers continued to believe that Islamism was too diverse to be looked at globally, and insisted it could be dealt with on a country-by-country basis. "We concluded that we couldn't have a policy toward political Islam," recalls Saunders.[2]

In the wake of the Iranian revolution there was a brief flurry of directives from Washington to CIA stations overseas to provide an evaluation of Iran's impact. Intelligence analysts at the CIA and the State Department took a look at countries that might be threatened with Khomeini-style revolution, and concluded that the internal threat seemed minimal. As long as existing, pro-U.S. regimes were not at risk, almost no U.S. officials raised alarm about the growing strength of political Islam, its effects within countries plagued by it, or the eventual possibility that radical Islamists might turn against the United States. "At first, there was the assumption that it was going to spread, that it was going to happen in Morocco, Jordan, and Saudi Arabia, that the monarchies were an anachronism," says a former CIA station chief in Morocco. "I got to Morocco and found nothing like that. There was a very small Islamist movement." In the CIA's field manual for Morocco, there were eight pages on Islam and politics, he says. "I'd tell my case officers: Know it cold. And when they were talking to an Islamist, I told them to say: 'I don't understand this or that.' And then listen."[3] The conclusion reached in Morocco, as for other states, was that there was nothing to worry about.

At the CIA, Martha Kessler was one of the few analysts who consistently paid attention to political Islam and the Muslim Brotherhood. In the field, she says, many CIA operatives missed it, because the most militant Islamists were organizing under the radar. "We had a World War II–era system of just plopping our officials down in capital cities, and the Islamist movement wasn't happening in those cities, it was happening out in the country and in small towns." In her opinion, it was taking on a decidedly anti-American character. She wrote an analysis at the time warning that when governments such as Egypt, Sudan, and Pakistan begin to play ball with Islamists, it would have profound consequences. "I said that when governments in the region started making efforts to co-opt the Islamists, it would change the character of those governments," she says. "I was of the school that it would be largely anti-Western in tone."[4] Needless to say, Kessler's analysis did not dissuade policy makers from the Afghan jihad.

The same view prevailed among U.S. government counterterrorism professionals. "After the Sadat assassination, I was in the counterterrorism center," says Robert Baer, a former CIA operative. "I came across some documents, some trial transcripts for [the assassins of Sadat], and I started asking, Who are these people? What's their agenda? What's the connection? I started looking for documents on the Muslim Brotherhood." But, he says, "It just wasn't in our consciousness to go after these people."[5]

Sadat, who had used the Muslim Brotherhood and the financial resources of its Islamic banking network to strengthen his grip on power after becoming president of Egypt in 1970, was least of all aware of how dangerous the Islamic right might be. Within days of the Soviet invasion of Afghanistan, Sadat enthusiastically joined the United States, Saudi Arabia, and Pakistan in sending jihadists to Peshawar, and war.

So the jihad in Afghanistan expanded into a full-scale war. And the

Reagan team, preoccupied with the Cold War, struck a deal with
Iran's ayatollahs in 1980, winked as Israel armed Iran from 1980 to
1987, gave Khomeini's regime secret intelligence about the Iranian
left, and finally, in the Iran-contra affair, actually sold U.S. arms to
Iran in search of mythical Islamist "moderates."

THE ARAB AFGHANS

The war in Afghanistan was fought, for the most part, by the
mujahideen of the fractious coalition backed by Pakistan and made up
mostly of guerrillas associated with one of four fundamentalist organizations. "In Afghanistan," says a former CIA official who ran the
covert operation, "there were about 300,000 fighters, all of whom,
with the exception of about 15,000 moderates, were Islamists."[6] The
vast majority were Afghans, but some were jihadists drawn to the
fighting from other parts of the world, especially from Egypt, Jordan,
Saudi Arabia, and the Gulf. These would be the raw material for
Osama bin Laden and the fledgling Al Qaeda organization that grew
out of the jihad. The so-called Arab Afghans included bin Laden himself, Ayman al-Zawahiri of Egypt's Islamic Jihad, Al Qaeda's second-
in-command, and tens of thousands of jihadists from the Arab states,
Indonesia, the Philippines, Chechnya, and other far-flung corners of
the Muslim world.

They were the guerrillas who, after the war was over, went home
to Algeria, to Egypt, to Lebanon, to Saudi Arabia, and to Central Asia
to continue the jihad. Many, of course, learned terrorism skills—
assassination, sabotage, car bombs—at the hands of the United States
and its allies.

In January 1980, Brzezinski visited Egypt to mobilize Arab support for the jihad. Within weeks of his visit, Sadat authorized Egypt's
full participation, giving permission for the U.S. Air Force to use
Egypt as a base, supplying stockpiles of Egyptian arms to the rebels,
and recruiting, training, and arming Egyptian Muslim Brotherhood
activists for battle. "Sadat and his government became, for a time, virtual recruiting sergeants and quartermasters to the secret army of

zealots being mustered to fight the Soviets in South and Central Asia."[7] U.S. cargo planes took off from Qena and Aswan in Egypt, ferrying supplies to the jihad bases in Pakistan, and, according to John Cooley, "Egypt's military inventories were being scoured for Soviet-supplied arms to send to the jihad. An old arms factory near Helwan, Egypt, was eventually converted to supply the same kind of weapons."[8]

Egypt—and other Arab countries—supplied more than weapons. A number of countries in the Muslim world decided it would be prudent to send Islamist militants to the Afghan war, perhaps thinking that they were killing two birds with one stone: they were pleasing the United States, which was looking for recruits, and they were getting rid of some troublemakers. Sadat, like other leaders, perhaps felt that most of them would be killed during the jihad. "Muslim governments emptied their prisons and sent these bad boys over there," says a CIA official who spent several years as station chief in Pakistan during the jihad.[9] Not only were they packaged and shipped to Afghanistan, but they received expert training from U.S. Special Forces. "By the end of 1980," wrote Cooley, "U.S. military trainers were sent to Egypt to impart the skills of the U.S. Special Forces to those Egyptians who would, in turn, pass on the training to the Egyptian volunteers flying to the aid of the mujahideen in Afghanistan."[10]

The British, for whom Afghanistan was the playground for the Great Game of the nineteenth century and who had long-standing colonial ties to Pakistan, had an extensive history of dealing with the tribes and religious leaders of the Pakistan-Afghanistan area. Gus Avrakotos, a CIA official closely involved with the jihad for years, reported that the British "have guys who have lived over there for twenty years as journalists or authors or tobacco growers, [and] when the Soviets invaded, MI6 activated these old networks." Added Avrakotos:

> The Brits were able to buy things that we couldn't, because it infringed on murder, assassination and indiscriminate bombings. They could issue guns with silencers. We couldn't do that because a silencer immediately implied assassination—and heaven forbid car bombs! No way I could even suggest it, but I could say to the

Brits, "Fadlallah [the radical Shiite leader] in Beirut was really effective last week. They had a car bomb that killed 300 people." I gave MI6 stuff in good faith. What they did with it was always their business.[11]

Much of this training in assassination, car bombs, and the like found its way to the Arab volunteers who eventually became Al Qaeda's foot soldiers. Some mujahideen were even trained to organize the low-tech, Afghan version of car bombs. "Under ISI direction, the mujahideen received training and malleable explosives to mount car bomb and even camel bomb attacks in Soviet-occupied cities, usually designed to kill Soviet soldiers and commanders," wrote Steve Coll. "[CIA Director] Casey endorsed these techniques despite the qualms of some CIA career officers."[12] And it was not just Soviet soldiers who were blown up by such devices. In at least one instance, the mujahideen carried out an extension of the battles that raged at Kabul University during the 1960s and 1970s, when a briefcase bomb exploded under a university dining room table.[13] "This is a rough business," said the CIA's Bill Casey. "If we're afraid to hit the terrorists because somebody's going to yell 'assassination,' it'll never stop."[14] Soon, the CIA and ISI were providing stealthlike explosive devices to the mujahideen, including bombs disguised as pens, watches, cigarette lighters, and tape recorders.[15] "Do I want to order bicycle bombs to park in front of an officers' headquarters?" asked Avrakotos. "Yes. That's what spreads fear."[16] Among the targets of mujahideen bombs were soft targets such as Kabul cinemas and cultural shows.

Although the Afghan mujahideen rebelled at the idea of suicide bombs, Arab volunteers did not:

> It was only the Arab volunteers—from Saudi Arabia, Jordan, Algeria, and other countries, who had been raised in an entirely different culture, spoke their own language, and preached their own interpretations of Islam while fighting far from their homes and families—who later advocated suicide attacks. Afghan jihadists, tightly woven into family, clan, and regional social networks, never embraced suicide tactics in significant numbers.[17]

Afghan mujahideen were also trained inside the United States, beginning in 1980 under Brzezinski's oversight, at various U.S. facilities on the East Coast, by Green Berets and U.S. Navy SEALs. "The deadly secrets which trainers of the Afghan holy warriors passed on numbered over sixty. They included the use of sophisticated fuses, timers and explosives, automatic weapons with armor-piercing ammunition, remote-control devices for triggering mines and bombs (later used in the volunteers' home countries and against the Israelis) [and] strategic sabotage, demolition, and arson."[18]

The Afghan war unfolded in several phases. It started slowly, and over the first five years the U.S. objective was not to win the war, not to defeat the Soviet Union and force its withdrawal, but simply to bleed the USSR, embarrass it, and win propaganda points. In 1984, however, prodded by Rep. Charlie Wilson and with Casey's enthusiastic support, CIA funding of the war—and Saudi Arabia's matching grants—rose rapidly. Funding for the jihad in 1984 totaled $250 million, "as much as all the previous years combined."[19] And it continued to skyrocket: $470 million in 1986, $630 million in 1987. The United States also worked hard to bring other countries into the war, including China. According to Charles Freeman, who served as U.S. ambassador to China, "From 1981 to 1984, there was about $600 million from Beijing in arms for Afghanistan," says Freeman.[20] Not only did Casey expand the funding for the war, but he grew more ambitious in his goals. Now seeking victory, he sought to provide more sophisticated weaponry to the mujahideen, including the Stinger ground-to-air missiles that allegedly had a decisive impact on the military dimension of the conflict.[21]

As the jihad expanded in both goals and scope, more and more Arabs and other foreigners were drawn in. Various Arab governments, including Egypt and Saudi Arabia, international organizations tied to the Islamic right—such as the Muslim Brotherhood, the Muslim World League, the International Islamic Relief Organization, and the Tablighi Jamaat, a Pakistan-based Islamic missionary organization—ran campaigns to recruit jihadis. It was Osama bin Laden's dream come true: Muslim fundamentalist groups mobilizing worldwide to find militant fighters, bring them to Pakistan, and then smuggle them into Afghanistan for a jihad. "Many were offered trips to Pakistan for religious studies," wrote Cooley:

> Usually, during about six weeks' religious studies, the new adepts were not offered military training immediately, or even briefed about the jihad against the Russian and Communist "enemies of God." This came at the end of the six-week period. ISI officers, usually in mufti, would then appear and offer opportunities for training. [Training was provided for] thousands of Algerians, Egyptians, Sudanese, Saudis, and others.[22]

According to Ahmed Rashid, a Pakistani journalist and author of *Taliban*, between 1982 and 1992 35,000 radical Islamists from forty-three countries fought alongside the mujahideen in the war and its aftermath, and tens of thousands of additional jihadis trained in the madrassas that General Zia created along the Pakistan-Afghanistan border. "Eventually more than 100,000 Muslim radicals were to have direct contact with Pakistan and Afghanistan and be influenced by the jihad."[23]

Some of the recruiting for the mujahideen took place inside the United States, in Arab and Muslim communities. At the Al Kifah Afghan Refugee Center in Brooklyn, many Arabs signed up for the jihad. "There were hard-to-trace suitcases full of cash and anonymous bearer cheques or bank drafts, from the Muslim World League, the Tablighi Jamaat, and other missionary and charitable organizations located in Pakistan."[24] One of the key individuals involved in the U.S. recruiting effort in the mid-1980s was Abdullah Azzam, a radical Palestinian Islamist who was bin Laden's professor and who would be the co-founder of the predecessor organization to Al Qaeda, the Services Bureau, which was established by bin Laden and Azzam in Peshawar, Pakistan, in 1984. The innocently named Services Bureau played the central role in moving Arab and foreign jihadis into the war.

Azzam, born in Jenin, Palestine, in 1941, joined the Muslim Brotherhood as a Palestinian youth in Syria, where he studied Islamic law in the early 1960s, when the Brotherhood was leading the anti-Nasser movement in the Arab world.[25] Although he initially belonged to the Palestine Liberation Organization, he split with the PLO during the showdown with King Hussein in Black September, 1970, when the Brotherhood backed the monarchy. He spent time at the Al Azhar mosque in Cairo, during the time that Anwar Sadat was bringing the Muslim Brotherhood back to Egypt, and ended up as a teacher of Islamic law at King Abdel Aziz University in Saudi Arabia, where bin Laden was his student. The Muslim World League hired Azzam to head its education section, and in 1980 he first traveled to Pakistan. In 1984, in addition to founding the Services Bureau, Azzam established *Al Jihad* magazine and wrote prolifically on the duties of Muslims. Providing an early road map to his plan for a global jihad, Azzam wrote the oft-quoted call to arms: "Jihad will remain an individual obligation until all other lands which formerly were Muslim come back to us and Islam reigns within them once again. Before us lie Palestine, Bukhara, Lebanon, Chad, Eritrea, Somalia, the Philippines, Burma, South Yemen, Tashkent, Andalusia."[26] To sweeten the pot, Azzam told potential jihad recruits that Osama bin Laden would pay $300 a month to Arabs who wanted to fight in Afghanistan.

Mike Scheuer is the CIA official who, in later years, would be in charge of U.S. efforts to hunt down Osama bin Laden. In 2002, under the name "Anonymous," he wrote *Through Our Enemies' Eyes*, a detailed account of the rise of bin Laden and Al Qaeda. In it, he described the role of the Services Bureau, also known by its Arabic acronym MAK:

Bin Laden got in on the ground floor of the development of Islamic NGOs for military-support activities when he joined with Shaykh Abdullah Azzam to found the *Makhtab al-Khidimat* (MAK)—or Service Bureau—in Peshawar in the mid-1980s. While the MAK provided relief to Afghan war victims, it also received, organized, and moved into Afghanistan the volunteers, arms, and money flowing to the mujahideen from the Muslim world. In the financial realm, *Al-Watan al-Arabi* has said that between 1979 and 1989 about $600 million was sent to bin Laden's organization through charitable institutions in the Gulf, especially those in Saudi Arabia, Kuwait, Oman, the UAE, Bahrain, and Qatar.[27]

According to Scheuer, bin Laden and Azzam were well connected to a host of other Islamic-right charities, including IIRO and the Muslim World League. According to CIA officials involved with the jihad, the CIA did not directly engage with Azzam and bin Laden in recruiting Arab volunteers, although the CIA did not oppose the effort. Robert Gates, then the CIA director, revealed that "the CIA examined ways to increase their participation." Although no action was taken, nothing was done to discourage the "Arab Afghans," either.[28]

As the CIA began to figure out long after the Afghan jihad was history, the joint U.S.-Saudi funding for the war was not the only source of cash for the mujahideen, as the $600 million that Scheuer refers to indicates. Private and semi-private donations from the Muslim Brotherhood and its apparatus poured into the jihad, and none of it was subject to even the minimal oversight that Pakistan's ISI provided over the distribution of the U.S. and Saudi largesse. According to *Afghanistan: The Bear Trap,* a riveting account of the jihad penned by a former Pakistani intelligence officer, Mohammad Yousaf, a parallel war supply system developed outside official channels, complete with freelancers and wheeler-dealers, and a significant part of it was funded with private Arab donations. "It was largely Arab money that saved the system," wrote Yousaf. "By this I mean cash from rich individuals or private organizations in the Arab world, not Saudi government funds. Without these extra millions the flow of arms actually getting to the Mujahideen would have been cut to a trickle. The problem is it all went to the four Fundamentalist parties, not the Moderates."[29]

In particular, Yousaf wrote, a lot of the cash went to Abdul Rasul Sayyaf, the chief Muslim Brotherhood activist in Afghanistan and one of the Islamist "professors" who helped to organize the secret society that emerged in the 1960s and early 1970s. It was Sayyaf, along with Gulbuddin Hekmatyar—the fanatical mujahideen leader whose Islamic Party was the largest and fiercest of the organizations in the jihad—who were closest to Osama bin Laden.

Sayyaf, Hekmatyar, and other fundamentalists got the lion's share of the Arab money because a large part of it was transferred to the mujahideen through the Muslim Brotherhood–linked Islamic Group of Pakistan, the Islamist political party that was created by Abul-Ala Mawdudi.[30] The Islamic Group (Jamaat-e Islami), founded in 1940, had spent much of the 1950s and 1960s battling Pakistan's left and secularists. In the 1970s, the Islamic Group became more powerful as it absorbed surplus petrodollars funneled its way by the Gulf Arabs, and it helped push Pakistan to the right in the 1970s, under Prime Minister Zulfiqar Ali Bhutto and General Zia ul-Haq. "The Muslim Brotherhood was spreading its money around," says Selig Harrison, an expert on south Asia and the co-author of *Out of Afghanistan*. According to Harrison, the head of the Islamic Group was related to Zia, and he worked closely with them and helped them, and many of the key players in the ISI and the military were members of the Islamic Group. Through the Muslim World League and other Muslim Brotherhood elements in the Gulf, money had started to flow to the coffers of the mujahideen even before the Soviet invasion of Afghanistan, says Harrison. "It was all done through Pakistan, with the help of Rabitat [the League], and the Jamaat-e Islami was getting rich, too."[31]

At the time, virtually no one sensed the importance of bin Laden and Azzam, and the non-Afghan jihad volunteers seemed like a minor part in the mobilization of several hundred thousand Afghan mujahideen. The CIA was so fixated on its Cold War jihad that it never stopped to consider the consequences of empowering a worldwide Islamist armed force. And, in the meantime, Bill Casey was busy opening a second front, pushing hard to expand the Afghanistan war into Central Asia—with resources that Zbigniew Brzezinski and Alexandre Bennigsen could never have dreamed of just a few years earlier.

ACROSS THE AMU RIVER

In carrying the Afghan jihad into the Soviet Union itself, Casey exhibited both a messianic, religiously inspired version of anti-communism and a high-stakes, high-risk approach to foreign policy. Within the Reagan administration, there were at least two competing schools of thought: The first, hewing to the traditional rules of U.S. diplomacy, saw the Soviet Union as a mighty competitor that needed to be challenged worldwide, in order to prevent Soviet gains; and the second, which included the neoconservatives and Casey, advocated a policy of rolling back the Soviet Union in the Third World, eastern Europe, and Central Asia. "The real split in the Reagan administration was not between liberals and conservatives," says Herb Meyer, who served as Casey's chief of staff at the CIA in the 1980s. "The real split was between those who wished not to lose the Cold War and those who wished to win it."[32] Casey was in the latter camp, and for him Afghanistan was the key.

In order to win the Cold War, Casey believed, it would take a strong working alliance among the countries of Brzezinski's "arc of Islam"—including Egypt, Pakistan, and Saudi Arabia—and Casey paid special attention to Saudi Arabia as the linchpin of the effort. The CIA director saw Saudi Arabia as more than a financial resource to support the jihad, and as more than the center of ultra-orthodox Islam. According to Meyer, Casey also mobilized Saudi Arabia's oil weapon against the USSR in the 1980s. "The Saudis were very helpful to us in winning the Cold War," says Meyer. Because the Soviet Union was so dependent on oil exports to earn hard currency, Casey asked Saudi Arabia to ramp up its oil output and collapse the price of oil. "Bill played a key role in working with the Saudis to get the price of oil down," says Meyer. "They hated the Soviets." Saudi Arabia expanded production, the price of oil dropped to historic lows, falling from $28 per barrel to $10 per barrel in a matter of weeks, and Soviet income was severely curtailed. "It was a body blow to the Soviets. It was the equivalent of stepping on their oxygen tube."[33]

Casey, a devout Catholic, combined a fierce belief in the power and importance of religion with a Machiavellian attitude toward the political utility of religious belief. "He was a deeply religious man, and he had a good working relationship with the pope," says Meyer. "Casey," wrote Coll, in *Ghost Wars,* "saw political Islam and the Catholic Church as natural allies in the 'realistic counter-strategy' of covert action he was forging at the CIA to thwart Soviet imperialism."[34] In this view, Casey was encouraged by his chief intelligence adviser on the Middle East, Robert Ames, who was the CIA's leading regional expert. In a speech, Casey credited Ames with having emphasized to him the importance of efforts by the Soviet Union and its allies in the Muslim world to extirpate organized religion, because of the threat that it supposedly posed to communist or nationalist party control. The communists wanted to "uproot and ultimately change the traditional elements of society," said Casey, citing Ames. "This meant undermining the influence of religion and taking the young away from their parents for education by the state." For that reason, the world's two great religions had to cooperate. "Because the Soviets saw all religious faith as an obstacle, they suppressed churches and mosques alike." Casey was convinced that "militant Islam and militant Christianity should cooperate in a common cause."[35]

Inside the CIA, Casey often infuriated professional colleagues by his nonchalant view of the growing power of political Islam. "I worked with Casey," says Richard Krueger, a former CIA operative who spent the last several years of the shah's reign working right inside the shah's own office. "After the revolution, I sponsored with Casey and the heads of all the intelligence agencies a futurist exercise at Camp Perry to analyze the Islamic movement." According to Krueger, John McMahon, Casey's deputy, clashed with Casey over the issue. "I can remember major, major unpleasantries between Casey and McMahon over the long-term implications of the Islamic revolution, with McMahon taking an almost alarmist position and Casey taking a couldn't-care-less position," recalls Krueger. "Casey wanted to just wave it off, and uncharacteristically McMahon jumped in. He was agitated, talking about how Islamic fundamentalism was going to spread to Indonesia, the Philippines. He believed the movement was a natural to internationalize, through all sorts of religious and social connections, and that it wouldn't appear to be state-sponsored." But Casey did not agree.[36]

Casey's views on religion and politics dovetailed with President Reagan's own rock-ribbed faith, and together the two men had no trouble seeing the Afghan jihad as a religious war in which Christianity and Islam were allies against the atheistic Soviet Union. Fawaz

Gerges wrote that Reagan continued the U.S. tradition of supporting Islamic religious forces in the Middle East:

> Under Reagan, U.S. policy remained wedded to supporting conservative religious elements against secular, socialist and third world nationalist forces. Whereas the administration's public statements were exceptionally hostile, no corresponding changes marked its actual behavior toward the new Islamists. . . . Reagan's flirtation with the Islamist mujahideen factions in Afghanistan should be situated within the context of the second phase of the Cold War. Like his predecessors in the 1950s and 1960s, President Reagan allied the United States with Islamist groups and states—Afghanistan, Saudi Arabia, and Pakistan—to combat what he called the 'evil empire' and its third world clients.[37]

Sometimes, Casey's willingness to encourage political Islam seemed strictly cynical. That was especially true when Casey dealt with Saudi Arabia's King Fahd. Gus Avrakotos recounted the story of a discussion about Casey's visit to Saudi Arabia to nail down that year's Saudi matching contribution to the jihad fund. "I told Casey that he should talk to the king about 'your Muslim brothers,' about using the money for food for families, for clothing, weapons, for repairing the mosques. You should talk to him about being 'keeper of the faith.'" Casey replied: "Jesus, fuck, I like that—'keeper of the faith.' Oh, fuck, I like that—'keeper of the faith.'"[38] A former CIA official involved in the jihad confirmed that story. "We would tell the Saudis what a good thing it was that the religious Afghans were expelling the atheistic communists," he adds. "It was the politic thing to say to King Fahd."[39]

Starting in 1984, Casey pushed the Saudi-Pakistan alliance to undertake a much more explosive strategy, launching propaganda, sabotage, and guerrilla activity across the Amu River into the Soviet Union's Muslim republics. "The borders in that part of the world are, well, sort of sloppy," says Meyer, Casey's aide. "So all sorts of interesting things happened."[40] A CIA official who worked with Casey at the time says: "There were occasional forays that took place within the territory of the Soviet Union, which scared the crap out of Moscow."[41] In taking such provocative steps, Casey drew on covert action plans that had originally been developed during the Carter administration, but which had been rejected because of the very real danger that the USSR would counterattack in unpredictable ways, including either a direct strike at Pakistan or an effort to foment a rebellion in Pakistan's unstable province of Baluchistan.

The ISI's Yousaf provides the most detailed account of the jihad's move across Afghanistan's northern border. "The people on both sides were Uzbeks, Tajiks, and Turkomans," he wrote. "They shared a common ethnic identity and, despite the communist clampdown on religious activities, they also shared the same faith, Islam."[42] Casey declared, according to Yousaf: "This is the soft underbelly of the Soviet Union." During a visit to ISI's headquarters, Casey "was the first person seriously to advocate operations against the Soviets inside their own territory. . . . He was convinced that stirring up trouble in this region would be certain to give the Russian bear a bellyache." At first, the effort was restricted to smuggling propaganda into the USSR's Muslim republics, seeking to stir up Islamic fervor. During the 1980s thousands of Korans were printed in Central Asian languages and covertly moved across the Afghan border. Some of the Korans were printed in Saudi Arabia, others by the CIA itself, using Muslim connections in Western Europe.

Saudi Arabia, especially, was interested in Central Asia because it saw Iran, and the new Khomeini regime there, as a competitor trying to spread its version of Shiite fundamentalism into Central Asia, against Saudi Arabia's ultra-orthodox Wahhabi brand of Sunni Islam. A former CIA operations officer who worked closely with Saudi Arabia says that Saudi intelligence officers told him about their idea of "colonizing the 'Stans":

> They wanted to get in there and steal a march on the Iranians, and undercut the Russians, and make sure that Sunni Islam prevailed over Shia Islam. The Saudis were ready to go. They said, "We've got to get in there, into the 'stans, we've got to work together, use Islam to break the grip of communism in the 'stans, in Kazakhstan, Uzbekistan, all through there." It was open season. Different Saudi princes and clerics would go up there or send stuff up there, Korans and other material.[43]

Beginning in 1984, however, it was more than just Korans and Islamist books and propaganda. "The United States put in train a major escalation of the war which, over the next three years, culminated in numerous cross-border raids and sabotage missions north of the Amu," wrote Mohammad Yousaf. "During this period we were specifically to train and dispatch hundreds of Mujahideen up to 25 kilometres deep inside the Soviet Union. They were probably the most secret and sensitive operations of the war." He added that the Soviet Union's "specific worry was the spread of fundamentalism and its influence on Soviet Central Asian Muslims."[44] The ISI official was prepared to "send teams over the river to carry out rocket attacks, mine-laying, derailment of trains or ambushes."[45] Teams that did cross the Soviet border sought contacts among Muslim activists in the region. "I was impressed by the number of reports of people wanting to assist," wrote Yousaf. "Some wanted weapons, some wanted to join the Mujahideen in Afghanistan, and others to participate in operations inside the Soviet Union."[46] According to Yousaf:

> These cross-border strikes were at their peak in 1986. Scores of attacks were made across the Amu from Jozjan to Badakshan Provinces. Sometimes Soviet citizens joined in these operations, or came back into Afghanistan to join the Mujahideen. . . . That we were hitting a sore spot was confirmed by the ferocity of the Soviets' reaction. Virtually every incursion provoked massive aerial bombing and gunship attacks on all villages south of the river in the vicinity of our strike.[47]

It was, of course, an offensive that not only risked inflaming latent Islamist sentiment inside the Soviet Union but which could have provoked Moscow to retaliate against Pakistan itself, something that could lead to a U.S.-Soviet global conflagration—and all of this unfolded secretly, without the knowledge of the American public. According to various accounts of the Afghan conflict, and from Yousaf's own testimony, eventually cooler heads in Washington got the upper hand, and the cross-border attacks were halted. "By 1985, it became obvious that the United States had got cold feet," mourned Yousaf. "Somebody at the top in the American administration was getting frightened." But, he asserted, "the CIA, and others, gave us every encouragement unofficially to take the war into the Soviet Union."[48]

In the end, the Casey-ISI offensive into the Soviet Union failed to provoke a Muslim uprising. The Brzezinski-Bennigsen theory of a restive Muslim population chafing to revolt against its Soviet over-lords, and loyal to an underground network of Sufi Islamists, proved flawed, at best. Yet there is no question that the Casey-ISI actions aided the growth of a significant network of right-wing Islamist extremists who, to this day, still plague the governments of the former Soviet republics, now led by regimes of varying authoritarian, but not Islamist, character. In particular, the Islamic Movement of Uzbek-istan, the Islamic Liberation Party (Hizb ut-Tahrir), the powerful Islamist groups in Chechnya and Dagestan, and the shadowy Al Qaeda presence in Central Asia all gained momentum in the 1980s, thanks to the spillover of the Afghan jihad.

No End to Jihad

The Afghan jihad did not end when the Soviet Union withdrew its forces. The United States had no exit strategy and no plan for Afghanistan in the wake of the war. Most policy makers in Washing-ton believed that the weak pro-Soviet government in Kabul that was left in place would collapse in short order, but it lingered on. The mujahideen, who fractured into factions after the war and fought amongst themselves, continued to fight. And Pakistan, which saw Afghanistan as its partner in a coalition against India, heavily sup-ported the Islamists in the shattered country.

None of this seemed to bother top U.S. officials at the time. "We knew we were involved with Islamic fundamentalists," said Caspar Weinberger, who served as President Reagan's secretary of defense. "We knew they were not very nice people, and they were not all people attached to democracy. But we had this terrible problem of making choices. . . . Remember what Churchill said, 'If Hitler invaded Hell, I would at least make a favorable reference to the Devil in the

House of Commons.' "[49] It was an apt characterization of U.S. policy toward Afghanistan, Central Asia, and the "arc of Islam" in the 1980s.

There is no question that the U.S. support for the mujahideen, most of which went to the hard-core Islamists, was a catastrophic miscalculation. It devastated Afghanistan itself, led to the collapse of its government, and gave rise to a landscape dominated by warlords, both Islamists and otherwise. It created a worldwide network of highly trained Islamist fighters from a score of countries, linked together and roughly affiliated to Osama bin Laden's soon-to-be established Al Qaeda organization. It left behind a shattered nation that played host to Al Qaeda and other assorted terrorist formations. And it set up conditions under which Pakistan's ISI could encourage the growth of the Taliban movement in the 1990s.

Yet advocates of the jihad, even those who in 2005 are the staunchest proponents of the global war on terrorism directed against Islamist groups, assert that it was correct policy. "I think it was the right thing do to," says Daniel Pipes, the prolific campaigner against political Islam and son of Richard Pipes, who coordinated the Nationalities Working Group in the early years of the Reagan administration. During those years, Daniel Pipes was a State Department and National Security Council official. "We supported Stalin against Hitler," he says, echoing Weinberger's theory of dealing with devils. "These are real-world choices." The most militant among the mujahideen were the best fighters, according to Pipes. "If anything, the radical Islamists were seen as more vehemently anti-Soviet."[50] It is a view echoed by numerous U.S. veterans of the Afghan war, including many CIA officials and policy makers. "The people we did support were the nastier, more fanatic types of mujahideen," said Stephen P. Cohen, who was a top State Department official in the 1980s. "If you want to win the Cold War and defeat the Soviets in Afghanistan, you can't use the Salvation Army."[51]

Needless to say, the "fanatic types" did not fade away after the Soviet Union decided to withdraw from Afghanistan, although the people sponsoring them changed dramatically: Bill Casey died, and both General Zia and the head of ISI were killed in an unexplained plane crash. But the Islamic right was entrenched in both Afghanistan and Pakistan. The Islamic Group of Pakistan was rich and powerful, and well connected with the Muslim Brotherhood's worldwide networks. Most of the top ISI officials were now confirmed Islamists with Muslim Brotherhood links. The Islamic Group and the Brotherhood, in turn, maintained strong ties to Gulbuddin Hekmatyar and the other militant Islamists in Afghanistan, and to the burgeoning mujahideen network from dozens of countries who came and went freely though the madrassa system. The Soviet withdrawal was celebrated as a tremendous victory at the CIA and the Pentagon, and for the most part they turned away from Afghanistan, assuming that the pro-Soviet regime that still ruled in Kabul, led by President Najibullah, would quickly fall. The CIA drew an analogy with how quickly the government of South Vietnam fell after the U.S. withdrawal there, and they assumed that Najibullah would collapse in short order. Still, an odd sort of morning-after queasiness developed in U.S. government circles.

At the State Department, and even at the CIA, there was some disquiet over the prospect of Hekmatyar and other fundamentalists taking over in Afghanistan. Soviet officials were among those warning Washington of the dangers inherent in the Islamist movement. Soviet Foreign Minister Eduard Shevardnadze tried to feel out Secretary of State George Shultz about the possibility of a U.S.-Soviet gentleman's agreement on the terms of a Soviet pullout, and he "asked for American cooperation in limiting the spread of 'Islamic fundamentalism.'" However, other than Shultz, the administration was unsympathetic and "no high-level Reagan administration officials ever gave much thought to the issue. They never considered pressing Pakistani intelligence to begin shifting support away from the Muslim Brotherhood–connected factions." Moscow was exceedingly worried about Islamic fundamentalism taking root along its southern frontier, however, and even Vladimir Kryuchkov, the head of the KGB, sat down with CIA Director Gates to explain why Soviet leaders were "fearful about the rise to power in Afghanistan of another fundamentalist government, a Sunni complement to Shiite Iran."[52] To no avail.

By default, the United States allowed Pakistan and the ISI to maintain control of the political levers in Afghanistan. The official Saudi spigot for cash had largely shut down, but the unofficial, private sources of funding—through various wealthy princes, through the Muslim World League, through the Muslim Brotherhood's networks—were still up and running. According to two U.S. ambassadors who served in Saudi Arabia at this time, the United States handled the end of the war badly. "Where I was, nobody was looking ahead at what would happen to these unemployed freedom fighters," says Walter Cutler, who was U.S. ambassador in Saudi Arabia during most of the 1980s. "I don't recall any discussion about, 'Gee, I wonder if these guys are going to pose any threat?' We didn't really focus that much on political Islam. It was the Cold War. The fact that you had these zealots, trained and armed with Stingers, didn't come up."[53]

"We start wars without figuring out how we would end them," says Charles Freeman, who was ambassador to Saudi Arabia at the end of the 1980s and during the first Gulf War in 1991. "Afghanistan was lurching into civil war, and we basically didn't care anymore." Adds Freeman:

> The Afghan struggle didn't stop. Some of us were concerned—I was, and so was [Robert] Oakley [U.S. ambassador in Pakistan], who was concerned about the ISI screwing around in Afghanistan and Kashmir, and that the Saudis were complicit in this. You couldn't really figure out if the Saudis were being used, or were witting. I talked to [Prince] Turki [the head of Saudi intelligence] about it, and to the CIA, and my message was, basically, that we need to start thinking about disentangling ourselves. But there was some question about whether Saudi Arabia had been captured by the ISI. The ISI would take their money and start implementing things, and we didn't know what they were doing. Certainly a lot of Saudi money was going to Hekmatyar. But we couldn't really figure out what the Saudi agenda was. There'd been up to $3 billion a year flowing into the war, in all, from the United States, Saudi Arabia, and others. You can't just turn the spigot off overnight. Both Bob and I thought we should have a serious dialogue about it, but we couldn't get anyone else interested, including [Robert] Gates and [William] Webster [both CIA directors]. Part of the attitude in Washington was, "Why should we go out

there and talk to people with towels on their heads?" So we weren't effective.[54]

According to Yousaf, who had a bird's-eye view of the end of the war from his post at ISI, as the dust cleared in Afghanistan some Americans did become alarmed at the prospect of Hekmatyar and his fellow fundamentalists taking power. "The Americans began to look at an Afghanistan without the Red Army," he wrote. "What they saw alarmed them." But, he said, Gen. Akhtar Abdel Rahman Khan, the ISI architect of the jihad, managed to counter the ineffectual U.S. efforts to strengthen potential Afghan non-fundamentalist groups, including the forces allied to the exiled king, Zahir Shah, and to other, less Islamist parties and individuals. "General Akhtar understood [the Americans'] aims and methods and opposed their every move." Akhtar also opposed what Yousaf calls "the Americans' bright idea of bringing back the long-exiled Zahir Shah to head a government of national reconciliation."[55]

Even had the United States wanted to exert itself to minimize the power of the fundamentalists after the war, and to enhance the strength of the moderates, centrists, and secularists, it would have been difficult— for the simple reason that most of them were dead. At the same time that the largely Islamist mujahideen were battling the USSR, they were also killing potential postwar Afghan opponents by the thousands, in a little-known second front of the jihad directed against non-communist Afghanis. "In Afghanistan, we made a deliberate choice," says Cheryl Benard, a RAND Corporation expert on political Islam, who is married to Zalmay Khalilzad, who served as U.S. ambassador in Kabul. "At first, everyone thought, There's no way to beat the Soviets. So what we have to do is to throw the worst crazies against them that we can find, and there was a lot of collateral damage. We knew exactly who these people were, and what their organizations were like, and we didn't care," she says. "Then, we allowed them to get rid of, just kill all the moderate leaders. The reason we don't have moderate leaders in Afghanistan today is because we let the nuts kill them all. They killed the leftists, the moderates, the middle-of-the-roaders. They were just eliminated, dur- ing the 1980s and afterward."[56]

SECRET DEALS WITH THE AYATOLLAHS

The wreckage left behind in Afghanistan could have been even worse had the Reagan administration's secret initiatives toward Iran from 1980 to 1986 borne fruit. There are three episodes in regard to Iran that paralleled America's alliance with fundamentalist Islam in Afghanistan: the so-called October Surprise in 1980, Israel's secret relationship with Iran during the 1980s, and the 1984–86 covert Reagan administration approach to Ayatollah Khomeini's Iran.

In 1980, as Carter administration officials frantically tried to secure the release of the U.S. hostages in Iran, it appears likely that members of the Reagan campaign team, including Casey, established contacts with Iranian officials, in an effort to postpone the hostages' release until after the election.

Gary Sick, a U.S. Navy officer who served on the National Security Council staff under Ford, Carter, and Reagan, concluded years later that the Reagan-Bush campaign did in fact enter into secret talks with Iranian leaders to prevent the release of the hostages and to promise to ship U.S. and Israeli arms to Iran in 1981. He penned a detailed account of his findings in the book *October Surprise: America's Hostages in Iran and the Election of Ronald Reagan*. In it, he concludes: "The Reagan-Bush campaign mounted a professionally organized intelligence operation to subvert the American democratic process."[57]

Sick suspected that the basis for the GOP-Iran talks was a promise that a Republican administration would look with favor on the shipment of Israeli and other arms to Iran, possibly including U.S. stockpiles of weapons that the shah had ordered and paid for. Iran desperately needed weapons for its fight with Iraq, which erupted into a full-scale war in September 1980. Israel, which had a long military relationship with Iran going back to the two countries' first major arms deal in 1966, was eager to supply Teheran's clerical regime with weapons, despite the hostage crisis. "Israel's almost frantic efforts to reopen an arms relationship with Iran were being thwarted by President Carter, who stubbornly refused to acquiesce to even token Israeli arms shipments until the hostages were free," wrote Sick.[58] Interestingly, the key Iranian broker for arms talks between Israel and Iran was Ahmed Kashani, the son of Ayatollah Seyyed Abolqassem Kashani, the cleric who received CIA payments in 1953 in order to organize mobs demanding the overthrow of Mossadegh and the return of the shah. Kashani visited Israel in 1980, according to Sick, who adds that "other channels between Israel and Iran were functioning long before he arrived." In the spring of 1980, a small Israeli arms shipment arrived in Iran.[59]

Sick provides a detailed account of contacts and meetings between Casey, other Reagan officials, and a host of Iranian go-betweens, several of whom would turn up as part of the 1984–86 Iran-contra scandal.[60] Some of them, in turn, had close contacts in Israel, and Israel and Iran began closer military cooperation in late 1980, including— most spectacularly—Israel's June 7, 1981, air raid that destroyed Iraq's Osirak nuclear facility, only days after the outbreak of the Iran-Iraq war. "Israel provided Iran with information on how to attack the nuclear facility but . . . the Iraqi air defense was too good for the Iranian air force," reported Sick.[61] So Israel did it.

Casey, according to Sick, helped Iran break the U.S. embargo on Israeli arms for Iran. "William Casey struck exactly the kind of unsentimental bargain with the Iranian clerics that the Iran lobby in Israel had been looking for," wrote Sick. "Israel was approached in August not only by Casey but by officials within the CIA who encouraged Israel to cooperate with the Republican initiative as a means of freeing the hostages."[62] At the NSC, Sick was getting reports of Israeli arms deliveries to Iran, in defiance of Carter's opposition. "The Israeli leadership, at the very highest level, had deliberately, almost contemptuously turned its back on Jimmy Carter's administration."[63] In the end, the hostages were freed, but only on January 20, 1981, minutes after Reagan was sworn in as America's fortieth president. "Few suspected," wrote Sick, that the release of the hostages "was the denouement of an elaborate plot that had been hatched months before by William Casey."[64]

The secret Reagan-Casey contacts with Iran in 1980–81 foreshadowed efforts during the Reagan administration to maintain covert ties with the Iranian ayatollahs. Some U.S. officials saw Iran as an ally in the growing war in Afghanistan, since Khomeini was bitterly opposed to the Soviet Union and wanted to extend Iranian influence into Afghanistan and Central Asia. Others saw Iran as a counterweight to Iraq, for two reasons: first, because of the Soviet Union's close ties to Baghdad, but second, and more important, because a powerful Iraq was seen as a threat to Israel.

During the Iran-Iraq war, the United States pursued two policies at the same time. Washington's main approach was the "tilt" toward Iraq during its war with Iran. Officials who supported the pro-Iraq tilt correctly saw Iran as the major threat to American interests in the region, since the defeat of Iraq by Iran's fundamentalist regime would open the way to Iranian domination of the entire Persian Gulf, including Kuwait and Saudi Arabia. Virtually the entire Arab world backed Iraq in its war with Iran, and the United States provided limited support to Iraq, including intelligence on Iran's capabilities and troop deployments.

But Israel—along with many U.S. neoconservative officials, including Casey—saw it differently.

From 1980 to 1987, even as the United States officially backed Iraq, the Israelis supplied Iran with a steady stream of arms, ammunition, and spare parts. Whether or not it was part of a secret deal between Casey, Israel, and Iran, the Reagan administration did nothing to get Israel to stop arming the ayatollahs. In doing so, Israel was drawing on its many contacts with Iran during the shah's rule. When the shah was toppled, the Israelis continued to work with Iranian army and intelligence officers they knew, even though the officers were now reporting to mullahs and ayatollahs. Israel's ties to Khomeini's Iran were multifaceted. They had links to Iran's armed forces and the successor organization to the shah's SAVAK secret service. In addition, thousands of Iranian Jews had long been active in the bazaar merchant class, many of whom had immigrated to Israel but maintained ties to Iran, including links to the families of the wealthier, conservative ayatollahs. Israel capitalized on those contacts, too.

"Israel was dealing with the regime in Iran as a semi-ally," says Patrick Lang, who headed the U.S. Defense Intelligence Agency's

Middle East section.[65] "They were dealing with the same people they dealt with under the shah. During these years, the Israelis were having meetings once a month in Europe with people from the Iranian air force." According to Lang, these Israel-Iran meetings took place for many years. Israel, he said, would ask Iran what sort of arms it needed, then take Teheran's shopping list to see what it could provide. At the time, the Reagan administration had instituted what was called Operation Staunch in 1984, to cut the arms flow to Iran and Iraq, but the Israelis flouted it and Reagan never used America's influence in Israel to get them to halt the arms deliveries. "The Israelis were doing this all along," Lang says. "At the Defense Intelligence Agency, we found out about it when an Iranian air force colonel defected to us and told us about it." Still, says Lang, President Reagan's team looked the other way. "My impression is that we didn't try too hard to stop it," says Lang. In just the immediate period after the release of the U.S. hostages, Israel supplied Iran with $300 million worth of military equipment. The shipments included spare parts for U.S. F-4 aircraft, M-48 tanks, and M-113 armored personnel carriers.[66]

An important incident in 1983 reveals the extent to which Casey's CIA worked with Iran's intelligence service when it was in both countries' mutual interest to do so. In 1982, Vladimir Kuzichkin, who had served as the station chief in Teheran for the Soviet KGB, defected to Great Britain. During the revolution, Kuzichkin had ably represented Soviet interests in Iran, but in fact the Soviet presence in Iran was quite small, and did not threaten either the United States or the shah. According to Kuzichkin, who later wrote a book about his experience, the KGB had a grand total of two agents in government and official Iranian circles. "I could not believe my eyes, but it was a fact, and facts do not go away," he wrote. "I was very surprised at the small number of agents in Iran."[67] Kuzichkin also wrote that the USSR valued the stability of Iran under the shah and that Moscow never had any contacts with either the Islamist revolutionaries or the so-called Islamic Marxist groups that briefly made common cause with Khomeini.[68] But the KGB station did support the small and ineffective Tudeh Communist Party in Iran.

When Kuzichkin defected, he decided to win favor in Anglo-

American circles by giving MI6 and the CIA everything he knew about the Tudeh and its members. "He provided the British with a list of several hundred Soviet agents operating in Iran," wrote James Bill. Almost immediately, MI6 and the CIA handed Kuzichkin's information to the Iranian intelligence service:

> Kuzichkin's information was shared with the Iranian authorities, who arrested over 1,000 Tudeh party members, many of whom had already been under surveillance. Those arrested included Nureddin Kianuri [the Tudeh leader, who admitted] that he had maintained contact with Soviet agents since 1945. This dramatic destruction of the Tudeh party in 1983 completed the dismantling of the Iranian left.[69]

None of this, of course, was made public at the time. Americans knew nothing about the CIA's sub rosa cooperation with Khomeini's Iran, nothing about Israel's ongoing arms supply to Iran, and, later, nothing about the Iran-contra initiative toward Iran, until it was revealed by a Lebanese newspaper. Mel Goodman, a former CIA analyst who headed the agency's team analyzing Soviet policy in the Third World, confirms that the CIA was part of the Kuzichkin-MI6 connection to Iran. "The CIA was involved in that, too," says Goodman. "They were working with the ayatollah to wrap up the Tudeh Party. There was a lot of [cable] traffic on it. Kuzichkin was being run by the British and he provided a lot of information." According to Goodman, the CIA and MI6 were working with Iranian intelligence officials who had been part of the old SAVAK organization, and who simply shifted loyalty to the new Islamic republic.[70]

Most notorious among the former SAVAK officials now cooperating with the new regime was Hossein Fardoust. Fardoust was a childhood friend of the shah, who had attended school in Switzerland with both the shah and future CIA director Richard Helms. Fardoust had risen to a high position in Iranian intelligence in the 1970s, and in 1976 he was named to head the Organization of Imperial Inspection, which was reconstituted by the shah. In his memoirs, the shah describes the inspectorate as "a modern version of what the ancient

Persians had called 'the eyes and ears of the king.' "[71] Its job was to keep track of political currents in the country, including among the clergy. But Fardoust joined the pro-Khomeini opposition, secretly. Princess Ashraf, the shrewd and ruthless sister of the shah, recalled in her memoirs that Fardoust failed, deliberately, to inform the shah of what the mullahs were doing:

> Curiously, SAVAK—the supposedly all-seeing, all-knowing intelligence source—made no reports on the extent and manner in which the mullahs were now using the sanctity of the pulpit to undermine the throne. . . . Each day my brother met with Hossein Fardoust, . . . the same Fardoust of childhood, whose assignment was to gather, evaluate, and distill all intelligence reports. . . . I am convinced that Fardoust must have withheld vital information from the Shah and was, in fact, in active negotiation with Khomeini during the last years of the regime. I think the events following the revolution support my view; at a time when anyone remotely connected with the Shah was being summarily executed, Hossein Fardoust remains alive and well, prospering under the new administration as one of the heads of SAVAMA (which is Khomeini's name for SAVAK).[72]

Whether it was the mysterious Fardoust or someone else, both the CIA and the Israelis had channels into Iran's intelligence service from the first days of the revolution through the start of the Casey-North conspiracy in the mid-1980s. Seen in this context, the Iran-contra affair is not some strange aberration, but simply an extension of a preexisting relationship that dated back to 1979. Within the Reagan administration, a small clique of conservatives, and neoconservatives, were most intimately involved in the Iran-contra initiative, especially those U.S. officials and consultants who were closest to the Israeli military and intelligence establishment.

The record of the Iran affair has been told and retold in various books, memoirs, and official government reports.[73] The entire business was complex and multilayered, and it tied U.S. and Israeli arms shipments to Iran to illegal financial support for the Nicaraguan guerrillas backed by the Reagan administration. Critics of the U.S.

approach to Iran accuse Reagan and his advisers of seeking to trade arms with Iran for the release of U.S. hostages in Lebanon held by Hezbollah, an Iranian cat's-paw. Indeed, to President Reagan himself, the deal with Iran may have appeared to be simply an effort to get the hostages released, although the president (in later testimony) said that he could not recall approving the arms transfers to Iran. To his advisers, however—especially to the neoconservatives and Casey—it had a much broader purpose, namely, an attempt to reengage with Iran, in direct opposition to the official U.S. policy of supporting Iraq in its resistance to Iranian expansionism.

The context for the secret Casey-North approach to Iran was the National Security Council's 1984 reevaluation of U.S. policy toward Iran. That reevaluation was pushed by a small clique of U.S. officials opposed to the American tilt in favor of Iraq during the Iran-Iraq war. Robert McFarlane, the national security adviser, ordered the NSC review, and several officials—including Howard Teicher and Donald Fortier at the NSC, Graham Fuller at the CIA, and others—began a two-year-long campaign to shift U.S. policy in favor of Iran. Their effort dovetailed nicely with parallel Israeli efforts to isolate Iraq and connect with Iran. At the time, Israel was supplying arms to Iran, backing the rise of the Islamic right in the occupied territories, fueling the Muslim Brotherhood's civil war in Syria, and fiercely supporting the Islamists in Afghanistan.

In 1985, Fuller—working along with Teicher and Fortier— produced an infamous Special National Intelligence Estimate (SNIE) that called for the United States to provide arms to the ayatollahs' regime and a draft policy paper that said that the United States should "encourage Western allies and friends to help Iran meet its import requirements . . . including provision of selected military equipment."[74] Both Secretary of State Shultz and Secretary of Defense Weinberger strongly opposed the idea, but CIA Director Casey backed it. In the midst of this internal battle, Israel stepped in, using intermediaries to propose a joint U.S.-Israeli effort to approach Iran and sell Teheran weapons. The U.S. contact for the Israeli intelligence scheme was Michael Ledeen, a neoconservative NSC consultant, who was sent to

Israel by McFarlane to discuss the idea. Specifically, Israel wanted to ship HAWK antiaircraft and TOW antitank missiles to the Iranians, weapons considered critical in Iran's war with Iraq, along with a U.S. commitment to resupply Israel with the missiles once they were sent. Israel's rationale was the release of the U.S. hostages, but of course Israel—and elements within the American administration—had broader, pro-Iranian strategic concerns, not related to the hostages.

Teicher, in particular, vehemently supported the Iran initiative. In 1980, when Iran and Iraq went to war, "I renewed my campaign against the nascent tilt toward Iraq," wrote Teicher in his memoirs. He added that some U.S. officials viewed the war as a way to undermine the Islamist threat from Iran, which at the time was holding fifty-three Americans captive. "The Arabists in the U.S. government saw the Iraqi invasion as an opportunity to eliminate the growing threat of Iranian-sponsored Islamic fundamentalism."[75]

Advocates for selling arms to Iran made two seriously flawed arguments. The first was that there were moderates inside Iran who wanted to deal with the United States, and who would look with favor upon a U.S. goodwill offer to replenish Iran's dwindling arsenal. The second was that Iran was internally weak and unstable, and ripe for a Soviet takeover that could bring the USSR into the Gulf. Both arguments were wildly inaccurate—and so was the belief that token arms shipments could win freedom for U.S. hostages in Lebanon. At the start of the Iran initiative, an Israeli intelligence official told McFarlane that "the Israelis planned to provide some arms to moderates in Iran who would oppose Khomeini." The idea that some powerful faction of Iranian moderates would emerge to greet the United States and Israel with open arms and take action against Khomeini captivated many of the U.S. participants in the Iran-contra affair, including Casey himself. But it was a mirage. According to a former senior CIA official, it took a lot of doing in the mid-1980s to convince Casey that the chimerical "moderates" were not there. "There were no moderates to speak of in 1986," says the CIA official. When Ollie North, McFarlane, and other U.S. and Israeli officials were planning a secret visit to Iran to try to make a deal, the official says, Casey—who had approved the plan—wanted to know if the plan would work. "Casey called me in and asked, Did I think this mission had a chance of success? I told him, 'Not much.' And there wasn't really a chance of success." Asked if Casey ultimately believed that Iranian moderates would respond in a positive way to the U.S. gambit, the official says: "Probably not after talking to me."[76] Says W. Patrick Lang, who was then director of the Defense Intelligence Agency's Middle East section: "Their view was that there were lots of moderates in Iran who are not what they seem to be, which was a bunch of jackasses. And I said, that's exactly what they are—jackasses."

The more significant argument, that Iran might fall to the USSR, was absurd on its face. The Soviet Union was battling insurgents in Afghanistan, it had little or no assets inside Iran, and Soviet leaders had no intention of crossing the red line into the Persian Gulf, a region that FDR, Eisenhower, and Carter had all proclaimed a zone of American predominance. Yet in a May 1985 memo to Casey, called "Toward a Policy toward Iran," the CIA's Fuller argued, "The Khomeini regime is faltering.... The U.S. has almost no cards to play; the USSR has many." According to Fuller, U.S. intelligence analysts felt that Moscow was making "progress toward developing significant leverage in Tehran" and that the U.S. policy forbidding arms sales to Iran "may now serve to facilitate Soviet interests more than our own." He added:

> It is imperative, however, that we perhaps think in terms of a bolder—and perhaps riskier—policy which will at least ensure greater U.S. voice in the unfolding situation. Right now, unless we are very lucky indeed, we stand to gain nothing and lose more in the outcome of developments in Iran, which are all outside our control.[77]

Fuller was developing a view that made him increasingly sympathetic to fundamentalist Islam, and in his testimony to the Tower Commission, a three-man panel, appointed by President Reagan and led by former senator John Tower of Texas, assigned to investigate the NSC's role in the Iran-contra scandal, he said that a problem was that "the Iranian regime perceived us as implacably hostile towards an

Islamic republic in principle."[78] In his controversial SNIE and other analyses, Fuller insisted the United States would drive Iran into the Soviet camp unless it allowed Israel and other allies to arm the mullahs. It said that to the extent that American "allies," including Israel, "can fill a military gap for Iran will be a critical measure of the West's ability to blunt Soviet influence."[79]

Fuller's analysis was hotly disputed by other intelligence officials. Fuller's SNIE said that "the Iran revolution was phony, that it was led by a bunch of agricultural reformers who didn't really care about Islam and that they would make common cause with the Soviet Union," says the DIA's Lang. "I got another NIE started, which was finished five months later. And it said exactly the opposite, but it didn't have the same impact." In the meantime, Fuller, Teicher, and others pressed ahead to translate Fuller's SNIE into U.S. policy, seeking to draft a presidential directive that called for "a vigorous policy designed to block Soviet advances in the short-term while trying to restore the U.S. position in Iran which existed under the shah." The directive, couched in anti-Soviet, Cold War terms, virtually called for an alliance with the Islamic Republic of Iran against the USSR, including "continued Iranian resistance to Soviet expansion (in particular, in Afghanistan)." The draft encouraged Israel and other U.S. allies to arm Iran, and it called for the United States to "establish links with, and provide support to, Iranian leaders who might be receptive to efforts to improve relations with the United States." It also called on the Voice of America to "increase efforts to discredit Moscow's Islamic credentials."

"Iran still represented the strategic prize in the modern Great Game," wrote Teicher. "McFarlane agreed with Fuller's analysis and directed Fortier and me to draft an NSDD [National Security Decision Directive]. The NSDD was based on Fuller's analysis [and it] argued that . . . the United States should establish a dialogue with Iranian leaders. The proposal included the provision of selected military equipment to Iran as determined on a case-by-case basis."[80] The Iran initiative proceeded but was later shot down by Shultz and Weinberger. The latter scribbled the word "absurd" on Teicher's draft

NSDD. "I also added that this is roughly like inviting Qaddafi over for a cozy lunch," said Weinberger.[81] According to Teicher, Vice President Bush and CIA Director Casey "strongly supported it."[82]

By the end of the Reagan administration, the Iran-contra initiative had come to light, and it was being investigated by journalists, a special prosecutor, and congressional committees. The olive branch to the Iranians had failed. Only a single hostage had been released during the initiative, and not necessarily because of it. No Iranian "moderates" spoke up, and those who cooperated with the Reagan administration and Israel in secret, such as Ali Akbar Hashemi-Rafsanjani, a future Iranian president, covered their tracks by appearing to become even more bellicose.

The Afghan jihad ended—or appeared to end—with the withdrawal of Soviet forces. But the legacy of that conflict, including well-trained terrorist operatives and a worldwide Islamist machine, would continue to plague the United States and the West. In the 1990s, Afghanistan fell to the Wahhabi Taliban movement; Algeria was engulfed in a civil war against the Islamic right; and Islamist terrorists wreaked havoc in Egypt, Saudi Arabia, and Lebanon; and Osama bin Laden put Al Qaeda together. Through it all, the United States struggled, unsuccessfully, to adopt a coherent policy toward political Islam. The consequences of its failure to do so, and its continued benign view of the Islamic right, would become painfully obvious on September 11, 2001.

12

CLASH OF CIVILIZATIONS?

THE COLD WAR ended in 1991. But, if the Cold War was World War III, does that mean, as some conservatives argue, that the United States is now engaged in World War IV, this time against Islam? Is Islamic fundamentalism the "new communism"? Is the war on terrorism the twenty-first-century equivalent of the global struggle against the Soviet Union? How serious, really, is the threat of Islamist terrorism? And how—if at all—did America's relationship to political Islam change with the end of the Cold War?

The central theme of this book is that the Islamic right was seen as a valuable U.S. ally during the Cold War. Was that alliance superseded, or rendered superfluous, by the disappearance of the U.S.-Soviet rivalry? With the elimination of its communist enemy, did the Islamic right direct its wrath instead toward the Great Satans of the secular West? Is the United States now facing a worldwide enemy, comprising a hydra-headed monster tied to a network of states—Iran, Syria, Libya, Sudan, and Saudi Arabia—that Michael Ledeen, the Iran-contra veteran, calls the "terror masters"?

Since September 11, 2001, the notion that the United States and the Muslim world are on a collision course has gained credence. If the first Iraq war in 1991 marked the start of the short-lived New World

Order, does the second Iraq war in 2003 symbolize an entirely different era: the Clash of Civilizations? Proponents of this view—popularized by Bernard Lewis and Samuel Huntington—see President Bush's war on terrorism not as a struggle against Al Qaeda and its radical allies, but as a titanic struggle pitting Judeo-Christian civilization against the Muslim world. Fittingly, in the Pentagon, the Global War on Terrorism is known by its acronym, G-WOT, pronounced "gee what," thus neatly rhyming with "jihad."

Leading neoconservatives, such as James Woolsey, the former CIA director and *Commentary*'s Norman Podhoretz proclaimed that the struggle against Islam was indeed World War IV. Joined by key Bush administration officials, they compared the power of the Islamic right—and sometimes, the religion of Islam itself—to that of fascism or communism. It was, they said, a globe-spanning opponent whose existence threatened America's survival, and because of it, previously unthinkable steps had to be taken. To fight World War IV would require a new U.S. doctrine of unilateral, preventive wars, an offensive posture that included wars against Afghanistan, Iraq, and then other nations, and vast increases in U.S. military and intelligence budgets. It would mean the creation of a surveillance state at home, with the Department of Homeland Security, the USA Patriot Act, the Pentagon's Northern Command for deploying the armed forces inside the United States, and new Justice Department rules giving the FBI, the police, and Joint Terrorism Task Forces in fifty-three U.S. cities significant new authority.

On closer examination, however, the clash of civilizations, the war on terror, and the Bush administration campaign to reshape the Middle East were rife with paradoxes, contradictions, and outright lies.

The enemy that attacked the United States on September 11 was not Islam, nor was it Islamic fundamentalism, nor was it the Muslim Brotherhood, Hezbollah, Hamas, or any other group of violence-prone militants on the Islamic right. Rather, it was Al Qaeda. Osama bin Laden's organization is not a global power, and it does not pose an existential threat to the United States. It is a group of fanatics with a tightly disciplined command structure demanding mafia-style, blood-oath loyalties. Its attack on New York and Washington in 2001 outraged the entire world, and an effective counterattack—using intelligence, legal action, political and diplomatic pressure, and highly selective military strikes—could have weakened and then destroyed it. Unquestionably, the destruction of Al Qaeda could have been accomplished without a war in Afghanistan, without a war in Iraq, and without a "war on terrorism."

But the Bush administration deliberately inflated the specific threat from Al Qaeda itself. Certainly, bin Laden's group has proved itself capable of inflicting severe damage. Since 9/11, it has struck targets in Saudi Arabia, Spain, Turkey, and elsewhere. Despite Attorney General Ashcroft's unsubstantiated claim in 2001 that thousands of Al Qaeda operatives had infiltrated the United States, however, in the almost four years after 9/11 not a single violent act by Al Qaeda occurred in America. And there is no shred of evidence that Al Qaeda has acquired or is about to acquire any nuclear, biological, or chemical weapons. In short, while bin Laden can launch terrorist strikes, and may do so again, the actual threat that Al Qaeda poses is circumscribed and manageable. Many other nations, including Israel, Ireland, and Italy, have weathered far more serious terrorist threats over many years.

Equally, neither Al Qaeda, nor its ideological comrades, nor the Islamic right as a whole—nor, for that matter, the entire Muslim world—present the kind of challenge to America's global hegemony that the Soviet Union clearly did. No combination of Middle East states, most of which are weak, impoverished, and wracked by internal divisions, is able to mount a threat to the United States in a manner that would justify an enterprise called "World War IV." But by describing the Islamist threat in such an exaggerated way, the Bush administration and its neoconservative allies created a pretext for an imperial expansion of the U.S. presence in the greater Middle East, including Pakistan, Central Asia, and the eastern Mediterranean/Red Sea/Indian Ocean region. It is fair to ask if the virtual U.S. occupation of the Middle East is related to goals other than anti-terrorism. Is it because neoconservatives want to anchor U.S. global hegemony by planting the flag in that vital, but unstable region? Is it because as much as two-thirds of the world's oil is in Saudi Arabia and Iraq? Is it because the Bush administration has forged such intimate ties to Ariel Sharon and the Israeli right?

The notion that Islamist terrorism is really the U.S. government's target is contradicted by the targets of the Bush administration's Middle East policy. Why, if the enemy is Islamist terrorism, did the administration invest so much energy against Iraq, Syria, and the PLO? Both Syria's president, Bashir Assad, and the late chairman of the PLO, Yasser Arafat, were implacable opponents of the Muslim Brotherhood, but they found themselves added incongruously to the list of Al Qaeda's allies. By attacking Iraq, the Bush administration also found an inappropriate target. Since coming to power in 1968, Saddam Hussein was a determined enemy of the Islamists, from Iran's Ayatollah Khomeini to terrorist Shiite groups to Al Qaeda itself. The Arab Baath Socialist Party, in both its Iraqi and Syrian branches, is resolutely secular, and the Bush administration's efforts to link Iraq to Al Qaeda were ridiculed by the CIA and the State Department. In fact, in invading Iraq, President Bush made common cause with the Islamic right: before, during, and after the invasion, the United States supported the Iraqi National Congress exile coalition, in which two Shiite fundamentalist parties, the Supreme Council for the Islamic Revolution in Iraq (SCIRI), and the Islamic Call (Al-Dawa), played prominent roles. Both SCIRI and Dawa had close ties to the Islamic Republic of Iran, and after the war, both worked closely with Ayatollah Ali al-Sistani.

Not only did the Bush administration pick the wrong targets, but its military-run war on terrorism is exactly the wrong way to reduce the appeal of the Islamic right. Putting Al Qaeda, Islamic Jihad, and similar terrorist groups to one side, the far broader constellation of right-wing Islamic groups, institutions, and political parties in the Muslim world does in fact represent a significant threat—not to U.S. national security but to governments, intellectuals, progressives, and other freethinkers in the swath of nations from Morocco to Indonesia. From Algeria's FIS to Egypt's Muslim Brotherhood to the Palestinian Hamas to Iraq's Shiite fundamentalists to Pakistan's Islamic Group, together with the support of ultra-orthodox Wahhabi clerics in Saudi Arabia, organizations such as the Muslim World League, and the Islamic banks, there is indeed a threat to the Middle East. It is, however, a threat that cannot be dealt with by military means. Indeed, it will get worse in precise proportion to the intrusiveness of the U.S. political, military, and economic presence in the region. Only by rapidly withdrawing from Afghanistan and Iraq, by reducing America's overweening presence in Saudi Arabia and the Gulf, and by reversing U.S. support for Israel's aggressive opposition to Palestinian nationalism can the United States undercut the anger, frustration, and resentment that fuels Islamism.

Reducing America's footprint in the Middle East is the polar opposite of the Bush administration's policy, however. Cynically perhaps, the administration has wielded the idea of a broad struggle against terrorism to pursue a policy aimed at redrawing the entire map of the Middle East. The radical, or "idealist" neoconservatives, from administration officials to armchair strategists at think tanks such as the American Enterprise Institute, the Hudson Institute, and the Project for a New American Century, announced that the wars in Afghanistan and Iraq were just the first two salvos in a sweeping plan to seize control of Iran, Syria, Saudi Arabia, and the Gulf states. Even the more mainstream Bush administration officials, while eschewing some of the neoconservatives' visions, support the idea of a greater U.S. military presence in the region from North Africa to Indonesia.

Astute critics of the Bush administration's military-based anti-terrorism policies and imperial pretensions have argued that it is a strategy guaranteed to backfire, and one that seems designed to create more terrorists than it kills. Anger against the occupation of Iraq and Afghanistan is likely to draw new jihadists into battle in those two countries, and the conflict could spread into both Pakistan and Saudi Arabia, where conservative, Islam-oriented governments could fall to far more radical dissident groups associated with bin Laden, the mujahideen, the Taliban, and a Wahhabi extremist underground.

A second prong of the Bush administration's Middle East policy is likely to prove equally counterproductive, namely, its vaunted call for democratic reform.

The administration's support for democracy in the region is, on the surface at least, a stunning about-face. For years, especially during the Cold War, the United States propped up dictators, kings, emirs, and presidents-for-life in the Middle East and around the world. In the Arab world—in Saudi Arabia, Jordan, Egypt, and the Gulf—many of these autocrats ruled in part by forging an alliance with the Islamic right, with the support of U.S. policy makers. Throughout these years, opposition to the region's kleptocracies and right-wing regimes came exclusively from the left—from American liberals, from the European left, from the Soviet Union. Certainly, the elimination of dictatorships and the establishment of fledgling democracies in the Arab world, Iran, Pakistan, Afghanistan, and Muslim Africa ought to be a valued goal.

But the Bush administration's version of democratic reform is suspect.

First, it is opportunistic. Much of the momentum for the Bush administration's emphasis on Arab democracy came only when the 2003 invasion of Iraq belied the White House's stated objectives in launching the war: to find Saddam's weapons of mass destruction and to uncover Iraq's supposed ties to Al Qaeda. When those two rationales proved to be fictional, President Bush shifted to a new one—that America's *raison de la guerre* was to bring democracy to Iraq.

Second, the Bush administration cynically distinguishes between pro-American dictatorships in the Middle East and anti-American ones, concentrating its pressure for democracy on the latter. In the context of the Bush administration's imperial Middle East policy, its call for imposing democracy can only be seen as a spearhead for intensified U.S. political and military involvement in the region. True democracies in the oil-producing countries would pursue bold, nationalist initiatives that are almost guaranteed to run afoul of the Bush administration's long-range plans for the region. Only the naïve believe that the United States, in pursuing a "regime change" strategy in a part of the world that contains two-thirds of the world's oil, desires the emergence of governments that might resist U.S. regional hegemony. Certainly, the Bush administration does not favor the development of Arab or Iranian democracies that would forge closer ties with, say, Russia or China at American expense. Instead, its calls for democratic change in the Middle East allow the Bush administration to apply greater or less pressure selectively on governments in the region in order to achieve particular U.S. national security goals.

Thus, Syria is now squeezed between Israel and U.S.-occupied Iraq, and Iran is positioned between Iraq and NATO-occupied Afghanistan. Since 2001, the United States has achieved a position of unparalleled supremacy in the region. The neoconservatives who argued successfully for war in Iraq want nothing more than a calibrated American effort toward forcible regime change in Syria and Iran, in order to create a block of new states in combination with Israel, Turkey, and Pakistan—but organized and managed under U.S. tutelage.

And what about the pro-American autocracies such as Saudi Arabia, Jordan, and Egypt? To the extent that President Bush extends his pressure for imperial democracy beyond Iraq, Syria, Iran, and the PLO to the pro-Western governments in the region, the effort must be taken with a grain of salt. Because it is comprised of constituencies with differing perspectives, the administration has sent mixed signals in regard to its two most important Arab allies. Mainstream U.S. policy makers, officials at the CIA and the State Department, and their allies with vested interests in the region—the oil companies, banks, and defense contractors—want the Bush administration to go slow on pressing Cairo and Riyadh for change. Others, more ideological, seem to exhibit the messianic belief that the experiment in Iraq must be forcibly replicated in both Egypt and Saudi Arabia. And some radical neoconservatives, such as Richard Perle and Michael Ledeen, roughly lump Saudi Arabia with Syria and Iran as a supporter of Al Qaeda and demand that Riyadh be added to the president's axis-of-evil enemies' list. All of them overlook the fact that both Egypt and Saudi Arabia have been under both internal and external pressure to liberalize their regimes for decades, and from time to time both have experimented, cautiously, with democratic reform—only to pull back. The need for delicacy in dealing with these two countries often escapes the Bush administration's more ideological partisans.

But in the context of examining U.S. policy toward the Islamic right, the twin cases of Egypt and Saudi Arabia are fraught with dangerous possibilities. Pressing too hard for liberalization in either country could result in bringing the Islamic right to power in both Cairo and Riyadh.

As during the Cold War, however, when the United States pre-ferred Islamism to Arab nationalism, the Bush administration and its neoconservative allies have sometimes expressed their preference for the Islamic right, too. If forced to choose between regimes in Egypt and Saudi Arabia led by left-leaning Arab nationalists or right-leaning Islamists, Washington will pick the Islamists every time. Despite their rhetoric about a clash of civilizations, the Bush administration has not been averse to seeking allies among the Islamic right. In Iraq, the Bush administration after the war found itself in a partnership with Ayatollah Sistani, two Iranian-connected parties, and the forces of organized Shiite fundamentalism. Leading neoconservatives also sup-ported the Shiite right elsewhere, including in Saudi Arabia, where they went beyond calls for democratic reform to demand the breakup of Saudi Arabia and the creation of a Shiite state in Saudi Arabia's eastern province, where Shiites comprise a majority. In Gaza and the West Bank, Ariel Sharon continued to toy with using Hamas, Islamic Jihad, and Hezbollah to undercut the PLO, and in 2005 Hamas emerged as the most powerful electoral force in Gaza. It seems that even those who issue the most dire warnings about a titanic, Islam-vs.-Christianity struggle readily manage to find accommodation with right-wing Islamists.

Still, for purposes of public relations, the Bush administration has been content to allow its Middle East policy to be portrayed as a clash of civilizations. Some of its allies, especially members of the Christian right, explicitly disparage Islam as an evil and violent religion. Pro-claiming that Islamic fundamentalists and bin Laden "hate our free-doms," rather than U.S. policies, Bush has framed the war on terrorism in the starkest terms, as a showdown between a God-fearing America and an "axis of evil." Despite the paradoxes of the war on terror, it is safe to say that millions of Americans have been sold on the idea that the Christian and Muslim worlds must battle each other to the end.

What happened between 1991 and 2001 to transform Islam from an ally to a malignant evil?

The easy answer is blame the shock that followed Al Qaeda's 2001 attacks. But 9/11 was preceded by a decade of confusion in the United States. To follow the transition from the New World Order to the clash of civilizations, it is necessary to touch on the three crises of political Islam during the nineties: Algeria, Egypt, and the rise of the Taliban. The twelve years from the first Iraq war to the second was a period of dizzying change for the Middle East. In Algeria, the Islamic right plunged the country into a brutal civil war when it was denied the fruits of an electoral victory in 1991. In Egypt, a terrorist underground, discreetly supported by the Muslim Brotherhood establishment, nearly toppled Mubarak in the mid-1990s. And then, in Afghanistan, the Pakistan-backed Taliban movement seized Kabul and imposed the world's strictest theocracy.

During these crises, the administrations of George Bush and Bill Clinton failed to develop a coherent policy toward political Islam. Even though the Muslim Brotherhood and right-wing political Islam had seized control of Iran, Afghanistan, Pakistan, and Sudan—and threatened Algeria, Egypt, Syria, and the Palestinian Authority—neither Bush nor Clinton grasped the implications. The U.S. intelligence system and its vaunted counterterrorism machinery first missed the rise of Al Qaeda and then, when the organization made its presence known with a series of spectacular attacks in the late 1990s, failed to stop it. Had they responded differently, had they realized the significance of the Islamist movement then, and had U.S. intelligence analysts and operatives more carefully tracked the violent offshoots of the Brotherhood and the Taliban, perhaps the events of 2001 and beyond would not have occurred. Certainly, had the United States mapped out a coherent policy toward Islamism during the 1990s, the dangerous notion that America is facing a clash of civilizations would never have gained traction.

The U.S. government, academia, and the world of policy-oriented think tanks were divided over how to respond to the Islamic resurgence at the end of the Cold War. Some wanted to develop a comprehensive policy toward Islamism, others demanded that it be treated on a country-by-country basis. Some wanted to confront the Islamists, others to co-opt or placate them. Pragmatists believed that U.S. policy ought to stick with support for the existing regimes in Cairo, Amman, Algiers, and elsewhere, but idealists supported the idea that democracy had to flower in the region, even if the Islamists were positioned to win elections. In the decade between 1991 and 2001, U.S. policy toward the Islamic right was confused and contradictory. When not ignoring it, everyone agreed that Islamist terrorism was bad, but that's where the agreement stopped. The end of the U.S.-Soviet struggle in the Middle East left the United States facing a region in which political Islam was a major player. The Islamic right covered a spectrum from the conservative Islamist regimes in Pakistan and Saudi Arabia, to the radical regimes in Iran and Sudan, to extra-governmental organizations such as the Muslim Brotherhood, the Taliban and Hezbollah, to radical-right terrorist cells such as Al Qaeda. Some were allies, some were vaguely threatening, some dangerously hostile. But how to tell friend from foe?

THREE CRISES IN THE 1990S

During the 1990s, the United States dealt uncertainly with flare-ups by the Islamic right, first in Algeria, then in Egypt, and finally, once again, in Afghanistan. In all three cases, the Islamists were able to draw on battle-hardened veterans of the U.S.-sponsored Afghan jihad, who applied the skills acquired in that war—including bomb-making, assassinations, and guerrilla-style attacks—in their struggle.

As the Soviet Union melted away, the Islamic right began to emerge as a threat to stability, security, and U.S. interests. "One year after Muslim rebels ousted the communist government in Afghanistan, the long Afghanistan war reverberates throughout the Islamic world, as veterans of the conflict take up arms to try to topple governments in Algeria, Egypt, and other Arab countries," the *New York Times* reported in 1993. "Western diplomats and Arab officials say thousands of Islamic militants engaging in clandestine, violent campaigns to overthrow governments in Algeria, Egypt, Yemen, Tunisia, Jordan, Turkey and other predominantly Muslim states currently use Afghanistan as a base."[1] Imbued with a new consciousness and the belief that their insurgency had defeated a superpower in Afghanistan, the Islamic right tested the limits of its newfound power.

Algeria

The 1992–99 crisis in Algeria triggered the first government-wide review of U.S. policy toward political Islam since the Iranian revolution. And, during the seven-year civil war in Algeria, U.S. policy was pulled this way and that by contradictory views—amid charges in Paris and elsewhere in Europe that Washington was cozying up to the Algerian Islamists in order to advance its own oil, gas, and industrial interests in North Africa, at Europe's expense.

The conundrum for the United States in Algeria was having to choose between an Islamist insurgency that had gained an electoral advantage and an entrenched, military-dominated but secular regime that then suspended democracy in order to block the Islamists' victory. The issue was not whether the United States should intervene directly—neither side in Algeria wanted that, and it was impractical in any case. But Washington had to choose between affirming its support for Algeria's experiment in democracy, thus aligning it with a radical Islamist movement, or siding with the Algerian army. Though Washington looked for a middle ground, in the end, correctly, it tolerated the army's suppression of the Islamists. It was not an entirely happy outcome. Yet had the United States condemned the Algerian regime and thrown its diplomatic support to the Islamic right, the consequences—in Algeria, and across the region—could have been catastrophic.

The usual version of the Algerian crisis starts in 1989, with the establishment of the Islamic Salvation Front, known by its French abbreviation, FIS. In June 1990, the FIS won a resounding victory in local elections. Then, in December 1991, FIS stunned the ruling party, the National Liberation Front (FLN), winning 118 parliamentary seats to the FLN's 16. But before the second round of the vote, and before the FIS took power, the army intervened to annul the vote, arresting 10,000 FIS members and supporters. Denied its victory, the FIS unleashed a campaign of terrorism. The president of Algeria was assassinated, ministries were bombed, and hundreds of security officials and policemen were killed by FIS gunmen. Civil war began.

During the decade, a second organization called the Armed Islamic Group (GIA) emerged, with a murky relationship to FIS. As the violence intensified, Islamist vigilantes and shadowy paramilitary groups carried out a campaign of horrifying slaughter, decimating villages, massacring women and children. Tens of thousands died.[2]

But the FIS did not emerge suddenly in 1989. As happened in Pakistan, Egypt, Syria, Sudan, and Afghanistan during the Cold War, the Islamic right built its power by battling the left and Algerian nationalists, especially on campuses. As in Afghanistan, where "the professors" tied to Egypt's Muslim Brotherhood built a secret society of Islamists in Kabul in the 1960s and 1970s, in Algeria a host of professors and teachers from Egypt, many of whom were members of the Muslim Brotherhood and who had studied in Saudi Arabia's Islamic universities, were imported to teach Arabic to the francophone Algerians. Mohammed al-Ghazali and Yusuf al-Qaradawi, two of Egypt's leading Islamic scholars who had fled to the Gulf, and who "were fellow travelers of the Muslim Brothers and very much in favor with the oil monarchies [and who encouraged] the 'Islamic awakening' at work" in Algeria in the mid-1980s.[3] Throughout the 1980s, this cadre of Islamic-right activists carried out a series of terrorist attacks against the Algerian government. Many of the terrorists involved had been to Afghanistan, or traveled back and forth to the jihad, and one of them, Abdallah Anas, joined forces with bin Laden and Azzam in the pre–Al Qaeda "Services Bureau." When Azzam was assassinated, Anas took over.

By the time the FIS was created, it had seized control of thousands of mosques across the country and built a political-religious machine. Like the Taliban, wherever FIS controlled municipal or provincial governments it instituted its version of Islamic cultural restrictions, forcing women to wear the veil, closing liquor and video stores, and often persecuting those who did not go along. The FIS denounced Algeria's educated, secular middle classes and announced its intent to "ban France from Algeria intellectually and ideologically."[4] One month before the December election that catapulted the FIS to victory, in November 1991, a supposedly independent or renegade band of Algeria's Islamists shocked the country with an outrageous act of terror:

Their first spectacular operation was a bloody assault on a frontier post, in the course of which a group of "Afghan" veterans cut off the heads of some wretched army conscripts. . . . The date was carefully chosen to celebrate within four days the second anniversary of the martyrdom of Abdullah Azzam in Peshawar. It marked the beginning of a jihad on Algerian soil.[5]

Many Algerians feared that an Islamist government would institute a reign of terror. Arab governments, including Egypt, Jordan, Tunisia and Morocco, were alarmed, fearing that an Islamist-run Algeria would be infectious. And for the United States, the Algerian army's action posed a delicate political problem: would Washington endorse the army's suppression of the election results, or defend the FIS and the Islamic right?

For the Bush administration, preoccupied with the New World Order, it was a puzzle. Bush and Secretary of State James Baker were uneasy about the prospect of Islamism in Algeria, and they sided semi-officially with the Algerian army, adopting a position that a Senate report called "something of a wink and a nod."[6] Baker, explaining his position later, said: "When I was at the State Department, we pursued a policy of excluding the radical fundamentalists in Algeria even as we recognized that this was somewhat at odds with our support of democracy."[7] But many other U.S. officials, including CIA officers who had contact with the FIS, did not agree with the Bush-Baker policy.

According to Robert Pelletreau, a former U.S. ambassador and senior official at the State Department, there was serious disagreement about the Bush-Baker policy of blocking the Islamists in Algeria. "In the immediate aftermath of the military's decision to block the election result, we were very critical," says Pelletreau. "Twenty-four hours later, we reversed ourselves, and took a much more nuanced view."[8]

The Bush administration, uncertain about how to deal with the Islamist challenge in Algiers, undertook a policy review. But it was a hodgepodge, an effort to forge a consensus about how to deal with a phenomenon little understood even by experts and about which politicians, top administration officials, and members of Congress were utterly ignorant. Battle lines had not yet hardened, but at least two currents had already started to emerge. One was an accommodationist point of view, whose adherents argued that the United States had nothing to fear from the Islamic right and that U.S. diplomats and CIA officials ought to begin a worldwide effort to open contacts with the Islamists who were willing, for the sake of dialogue, to eschew violence. A second (still nascent) point of view was the clash-of-civilizations school, which believed that the Muslim world was unalterably and fundamentally hostile to the West. According to them, the enemy of the United States was not just Al Qaeda, and not even right-wing political Islam, but the very nature of the Muslim faith, the Koran, and Islamic civilization as it had evolved over thirteen centuries. Throughout the 1990s, these two schools would gain momentum and confront each other. Two leading academics would come to represent the two sides: for the accommodationists, John Esposito of Georgetown University; and for the clash of civilizations, Bernard Lewis of Princeton University.

In 1992, a decision was taken to have Edward Djerejian, then assistant secretary of state for Near East affairs, spearhead the effort to invent a policy toward Islam, and he was chosen to deliver a speech in June 1992, at Meridian House in Washington. "The State Department came to me and said, 'We need an Islam policy,'" says David Mack, then Djerejian's deputy. According to Mack, the speech was partly designed to counter administration officials who were starting to argue that the United States should treat Islam as a new global enemy. "Some of the folks, especially Richard Schifter of the bureau of human rights, were saying that Islam was dangerous, and of course this was the time when the thesis of the clash of civilizations was starting to surface," says Mack. "Well, we pretty much managed to head it off. We had a big, in-house conference, with people from [Near East affairs], [the Bureau of Intelligence and Research], human rights, and a lot of outside experts on Islam. And I drafted a speech for Djerejian. We brought it to Jim Baker, who said, 'Okay, fine, if you want to do this.'"[9]

Schifter, the assistant secretary of state for human rights, says that he adheres to Jeanne Kirkpatrick's distinction between "authoritarian" and "totalitarian" regimes. In the Algerian crisis, he says that he supported the view that the United States ought to back the Algerian army's suppression of the Islamists. But for Schifter, and for many hard-liners and neoconservatives, the issue was much larger than Algeria. "What I saw was the development of a movement similar to communism," he says. "It's the third totalitarian attack on democracy, after fascism and communism."[10] According to Mack, Schifter wanted a much tougher line in the speech than was adopted. "Schifter and the bureau of human rights felt it was a soft-minded approach," says Mack.[11]

In the end, Djerejian's speech laid down some important markers, but it also avoided crucial questions. Djerejian rejected out of hand the clash-of-civilizations idea. "The U.S. government does not view Islam as the new 'ism' confronting the West or threatening world peace," he said. "The Cold War is not being replaced with a new competition between Islam and the West. The Crusades have been over for a long time. Americans recognize Islam as a historic civilizing force among the many that have influenced and enriched our culture." But he went further:

> Much attention is being paid to a phenomenon variously labeled political Islam, the Islamic revival, or Islamic fundamentalism. . . . In countries throughout the Middle East and North Africa, we thus see groups or movements seeking to reform their societies in keeping with Islamic ideals. . . . We detect no monolithic or coordinated international effort behind these movements. What we do see are believers living in different countries placing renewed emphasis on Islamic principles and governments accommodating Islamist political activity to varying degrees and in different ways.

Djerejian went on to add that the United States wanted free elections and enhanced civil rights in the region, but said, in an obvious reference to the crisis in Algeria: "We are suspect of those who would use the democratic process to come to power, only to destroy that very process in order to retain power and political dominance." And he said that the United States was opposed to those who engage in violence, repression, or "religious and political confrontation."[12]

In other forums, Djerejian spoke favorably, but vaguely, about "moderate Islamists," although he failed to define what he meant by "moderate."[13] While Djerejian condemned terrorism and noted that the United States has good relations with countries "whose systems of government are firmly grounded in Islamic principles," such as Saudi Arabia and Pakistan, he completely avoided any discussion of the Islamic right itself and its manifestations. "Unfortunately," Gerges wrote, "the Meridian address did not clarify the Bush administration's approach toward those very Islamist groups."

If Djerejian's speech failed as an outline of American policy toward political Islam, it worked well as a more particular response to events in Algeria, where the United States tacitly supported the army's suspension of democracy. But the situation went from bad to worse, as Algeria was engulfed in a cycle of violent attacks and counterattacks pitting the army against battle-hardened jihad veterans.

In 1993, the Clinton administration tried to encourage a dialogue between the Algerian authorities and elements of the Islamist opposition. But Western Europe, particularly France, accused the United States of using its dialogue with the Algerian Islamists to secure a political and commercial advantage in Algeria in the wake of what many expected would be an Islamic revolution. "The French attacked American motives for meeting with Islamists, suspecting the U.S. government of favoring the FIS over the Algerian regime," according to Gerges, who reports that Charles Pasqua, the French interior minister, accused Washington of harboring "fundamentalist terrorists."[14] That was a reference to Anwar Haddam, the FIS representative in Washington, who maintained on-and-off contacts with U.S. officials in the early 1990s. "The French wanted us to expel the FIS guy here," says Pelletreau, who served under Clinton as assistant secretary of state for Near East affairs. "But we never had any call to expel him."[15]

The loudest voice calling for a reconciliation with Algeria's Islamists was none other than Graham Fuller, the former CIA analyst who had worked with Casey to build a justification for the 1984–86 Iran-contra approach to Teheran. Then ensconced at the RAND Corporation, Fuller wrote a book entitled *Algeria: The Next Fundamentalist State?* In it, he virtually endorsed FIS as Algeria's next rulers and urged the United States not to worry. "The FIS is unlikely to present a massive challenge to U.S. and Western interests," wrote Fuller. "Is the United States willing to inaugurate democratic processes in which the

Islamists stand a very good chance of gaining a significant voice in power?"[16] Fuller admitted that FIS would suppress women's rights and spread the gospel abroad, "emboldening other Islamist movements in Egypt, Tunisia, Libya, and Morocco [with] asylum, financial aid, even weapons."[17] But he argued that its momentum was unstoppable. "It will be very difficult, if not almost impossible, to stop Islamist forces," said Fuller. "Islamist governments in the Middle East are likely to multiply in the years ahead, taking numerous different forms. They, and the West, are going to have to learn to live with each other."[18] Fuller argued that FIS "is likely to welcome U.S. private sector investment in Algeria and to undertake close commercial relations with the United States. . . . The FIS has long had good ties with Saudi Arabia and received a great deal of Saudi funding until recent years."[19] Fuller's monograph was written for and sponsored by the U.S. Army.

To Fuller, the FIS movement in Algeria was a grand experiment, and one that the United States ought not to turn away from—and his views were certainly influential during the Clinton administration. But many Algerians, especially veterans of the revolution that ended in 1962, were not so ready to abandon secularism and socialism for free-market Islamism. "It's fine for others to talk about conducting a grand political experiment in Algeria," said Maloud Brahimi, former head of Algeria's League of Human Rights. "But what do we look like—white rats?"[20]

Egypt

On the heels of the Algerian explosion, a dire Islamist threat to Egypt emerged in the 1990s, creating another dilemma for the Clinton administration. Was Egypt, the original home of the Muslim Brotherhood, about to fall to an Islamist revolution? And if so, what should U.S. policy be? The Bush administration's 1992 review, and the task force that Djerejian created, did not provide much guidance. Unlike Algeria, which after all was on the periphery of the Middle East, Egypt was its very heart—and President Mubarak a staunch ally.

In the 1990s, Egyptian Islamists waged an assault on the Egyptian regime strong enough to threaten the country's stability. Hundreds of people were killed by armed militants, including military and police officers, government officials, and leading Egyptian writers and intellectuals. Despite heavy repression after the death of Sadat in 1981, and periodic crackdowns in the 1980s, the Brotherhood had made steady gains, especially in civil society. The organization won control of many of Egypt's professional associations—doctors, lawyers, engineers, and, of course, student groups, its traditional stronghold. In 1993, the *Sunday Times* of London reported that the CIA issued a National Intelligence Estimate warning that "Islamic fundamentalist terrorists will continue to make gains across Egypt, leading to the eventual collapse of the Mubarak government."[21]

James Woolsey was the CIA director at the time. "We were very worried, and as I remember we offered Egypt whatever assistance we could reasonably provide," he says. "Generally speaking, there was a substantial amount of support in the U.S. government, certainly in the intelligence community, for Mubarak doing whatever he had to do to prevent an Islamist takeover."[22] The United States provided security assistance to Egypt's police and intelligence service. "In Egypt we'd trained a Special Operations group among the Egyptian authorities, with the help of the CIA," says Edward W. Walker, the U.S. ambassador from 1994 to 1997. "They were used in cleaning up a few of these cells."[23]

The truth, however, is that even though the United States cooperated with Egypt to a degree in combating Islamist terrorism in Egypt, that cooperation was far less than it ought to have been, for several reasons. First, within the U.S. government, there was a persistent belief that the Muslim Brotherhood was a potentially useful partner in efforts to bring democracy to Egypt, and throughout the 1990s that belief undercut U.S. assistance to Egypt's security and intelligence agencies. Second, the Mubarak regime's often very heavy-handed repression of its opponents, including arrests of all manner of dissidents and the use of torture against prisoners, made the United States skittish about helping Cairo. Both Woolsey and Walker say that the United States had strong reservations about the harshness of Egyptian methods. "They were very aggressive, more aggressive than we were willing to support. Some of the people they seized were found shot with their hands tied," says Walker. "We had to stop the program."[24] And third, there was sharp disagreement among U.S. intelligence and diplomatic officials about the nature of the Brotherhood itself: Was the organization cooperating with the radical, openly terrorist sub-groups like Al Gamaa or Islamic Jihad, whose leaders included Ayman al-Zawahiri, Osama bin Laden's future chief aide? Or was the Brotherhood a moderate, even establishment group whose rhetorical commitment to democracy could be relied upon?

For Mubarak, at least, the answer was provided by Algeria. The Egyptian leader watched in horror as that country plunged into civil war, and he vowed not to allow the Islamists in Egypt to gain enough strength to mount a frontal challenge to his regime. Beginning in the 1980s and continuing through September 11, 2001, Mubarak criticized the United States repeatedly for its failure to take action against the Islamic right in its bases in Western Europe and in the United States itself. Those included overt Muslim Brotherhood organizational units in London and Germany, Said Ramadan's Islamic Center in Geneva, New York–New Jersey cells such as the one affiliated with blind sheikh Omar Abdul Rahman, the ringleader of the 1993 attack on the World Trade Center, and other U.S.-based cells, mosques, and Islamic centers. Until 2001, no concerted U.S. effort to investigate these networks was undertaken.

"Neither Europe nor the United States were cooperating with Egypt, not until 9/11," says Abdel Moneim Said of the Al Ahram Center in Cairo:

> Omar Abdel Rahman was being harbored in the United States, having escaped in between trials and going to Sudan. The United States was not cooperating. They'd say to us, "You are not a democracy, you are not making reforms." So they were creating a worldwide terrorist network, and we were practically on our own during this period. We wanted the United States to give these guys to us, to sabotage their propaganda networks, to sabotage their financial networks, to disturb their connection with the trouble spots in Afghanistan. We tried several times to get the United States involved, first in 1986, when President Mubarak called for an international conference on terrorism, announcing it at a meeting

of the European parliament in Strasbourg. We knew a lot by then: that the international centers for this movement were in London, New Jersey, Frankfurt, with other centers in Hamburg, Geneva, Copenhagen. They were not at all sensitive to this in Europe in the 1980s and 1990s.[25]

The two U.S. ambassadors to Egypt during this period had conflicting views about the Muslim Brotherhood. Walker, who served from 1994 to 1997, was skeptical of the Muslim Brotherhood and mostly sympathetic to Mubarak's crackdown. Pelletreau, who served in Cairo from 1991 to 1993, was more apt to see the Brotherhood in a favorable light—even if it attracted the attention of Egypt's intelligence service. "Ned [Walker] and I had different policies," says Pelletreau. "I felt we had to be talking to members of the Muslim Brotherhood. I did [talk to them]." Pelletreau's contacts with the Brotherhood angered Mubarak. "At one point I received a very strong message from the [Egyptian] government, demanding that I break off those contacts. I said that I would not. I didn't meet with them myself, but people from the political section did. We developed people as contacts who were inside the movement. But in Egypt you have to be very careful, because the Egyptians have a very, very effective counterintelligence capability."[26]

Pelletreau recalls a visit to Washington by Mubarak in which the Egyptian president lost his temper over U.S. inaction:

> Soon afterward, Mubarak came to Washington, and the secretary of state invited him to lunch. Warren Christopher asked Mubarak about the best way to deal with the Islamists. I'll never forget what happened next. Mubarak sat up sharply, rigidly. "This is not a new phenomenon in Egypt," he said, getting angry. "These people killed my predecessor!" Then he raised this huge fist, and he slammed it down on the table hard, and everything on the table jumped and rattled. Bang! "When they come out, we have to hit them!"[27]

But Pelletreau says: "I told Mubarak that it was the right policy to crack down on terrorists, but not on the Muslim Brotherhood." The question of how to tell the difference was something that U.S. intelligence could not answer, according to U.S. diplomats and intelligence officers. The line between the overtly terrorist organizations and the more establishment Muslim Brotherhood was not a clear one. The Brotherhood ran clinics, social welfare centers, and mosques, had a powerful presence among professional groups, and set up a semi-official political party.

According to Pelletreau and Walker, the link between the official Muslim Brotherhood and the underground terrorist cells was probably organized through independent mosques and Islamic centers in Egypt run by "emirs." They apparently maintained a membership in the Brotherhood, which was a secret society, while giving encouragement, support, and theological justification to the terrorists. "The Egyptians claimed that they discovered some links, and I guess you could say that the whole line became blurred between the Muslim Brotherhood and the armed groups," says Pelletreau. "A lot of independent emirs start popping up here and there, in various parts of Cairo, and some of the clerics develop a group of followers. They don't usually engage in acts of violence themselves, but they can condone violence. Say, someone will come to them and say, 'Is it permitted to do such and such?' and they will say, 'Yes, according to Islam.'"

Walker, who followed Pelletreau, had a somewhat different view. "We'd realized it was a much bigger problem," he says. "We were very close to the Europeans in cooperating to roll up these threats. We created flow charts of how these groups interacted with each other. A lot of the leaders were in places like Italy and London, and we'd cooperate by intercepting communications back into Egypt, and then the Egyptians would roll them up." But, Walker says, Egypt was not satisfied with U.S. and European cooperation. "I can't count the number of times that Mubarak yelled at me about how the British were giving the Muslim Brotherhood and other Islamists safe haven," he says. "In Egypt, everybody seemed to see it as a problem, but they couldn't convince us."[28]

Like Pelletreau, Walker maintained a relationship with the Muslim

Brotherhood. "When I was there in Egypt we engaged with members of the Muslim Brotherhood, as individuals, on the level of the embassy political counselor. But it was an illegal organization, so it was sensitive. The Muslim Brotherhood was more acquiescent than some of the other groups, such as Islamic Jihad. The Muslim Brotherhood had a lot of sympathy from some people in Washington, who held it should be accommodated," he says. "For many of those who support bringing democracy to the region, the Muslim Brotherhood was seen as a legitimate domestic opposition force." Walker, and some CIA officers, didn't agree. "Terrorism had two sources. One was the Palestinians, and one, the Muslim Brotherhood. They had a checkered history. One day you're friends, and then they try to assassinate you," Walker says. "Our intelligence people saw it as a kind of international fraternity of terrorists. Some specific mosques were involved. It is not a coherent organizational structure. But if someone comes along, they help them."[29]

Mubarak repeatedly slammed the United States in public, too, especially after the Islamists mounted an assassination attempt against him in 1995, murdered several Egyptian government officials abroad, and bombed Egypt's embassies. To Americans who urged him to cooperate with moderate Islamists, including the Muslim Brotherhood, Mubarak dripped with scorn. "Who are the moderates?" he said. "Nobody has succeeded in defining them for me." He ridiculed the effectiveness of dialogue with the Islamists. "Dialogue with whom? It will be the dialogue of the deaf. We had a dialogue with them for fourteen years, and every time we engaged them, they became stronger. Dialogue is old-fashioned. The ones who are asking for dialogue do not know [Islamists]. We know them better."[30]

The shadow of Iran's 1979 revolution haunted Mubarak. Again and again, he accused the United States of conducting secret talks with the Brotherhood. "You think you can correct the mistakes that you made in Iran, where you had no contact with the Ayatollah Khomeini and his fanatic groups before they seized power," Mubarak said. "But, I can assure you, these groups will never take over this country, and they will never be on good terms with the United States."[31] To a large extent, Mubarak was right that many U.S. officials expected that the Islamists would seize control of Egypt, and so they sought an inside track with the Islamic right. Foreshadowing the neoconservative dreams after 2001 of reshaping the Middle East and imposing some new democratic order there, an official at the National Security Council said in early 1995 that Egypt's Islamists were the wave of the future:

> The existing Middle Eastern regimes, said this official, are bound to disappear in the future because change is inevitable; one of Washington's major policy objectives is to manage the transition to a new Middle Eastern political order with minimal cost. The United States views Islamists as integral players among the broad social forces operating in the region. Thus, to survive, the dominant ruling elites will have to broaden their social base by integrating Islamists into the political field. This reality explains the rationale for the Clinton administration's early decision to maintain a discreet dialogue with the Algerian and Egyptian Islamists.[32]

Neither Algeria's government nor Mubarak thought much of that "reality," however, and they acted to crush the Islamist insurgency. Following the 1995 assassination attempt, Mubarak launched an assault against the Muslim Brotherhood that recalled the 1954 and 1964–66 crackdowns by Nasser. Hundreds of Muslim Brotherhood leaders were arrested, their institutions were dismantled, professional syndicates closed, and show trials held. Some U.S. officials predicted that the repression would backfire, but instead, during the second half of the 1990s, the Islamic right in Egypt retreated with one glaring exception: a series of spectacular terrorist acts directed against tourists in Egypt in 1997. The Islamic right in Egypt had, once again, been beaten into submission. But it did not go away. Its violence-oriented underground scattered, or went into hiding. Its moderate-seeming ideologues, preachers, and politicians sought alliance with Egypt's democratic opposition, declaring their support for elections to replace Mubarak. Many U.S. government officials, sympathetic Orientalists, and think tanks—from the Brookings Institution to the U.S. Institute for Peace—insisted that the Muslim Brotherhood was a promising partner in a reformed Egypt.

The Taliban

The third Islamist eruption to confront U.S. policy makers was the meteoric rise of the Taliban in war-shattered Afghanistan.

The most incisive account of the founding, growth and victory of the Taliban is Ahmed Rashid's *Taliban: Militant Islam, Oil, and Fundamentalism in Central Asia*. A veteran Pakistani reporter, Rashid spent years covering Afghanistan and Pakistan's ISI. According to Rashid, from the start the Taliban had strong support not only from Saudi Arabia, which financed it, and from Pakistan, whose ISI intelligence service was the primary force behind the Taliban's conquest of warlord-dominated Afghanistan, but from the United States as well. "Between 1994 and 1996, the U.S.A. supported the Taliban politically through its allies Pakistan and Saudi Arabia, essentially because Washington viewed the Taliban as anti-Iranian, anti-Shia, and pro-Western," he wrote. "Between 1995 and 1997 U.S. support was even more driven because of its backing for the Unocal project [for an energy pipeline from Turkmenistan through Afghanistan]." Many U.S. diplomats, he wrote, "saw them as messianic do-gooders—like born-again Christians from the American Bible Belt."[33]

The U.S. support for the Taliban was strategic. It precisely echoed Brzezinski's "arc of Islam" policy and Casey's dream of using Islam to penetrate the Soviet Union. Even in the post–Cold War world, the United States sought to gain advantage in oil-rich Central Asia, and throughout the 1990s Washington jockeyed for position. In the American view, its allies were Saudi Arabia and Pakistan, and its competitors were Russia, China, India, and Iran. A 1996 State Department memo, written just before the Taliban captured Kabul, warned that Russia, Iran, and India—all of which feared Sunni fundamentalism in the region—would back an anti-Taliban force in Afghanistan,[34] and that is precisely what did happen, as the Ahmed Shah Massoud–led Northern Alliance emerged in the late 1990s as the chief opponent of the Taliban's fanatical regime. (Ironically, it would be the Northern Alliance that would be the chief ally of the United States when, after the attack on the World Trade Center and the Pentagon, the United States invaded Afghanistan.)

Graham Fuller, in *The Future of Political Islam,* accurately described how the Taliban threatened nations competing with the United States in Central Asia:

> Important external forces that shared a stake in Afghan events were disturbed at the implications of a Taliban takeover: Iran because the Taliban were fiercely anti-Shiite and treated the Shiite Hazara population with extreme harshness; and Russia, Uzbekistan, and Tajikistan because they feared the Taliban would turn their sights toward expanding Islamist movements north into central Asia. India, too, geopolitically sought to deny Pakistan strategic dominance in Afghanistan, which a Taliban victory would represent. Washington was initially neutral and hoped, with Pakistani urging, that the Taliban had no anti-U.S. agenda, could at last unify the country so long wracked by civil war; could facilitate the passage of Turkmen gas pipelines through Afghanistan to the Indian Ocean, skirting Iran; could impose control over the rampant poppy production, and crack down on the presence of Muslim guerrillas and training camps in the country since the anti-Soviet jihad.[35]

Cold War or not, the United States explicitly stated its intention to challenge Russian hegemony in Central Asia and Afghanistan. U.S. policy, said Sheila Haslin, an NSC official, was to "promote the independence of these oil-rich countries, to in essence break Russia's monopoly control over the transportation of oil from that region, and frankly, to promote Western energy security through diversity of supply."[36] Unocal, the prime backer of plans for a pipeline to guarantee that diversity, hired numerous former U.S. officials to promote its scheme, from Henry Kissinger to Zalmay Khalilzad, the future U.S. ambassador in Kabul. Khalilzad, a specialist at the RAND Corporation, said in 1996: "The Taliban does not practice the anti-U.S. style of fundamentalism practiced by Iran—it is closer to the Saudi model. The group upholds a mix of traditional Pashtun values and an orthodox interpretation of Islam."[37]

Besides Saudi Arabia and Pakistan, two other U.S. allies joined in the regional strategy for ousting Russia and containing Iran: Israel and Turkey. In the 1990s, Turkey—which was increasingly falling under the spell of its own Muslim Brotherhood–linked Islamist movement—was being encouraged by Washington to extend its influence into Central Asia, where a large Turkic population was, they thought, ready to respond to a Turkish-led bloc stretching from the Bosporus to China.

At exactly the same time that Osama bin Laden was setting up headquarters in Afghanistan, after being asked to leave Sudan in 1996, the Taliban leaders who hosted him, and who were becoming increasingly dependent on bin Laden's financial support, were crisscrossing the United States, meeting U.S. officials, oil men, and academics. Protests against the Taliban from women's groups, who opposed the Taliban's hateful treatment of Afghan women, were (at first) overlooked by the Clinton administration and by Unocal, who preferred to see the Taliban as a mini-version of Saudi Arabia's ruling elite. "The Taliban," said a State Department official, "will probably develop like the Saudis. There will be Aramco, pipelines, an emir, no parliament, and lots of sharia law. We can live with that."[38]

During the U.S.-Taliban era of cooperation from 1994 to 1998—which ended with the bombings of two U.S. embassies in Africa, when the United States targeted not only bin Laden but his Afghan allies as well—a key Unocal consultant was a University of Nebraska academic named Thomas Gouttierre, director of the Center for Afghanistan Studies there. During and after the Afghan jihad, Gouttierre's center secured more than $60 million in federal grants for "educational" programs in Afghanistan and Pakistan. Although the funding for Gouttierre's work was funneled through the State Department's Agency for International Development, the CIA was its sponsor. And it turned out that Gouttierre's education program consisted of blatant Islamist propaganda, including the creation of children's textbooks in which young Afghanis were taught to count by enumerating dead Russian soldiers and adding up Kalashnikov rifles, all of it imbued with Islamic fundamentalist rhetoric. The Taliban liked Gouttierre's work so much that they continued to use the textbooks he created, and when a delegation of Taliban officials visited the United States in 1997 they made a special stop in Omaha to pay homage to Gouttierre. In 1999, another Taliban delegation, which included military commanders with ties to bin Laden and Al

Qaeda, was escorted by Gouttierre on a tour of Mount Rushmore.[39] "You sit down with them and they are relatively regular Joes," said Gouttierre, according to the *Omaha World Herald*.[40] When the United States invaded Afghanistan in 2001, one of its tasks was to purge and replace Gouttierre's Taliban-endorsed (and CIA-funded) Islamists text-books in the schools. "The primers," the *Washington Post* reported, "were filled with talk of jihad."[41]

A CLASH OF CIVILIZATIONS?

By the end of the 1990s, a tense stalemate existed respecting the power of the Islamic right in the Middle East and south Asia. In Egypt and Algeria, the Islamists had been beaten into submission, but they maintained a low-level presence. In Afghanistan, Iran, and Sudan they held the high ground, controlling radical Islamic republics under dic-tatorial regimes. In Pakistan and Saudi Arabia, the Islamists exercised extraordinary power in alliance with ruling elites, although the royal family in Saudi Arabia and the army in Pakistan were increasingly edgy about their respective deals with the devil. Islamism was making unprecedented gains in Turkey, whose seventy-year secular tradition reaching back to Kemal Ataturk was threatened by right-wing Islamists tied to the Muslim Brotherhood and the Naqshbandi Sufi secret society.

In the United States, from the Iranian revolution until the late 1990s, almost no one gave a thought to the problems in the Middle East caused by Islamism. Even that violent subset of Islamism— namely, Islamic terrorist groups—was essentially ignored, according to Woolsey and other CIA officials, with the exception of Hezbollah. The CIA and U.S. counterterrorism officials finally responded to a series of wake-up calls (the 1996 destruction of the U.S. military's Khobar Towers facility in Saudi Arabia, the 1998 car bombing of U.S. embassies in Kenya and Tanzania, and the 2000 attack on the U.S.S. *Cole* off the coast of Yemen) by creating a series of task forces dedi-cated to Osama bin Laden, Al Qaeda, and its allies, who became Pub-lic Enemy No. 1.

But the U.S. effort to find and eliminate bin Laden was laughably incompetent. A $27 billion U.S. intelligence system, with perhaps 100,000 employees spread among a dozen agencies, with a vast array of satellites, surveillance devices, spies, agents, and informers, failed to find him. At the same time, however, countless journalists from the United States and Europe, including television reporters from CNN and *Frontline,* found him with ease and conducted lengthy interviews. Would-be terrorists with questionable bona fides, such as John Walker Lindh, managed to get close to bin Laden, but the CIA couldn't replicate the feat. Cruise missile attacks against alleged bin Laden hideouts in Afghanistan failed miserably, and attacks on facilities in Sudan allegedly tied to Al Qaeda efforts to produce weapons of mass destruction managed to destroy that country's only factory for producing medicines. A scheme to kidnap bin Laden, meticulously planned, was aborted.

Then, on September 11, 2001, those who believed in the clash of civilizations got the opening they needed. Their views, until then considered odd at best and extremist at worst, won a far wider following. And the Bush administration, while not endorsing the idea of a struggle between Christianity and Islam, seized the notion of a clash of civilizations to propel the United States into an unprecedented expansion of its imperial presence in the Middle East.

Lewis and Huntington

Until that date, the two men most responsible for popularizing the idea of a clash of civilizations, Bernard Lewis and Samuel Huntington, were regarded as curiosities by mainstream national security and foreign policy experts. Their Ivy League credentials and access to prestigious publications such as *Foreign Affairs,* and the edgy radicalism of their theories, guaranteed that they would generate controversy, and they did. But few took their ideas seriously, except for a scattered array of neoconservatives, who, in the 1990s, resided on the fringe themselves. The Lewis-Huntington thesis was hit by a withering salvo of counterattacks from many journalists, academics, and foreign policy gurus.

Samuel Huntington, whose controversial book *The Clash of Civilizations* amounted to a neoconservative declaration of war, wrote that the enemy was not the Islamic right, but the religion of the Koran itself:

> The underlying problem for the West is not Islamic fundamentalism. It is Islam, a different civilization whose people are convinced of the superiority of their culture and are obsessed with the inferiority of their power. The problem for Islam is not the CIA or the U.S. Department of Defense. It is the West, a different civilization whose people are convinced of the universality of their culture and believe that their superior, if declining power imposes on them the obligation to extend that culture throughout the world.[42]

What followed from Huntington's manifesto, of course, was that the Judeo-Christian world and the Muslim world were locked in a state of permanent cultural war. The terrorists—such as Al Qaeda, which was still taking shape when Huntington's book came out—were not just a gang of fanatics with a political agenda, but the manifestation of a civilizational conflict. Like a modern oracle of Delphi, Huntington suggested that the gods had foreordained the collision, and mere humans could not stop it.

Huntington acknowledged—without mentioning the role of the United States—that Islam had been a potent force against the left during the Cold War. "At one time or another during the Cold War many governments, including those of Algeria, Turkey, Jordan, Egypt, and Israel, encouraged and supported Islamists as a counter to communist or hostile nationalist movements," he wrote. "At least until the Gulf War, Saudi Arabia and other Gulf states provided massive funding to the Muslim Brotherhood and Islamist groups in a variety of countries."[43] But he had a neat explanation of how the alliance between the West and the Islamists unraveled. "The collapse of communism removed a common enemy of the West and Islam and left each the perceived major threat to the other," he wrote.[44] "In the 1990s many saw a 'civilizational cold war' again developing between Islam and the West."[45] Huntington, who is not an expert on Islam, observed a "connection between Islam and militarism,"[46] and he asserted: "Islam has from the start been a religion of the sword and it glorifies military virtues."[47] Just to make sure that no one could miss his point, he quoted an unnamed U.S. Army officer who said, "The southern tier"—i.e., the border between Europe and the Middle East—"is rapidly becoming NATO's new front line."[48]

Huntington quotes his guru on matters Islamic, Bernard Lewis, in order to prove that Islam presents an existential threat to the very survival of the West:

> "For almost a thousand years," Bernard Lewis observes, "from the first Moorish landing in Spain to the second Turkish siege of Vienna, Europe was under constant threat from Islam." Islam is the only civilization which has put the survival of the West in doubt, and it has done that at least twice.[49]

How exactly the weak, impoverished, and fragmented countries of the Middle East and south Asia could "put the survival of the West in doubt" was not explained. But it was a thesis that Bernard Lewis had been refining since the 1950s.

Lewis, a former British intelligence officer and longtime supporter of the Israeli right, has been a propagandist and apologist for imperialism and Israeli expansionism for more than half a century. He first used the term "clash of civilizations" in 1956, in an article that appeared in the *Middle East Journal,* in which he endeavored to explain "the present anti-Western mood of the Arab states." Lewis asserted then that Arab anger was not the result of the "Palestine problem," nor was it related to the "struggle against imperialism." Instead, he argued, it was "something deeper and vaster":

> What we are seeing in our time is not less than a clash between civilizations—more specifically, a revolt of the world of Islam against the shattering impact of Western civilization which, since the 18th century, has dislocated and disrupted the old order. . . . The resulting anger and frustration are often generalized against Western civilization as a whole.[50]

It was a theme he would return to again and again. By blaming anti-Western feeling in the Arab world on vast historical forces, Lewis absolved the West of its neocolonial post–World War II oil grab, its support for the creation of a Zionist state on Arab territory, and its ruthless backing of corrupt monarchies in Egypt, Iraq, Libya, Jordan, Saudi Arabia, and the Gulf. In his classic 1964 book, *The Middle East and the West,* he repeated his nostrum: "We [must] view the present discontents of the Middle East not as a conflict between states or nations, but as a clash of civilizations."[51] Lewis explicitly made the point that the United States must not seek to curry favor with the Arabs by pressuring Israel to make peace. "Some speak wistfully of how easy it would all be if only Arab wishes could be met—this being usually interpreted to mean those wishes that can be satisfied at the expense of other parties," i.e., Israel.[52] Instead, he demanded, the United States should simply abandon the Arabs. "The West should ostentatiously disengage from Arab politics, and in particular, from inter-Arab politics," wrote Lewis. "It should seek to manufacture no further Arab allies."[53] Why seek alliance with nations whose very culture and religion make them unalterably opposed to Western civilization?

Over several decades, Lewis played a critical role as professor, mentor, and guru to two generations of Orientalists, academics, U.S. and British intelligence specialists, think tank denizens, and assorted neoconservatives, while earning the scorn of countless other academic specialists on Islam who considered Lewis hopelessly biased in favor of a Zionist, anti-Muslim point of view. A British Jew born in 1916, Lewis spent five years during World War II as a Middle East operative for British intelligence, and then settled at the University of London.[54] In 1974 he migrated from London to Princeton, where he developed ties to people who would later lead the fledgling neoconservative movement. "Lewis became [Senator Henry] Jackson's guru, more or less," said Richard Perle,[55] a former top Pentagon official who, as chairman of the Pentagon's Defense Policy Board, was the most prominent advocate for war with Iraq in 2003, and who is a longtime acolyte of Lewis's. Lewis also became a regular visitor to the Moshe Dayan Center at Tel Aviv University, where he developed close links to Ariel Sharon.

By the 1980s, Lewis was hobnobbing with top Department of Defense officials. According to Pat Lang, the former DIA official,

Bernard Lewis was frequently called down from Princeton to provide tutorials to Andrew Marshall, director of the Office of Net Assessments, an in-house Pentagon think tank.[56] Another of Lewis's students was Harold Rhode, a polyglot Middle East expert who went to work in the Pentagon and stayed for more than two decades, serving as Marshall's deputy. Over the past twenty years, Lewis has served as the in-house consultant on Islam and the Middle East to a host of neoconservatives, including Perle, Rhode, and Michael Ledeen. Asked whom he drew on for expertise during his tenure as CIA director, James Woolsey says, "We had people come in and give seminars. I remember talking to Bernard Lewis."[57]

Although Lewis maintained a veneer of academic objectivity, and though many scholars acknowledged Lewis's credentials as a primary-source historian on the history of the Ottoman Empire, Lewis abandoned all pretense of academic detachment in the 1990s. In 1998, he officially joined the neocon camp, signing a letter demanding regime change in Iraq from the ad hoc Committee for Peace and Security in the Gulf, co-signed by Perle, Martin Peretz of *The New Republic,* and future Bush administration officials, including Paul Wolfowitz, David Wurmser, and Dov Zakheim. He continued to work closely with neoconservative think tanks, and in the period after September 11, 2001, Lewis was ubiquitous, propagating his view that Islam was unalterably opposed to the West. Two weeks after 9/11, Perle invited Lewis and Ahmed Chalabi to speak before the influential Defense Policy Board, inaugurating a two-year effort by neoconservatives to prove a nonexistent link between Osama bin Laden and Saddam Hussein. Chalabi, a friend of Perle's and Lewis's since the 1980s, led an exile Iraqi opposition group, the Iraqi National Congress, and Chalabi was responsible for feeding reams of misleading information to U.S. intelligence officers that helped the Bush administration exaggerate the extent of the threat posed to the United States by Iraq.

Less than a month after Lewis and Chalabi's appearance, the Pentagon created a secret rump intelligence unit led by Wurmser, which later evolved into the Office of Special Plans (OSP). It was organized by Rhode and Douglas Feith, the undersecretary of defense for policy. "Rhode is kind of the Mikhail Suslov of the neocon movement," says

Lang, referring to the late chief ideologue for the former Soviet Communist Party. "He's the theoretician."[58] It was Rhode and Feith's OSP, under neocon Abram Shulsky, which manufactured false intelligence that blamed Iraq for ties to Al Qaeda. And it was the OSP which created talking-points papers for Vice President Cheney, Secretary of Defense Donald Rumsfeld, and other top Bush administration officials claiming that Iraq had extensive stockpiles of chemical and biological weapons, long-range missiles, unmanned aerial vehicles, and a well-developed nuclear program.[59] Chalabi's falsified intelligence fed directly into the OSP, from whence it ended up in speeches by Cheney, Rumsfeld, and other top Bush administration officials. On the eve of the Iraq war, Lewis, who was close to Cheney, had a private dinner with the vice president to discuss plans for the war in Iraq,[60] and, in 2003, Lewis dedicated his book *The Crisis of Islam* "To Harold Rhode."

The War on Terror

In going to war, first in Afghanistan and then in Iraq, and in declaring the start of a global war on terrorism with no end in sight, President Bush was careful not to embrace fully the Lewis-Huntington theory of a civilizational clash. In speech after speech—and despite an initial clumsy reference to the campaign in the Middle East as a "crusade"— the president insisted that the United States was engaged in a war against terrorists, not a war against the people of the Koran. In fact, however, Bush's war on terrorism is merely an excuse to implement a radical new approach to the Middle East and Central Asia. It is not a policy toward Islam, or Islamic fundamentalism, or even toward terrorism, Islamic or otherwise.

From the start, the president's response to 9/11 displayed a broad imperial vision. He imagined a domino-like series of regime changes in the Middle East, tied to an expanded U.S. military and political presence in the region: First the Taliban, then Saddam Hussein, then regimes in Iran, Syria, Saudi Arabia, and beyond would fall before the onslaught of an imperial democracy. The Bush administration was heavily influenced by neoconservatives inside and outside who preached the gospel of sweeping regional change. Inside were Wolfowitz, Feith, Perle, Marshall, Wurmser, and Shulsky, along with other key officials in the Pentagon, such as Michael Rubin and William Luti, Lewis Libby in Vice President Cheney's office, John Bolton at the State Department, Elliott Abrams at the NSC, and many others; outside were a host of think tank and media activists, including Tom Donnelly and Gary Schmitt of the Project for a New American Century, William Kristol of the *Weekly Standard,* Michael Ledeen of the American Enterprise Institute, Max Singer of the Hudson Institute, and *The New Republic*'s Peretz and Lawrence F. Kaplan, and James Woolsey.

"The mission begins in Baghdad, but it does not end there," wrote Kaplan and Kristol in *The War Over Iraq.* "We stand at the cusp of a new historical era. . . . This is a decisive moment. . . . It is so clearly about more than Iraq. It is about more even than the future of the Middle East and the war on terror. It is about what sort of role the United States intends to play in the world in the twenty-first century."[61] At a press conference on the eve of the invasion of Iraq, Ledeen put the strategy even more bluntly. "I think we are going to be obliged to fight a regional war, whether we want to or not," he said, asserting that the war could not be limited to Iraq. "It may turn out to be a war to remake the world."[62]

Such grandiose ideas had long marked the neoconservative vision of the world. In the infamous blueprint for their strategy, drafted in 1996 as a policy memorandum to then–Prime Minister Netanyahu of Israel, Perle, Feith, Wurmser, and others described a comprehensive regional policy. The memo, entitled, "A Clean Break: A New Strategy for Securing the Realm," called on Israel to work with Turkey and Jordan to "contain, destabilize, and roll back" various states in the region, overthrow Saddam Hussein, press Jordan to restore a scion of its Hashemite dynasty in Baghdad, and launch military action against Lebanon and Syria as a "prelude to a redrawing of the map of the Middle East [to] threaten Syria's territorial integrity." Nowhere, in the long memo, did it suggest a policy of countering fundamentalist Islam, the Muslim Brotherhood, or even Al Qaeda.[63]

Nor is democracy the real objective of the Bush administration in the Middle East, despite the central place that idea occupies in the president's rhetoric. Neoconservatives want to control the Middle East, not reform it, even if that means tearing countries apart and replacing them with rump mini-states along ethnic and sectarian lines. The Islamic right, in this context, is just one more tool for dismantling existing regimes, if that is what it takes. In "Rethinking the Middle East" in *Foreign Affairs*, Bernard Lewis forthrightly described a process he called "Lebanonization":

> [A] possibility, which could even be precipitated by fundamentalism, is what has of late been fashionable to call "Lebanonization." Most of the states of the Middle East—Egypt is an obvious exception—are of recent and artificial construction and are vulnerable to such a process. If the central power is sufficiently weakened, there is no real civil society to hold the polity together, no real sense of common identity. . . . The state then disintegrates—as happened in Lebanon—into a chaos of squabbling, feuding, fighting sects, tribes, regions and parties.[64]

That, of course, is indeed one possible future for Iraq in the wake of the U.S. invasion, one foreseen by Chas Freeman. "The neoconservatives' intention in Iraq was never to truly build democracy there," he says. "Their intention was to flatten it, to remove Iraq as a regional threat to Israel."[65]

Not only Iraq is vulnerable to disintegration, but the neoconservatives have made explicit their intention to collapse Saudi Arabia, too. In their book, *An End to Evil: How to Win the War on Terror*, Richard Perle and David Frum, both fellows at the American Enterprise Institute, suggest mobilizing Shiite fundamentalists against the Saudi state. Because the Shiites are a powerful force along the shore of the Persian Gulf, where Saudi oil fields are, Perle and Frum note that the Saudis have long feared "that the Shiites might someday seek independence for the Eastern Province—and its oil." They add:

> Independence for the Eastern Province would obviously be a catastrophic outcome for the Saudi state. But it might be a very good outcome for the United States. Certainly it's an outcome to ponder.

Even more certainly, we would want the Saudis to know we are pondering it.[66]

Max Singer, the co-founder of the Hudson Institute, has repeatedly suggested that the United States seek to dismantle the Saudi kingdom by encouraging breakaway states in both the Eastern Province and the western Hijaz. "After [Saddam] is removed, there will be an earthquake in the region," says Singer. "If this means the fall of the [Saudi] regime, so be it."[67] Ledeen wrote that the fall of the House of Saud could lead to the takeover of the country by pro–Al Qaeda radicals. "In that event," he says, "we would have to extend the war to the Arabian Peninsula, at the very least to the oil-producing regions."[68] James Akins, the former U.S. ambassador in Riyadh, says: "I've stopped saying that Saudi Arabia will be taken over by Osama bin Laden or a bin Laden clone if we go into Iraq. I'm now convinced that that's exactly what [the neoconservatives] want to happen. And then we take it over."[69]

During the first four years of Bush's war on terror, many critics argued that by invading Afghanistan and Iraq and by raising America's profile in the Middle East so high, the Bush administration was creating a new generation of radical Islamists who would blame the United States for all the ills in the Middle East. Despite its rhetoric about combating Islamist-inspired terrorism, in neither Afghanistan nor Iraq did the Bush administration demonstrate a successful strategy for reversing the spread of Islamic fundamentalism. Michael Scheuer, writing as "Anonymous" in *Imperial Hubris,* stated the case most forcefully:

> U.S., British, and other coalition forces are trying to govern apparently ungovernable postwar states in Afghanistan and Iraq while simultaneously fighting growing Islamist insurgencies in each—a state of affairs our leaders call victory. In conducting these activities, and the conventional military campaigns preceding them, U.S. forces and policies are completing the radicalization of the Islamic world, something Osama bin Laden has been trying to do with but incomplete success since the early 1990s. As a result, I

think it is fair to conclude that the United States of America remains bin Laden's only indispensable ally.[70]

Whether or not Afghanistan can defeat the remnants of the Taliban, reverse decades of Islamization, dismantle the underground forces of the Islamic right, and create a stable, secular state remains to be seen. Whether Iraq can produce a secular government, crush the forces associated with Al Qaeda that have collected there, suppress Shiite fundamentalist parties such as SCIRI and Al Dawa that have dominated postwar Iraq, and hold off efforts by Iran's ayatollahs to exercise influence inside the territory of their Arab neighbor is also an open question. Chances are at least fifty-fifty that in the not-too-distant future Afghanistan will fall back under the sway of hard-core Islamists and that Iraq will end up with a theocracy only slightly less militant that Iran's. By the same token, the clerical leadership in Teheran appears to have consolidated its iron grip over power in the Islamic Republic of Iran. In Pakistan, President Musharraf—who already tolerates the muscular influence of Islamists in Karachi—could at any moment fall to an Islamist coup d'état from the army and the ISI, in alliance with the Muslim Brotherhood or other militant parties and groups on the Islamic right. Indonesia and Bangladesh are facing Islamist insurgencies, Turkey has been drifting into the Islamist camp for more than a decade, and Syria, Lebanon, Jordan, and Palestine are all facing severe pressure from the Muslim Brotherhood. The heart of the Arab world, Egypt and Saudi Arabia, are both facing pressure to open up their political systems, which many observers believe could lead to the establishment of Islamic republics in both countries.

The case of Iraq is most startling. President Bush went to war in Iraq after accusing Saddam Hussein of forging an alliance with Al Qaeda. He warned that Saddam might be inclined to give weapons of mass destruction to bin Laden's cells. But, as became evident in 2003, Saddam's regime had no ties to Al Qaeda and no weapons of mass destruction to distribute. The regime in Baghdad, dictatorial though it was, was a secular one whose Baath Party leadership was a confirmed enemy of the Islamists—both the Shiite variety and the Sunni Muslim

Brotherhood. But Bush, consciously and with deliberation, encouraged Iraq's Islamists to reach for power. American forces and the CIA brought an ayatollah from London to Najaf, Iraq, and forged a pragmatic alliance with another ayatollah, Ali al-Sistani, an Iranian cleric who became the kingmaker in Iraq after the war. The United States worked with a radical Iraqi cleric, Abdel-Aziz al-Hakim, who commanded the 20,000-strong paramilitary Badr Brigade, a force that was armed and trained by Iran. And it promoted a terrorist group called the Islamic Call, or Al Dawa, a group that over its forty-year history had conducted bombings, assassinations, and other violent attacks, including an attack against the American embassy in Kuwait in the early 1980s. On the Sunni front, in central Iraq, the chief political party to emerge after the war in 2003 was the Iraqi Islamic Party, the Muslim Brotherhood's official branch in Iraq.

The Bush administration has set into motion a chain of events that could lead to a reprise of the Algeria crisis of 1992 in countless states in the region. Even tiny states such as Kuwait, where the Brotherhood is strong, and Bahrain, with its Sunni royal family and its Shiite majority population, are vulnerable to Islamic revolution or ballot-box Islamist triumphs—or both.

Reuel Marc Gerecht is a former CIA officer with experience in Iraq and the Middle East, a fellow at the American Enterprise Institute, and a neoconservative hard-liner who was a leading voice in support of the U.S. invasions of Afghanistan and Iraq. For three years after 2002, he appeared at AEI forums alongside Perle, Ledeen, and other neoconservatives, while writing for the *Weekly Standard* and many other right-wing publications, including the *Wall Street Journal's* op-ed page. Early in 2005 Gerecht dropped all pretense of opposing the Islamic right, issuing a clarion call for the United States to encourage both Sunni and Shiite fundamentalism throughout the entire Middle East.

In a January 2005 appearance at AEI, Gerecht announced the release of his new book, *The Islamic Paradox: Shiite Clerics, Sunni Fundamentalists, and the Coming of Arab Democracy*. In it, Gerecht declared that the future of the Middle East lies with the Islamic right, and that the United States ought to welcome it. Although many Americans hope that moderate, secular Muslims are the silent majority in the Middle East, Gerecht says, " 'Moderate Muslims' may not be the key to a new, less threatening Middle East."[71] He added:

> Most American liberals and conservatives will strongly resist the idea that Islam's clergymen and lay fundamentalists, who usually dislike, if not detest, the United States, Israel, and progressive causes like women's rights, are the key to liberating the Muslim Middle East from its age-old reflexive hostility to the West. These men, not the much-admired liberal Muslim secularists who are always praised and sometimes defended by the American government and press, are the United States' most valuable potential democratic allies.[72]

Gerecht compares Khomeini favorably to Mubarak:

> Khomeini submitted the idea of an Islamic republic to an up-or-down popular vote in 1979, and regular elections with some element of competition are morally essential to the regime's conception of its own legitimacy, something not at all the case with President Husni Mubarak's dictatorship in Egypt.[73] . . . Anti-Americanism is the common denominator of the Arab states with "pro-American" dictators. By comparison, Iran is a profoundly pro-American country.[74]

And after acknowledging the direct intellectual connections between Hassan al-Banna's Muslim Brotherhood and Osama bin Laden's Al Qaeda, he concludes, astonishingly, that a Muslim Brotherhood dictatorship in Egypt would be better than Mubarak's regime:

> Egypt is probably the Arab country that has the best chance of quickly marrying fundamentalism and democracy. It is certainly possible that fundamentalists, if they gained power in Egypt, would try to end representative government. The democratic ethic, although much more common in Egypt than many Westerners believe, is not as well anchored as it is among the Shiites of Iran or in the fatwas of Grand Ayatollah Sistani. But the United States would still be better off with this alternative than with a secular dictatorship.[75]

Sixty years earlier, when the United States began its odyssey in the Middle East, there were other voices who wanted conservative Islam, and early fundamentalist groups associated with the nascent Islamic right, to do battle with the secular left, with Nasser, with Arab communists and socialists. Now, six decades later, the Bush administration is pursuing a strategy in the Middle East that seems calculated to boost the fortunes of the Islamic right. The United States is counting on Shiite fundamentalists in Iraq to save its failed policy in that country, and a major theoretician of that campaign explicitly calls for the United States to cast its lot in with ayatollahs and the Muslim Brotherhood.

The devil's game continues.

NOTES

1: Imperial Pan-Islam

1. The proposal to London from Jamal Eddine al-Afghani was reported by a British Orientalist and author of the time, W. S. Blunt, a friend of Afghani's. It is cited in C. C. Adams, *Islam and Modernism in Egypt* (New York: Russell and Russell, 1933), p. 10, n. 1.

2. Elie Kedourie, *Afghani and Abduh: An Essay on Religious Unbelief and Political Activism in Modern Islam* (New York: The Humanities Press, 1966), p. 30.

3. Kedourie, p. 6.

4. Ibid., p. 13.

5. Cited in Kedourie, p. 45.

6. Ibid.

7. Afghani's views on religion are quoted at length in Kedourie, p. 44.

8. Cited in Kedourie, p. 4. Kedourie commented wryly on Gibb's view, saying: "Afghani would no doubt have been much gratified to see that half a century after his death, his pretentions to 'sound Koranic orthodoxy' were still being unquestioningly accepted."

9. Wilfred Cantwell Smith, *Islam in Modern History* (New York: New American Library, 1957), p. 54.

10. Smith, pp. 56–57.

11. Ibid., p. 55.

12. Richard P. Mitchell, *The Society of the Muslim Brothers* (London: Oxford University Press, 1969), p. 321.

13. Nikki Keddie, "Afghani in Afghanistan," *Middle Eastern Studies* (1) 4.

14. Kedourie, pp. 20–21.

15. Ibid., p. 8.

16. Adams, p. 54.

17. Ibid., pp. 30–31.

18. Adams, p. 18.

19. Ibid., p. 39. Wrote Kedourie: "It is, at any rate, reasonable to presume that having offered his services to the British, Afghani would offer them again to the French." In any case, France tolerated *The Indissoluble Bond,* while Great Britain, Egypt, and India banned it.

20. Adams, p. 9, n. 5.

21. Kedourie, p. 54.

22. Ibid., p. 58.

23. Quoted in Adams, pp.59–60.

24. Kedourie, p. 14.

25. Adams, p. 83.

26. Ibid., p. 79.

27. Kedourie, p. 56.

28. Cited in Kedourie, p. 57.

29. E. G. Browne, *A Year amongst the Persians* (London: Adam and Charles Black, 1950), pp. 13–14.

30. For an account of the relationship between Khan and Afghani, see Kedourie, pp. 22–23.

31. Adams, p. 11.

32. Kedourie, p. 4.

33. Ibid., p. 5.

34. David Long, *The Kingdom of Saudi Arabia* (Gainesville: University Press of Florida, 1997), p. 22.

35. In Arabic, *muwahhidin.* See Long, p. 23.

36. Hamid Algar, *Wahhabism: A Critical Essay* (Oneonta, N.Y.: Islamic Publications International, 2002), p. 5.

37. Algar, pp. 14–16.

38. William Gifford Palgrave, *Personal Narrative of a Year's Journey through Central and Eastern Arabia (1862–1863)* (London: Macmillan and Co., 1993), p. 184.

39. Algar, pp. 20–22.

40. Ibid., pp. 23–25.

41. Ibid.

42. John Esposito, *Unholy War: Terror in the Name of Islam* (New York: Oxford University Press, 2002), p. 108.

43. Algar, p. 38.

44. Daniel Yergin, *The Prize: The Epic Quest for Oil, Money, and Power* (New York: Simon & Schuster, 1991), p. 284.

45. Ibid., p. 285.

46. The word *ikhwan* is the plural of *akh* (brother) and can be translated as brothers or brotherhood.

47. David Holden and Richard Johns, *The House of Saud* (New York: Holt, Rinehart and Winston, 1981), pp. 50–51.

48. Ibid., pp. 11–26.

49. Elizabeth Monroe, *Philby of Arabia* (New York: Pitman Publishing Corporation, 1973), p. 24.

50. Ibid., p. 70.

51. Cited in Monroe, p. 104.

52. Cited in Monroe, p. 127.

53. Philby's critics disparaged his supposed pro-republican stance. Says Monroe: "They were quick to point out, too, that his republican nostrum for the Arab world did not tally with his unstinted praise for the absolute rule of his hero, Ibn Saud." Ibid., p. 139.

54. Ibid., p. 139.

55. Algar, p. 42.

56. Cited in John S. Habib, *Ibn Saud's Warriors of Islam* (Leiden: E. J. Brill, 1978), p. 14.

57. Ibid., p. 20.

58. Ibid., pp. 26–27.

59. Percy Cox, cited in Dore Gold, *Hatred's Kingdom* (Washington: Regnery Publishing, 2003), pp. 44–45.

60. The term *hijra* means "immigration," but in this case it refers to the notion that a Muslim must "immigrate" to Islam, by abandoning his nomadic ties and tribal connections.

61. Habib, p. 32.

62. Ibid., p. 76.

63. Monroe, p. 135.

64. Bernard Lewis, *The Crisis of Islam* (New York: The Modern Library, 2003), pp. 125–26.

65. Habib, p. 119.

2: England's Brothers

1. In Arabic, *Al Manar.*

2. A detailed account of Rashid Rida's work is found in C. C. Adams, *Islam and Modernism in Egypt* (New York: Russell and Russell, 1933), pp. 177–204.

3. Cited in Adams, p. 185.

4. Ibid., p. 186.

5. Ibid., p. 222.

6. Richard P. Mitchell, *The Society of the Muslim Brothers* (London: Oxford University Press, 1969), p. 9. The source Mitchell uses is al-Banna's autobiography.

7. Ibid., p. 5.

8. Ibid., p. 322.

9. Ibid., p. 321.

10. Ibid., p. 186.

11. Gilles Kepel, *Jihad: The Trail of Political Islam* (Cambridge, Mass.: Belknap Press, 2002), p. 27.

12. Mitchell, p. 246.

13. Ibid., p. 14.

14. In Arabic, *kataib*. Interestingly, the same word was used by the fascist Christian Lebanese Phalangists led by the Gemayel family of warlords, themselves, like many Islamists, admirers of Hitler.

15. Mitchell, pp. 13–16.

16. Joel Gordon, interview with author, June 2004.

17. Mitchell, pp. 40–42.

18. Ibid., p. 27.

19. Zvi Kaplinsky, "The Muslim Brotherhood," *Middle Eastern Affairs,* December 1954, p. 378.

20. Mitchell, p. 32.

21. Kaplinsky, p. 378.

22. Stephen Dorril, *MI6* (New York: The Free Press, 2000), p. 538.

23. Mitchell, p. 39.

24. Ibid., p. 40.

25. Said K. Aburish, *Nasser: The Last Arab* (New York: Thomas Dunne Books, St. Martin's Press, 2004), p. 18.

26. Anwar Sadat, *In Search of Identity* (New York: Harper & Row, 1977). Sadat's version must be taken with a grain of salt, however. Written in the mid-1970s, at a time when Sadat was engaged in a delicate effort to forge a political alliance with the revived Muslim Brotherhood, the book undoubtedly leaves out some important details.

27. Sadat, p. 22.

28. Ibid.

29. Miles Copeland, *The Game of Nations* (New York: Simon & Schuster, 1969), p. 184.

30. Ibid.

31. Mitchell, p. 47 and passim.

32. Mitchell, p. 55.

33. Joseph B. Schechtman, *The Mufti and the Fuehrer* (New York: Thomas Yoseloff, 1965), p. 287.

34. Ibid., p. 21.

35. *Political Dictionary of the Middle East in the 20th Century* (Jerusalem: The Jerusalem Publishing House Ltd., 1972), p. 260.

36. Schechtman, pp. 23–24.

37. Ibid., p. 45.

38. Ibid., p. 106.

39. Ibid., p. 172.

40. Clifton Daniel, "A New Chapter for the Mysterious Mufti," *New York Times Magazine,* August 25, 1946.

41. Joseph Alsop, "Crafty Fanatic Organizes Trouble in Palestine," *Boston Evening Globe,* December 17, 1947.

42. Dorril, p. 537.

43. Ibid., p. 540.

44. Andrew Roth, "The Mufti's New Army," *The Nation,* November 16, 1946.

45. Schechtman, p. 223.

46. Ibid., p. 234.

47. No one was ever arrested in the assassination of Banna. According to most historians, his death was ordered by the Egyptian government and carried out by government security officers.

3: *Islam Meets the Cold War*

1. This account is taken from an April 2004 interview with Hermann Eilts, one of America's leading Arabists and the former U.S. ambassador to Egypt, who served in several posts in the Persian Gulf and Arabian Peninsula early in his career.

2. Said K. Aburish, *Nasser: The Last Arab* (New York: Thomas Dunne Books, St. Martin's Press, 2004), p. 30. Other estimates put the number of Brotherhood members at several hundred thousand.

3. Miles Copeland, *The Game of Nations* (New York: Simon and Schuster, 1969), p. 48.

4. Elizabeth Monroe, *Philby of Arabia* (New York: Pitman Publishing Corporation, 1973), p. 162.

5. Ibid., p. 164.

6. Ibid., p. 168.

7. Ibid., p. 211.

8. Daniel Yergin, *The Prize: The Epic Quest for Oil, Money, and Power* (New York: Simon & Schuster, 1991), p. 291.

9. Standard Oil of California, or Socal, was originally part of the Rockefeller Standard Oil monopoly. The Texas Oil Company, or Texaco, would eventually merge with Socal (renamed Chevron) to become today's ChevronTexaco. Two other Rockefeller entities, Standard Oil of New Jersey (Esso, later Exxon) and Standard Oil of New York (Socony, later Mobil) would also merge to form ExxonMobil.

10. Executive Order 8926, February 18, 1943. Quoted in David Holden and Richard Johns, *The House of Saud* (New York: Holt, Rinehart and Winston, 1981), p. 123.

11. Yergin, p. 394.

12. Ibid., p. 397.

13. Ibid., p. 401.

14. Ibid.

15. Elliott Roosevelt, *As He Saw It* (New York: Duell, Sloan and Pearce, 1946), p. 244.

16. Cited in Yergin, pp. 404–5.

17. David Long, *The Kingdom of Saudi Arabia* (Gainesville: University Press of Florida, 1997), p. 116.

18. The single best account of how the United States saw national security issues in the Middle East from 1945 to 1958 is John C. Campbell's *The Defense of the Middle East* (New York: Frederick C. Praeger, 1960).

19. The photograph is found in the September 1953 proceedings of the Colloquium on Islamic Culture, held at Princeton University and in Washington, D.C.

20. The Jamaat-e Islami. Throughout, I try to use English translations of organizational names that are usually left untranslated from the original Arabic, Farsi, Urdu, Turkish, or other Middle Eastern languages.

21. This and other details of Ramadan's life and career can be found in *Dr. Said Ramadan, 1926–1995*, a useful biographical sketch published on the Internet by the Islamic Center of Geneva, which was founded by Ramadan in 1961. See www.cige.org/historique.htm.

22. Ziad Abu Amr, *Islamic Fundamentalism in the West Bank and Gaza* (Bloomington: Indiana University Press, 1994), pp. 1–5.

23. Alain Gresh and Dominique Vidal, *The New A-Z of the Middle East* (London: I. B. Tauris & Co. Ltd., 2004), p. 107.

24. Ibid.

25. Richard P. Mitchell, *The Society of Muslim Brothers* (London: Oxford University Press, 1969), p. 270.

26. Ibid.

27. Islami Jamaat-i Tulabah, the student wing of the Jamaat-e Islami (Islamic Group). For a detailed discussion of the IJT, see Seyyed Vali Reza Nasr, *The Vanguard of the Islamic Revolution* (Berkeley: University of California Press, 1994), p. 64ff.

28. Ibid., p. 65.

29. Also known by its Arabic name, the Hizb ut-Tahrir al-Islami.

30. Marion Boulby, *The Muslim Brotherhood and the Kings of Jordan* (Atlanta, Ga.: Scholars Press, 1999), pp. 37–43.

31. *Conference on Islamic Civilization,* U.S. Department of State, International Information Administration. This is a memo intended for Secretary of State John Foster Dulles. Washington, D.C.: National Security Archive, April 30, 1953.

32. Jefferson Caffery, U.S. Department of State, *Colloquium on Islamic Culture and Saeed Ramadhan.* Foreign Service Dispatch. Washington, D.C.: National Security Archive, July 27, 1953.

33. Ibid.

34. Ibid.

35. Sylvain Besson, "When the Swiss Protected Radical Islam in the Name of Reasons of State," *Le Temps,* October 26, 2004.

36. Bernard Lewis, "Communism and Islam," in The *Middle East in Transition,* ed. Walter Laqueur (New York: Frederick A. Praeger, 1958), pp. 311–24.

37. *Colloquium on Islamic Culture,* pp. 86–89.

38. Kenneth Cragg, "The Intellectual Impact of Communism upon Contemporary Islam," *Middle East Journal* 8 (2) (Spring 1954), pp. 127–38.

39. Campbell, p. 299. A quarter century later, however, Campbell would modify his view somewhat. Writing in the spring 1984 issue of *American-Arab Affairs* (No. 8, p. 80), Campbell would say: "Khomeini seems to enjoy humiliating the 'atheistic' Soviet Union regardless of the actuality of the threat. The Soviets have been whipsawed by the emergence of Islam as a growing and powerful political force in the Middle East. . . . The regime in Iran [has] supported counter-revolutionary Islamic reactionaries in Afghanistan. The swirling currents of Islamic reassertion are not without impact on the Muslims of Soviet central Asia." A lot would change in the twenty-five years between Campbell's CFR task force and the revolution in Iran.

40. S. A. Morrison, "Arab Nationalism and Islam," *Middle East Journal* (April 1948), pp. 147–59.

41. "Anti-Communist Poster Material Prepared by USIS Baghdad," March 10, 1951. National Security Archive.

42. Copeland, p. 58.

43. Ibid., p. 184.

44. Ibid., pp. 185–86.

45. William A. Eddy, letter to Dorothy Thompson, June 7, 1951. National Security Archive.

46. Patrick O'Donnell, *Operatives, Spies, and Saboteurs* (New York: The Free Press, 2004), pp. 31–32.

47. "Conversation with Prince Saud," March 10, 1952. National Security Archive.

48. David Long, interview with author, April 2004.

49. The Middle East Institute, "Islam in the Modern World," March 9–10, 1951, p. 72.

50. Ibid., pp. 15–18.

51. Ibid., pp. 13–14.

4: *The War against Nasser and Mossadegh*

1. Quoted in Said K. Aburish, *Nasser: The Last Arab* (New York: Thomas Dunne Books, St. Martin's Press, 2004), p. 314.

2. Ibid.

3. Ibid., p. 315.

4. Ed Kane, interview with author, May 2004.

5. Ibid.

6. Miles Copeland, *The Game of Nations* (New York: Simon & Schuster, 1969), p. 62.

7. Ibid., p. 63.

8. Ibid., p. 65.

9. Joel Gordon, *Nasser's Blessed Movement* (New York: Oxford University Press, 1992), p. 158.

10. Copeland, p. 74.

11. The most detailed account of this period is in Gordon's *Nasser's Blessed Movement*, pp. 98–106 and 175–90.

12. Gordon, p. 103.

13. Stephen Dorril, *MI6* (New York: The Free Press, 2000), p. 610.

14. Ibid., p. 613.

15. Gordon, p. 105.

16. Ibid., p. 106.

17. Robert Baer, *Sleeping with the Devil* (New York: Crown Publishers, 2003), p. 99.

18. Bernard Lewis, *The Middle East and the West* (New York: Harper & Row, 1964), pp. 112–13.

19. Richard Mitchell, *The Society of the Muslim Brothers* (London: Oxford University Press, 1969), pp. 141–42.

20. Dorril, pp. 633–34.

21. Cited in Gordon, p. 186. From *The New York Times*, November 17, 1954.

22. Copeland, p. 183.

23. Dorril, p. 629.

24. Copeland, p. 282.

25. Ibid., p. 184.

26. John Voll, interview with author, March 2004.

27. Interviews with former Iranian officials.

28. Ashraf Pahlavi, *Faces in a Mirror: Memoirs from Exile* (Englewood Cliffs, N.J.: Prentice-Hall, 1980), pp. 8–9.

29. For an account of the secularizing measures undertaken by Shah Reza Pahlavi, see Dilip Hiro, *Holy Wars* (New York: Routledge, 1989), p. 153.

30. Mohammed Reza Pahlavi, *Answer to History* (New York: Stein and Day, 1980), p. 84.

31. Fereydoun Hoveyda, interview with author, May 2004.

32. Ashraf Pahlavi, p. 6.

33. Ibid., p. 47.

34. Mohammed Reza Pahlavi, p. 59.

35. Mark J. Gasiorowski, *U.S. Foreign Policy and the Shah: Building a Client State in Iran* (Ithaca, N.Y.: Cornell University Press, 1991), p. 68.

36. Central Intelligence Agency, "Prospects for Survival of Mossadeq Regime in Iran," October 14, 1952, p. 2.

37. U.S. State Department, "C. C. Finch conversation with Dr. Sepahbodi," December 10, 1952.

38. Dorril, p. 566.

39. Ibid., p. 565. Dorril's book provides extensive detail of the Anglo-American action in 1953, including support for the Islamists. More detail is provided in Gasiorowski's *U.S. Foreign Policy and the Shah,* especially pp. 67–79. See also Gasiorowski, "The 1953 Coup d'état in Iran," *International Journal of Middle East Studies* 19 (1987).

40. John Waller, interview with the author, February 2004.

41. Dorril, p. 585.

42. Waller, interview.

43. Dorril, p. 592.

44. Ibid.

45. Ibid., pp. 592–93.

46. Hoveyda, interview.

47. The information about the early years of Khomeini's political life is taken largely from the brilliant biography of the ayatollah by Baqer Moin, *Khomeini: Life of the Ayatollah* (New York: Thomas Dunne Books, St. Martin's Press, 1999).

48. Moin, p. 60.

49. Ibid., pp. 63–64.

5: The King of All Islam

The epigraph is from Miles Copeland, *The Game of Nations* (New York: Simon & Schuster, 1969), p. 216.

1. Cited in Fred Halliday, *Arabia without Sultans* (New York: Vintage Books, 1975), p. 66.

2. David Holden and Richard Johns, *The House of Saud* (New York: Holt, Rinehart and Winston, 1981), p. 193.

3. Dwight Eisenhower, *The White House Years, Vol. II: Waging Peace* (London: Heinemann, 1965), pp. 115–16.

4. Malcolm H. Kerr, *The Arab Cold War, Gamal Abd al-Nasir and His Rivals, 1958–1970* (London: Oxford University Press, 1971). More recently, see Adeed Dawisha, *Arab Nationalism in the Twentieth Century: From Triumph to Despair* (Princeton, N.J.: Princeton University Press, 2003).

5. James E. Akins, interview with author, June 2004.

6. Holden and Johns, p. 177.

7. Nathan J. Citino, *From Arab Nationalism to OPEC: Eisenhower, King Saud, and the Making of U.S.-Saudi Relations* (Bloomington: Indiana University Press, 2002), p. 95.

8. Ibid.

9. Ibid., p. 126.

10. John Waller, interview with author, February 2004.

11. Donald N. Wilber, *Adventures in the Middle East: Excursions and Incursions* (Princeton, N.J.: Darwin, 1986), p. 195.

12. Ibid.

13. Citino, p. 96.

14. Holden and Johns, p. 194.

15. The late-1950s CIA action against Syria has been widely reported. Its existence was confirmed to me in interviews by several former CIA officials who were involved, among them Ray Close.

16. Retired CIA operations officer, interview with author, July 2004.

17. David Long, interview with the author, April 2004.

18. John Voll, interview with the author, March 2004.

19. Ray Close, interview with the author, April 2004.

20. Hermann Eilts, interview with the author, April 2004.

21. Reinhard Schulze, *A Modern History of the Islamic World,* trans. Azizeh Azodi (New York: New York University Press, 2000), p. 127.

22. Dore Gold, *Hatred's Kingdom* (Washington, D.C.: Regnery Publishing, 2003), p. 91.

23. Holden and Johns, p. 262.

24. Gold, p. 110.

25. Gilles Kepel, *Jihad* (Cambridge, Mass.: Belknap Press, 2002), p. 51.

26. Ibid., p. 78.

27. Eilts, interview.

28. Martha Kessler, interview with author, April 2004.

29. Charles Freeman, interview with the author, April 2004.

30. For a complete list of the founding members of the Muslim World League, see Schulze, p. 172.

31. Schulze, p. 173.

32. John Esposito, *Unholy War: Terror in the Name of Islam* (New York: Oxford University Press, 2002), pp. 106–8.

33. Kepel, p. 52.

34. Retired CIA official, interview with the author, June 2004.

35. Charles Waterman, interview with the author, July 2004.

36. Gold, pp. 76–79.

37. Quoted in "Secrets of the Financial Holy War," *Le Nouvel Observateur,* January 31, 2004.

38. Hani Ramadan, interview with Valentina Marano, September 2004.

39. The Call (Al Dawa) was founded in 1957, expanded in the 1960s, carried out terrorist sabotage in the 1980s and 1990s—including an attack on the U.S. embassy in Kuwait—and, in 2003, emerged as an overt force in post–Saddam Hussein Iraq.

40. Gilles Kepel, *Muslim Extremism in Egypt* (Berkeley: University of California Press, 1993), pp. 33–34.

41. Sylvain Besson, *Le Temps,* October 26, 2004.

42. Esposito, p. 106.

43. Eilts, interview.

44. Talcott Seelye, interview with the author, June 2004.

45. Cited in Warren Bass, *Support Any Friend* (New York: Oxford University Press, 2003), p. 77, from *Foreign Relations of the United States 1961–1963, Vol. 17,* pp. 164–66.

46. Bass, p. 79.

47. Ibid., p. 53.

48. Ibid., p. 99.

49. Ibid., p. 102.

50. Seelye, interview.

51. Cited in Bass, pp. 103–4.

52. Ibid., p. 43.

53. Stephen Dorril, *MI6* (New York: The Free Press), 2000, p. 680.

54. Ibid., pp. 680–85.

55. Howard Teicher and Gayle Radley Teicher, *Twin Pillars to Desert Storm* (New York: William Morrow, 1993), p. 94.

56. Bass, p. 114.

57. Charles Freeman, interview with the author, April 2004.

58. Shireen Hunter, *The Future of Islam and the West* (Westport, Conn.: Praeger, 1988), pp. 156–57.

59. Bass, p. 141.

60. Holden and Johns, p. 271.

61. Saudi Ministry of Information, *Faisal Speaks* (undated collection of King Faisal's speeches).

62. Ibid.

63. Ibid.

64. Hunter, p. 159.

65. Gold, p. 93.

66. Long, interview.

67. Holden and Johns, p. 290.

68. Abdullah M. Sindi, "King Faisal and Pan-Islamism," in Willard A. Beling, *King Faisal and the Modernisation of Saudi Arabia* (London: Croom Helm, 1980), p. 190.

69. Long, interview.

6: *The Sorcerer's Apprentice*

1. David Long, interview with the author, April 2004.

2. Anwar Sadat, *In Search of Identity* (New York: Harper & Row, 1977), p. 215.

3. Michael Dunn, interview with the author, February 2004.

4. Reinhard Schulze, *A Modern History of the Islamic World* (New York: New York University Press, 2000), p. 189.

5. David Holden and Richard Johns, *The House of Saud* (New York: Holt, Rinehart & Winston, 1981), p. 289.

6. Ibid.

7. Ibid., p. 292.

8. Mohammed Heikal, *The Sphinx and the Commissar* (New York: Harper & Row, 1978), p. 219.

9. Holden and Johns, p. 293.

10. Henry Kissinger, *The White House Years* (London: Weidenfeld and Nicolson, 1979), p. 1293.

11. Sadat, p. 224.

12. Raymond Close, interview with the author, April 2004.

13. Gilles Kepel, *Muslim Extremism in Egypt* (Berkeley: University of California Press, 1993), p. 105.

14. In Arabic, *jama'at islamiyya.*

15. John Esposito, *Unholy War: Terror in the Name of Islam* (New York: Oxford University Press, 2002), p. 86.

16. Kepel, p. 133.

17. Ibid., p. 129.

18. Much of the information and quotes in this paragraph are taken from Kepel, pp. 133–40, whose work on Islamism in Egypt during this period is definitive.

19. Schulze, p. 201.

20. Daniel Pipes, *In the Path of God* (New York: Basic Books, 1983), p. 209.

21. Abdel Moneim Said, interview with the author, July 2004.

22. Hermann Eilts, interview with the author, April 2004.

23. Close, interview.

24. Martha Kessler, interview with the author, April 2004.

25. The Liberation Party is known in Arabic as Hizb ut-Tahrir. It still exists. The party fled the Middle East, relocated to Germany, and then built a power base in Soviet Central Asia.

26. Kepel, pp. 92–94.

27. Said, interview.

28. Eilts, interview.

29. Said, interview.

30. Eilts, interview.

31. Ibid.

32. Former CIA officer, interview with the author, June 2004.

33. Kathy Christison, interview with the author, March 2004.

34. Eilts, interview.

35. Retired CIA officer, interview with the author, June 2004.

36. Kepel, p. 108.

37. Ibid., pp. 108–9.

38. Samer Soliman, "The Rise and Decline of the Islamic Banking Model in Egypt," in *The Politics of Islamic Finance,* ed. Clement M. Henry and Rodney Wilson (Edinburgh: Edinburgh University Press, 2004), p. 266.

39. Said, interview.

40. Monzer Kahf, "The Rise of a New Power Alliance," in Henry and Wilson, p. 22.

41. Ibrahim Warde, *Islamic Finance in the Global Economy* (Edinburgh: Edinburgh University Press, 2000), p. 211.

42. Soliman, in Henry and Wilson, p. 273.

43. Ibid., p. 270.

44. Ibid., pp. 270–71. Egypt's tolerance of Islamic banking was scaled back in the 1980s, after the assassination of Sadat made it clear how dangerous the Islamist movement could be.

45. Kahf, in Henry and Wilson, p. 211.

46. Soliman, in Henry and Wilson, p. 276.

47. Cited in Richard Labeviere, *Dollars for Terror: The United States and Islam* (New York: Algora Publishing, 2000), p. 138. Labeviere presents a detailed picture of Al Taqwa's involvement in Egypt, Turkey, and elsewhere.

48. Ibid., p. 139.

49. Douglas Farah, *Blood from Stones: The Secret Financial Network of Terror* (New York: Broadway Books, 2004), p. 148.

50. Warde, p. 84.

51. Soliman, in Henry and Wilson, p. 273.

7: The Rise of Economic Islam

1. For details on the mechanisms of Islamic finance sans interest (in Arabic, *riba*), see Clement M. Henry and Rodney Wilson, eds., *The Politics of Islamic Finance* (Edinburgh: Edinburgh University Press, 2004); and Rodney Wilson, *Islamic Financial Markets* (London: Routledge, 1990). Another well-written book is Timur Kuran's *Islam and Mammon* (Princeton, N.J.: Princeton University Press, 2004). Finally, a wonderfully complete book is Ibrahim Warde's *Islamic Finance in the Global Economy* (Edinburgh: Edinburgh University Press, 2000).

2. Warde, p. 108.

3. See "Hopes for the Future of Islamic Finance," by Abbas Mirakhor, an executive director of the International Monetary Fund and an Islamic scholar from the Islamic Republic of Iran.

4. Ibrahim Warde, interview with Barbara Dreyfuss, August 2004.

5. Clement Henry, "Islamic Financial Movements: Midwives of Political Change in the Middle East?" (paper presented to the 2001 Annual Meeting of the American Political Science Association, University of Texas at Austin), p. 6.

6. Warde, p. 107.

7. Warde, p. 99.

8. Clement Henry, "Islamic Financial Movements: Midwives of Political Change in the Middle East?"

9. Warde, interview.

10. Nizam Ali, interview with Barbara Dreyfuss, August 2004.

11. Peter Ferrara and Khaled Saffuri, "Islam and the Free Market," Islamic Free Market Institute Foundation, at http:www.islamicinstitute.org/freemrkt.htm. Accessed September 2004.

12. Graham Fuller, *The Future of Political Islam* (New York: Palgrave Macmillan, 2003), p. 26.

13. Ibid.

14. Ibid., p. 35.

15. Ibid., p. 141.

16. Agence France Presse, "Islamic Banks, Institutions Boast Assets of 260 Billion Dollars," April 25, 2004.

17. Hanna Batatu, "Iraq's Underground Shi'a Movements," *Middle East Journal 35* (Autumn 1981), 4, p. 578.

18. Graham Fuller and Rend Rahim Francke, *The Arab Shi'a: The Forgotten Muslims* (New York: Palgrave/St. Martin's Press, 1999), p. 47. Fuller, a former CIA official, is a vocal apologist for fundamentalist Islam. Francke, former head of the Iraq Foundation, would be named the first post–Saddam Hussein ambassador to the United States from Iraq under the interim government of Prime Minister Iyad Allawi in 2003.

19. Ibid., p. 48.

20. For a complete account of the Oudh Bequest, see Yitzhak Nakash, *The Shi'is of Iraq* (Princeton, N.J.: Princeton University Press, 1994), pp. 211–29.

21. Fuller and Francke, p. 48.

22. Nakash, p. 135.

23. Samer Soliman, "The Islamic Banking Model in Egypt," in Henry and Wilson, p. 267.

24. Soliman, in Henry and Wilson, p. 267.

25. Jamal al-Banna, foreword, in unpublished book manuscript by Ahmed al-Najjar, translated by Rubah Elfattouh and Abdel Kader Thomas.

26. Najjar, unpublished manuscript, chapter 3.

27. Mohammed Malley, "The Political Implications of Islamic Finance in Jordan" (paper prepared for the 2001 annual meeting of the Middle East Studies Association, University of Texas at Austin).

28. Monzer Kahf, "The Rise of a New Power Alliance," in Henry and Wilson, p. 19.

29. Najjar, unpublished manuscript, chapter 4.

30. Interview with Barbara Dreyfuss, August 2004.

31. Najjar, unpublished manuscript, chapter 9.

32. Richard Labeviere, *Dollars for Terror: The United States and Islam* (New York: Algora Publishing, 2000), p. 240.

33. Kahf, in Henry and Wilson, p. 24.

34. Andre Stiansen, "Interest Politics: Islamic Finance in the Sudan, 1977–2001," in Clement and Henry, p. 157.

35. *New York Times,* August 12, 2004.

36. Monzer Kahf, "Strategic Trends in the Islamic Banking and Finance Movement" (paper presented at the Harvard Forum on Islamic Finance and Banking, Harvard University, Cambridge, Mass., April 6–7, 2002).

37. Ibid.

38. Talcott Seelye, interview with the author, June 2004.

39. Former CIA official, interview with the author, June 2004.

40. Ibid.

41. Kristin Smith, "The Kuwait Finance House and the Islamization of Public Life in Kuwait," in Henry and Wilson, pp. 168–90.

42. Ibid., p. 172.

43. Ibid., p. 169.

44. Shafeeq N. Ghabra, "Balancing State and Society: The Islamic Movement in Kuwait," *Middle East Policy* (May 1977), pp. 61–62.

45. Ibid., p. 60.

46. Smith, in Henry and Wilson, p. 178.

47. Ibid. One of Kuwait's charities was placed on the U.S. government's list of organizations suspected of ties to Osama bin Laden, according to an Associated Press story, "Kuwait Questions Islamic Charity on Allegation of Funding Terrorists," December 29, 2001.

48. Smith, in Henry and Wilson, p. 181.

49. Ghabra, p. 61.

8: Israel's Islamists

1. Charles Freeman, interview with the author, July 2004.

2. Khaled Hroub, *Hamas: Political Thought and Practice* (Washington, D.C.: Institute for Palestine Studies, 2000), p. 15.

3. Ziad Abu-Amr, *Islamic Fundamentalism in the West Bank and Gaza* (Bloomington: Indiana University Press, 1994), p. 3.

4. Hroub, p. 16.

5. Ibid., p. 20.

6. Marion Boulby, *The Muslim Brotherhood and the Kings of Jordan* (Atlanta, Ga.: Scholars Press, 1999), pp. 37–43.

7. Ibid., p. 43.

8. Ibid., p. 61.

9. Cited in Abu-Amr, p. 5.

10. Hroub, pp. 21–23.

11. Former CIA official who served in Kuwait in the 1950s and who knew many of the PLO leaders, interview with the author, 2004.

12. Hroub, pp. 25–27.

13. Shaul Mishal and Avraham Sela, *The Palestinian Hamas* (New York: Columbia University Press, 2000), p. 17.

14. Ibid., p. 18.

15. Abu-Amr, p. 17.

16. Ray Hanania, "Sharon's Terror Child," *Counterpunch,* January 18–19, 2003.

17. David Shipler, *Arabs and Jews: Wounded Spirits in a Promised Land* (New York: Penguin, 1987), p. 177.

18. Mishal and Sela, p. 21.

19. Abu-Amr, pp. 29, 31.

20. Martha Kessler, interview with the author, April 2004.

21. Ibid.

22. David Long, interview with the author, April 2004.

23. Philip Wilcox, interview with the author, March 2004.

24. Dilip Hiro, *Holy Wars* (New York: Routledge, 1989), p. 87.

25. Hiro, in chapter 4, presents a detailed account of the Muslim Brotherhood's growth in Syria from the 1930s through the 1976–82 civil war in Syria.

26. Hiro, chapter 4.

27. BBC Summary of World Broadcasts, September 29, 1981, quoting Marj Uyun, "Voice of Hope," in Arabic.

28. BBC Summary of World Broadcasts, February 28, 1981, citing Damascus radio.

29. BBC Summary of World Broadcasts, March 11, 1981, citing Damascus radio.

30. BBC Summary of World Broadcasts, April 10, 1981, citing Damascus radio.

31. BBC Summary of World Broadcasts, December 4, 1981, citing Damascus radio.

32. Steven Strasser, "A Brotherly Bomb in Damascus," *Newsweek,* December 14, 1981.

33. Long, interview.

34. Kessler, interview.

35. Talcott Seelye, interview with the author, June 2004.

36. "Jordan Ends Shelter for Assad's Enemies," *London Times,* November 12, 1985.

37. Charles P. Wallace, "Visit to Damascus Moves Jordan, Syria Closer," *Los Angeles Times,* November 13, 1985.

38. BBC Summary of World Broadcasts, November 18, 1985.

39. Robert Baer, *Sleeping with the Devil* (New York: Crown Publishers, 2003), pp. 95–97.

40. Robert Baer, interview with the author, March 2004.

41. Seelye, interview.

42. Judith Miller, *God Has Ninety-nine Names* (New York: Simon & Schuster, 1996), p. 295.

43. "Bloody Challenge to Assad," *Time,* March 8, 1982.

44. Seelye, interview.

45. Patrick Lang, interview with the author, March 2004.

46. See Victor Ostrovsky and Claire Hoy, *By Way of Deception* (New York: St. Martin's Press, 1990), and Victor Ostrovsky, *The Other Side of Deception* (New York: HarperCollins, 1994). Ostrovsky is a highly controversial, polarizing figure, and some of his assertions seem far-fetched. He refused to talk to me when I called him for elaboration. His charges about Islamism, however, are coherent with other sources.

47. Ostrovsky, *The Other Side of Deception,* pp. 196–97.

48. Ibid., p. 197.

49. Abu-Amr, pp. 43–44.

50. Ibid., p. 49.

51. Mishal and Sela, p. 34.

52. Wilcox, interview.

53. Freeman, interview.

54. Patrick Lang, interview with the author, March 2004.

55. *Corriere della Sera,* December 11, 2001.

56. Hanania, pp. 9, 14.

57. Ibid., p. 9.

58. Sara Roy, "Hamas and the Transformation of Political Islam in Palestine," *Current History,* January 2003, p. 14.

59. Ibid., pp. 18–19.

60. Ibid., p. 20.

9: Hell's Ayatollah

1. George Lambrakis, "Understanding the Shiite Islamic Movement," "confidential" dispatch, February 2, 1978.

2. James Bill, "Iran and the Crisis of 1978," *Foreign Affairs,* Winter 1978–79, p. 340.

3. Henry Precht, interview with the author, April 2004.

4. Thomas Ahern, interview with the author, June 2004.

5. Cited in James Bill, *The Eagle and the Lion: The Tragedy of American-Iranian Relations* (New Haven: Yale University Press, 1988), p. 133.

6. Retired CIA official, interview with the author, May 2004.

7. Bill, *The Eagle and the Lion,* p. 137.

8. Baqer Moin, *Khomeini: Life of the Ayatollah* (New York: Thomas Dunne Books, St. Martin's Press, 1999), p. 80. Moin's biography of Khomeini is an amazingly detailed and well-written portrait of the man, far and away the best book in English about Khomeini.

9. Moin, p. 88.

10. Cited in Gary Sick, *All Fall Down: America's Tragic Encounter with Iran* (New York: Random House, 1985), p. 22.

11. Bill, *The Eagle and the Lion,* p. 228.

12. Interview with Charles Cogan, Episode 20, *Soldiers of God,* at: www.gwu.edu/~nsarchiv/coldwaar/interviews/episode-20/cogan2.html. Accessed May 2004.

13. Juan Cole, interview with the author, July 2004.

14. Charles Naas, interview with the author, June 2004.

15. Mohammed Reza Pahlavi, *Answer to History* (New York: Stein and Day, 1980), p. 165.

16. Former CIA operations officer, interview with the author, June 2004.

17. Former State Department official, interview with the author, July 2004.

18. Anonymous U.S. State Department report, "Religious Circles," May 1972. Included in documents released by Iran from those captured in the takeover of the U.S. embassy in 1979.

19. The CIA reports were declassified and made the subject of a congressional investigation that released a public report in January 1979. The citations I used are taken from Sick.

20. Sick, p. 90.

21. Stansfield Turner, e-mail to the author, April 2004.

22. Walter Cutler, interview with the author, May 2004.

23. Retired CIA officer, interview, May 2004.

24. Precht, interview, May 2004.

25. Ibid.

26. Fereydoun Hoveyda, interview with the author, May 2004.

27. Interview with Charles Cogan, Episode 20, *Soldiers of God,* at: www.gwu .edu/~nsarchiv/coldwaar/interviews/episode-20/cogan1.html. Accessed May 2004.

28. Charles Cogan, interview with the author, May 2004.

29. Retired CIA official, interview with the author, May 2004.

30. David Long, interview with the author, April 2004.

31. Retired CIA officer, interview, May 2004.

32. William Sullivan, *Mission to Iran* (New York: W. W. Norton, 1981), p. 142.

33. William Sullivan, "Straws in the Wind: Intellectual and Religious Opposition in Iran," Confidential dispatch from Teheran to Washington, July 25, 1977.

34. Sullivan, *Mission to Iran* p. 92.

35. John Waller, interview with the author, February 2004.

36. Memorandum of Conversation, "The Iranian National Liberation Front," May 8, 1978, Secret. From the National Security Archives.

37. Memorandum of Conversation, "Further Discussions with the Liberation Movement of Iran (LMI) officials," May 30, 1978, Secret. From the National Security Archives.

38. Letter from Charles Naas to Henry Precht, June 6, 1978, Secret. From the National Security Archives.

39. Precht, interview. See also Precht's oral history in the *Middle East Journal* 58 (Winter 2004).

40. Walter Cutler, interview with the author, May 2004.

41. Ibid.

42. Bruce Laingen, interview with the author, June 2004.

43. Thomas Ahern, interview with the author, June 2004.

44. John Limbert, interview with the author, May 2004.

45. Laingen, interview.

46. Ahern, interview.

47. Retired CIA official, interview with the author, July 2004.

48. Laingen, interview.

49. Retired CIA official, interview, July 2004.

50. Precht, interview.

51. Zbigniew Brzezinski, *Power and Principle* (New York: Farrar Straus & Giroux, 1983), pp. 446–47.

52. Richard Cottam, "U.S. and Soviet Responses," in *Neither East nor West,* ed. Nikkie R. Keddie and Mark Gasiorowski (New Haven: Yale University Press, 1990), pp. 276–78.

53. Vladimir Kuzichkin, *Inside the KGB: My Life in Soviet Espionage* (New York: Ivy Books, 1990), p. 293.

54. Hamilton Jordan, *Crisis: The Last Year of the Carter Presidency* (New York: G. P. Putnam's Sons, 1982), pp. 35, 51.

10: *Jihad I: The "Arc of Islam"*

1. James E. Akins, interview with the author, November 2002.

2. Former CIA official, interview with the author, May 2004.

3. James Critchlow, interview with Kathleen Klenetsky, July 2004.

4. Charles W. Hostler, "The Turks and Soviet Central Asia," *Middle East Journal* (1958), pp. 268-69.

5. Gene Sosin, *Sparks of Liberty: An Insider's Memoir of Radio Liberty* (University Park: Pennsylvania University State Press, 1999), p. 115.

6. Robert Gates, *From the Shadows* (New York: Simon & Schuster, 1996), p. 93.

7. In 1961, Bennigsen wrote *The Evolution of Muslim Nationalities in the USSR;* in 1967, *Islam in the Soviet Union;* and in 1983, together with his daughter, Marie Broxup, associate editor of *Central Asian Survey,* the classic *The Islamic Threat to the Soviet State.*

8. Alexandre Bennigsen and Marie Broxup, *The Islamic Threat to the Soviet State* (New York: St. Martin's Press, 1983), p. 64.

9. Ibid., p. 48.

10. Ibid., p. 73.

11. Ibid., p. 77.

12. Ibid., p. 150.

13. Jeremy Azrael, interview with Kathleen Klenetsky, August 2004.

14. Zalmay Khalilzad, "The Return of the Great Game" (California Seminar on International Security and Foreign Policy, Discussion Paper No. 88, 1980), p. 41.

15. Ibid., pp. 70–71.

16. In 1983, Henze wrote a book, *The Plot to Kill the Pope,* promoting his theory.

17. Paul B. Henze, "The Shamil Problem," in *The Middle East in Transition,* ed. Walter Z. Laqueur (New York: Praeger, 1958), p. 442.

18. Richard Pipes, "Muslims of Soviet Central Asia: Trends and Prospects," Part II, *Middle East Journal* (Summer 1955), p. 308.

19. Richard Pipes, *Survival Is Not Enough: Soviet Realities and America's Future* (New York: Simon & Schuster, 1984), p. 185.

20. Fawaz Gerges, *America and Political Islam* (Cambridge: Cambridge University Press, 1999), p. 68.

21. Retired CIA official, interview with the author, May 2004.

22. Rose Bannigan, interview with the author, July 2004.

23. Olivier Roy, *Islam and Resistance in Afghanistan* (Cambridge: Cambridge University Press, 1985), pp. 69–70.

24. Ibid., p. 71.

25. U.S. State Department, "Afghanistan's Clerical Unrest: A Tentative Assessment," confidential, declassified, June 24, 1970.

26. Ibid., p. 73.

27. U.S. embassy in Kabul, "Portrait of a Moslem Youth Extremist," confidential, declassified, May 29, 1972.

28. Robert Wirsing, *Pakistan's Security under Zia, 1977–1988* (New York: St. Martin's Press, 1991), p. 73, n. 26.

29. Diego Cordovez and Selig Harrison, *Out of Afghanistan* (Oxford: Oxford University Press, 1995), p. 15.

30. Ibid., p. 16.

31. U.S. State Department, "Year End Afghan Internal Assessment," confidential telegram, from U.S. embassy in Kabul, December 1975.

32. Ibid., p. 23.

33. U.S. State Department, "CENTO Council of Deputies Meeting," telegram to Middle East embassies, secret, declassified, June 1978.

34. Bruce Amstutz, U.S. State Department confidential analysis, April 11, 1979.

35. U.S. State Department, "Current Status of the Insurrection in Afghanistan," telegram, June 1979.

36. Quotes from Brzezinski from *Le Nouvel Observateur,* January 15–21, 1998.

37. Gates, p. 132.

38. Ibid., p. 144.

39. Ibid.

40. Steve Coll, *Ghost Wars* (New York: The Penguin Press, 2004), p. 63.

41. Shireen T. Hunter, *The Future of Islam and the West* (Westport, Conn.: Praeger, 1988), p. 159.

42. George Crile, *Charlie Wilson's War* (New York: Atlantic Monthly Press, 2003), p. 222.

43. Ibid.

44. Ibid., p. 212.

45. Cordovez and Harrison, p. 162.

46. Former CIA official, interview with the author, March 2004.

47. Coll, pp. 120–21.

48. Dilip Hiro, *Holy Wars* (New York: Routledge, 1989), p. 259.

49. Coll, p. 119.

11: *Jihad II: Into Central Asia*

1. Harold Saunders, interview with the author, March 2004.

2. Saunders, interview.

3. Retired CIA official, interview with the author, March 2004.

4. Martha Kessler, interview with the author, April 2004.

5. Robert Baer, interview with the author, March 2004.

6. Former CIA official, interview with the author, March 2004.

7. John Cooley, *Unholy Wars* (London: Pluto Press, 1999), pp. 31–32.

8. Ibid., p. 32.

9. Retired CIA official, interview with the author, June 2004.

10. Cooley, p. 32.

11. George Crile, *Charlie Wilson's War* (New York: Atlantic Monthly Press, 2003), pp. 197, 201.

12. Steve Coll, *Ghost Wars* (New York: The Penguin Press, 2004), p. 129.

13. Ibid., p. 132.

14. Ibid., p. 129.

15. Ibid., p. 132.

16. Ibid., p. 136.

17. Ibid., p. 134.

18. Cooley, pp. 88–89.

19. Coll, pp. 102, 151.

20. Charles Freeman, interview with the author, April 2004.

21. Some analysts argued that the Soviet Union was already looking for a way out of Afghanistan and planning its withdrawal, under Mikhail Gorbachev, when the Stingers were introduced, and that the missiles themselves had only a marginal impact. The supply of the Stingers did, however, create a big problem for the CIA after the war ended, and the agency scrambled to buy back excess Stingers rather than let them fall into the hands of terrorists around the world.

22. Cooley, p. 85.

23. Ahmed Rashid, *Taliban: Militant Islam, Oil, and Fundamentalism in Central Asia* (New Haven, Conn.: Yale University Press, 2000), p. 130.

24. Ibid., p. 87.

25. This story of Azzam is drawn from Gilles Kepel, *Jihad: The Trail of Political Islam* (Cambridge, Mass.: The Belknap Press, 2002), pp. 144–47.

26. Ibid., p. 147.

27. Anonymous, *Through Our Enemies' Eyes* (Washington, D.C.: Brassey's, 2002), p. 41.

28. Coll, pp. 135–36.

29. Mohammad Yousaf and Mark Adkin, *Afghanistan: The Bear Trap* (Havertown, Penn.: Casemate, 1992), p. 106.

30. Kepel, p. 142.

31. Selig Harrison, interview with the author, June 2004.

32. Herbert Meyer, interview with the author, October 2004.

33. Ibid.

34. Coll, p. 97.

35. Ibid., p. 98.

36. Richard Krueger, interview with the author, March 2004.

37. Fawaz Gerges, *America and Political Islam* (Cambridge: Cambridge University Press, 1999), p. 71.

38. Crile, pp. 340–41.

39. Former CIA official, interview with the author, March 2004. Fahd, of course, a notorious playboy, may have had his own cynical interpretation of his role as "keeper of the faith."

40. Meyer, interview.

41. Former CIA official, interview with the author, June 2004.

42. Yousaf and Adkin, p. 47.

43. Former CIA official, interview with the author, July 2004.

44. Yousaf and Adkin, pp. 189–90.

45. Ibid., p. 193.

46. Ibid., p. 195.

47. Ibid., p. 200.

48. Ibid., p. 195.

49. Ibid., p. 164.

50. Daniel Pipes, interview with the author, April 2004.

51. Cited in *Omaha World Herald,* September 16, 2001, p. 12A.

52. Coll, pp. 168–69.

53. Walter Cutler, interview with the author, May 2004.

54. Freeman, interview.

55. Yousaf and Adkin, pp. 208–9.

56. Cheryl Benard, interview with the author, July 2004.

57. Gary Sick, *October Surprise: America's Hostages in Iran and the Election of Ronald Reagan* (New York: Times Books, 1991), p. 226.

58. Ibid., p. 59.

59. Ibid., pp. 69–71.

60. Additional, exhaustive tracking of the evidence for a Republican initiative toward Iran during the hostage crisis was compiled by journalist Robert Parry, in *Trick of Treason: The October Surprise Mystery* (New York: Sheridan Square Press, 1993).

61. Ibid., p. 115.

62. Ibid., p. 142.

63. Ibid., p. 167.

64. Ibid., p. 192.

65. Interview with Patrick Lang, March 2004.

66. Sick, p. 200.

67. Vladimir Kuzichkin, *Inside the KGB* (New York: Ivy Books, 1990), pp. 104–5.

68. Ibid., pp. 200–201.

69. James Bill, *The Eagle and the Lion* (New Haven: Yale University Press, 1988), p. 273.

70. Mel Goodman, interview with the author, March 2004.

71. Mohammed Reza Pahlavi, *Answer to History* (New York: Stein and Day, 1980), p. 125.

72. Ashraf Pahlavi, *Faces in a Mirror: Memoirs from Exile* (Englewood Cliffs, N.J.: Prentice-Hall, 1980), pp. 195–96.

73. See especially *Report of the Congressional Committees Investigating the Iran-Contra Affair,* November 1987; *The Tower Commission Report* by the President's Special Review Board, John Tower, chairman (New York: Times Books, 1987); *Firewall* by Lawrence E. Walsh, the independent counsel in the Iran-contra investigation (New York: W. W. Norton, 1997).

74. *Tower Commission Report,* p. 21.

75. Howard Teicher and Gayle Radley Teicher, *Twin Pillars to Desert Storm* (New York: William Morrow and Co., 1993), pp. 102–3.

76. Former CIA official, interview with the author, July 2004.

77. *Tower Commission Report*, pp. 112–13.

78. Ibid., p. 114.

79. Ibid., p. 115.

80. Teicher and Teicher, pp. 331–32.

81. *Tower Commission Report*, p. 119.

82. Teicher and Teicher, p. 332.

12: *Clash of Civilizations?*

1. Chris Hedges, "Muslim Militants Share Afghan Link," *New York Times,* March 28, 1993, p. 14.

2. For a blow-by-blow account of the complicated civil war in Algeria, 1992 to 1999, see chapter 11, "The Logic of Massacre in the Second Algerian War," in Gilles Kepel, *Jihad: The Trail of Political Islam* (Cambridge, Mass.: Harvard University Press, 2002), pp. 254–75.

3. Kepel, p. 165.

4. Ibid., p. 170.

5. Ibid., p. 174.

6. Senate Committee on Foreign Relations, *The Battle Looms: Islam and Politics in the Middle East* 1993, pp. 2, 6; cited in Fawaz Gerges, *America and Political Islam* (Cambridge: Cambridge University Press, 1999), p. 75.

7. "Interview with James A. Baker III," *Middle East Quarterly* (September 1994), p. 83.

8. Robert Pelletreau, interview with the author, April 2004.

9. David Mack, interview with the author, April 2004.

10. Richard Schifter, interview with the author, May 2004.

11. Mack, interview.

12. Edward Djerejian, "The United States and the Middle East in a Changing World" (address at Meridian House International, U.S. Department of State, June 2, 1992).

13. Gerges, pp. 80–81.

14. Ibid., p. 155.

15. Pelletreau, interview.

16. Graham Fuller, *Algeria: The Next Fundamentalist State?* (Santa Monica: RAND Corporation, 1996), p. xx.

17. Ibid., p. xiv.

18. Ibid., p. 4.

19. Ibid., p. xv.

20. Judith Miller, "The Islamic Wave," *New York Times Magazine,* May 31, 1992, p. 23.

21. Gerges, p. 171.

22. James Woolsey, interview with the author, May 2004.

23. Edward W. Walker, interview with the author, February 2004.

24. Ibid.

25. Abdel Moneim Said, interview with the author, June 2004.

26. Pelletreau, interview.

27. Ibid.

28. Walker, interview.

29. Ibid.

30. Gerges, pp. 174–75.

31. Ibid., p. 175.

32. Ibid., p. 178.

33. Ahmed Rashid, *Taliban: Militant Islam, Oil, and Fundamentalism in Central Asia* (New Haven, Conn.: Yale University Press, 2000), pp. 176–77.

34. Ibid., p. 177.

35. Graham Fuller, *The Future of Political Islam* (New York: Palgrave Macmillan, 2003), p. 115.

36. Sheila Heslin, testimony at Senate hearings into illegal fund-raising activities, September 17, 1997; cited in Rashid, p. 174.

37. Cited in Jean-Charles Brisard and Guillaume Dasquie, *Forbidden Truth* (New York: Thunder's Mouth Press/Nation Books, 2002), p. 21.

38. Rashid, p. 179.

39. Michael J. Berens, "University Helped U.S. Reach Out to Taliban," *Chicago Tribune,* October 21, 2001.

40. Stephen Buttry and Jake Thompson, "UNO's Connection to Taliban Centers on Education," *Omaha World Herald,* September 16, 2001.

41. Joe Stephens and David B. Ottaway, "From U.S., the ABC's of Jihad," *Washington Post,* March 23, 2002, p. A1.

42. Samuel Huntington, *The Clash of Civilizations* (New York: Simon & Schuster, 1996), p. 218.

43. Ibid., p. 115.

44. Ibid., p. 211.

45. Ibid., p. 207.

46. Ibid., p. 258.

47. Ibid., p. 263.

48. Ibid., p. 215.

49. Ibid., p. 210.

50. Bernard Lewis, "The Middle Eastern Reaction to Soviet Pressures," *Middle East Journal* 10 (Spring 1956), pp. 130–31.

51. Bernard Lewis, *The Middle East and the West* (New York: Harper & Row, 1964), p. 135.

52. Ibid., p. 133.

53. Ibid., p. 140.

54. Peter Waldman, "A Historian's Take on Islam Steers U.S. in Terrorism Fight," *Wall Street Journal,* February 3, 2004, p. 1.

55. Ibid.

56. Patrick Lang, interview with the author, March 2004.

57. Woolsey, interview.

58. Lang, interview.

59. For a detailed account of the founding and role of the OSP, see Robert Dreyfuss and Jason Vest, "The Lie Factory," *Mother Jones,* January–February 2004, p. 34.

60. Waldman, *Wall Street Journal.*

61. Lawrence F. Kaplan and William Kristol, *The War over Iraq* (San Francisco: Encounter Books, 2003), p. 124 and pp. vii–viii.

62. Benador Associates, press conference, Washington, D.C., February 13, 2003.

63. The full text of the memo is at http:www.israeleconomy.org/strat1.htm.

64. Bernard Lewis, "Rethinking the Middle East," *Foreign Affairs* (Fall 1992), pp. 99ff.

65. Charles Freeman, interview with the author, May 2003.

66. David Frum and Richard Perle, *An End to Evil: How to Win the War on Terror* (New York: Random House, 2003), pp. 140–41.

67. Max Singer, interview with the author, February 2003.

68. Michael Ledeen, *The War against the Terror Masters* (New York: Truman Talley Books, St. Martin's Press, 2002), pp. 208–9. In the book, Ledeen thanks Bernard Lewis for "personal guidance," and adds: "Harold Rhode, at the Pentagon's Office of Net Assessments, has been my guru on the Middle East for nearly twenty years. His boss, Andy Marshall, has been a constant source of good ideas," p. 240.

69. James E. Atkins, interview with author, January 2003.

70. Anonymous, *Imperial Hubris* (Washington: Brassey's, 2004), p. xv.

71. Reuel Marc Gerecht, *The Islamic Paradox: Shiite Clerics, Sunni Fundamentalists, and the Coming of Arab Democracy* (Washington, D.C.: The AEI Press, 2004), p. 10.

72. Ibid., p. 18.

73. Ibid., p. 41.

74. Ibid., p. 50.

75. Ibid., p. 53.

ACKNOWLEDGMENTS

MANY, MANY PEOPLE helped me find my way through what often seem to be the trackless wastelands of Middle East politics, as well as the shifting sands of U.S. policy toward that battle-scarred region. If I've gotten lost, it is my own fault. But I've had navigational guidance from experienced foreign service officers, intelligence officers, military men, and Middle East experts of all kinds. Some of them can't be named, because they've requested anonymity. But many others can be cited by name.

Among the very most helpful: Thomas Ahern, James Akins, Robert Baer, Amatzia Baram, Cheryl Benard, Vincent Cannistraro, Raymond Close, Charles Cogan, Walter Cutler, Michael Dunn, Hermann Eilts, Melvin Goodman, Joel Gordon, Charles Freeman, Selig Harrison, Fereydoun Hoveyda, Martha Kessler, Dick Krueger, Bruce Laingen, Patrick Lang, John Limbert, David Long, David Mack, Charles Naas, Yitzhak Nakash, Robert Pelletreau, Henry Precht, Abdel Moneim Said, Harold Saunders, Richard Schifter, Talcott Seelye, Peter Singer, John Voll, Edward Walker, John Waller, Charles Waterman, Philip Wilcox, James Woolsey, and Judith Yaphe.

Some people need to be singled out for special mention. First of all, I want to thank Ruth Van Laningham and the staff of the library at the Middle East Institute, who provided patient assistance and usually looked the other way on late fees for overdue books. I want to thank Sylvain Besson of *Le Temps* (Geneva) for his help on Said Ramadan and the Muslim Brotherhood in Europe. And Juan Cole, the University of Michigan historian, continually provided important insights.

I had research help from several people, whose work I value highly and to whom I am eternally grateful. Valentina Marano conducted interviews and provided deft, and quick, research in a wide range of areas and was a pleasure to work with. Kathleen Klenetsky provided a steady stream of information, wonderful insights, and important interviews on U.S. misadventures in Central Asia. And Laura Rozen helped to gather important research materials and sort out the mysteries of the Iran-contra episode. Of course, I emphasize that my conclusions, right or wrong, are mine alone.

This book would never have been written except for Steve Fraser and Tom Englehardt, the originators of the American Empire Project. I don't have an agent and hadn't intended to write a book until I got a probing phone call from Steve sometime in the spring of 2003. Steve shepherded the book from germ of an idea to proposal to manuscript, and he provided invaluable advice about how to organize the material—which, for someone used to writing magazine-length pieces, was far trickier than I had suspected. Sara Bershtel, the associate publisher at Metropolitan Books, for some reason believed that I could produce my first book, and she and her assistant, Kate Levin, were a joy to work with.

Most of all, of course, I have to thank Barbara Dreyfuss, who put up with my anxieties and long hours shut in my office and who read my chapters as they emerged. She also served as an unofficial research assistant, especially in regard to the complex machinations of the world of Islamic banking. And to my two children, to whom the book is dedicated, and who must have wondered from time to time where their father was, You performed the most important service of all: you kept me smiling.

INDEX

ABOUT THE AUTHOR

ROBERT DREYFUSS covers national security for *Rolling Stone*. He has written extensively on Iraq and the war on terrorism for *The
Nation, The American Prospect,* and *Mother
Jones* and has appeared on NPR, MSNBC,
CNBC, and many other broadcast outlets. He
is a graduate of Columbia University and currently lives in Alexandria, Virginia.

THE AMERICAN EMPIRE PROJECT

In an era of unprecedented military strength, leaders of the United States, the global hyperpower, have increasingly embraced imperial ambitions. How did this significant shift in purpose and policy come about? And what lies down the road?

The American Empire Project is a response to the changes that have occurred in America's strategic thinking as well as in its military and economic posture. Empire, long considered an offense against America's democratic heritage, now threatens to define the relationship between our country and the rest of the world. The American Empire Project publishes books that question this development, examine the origins of U.S. imperial aspirations, analyze their ramifications at home and abroad, and discuss alternatives to this dangerous trend.

The project was conceived by Tom Engelhardt and Steve Fraser, editors who are themselves historians and writers. Published by Metropolitan Books, an imprint of Henry Holt and Company, its titles include *Hegemony or Survival* by Noam Chomsky, *The Sorrows of Empire* by Chalmers Johnson, *Crusade* by James Carroll, *How to Succeed at Globalization* by El Fisgón, *Blood and Oil* by Michael Klare, and *Dilemmas of Domination* by Walden Bello.

For more information about the American Empire Project and for a list of forthcoming titles, please visit www.americanempireproject.com.